DEPOSITIONS
IN A NUTSHELL

By

ALBERT J. MOORE
Professor of Law
University of California, Los Angeles

DAVID A. BINDER
Professor of Law
University of California, Los Angeles

PAUL BERGMAN
Professor of Law
University of California, Los Angeles

JASON LIGHT
Lecturer in Law
University of California, Los Angeles

WEST®
A Thomson Reuters business

Mat #40755033

Nutshell Series, In a Nutshell and the Nutshell Logo are trademarks registered in the U.S. Patent and Trademark Office.

© 2011 Thomson Reuters

    610 Opperman Drive
    St. Paul, MN 55123
    1–800–313–9378

Printed in the United States of America

ISBN: 978–0–314–19489–3

ACKNOWLEDGEMENTS

To our research assistants Elizabeth Bosch and Kevin Sanders our sincerest thanks for your hard work and your dedication. Our thanks also to the UCLA Academic Senate and the Law School Dean's Fund for their financial support.

We also want to thank all the volunteers in the UCLA witness program, who have played the role of deponents in countless simulations, and the students and clients in our Depositions courses at UCLA Law School. We learned more from you than you did from us.

ALBERT J. MOORE
DAVID A. BINDER
PAUL BERGMAN
JASON LIGHT

Los Angeles, Calif.
August 2010

THE SCOPE OF THIS BOOK

This book focuses on deposition questioning strategies and techniques that maximize the likelihood that you can:

* Obtain helpful answers to critical questions.

* Find out everything deponents know about important topics and events.

* Undercut harmful testimony that emerges at deposition.

* Obtain information from deponents who claim not to understand your questions or who interpret your questions in a hypertechnical way.

* Exploit deponents' conflicting statements.

* Respond to opposing counsel's objections and obstructionist tactics.

* Undermine adverse experts' opinions.

The book has the following four parts.

Part One:
Deposing Adverse Witnesses

Part One illustrates common questioning strategies and techniques you might employ in the context of the most common type of deposition, the deposition of an adverse percipient witness. This part discusses strategies and techniques for (a) obtaining complete information, (b) encouraging deponents to provide your desired answer, (c) responding to incomplete, evasive or non-responsive answers, (d) undermining harmful testimony and (e) responding to inconsistent or implausible statements. Part One concludes with a discussion of how to respond to objections, instructions not to answer and obstructionist behavior of opposing counsel.

Part Two:
Preparing to Depose Adverse Witnesses

Part Two describes techniques and strategies for preparing yourself to take a deposition of an adverse witness. Experienced readers have undoubtedly developed their own system for preparation. Those readers can use the strategies and techniques in Part One whether or not they choose to employ the approach to deposition preparation described in this Part Two. This Part concludes with a discussion of the rules and procedures for arranging for depositions.

Part Three:
Special Depositions

Part Three focuses on taking "special" depositions, including those of an adverse expert, a Rule 30 (b) (6) deponent, and those to preserve the testimony of your own witness for trial.

Part Four:
Defending Depositions.

Part Four explores strategies and techniques for preparing a client or witness for a deposition and for defending at depositions taken by opposing counsel.

OUTLINE

Page

ACKNOWLEDGEMENTS ----------------------------------- III
THE SCOPE OF THIS BOOK ----------------------------- V
TABLE OF CASES ------------------------------------- XXXI

PART ONE. DEPOSING ADVERSE WITNESSES

Chapter 1. Three Primary Deposition Goals ----------------------------------- 2
1. Goal #1—Obtain an Adverse Witness' Version of Significant Events -------------- 2
   A. The Benefits of Obtaining an Adverse Witness' Version of Events ----------- 4
   B. The Risks of Obtaining an Adverse Witness' Version of Events ------------- 5
2. Goal #2—Searching for and Confirming Helpful Evidence ----------------------- 6
3. Goal #3—Uncovering and Undermining Harmful Evidence ------------------------ 7
4. The Order of Inquiry -------------------------- 10
5. Goals When Deposing "Neutral" Witnesses ----------------------------------- 10

Page

Chapter 2. Obtaining Complete Information: The T–Funnel Questioning Pattern ... 12

1. The T–Funnel Questioning Pattern ... 12
   A. An Illustration of the T–Funnel Pattern ... 14
   B. Using a Series of T–Funnels ... 15
   C. T–Funnels and Note Taking ... 19
2. Benefits of the T–Funnel Pattern ... 20
3. Avoiding Problems in T–Funnel Questioning ... 22
   A. Problem #1: Failure to Go to the Bottom of a T–Funnel ... 22
   B. Problem #2: The T–Funnel Is Too Vague or Too Broad ... 26
4. Consciously Omitting Closed Questions at the Bottom of the T to Limit Damaging Testimony ... 27
5. Inverted T–Funnels ... 30
6. Common T–Funnels ... 32
   A. "Everything That Happened During a Given Event" T–Funnels ... 32
   B. "Clumped Events" T–Funnels ... 33
   C. "Everything That You Did or Said" T–Funnels ... 37
   D. "All the Reasons" T–Funnels ... 38
   E. "Basis for a Conclusion, Opinion or Belief" T–Funnels ... 38
   F. "Reactions to an Occurrence or Event" T–Funnels ... 39
   G. "Do You Have Information to Help Prove My Case" T–Funnels ... 40
   H. "All the Documents" T–Funnels ... 43

Page

Chapter 3. Obtaining Complete Information: The Timeline Questioning Pattern ------------------------------------- 44
1. What Are Timelines? ----------------------------- 44
2. The Basic Timeline Questioning Pattern --- 45
3. An Illustrative Example of a Timeline Pattern --- 47
4. Benefits of Eliciting a Timeline --------------- 49
5. Refining Your Timeline Techniques -------- 51
   A. Problem: The Subject of Your Timeline Is Vague or Too Broad ----------- 52
   B. Problem: The Deponent Does Not Understand That You Want a Timeline (i.e. A Chronology About a Specific Subject) ----------------------------------- 53
   C. Problem: Creating Timeline Gaps When a Deponent Mentions a Future Event -------------------------------- 56
   D. Problem: Becoming Sidetracked into Non–Timeline Subjects ----------------- 57
   E. Problem: Uncertainty About a Timeline's Beginning --------------------------- 59
   F. Problem: Uncertainty About a Timeline's End --------------------------------- 60
6. Eliciting the Details of Timeline Events—Combining Timelines and T–Funnels ---- 61
7. Abandoning the Timeline When the Deponent Can Not Remember the Order in Which Events Occurred ---------------------- 66

Chapter 4. Obtaining Helpful Answers --- 72
1. Leading Questions ------------------------------- 73
2. Plausibility Chains ------------------------------- 74

Page

A. An Illustrative Example 74

B. Common Features of Questions in a Plausibility Chain 77

C. Accepting Less Than Perfect Answers 79

D. Plausibility Chains and Prior Statements 80

  1. Deponents' Prior Written Statements 81

  2. Deponents' Prior Oral Statements 85

  3. Statements of Third Persons 87

3. Exploiting Bias 89

4. Risks of Plausibility Chains and Exploiting Bias 94

5. Masking—Obscuring the Significance of Questions 94

A. Masking During Background Questioning 98

B. Combining Masking and Plausibility Chains 104

C. Masking to Create an Opportunity for Impeachment 107

6. Preparation Versus Seeking Admissions on the Fly 110

Chapter 5. Cementing Helpful Answers .. 112

1. Cementing Defined 112

2. Benefits of Cementing 113

3. Potential Risks of Cementing 115

4. Basic Cementing Techniques 115

A. Isolate Cemented Testimony 115

B. Occasionally Use Non–Leading Questions 122

Page

C. Obscure Your Purpose by Cementing "Surrounding Evidence" 122

D. Obscure Your Purpose by Delaying Cementing 124

E. Cement in the Deponent's Own Words 125

F. Offer a Neutral Explanation for Cementing 125

G. Obtain a Foundation 126

5. Cementing "That's All" 127

6. Responding to an "Asked and Answered" Objection 128

Chapter 6. Undermining Harmful Answers 130

1. Strategy #1—Challenge Accuracy 130

A. Inconsistent Behavior 131

B. Absence of Corroborative Evidence 132

C. Inability to Recall 133

1. Routine or Fungible Events 133

2. "Ancient" Occurrences.............. 136

3. No Reason to Recall 138

D. Unable to Provide the Details of Unique Occurrences 138

E. Inability to Perceive 139

F. No Reason or Motive for Behavior 140

G. Special Bias 141

H. Conclusion 143

2. Strategy #2—Attack the Inference.......... 143

3. Strategy #3—Aggrandize the Lie 145

4. Undermining Opinions and Conclusions ... 148

5. Undermining Conclusions About Conditions or Behavior Over Time 150

Page

6. Delaying Attempts to Undermine Harmful Evidence 152
7. Undermining With Conflicting Witnesses and Documents 152

Chapter 7. Responding to Inconsistent Statements 155
1. A Deponent's Testimony Conflicts With the Deponent's Prior Statement 155
   A. Option #1—Ask the Deponent for an Explanation.. 155
   B. Option #2—Ignore the Inconsistency.. 158
   C. Option #3—Aggrandize the Lie.......... 159
   D. Option #4—Encourage the Deponent to Affirm the Helpful Statement and Recant the Other One...................... 161
2. Deponent's Deposition Testimony Conflicts With Another Witness' Statement 164

Chapter 8. Responding to Implausibilities 169
1. What Makes Testimony Implausible? 169
2. Magnifying Implausibilities Through the "Especially When" Technique 170
3. Defer Inquiries into Topics That Might Magnify an Implausibility 171
4. Checking for Explanations 172

Chapter 9. Responding to Evasive, Forgetful or Uncertain Deponents 175
1. Evasive Deponents...................................... 175
   A. Non–Responsive Answers 175
   B. "Hints" in Lieu of Complete Answers 176

Page

C. "What Do You Mean By...." Answers 178

D. Overly Literal or Hyper–Technical Deponents 180

   1. Use a Series of Questions Containing Synonyms 181

   2. Ask for Information From All Sources 183

      a. Ask "Are You Aware of Any Information From Any Source That Might Indicate..." 184

      b. Ask Separately About "See" and "Hear" 185

      c. Potential Risks of Asking for Information From All Sources 186

2. Forgetful and Uncertain Deponents 186

  A. Probing for Recall 188

    1. Convey an Expectation That Recall Is Possible 188

    2. Bracket to Obtain a Best Estimate 189

    3. Use Documents 192

    4. Use Closed or Leading Questions 193

  B. Probing for Alternative Sources of Information 194

3. Responding to "I Don't Know" Answers 196

Chapter 10. Using Documents and Diagrams 198

1. Maintaining a Clear Record 198

  A. Use Exhibit Numbers and Precise Segment References 198

Page

   B. Provide Copies of Documents to Opposing Counsel 201

2. Common Uses of Documents 202

   A. Laying a Foundation for Later Use of Documents in Pre–Trial Motions or at Trial.. 202

       1. Authentication 202

       2. Satisfying Evidentiary Requirements 204

   B. Memory Stimulation............................. 205

   C. Develop a Deponent's Version of Events.. 206

   D. Explanations of Words and Phrases 210

   E. Preparation and Distribution History.. 211

   F. Obtaining Helpful Answers.................. 213

3. Diagrams... 214

Chapter 11. Questioning Tips 219

1. Ask for Hearsay 219

2. Ask "Why" Questions Concerning Deponents' Own Behavior............................... 220

3. Ask "Why" Questions Concerning a Third Person's Behavior..................................... 222

4. Ask "Have You Now Told Me Everything?" 224

5. Elicit the Bases of Conclusions and Opinions 225

6. Seek Out Opinions.................................... 226

7. Elicit the "Details" Rather Than the "Substance" of Occurrences.................... 228

8. Don't Conflate Discrete Occurrences 229

9. Seek Examples of Behavior Over Time 230

Page

10. Clarify Ambiguous References and Physical Gestures 231
11. Be Solicitous of the Court Reporter 232

Chapter 12. Communicating Arguments 233
1. Communicating Arguments by Marshaling Evidence With Leading Questions 234
2. Deciding Which Arguments to Communicate 238
3. When to Communicate Arguments 243

Chapter 13. Beginning and Concluding Depositions 244
1. Beginning Depositions 244
   A. Stipulations 244
   B. Admonitions 247
   C. Questions Regarding a Deponent's Preparation 260
      1. Documents a Deponent Used to Refresh Recollection 260
      2. Persons With Whom a Deponent Talked 264
   D. Background Questioning 265
      1. Employment History 266
      2. Educational Background 267
2. Concluding Depositions 267

Chapter 14. Professional Demeanor and Rapport Building 271
1. Maintain a Professional Demeanor With Deponents and Opposing Counsel 271
2. Building Rapport With the Deponent......... 273

Page

Chapter 15. Responding to Objections and Other Actions of Opposing Counsel ------------------------------------- 277

1. Instructions Not to Answer -------------------- 277
   A. The Propriety of Instructions Not to Answer ------------------------------------- 277
   B. Responding to Invalid Instructions Not to Answer --------------------------- 278
      1. On the Record, Ask Your Adversary to Withdraw the Instruction 279
      2. Put the Deponent's Refusal to Answer on the Record ------------------- 280
      3. Complete Your Questioning With Respect to the Subject Matter of the Question the Deponent Refuses to Answer ----------------------- 280
   C. Obtain an Order Compelling an Answer --- 287
2. Responding to Objections --------------------- 290
   A. Step One: Obtain an Answer ------------- 291
   B. Step Two: Decide Whether a Valid Objection Is Curable ------------------------ 294
3. Objections Commonly Raised at Deposition --- 298
   A. Common Objections That Can Often Be Cured --------------------------------- 299
   B. Objections That Usually Need Not Be Cured -- 306
4. Objections to Improper Answers ------------- 308
   A. The Answer Is Non–Responsive -------- 309
   B. The Objection to the Answer Raises a Potential Problem With the Question --- 310

Page

5. Responding to Inappropriate Behavior by Opposing Counsel 311
   A. Disruptive Statements or Objections ... 312
      1. Ignore the Improper Tactics and Obtain an Answer 314
      2. Cure a Valid Underlying Objection 316
      3. Cite the Rules and Threaten to Seek a Protective Order 316
      4. Offer to Stipulate That "All Objections Are Preserved" 319
      5. Terminate the Deposition and Move for a Protective Order 320
   B. Attempts to Coach the Deponent 321
      1. Speaking Objections 322
      2. Conferences With a Deponent 324
      3. Conferences With the Deponent During a Recess 328
   C. Resolving Disputes Via Telephone 330
   D. Visually Recording Depositions 330
   E. A Cautionary Note About Protective Orders 331

PART TWO. PREPARING TO DEPOSE ADVERSE WITNESSES

Chapter 16. Deposition Preparation 334
1. Step One—Identify Crucial Factual Contentions 335
2. Step Two—Identify the Topics, Events and Documents to Explore at the Deposition 338
   A. Technique #1—Review Documents & Deposition Transcripts 338

Page

B. Technique #2—Review a Case Chronology 340
  1. Create a Case Chronology 341
  2. Review Your Case Chronology 343
C. Technique #3—Brainstorming............ 344
  1. Brainstorming With Historical Reconstruction................................. 344
    a. Breaking Historical Reconstruction into Multiple Time Periods... 346
  2. Brainstorming With Generalizations 346
D. Technique #4—Use an Expert 349
E. Technique #5—Undermine Existing Harmful Evidence 350
F. Technique #6—Use Direct Inquiries ... 351
G. Technique #7—Anticipate Your Cross Examination.................................... 353
H. Technique #8—Anticipate Your Important Arguments............................. 354
I. Technique #9—Use a Pre–Fab Checklist 355
J. Technique #10—Computer Searches to Gather Background Information About the Deponent 356
3. Organize a Deposition Outline.................... 357
A. How Should You Organize Your Outline? 357
B. What Questioning Techniques Should You Use for Important Areas of Inquiry?.. 358

Page

C. Should You Include Questioning Prompts or Specific Questions in Your Outline? ---------------------------- 359

D. Should You Omit Topics to Avoid Educating Your Opposition? ----------------- 362

E. Should You Avoid Putting Harmful Evidence on the Record? --------------- 363

F. Might You Enhance Settlement? -------- 363

G. Do You Need to Prioritize to Comply With the Seven–Hour Rule? ----------- 364

Chapter 17. Arranging for Depositions --- 366

1. Who May You Depose? ------------------------ 366
2. Number of Depositions ------------------------ 367
3. Length of Depositions -------------------------- 367
4. Necessity of a Notice ------------------------- 367
5. Contents of a Notice ------------------------- 369
6. When You May Take Depositions ------------ 370
7. Where You May Take Depositions ----------- 371
8. Securing a Deponent's Attendance ---------- 372
9. Arranging for Document Production ------- 373
   A. Production at a Deposition --------------- 373
   B. Production Prior to a Deposition ------- 374
10. Ensuring a Presiding Officer's Attendance 376
11. Ensuring That a Deposition Is Recorded --- 376
12. Waiving FRCP Requirements ----------------- 377

PART THREE. SPECIAL DEPOSITIONS

Chapter 18. FRCP 30(b)(6) "Subject Matter" Depositions ---------------------- 380

1. Why Take a Subject Matter Deposition?----- 381

2. How Many 30(b)(6) Depositions Can You Take? --------------------------------- 382

3. The Importance of Comprehensive 30(b)(6) Notices ------------------------------ 382

4. Questioning 30(b)(6) Designees -------------- 383

   A. Is the Designee Knowledgeable? -------- 383

   B. Inquire About an Entity's Actions Rather Than a Designee's ------------- 388

5. Going Beyond the Subjects in a Notice ------ 389

6. Can You Depose a 30(b)(6) Designee Twice? ---------------------------------- 390

7. Using a 30(b)(6) Deposition to Obtain the Bases for an Adverse Party's Contentions ----------------------------------- 391

Chapter 19. Inquiring About Practices and Policies ----------------------------- 394

1. Distinguishing "Practices" From "Policies" -------------------------------------- 395

2. Purposes of Practice and Policy Inquiries -- 396

3. Who to Depose ------------------------------- 397

4. Questioning Strategies Regarding Practices --- 399

   A. Responding to "It Depends" Answers 399

   B. Inquire About Exceptions ----------------- 401

   C. Inquire About Prior and Subsequent Changes ----------------------------------- 404

   D. Distinguish Between the Entity's Practice and That of the Deponent 405

5. Questioning Strategies Regarding Policies 405

6. Inquiring About Discrepancies Between Practices and Policies ----------------------- 408

Page

7. Inquiring About Discrepancies Between Practices & Policies and What Happened in Your Client's Case 409

Chapter 20. Deposing Experts 410
 1. Mandatory Disclosures 411
 2. Beginning Adverse Expert Depositions 412
    A. Give Admonitions............................ 412
    B. Confirm That You Have All Relevant Documents........................... 413
    C. Obtain Background Information.......... 414
 3. Obtain a Chronology of Case Related Activities 416
 4. Obtain All Expert Opinions.................... 422
 5. Obtain the Basis for Each Opinion 423
    A. Obtain the **Evidentiary** Basis for Each Opinion 424
    B. Obtain the **Specialized Knowledge** Underlying Each Opinion 426
 6. Undermining an Expert Opinion............... 427
 7. Challenge #1—An Expert's Specialized Knowledge Is Inadequate.................... 428
 8. Challenge #2—"Exceptions" Detract From an Opinion's Accuracy 432
 9. Challenge #3—Conflicting Authorities Undermine an Opinion..................... 436
10. Challenge #4—An Opinion Is Based on Inaccurate Information From Third Parties........................... 437
11. Challenge #5—Undermine the Results of Scientific Tests or Technical Procedures 441
12. Challenge #6—An Investigation Is Incomplete or Untimely 444

		Page
13.	Challenge #7—An Expert Is Biased	445
14.	Garner Support for Your Expert's Opinion	446
15.	Opposing Party's Duty to Supplement Expert's Deposition Testimony	448
16.	Preparing Your Own Expert for Deposition	449
17.	Deposing Percipient Experts	449

Chapter 21. Deposing Your Own Witness or a Neutral Witness 452

1.	Pre–Deposition Preparation	453
2.	Questioning Strategies and Techniques	454
	A. Elicit Background Evidence	455
	B. Elicit a Selective Chronology	456
	C. Elicit Important Testimony Through Open Questions	458
	D. Emphasis Techniques	459
	1. Incorporate Important Evidence into Subsequent Questions	459
	2. Front Load Important Testimony	461
	3. Elicit a String of Denials	462
	E. Help Forgetful Deponents	463
	1. Follow a Closed/Open Questioning Sequence	463
	2. Use Documents to Refresh Recollection	467
	F. Consider Steering Around Unfavorable Testimony	469
3.	Redirect Examination	471
4.	Responding to Objections	472

Page

Chapter 22. Visually Recorded Depositions --- 475
1. Ground Rules for Visually Recorded Depositions Under the FRCP --------------------- 475
2. Advantages of Visually Recording Depositions -- 478
   A. Adds Impact to Impeachment at Trial 478
   B. Adds Impact to an Adverse Party's Helpful Deposition Testimony -------- 479
   C. Adds Impact to Preserved Testimony of a Friendly, Unavailable Witness 480
   D. Adds Impact to Demonstrations or Re–Enactments --------------------------- 480
   E. Creates Illustrative Exhibits for Trial or Settlement ----------------------------- 481
   F. Discourages Inappropriate Behavior by Opposing Counsel --------------------- 482
   G. Reduces Deposition Costs ----------------- 482
   H. Improves Feedback From Mock Jury Trials --- 483
   I. Improves Your Witness' Trial Testimony --- 483
3. Disadvantages of Visually Recording Depositions --- 484
   A. The Visual Recording of Your Witness Will Be Available for Your Adversary's Use at Trial ----------------------- 484
   B. The Visually Recording of an Adverse Witness May Be Available for Your Adversary's Use at Trial -------------- 485
   C. Technological Risks ------------------------- 486
   D. Increased Expense -------------------------- 486
   E. Inconvenient to Review -------------------- 487
4. Strategies for Preparing Friendly Deponents --- 488

Page

A. Visually Record a Practice Session 488
B. Show a "Good" Performance 489
C. Discuss What to Wear 489
5. Strategies for Taking Visually Recorded Depositions Effectively 489
A. Complying With FRCP 30(b)(4) 489
B. Bring an Assistant to the Deposition ... 492
C. Monitoring Your Own Conduct 493
6. Strategies for Defending Visually Recorded Depositions 493
A. Visually Record a Practice Session 493
B. Ensuring Fair Visually Recordings...... 494
C. Avoid Conferences While on the Record 496
D. Make Objections as You Would Before a Jury................................. 497
E. Take Adequate Breaks 498
F. Prohibit Improper Use of the Recording 498

PART FOUR. DEFENDING DEPOSITIONS

Chapter 23. Preparing Deponents 500
1. Your Pre–Meeting Preparation 500
A. Review the Validity of Document Requests................................. 500
B. Review Pertinent Documents............ 501
C. Prepare a Case Chronology.............. 501
D. Help Identify FRCP 30(b)(6) Deponents................................. 501
E. Arrange to Meet the Client 502

Page

2. Tell Clients What Documents to Review ... 503
3. Conducting Preparation Meetings 505
   A. Explain What a Meeting Entails 505
   B. Review a Client's Version of Events 506
   C. Briefly Explain What Will Occur During the Deposition 507
   D. Conduct a Practice Session 508
      1. Devote Practice Questioning to Selected Topics 509
      2. Explain the "Golden Rules" for Answering Questions 509
      3. Ask Questions as Deposing Counsel 513
      4. Improve Answers With Feedback and Advice 514
   E. Concluding Preparation Sessions 519
      1. Explain Objections and Instructions Not to Answer 519
      2. Final Instructions 520
4. Preparation Meetings With Non–Clients ... 520

Chapter 24. Defending Depositions 524
1. Defending Depositions of Your Witnesses .. 525
   A. Objections 525
      1. Purpose of Objections..................... 525
      2. "Curable" and "Non–Curable" Objections 529
         a. Objections That Commonly Are Curable 530
         b. Common "Incurable" Objections That You Can Raise Later Even if You Don't Make Them at Deposition 538

Page

    3. Objections to Deponent's Improper
       Answers 540
    4. Objecting to Improve a Deponent's
       Answers 542
    5. Forgoing Objections 543
    6. Phrasing Objections Properly 545
B. Instructions Not to Answer 547
    1. Instructions Not to Answer to Pre-
       serve a Privilege 548
    2. Instructions Not to Answer Based
       on a Prior Court Order 550
    3. Instructions Not to Answer to Sus-
       pend a Deposition to Seek a Pro-
       tective Order 550
    4. Risks of Improper Instructions Not
       to Answer 551
    5. An "Early Warning System" Alter-
       native Strategy 553
C. Consulting With Deponents 556
    1. Conferences   During   Deposing
       Counsel's Examination 556
    2. Conferences During a Recess or
       Break 559
D. Resolving Disputes Via Telephone 560
E. Should You Ask Questions? 560
    1. The Deponent May Be Unavailable
       at Trial 561
    2. The   Deponent's Answers Have
       Been Inaccurate 561
       a. Explicit Reference to Incorrect
          Testimony 563
       b. Cover Same Subject Matter 564
    3. Bringing Out Helpful Evidence 566

OUTLINE

	Page
2. Defending Non–Party Clients	567
3. Defending Depositions When You Do Not Represent the Deponent	569
A. Making Objections	569
B. Instructions Not to Answer	570
C. Consulting With a Neutral Witness During the Deposition	571
D. Should You Question a Neutral Witness?	571
4. Defending an Adversary's Deposition to Preserve Testimony	573
5. Terminating a Deposition That Exceeds the "One Day of Seven Hours" Time Limit	574
6. Requesting That the Deponent Have a Right to Review the Transcript	578
7. Supplementing Deposition Testimony After the Deposition Is Signed	579
INDEX	583

TABLE OF CASES

References are to Pages

A

Al–Rowaishan Establishment Universal Trading & Agencies, Ltd. v. Beatrice Foods Co., 92 F.R.D. 779 (S.D.N.Y.1982), *263, 504*

Amari Co., Inc. v. Burgess, 2009 WL 1269704 (N.D.Ill.2009), *291, 323, 525, 547*

Ambrosini v. Labarraque, 101 F.3d 129, 322 U.S.App.D.C. 19 (D.C.Cir.1996), *415*

American Directory Service Agency, Inc. v. Beam, 131 F.R.D. 15 (D.D.C.1990), *547, 559*

Amezaga, In re, 195 B.R. 221 (Bkrtcy.D.Puerto Rico 1996), *311, 324, 496, 556*

Amtower v. Photon Dynamics, Inc., 71 Cal.Rptr.3d 361 (Cal.App. 6 Dist.2008), *413, 422*

Applied Telematics, Inc. v. Sprint Corp., 1995 WL 79237 (E.D.Pa. 1995), *129, 307, 538*

Arkwright Mut. Ins. Co. v. National Union Fire Ins. Co. of Pittsburgh, Pa., 1993 WL 34678 (S.D.N.Y.1993), *351, 391*

Armstrong v. Hussmann Corp., 163 F.R.D. 299 (E.D.Mo.1995), *245, 290, 311, 321, 365, 496, 547, 557, 575*

Auto Owners Ins. Co. v. Totaltape, Inc., 135 F.R.D. 199 (M.D.Fla. 1990), *261, 503*

B

Bagley, United States ex rel. v. TRW, Inc., 212 F.R.D. 554 (C.D.Cal.2003), *263, 504*

Bahamas Agr. Industries Ltd. v. Riley Stoker Corp., 526 F.2d 1174 (6th Cir.1975), *528, 540*

Baker v. State, 35 Md.App. 593, 371 A.2d 699 (Md.App.1977), *468*

Banks v. Office of Senate Sergeant-at-Arms, 241 F.R.D. 376 (D.D.C.2007), *278, 548*

BB & T Corp. v. United States, 233 F.R.D. 447 (M.D.N.C.2006), *352*

B.C.F. Oil Refining, Inc. v. Consolidated Edison Co. of New York, Inc., 171 F.R.D. 57 (S.D.N.Y.1997), *418*

Biovail Laboratories, Inc. v. Anchen Pharmaceuticals, Inc., 233 F.R.D. 648 (C.D.Cal.2006), *551*

Birdine v. City of Coatesville, 225 F.R.D. 157 (E.D.Pa.2004), *324, 557*

Bogosian v. Gulf Oil Corp., 738 F.2d 587 (3rd Cir.1984), *263, 504*

Bongiovanni v. N. V. Stoomvaart–Matts "Oostzee", 458 F.Supp. 602 (S.D.N.Y.1978), *269, 579*

Bronston v. United States, 409 U.S. 352, 93 S.Ct. 595, 34 L.Ed.2d 568 (1973), *512*

Brown, United States v., 603 F.2d 1022 (1st Cir.1979), *15, 74, 302, 532*

C

Cabello v. Fernandez–Larios, 402 F.3d 1148 (11th Cir.2005), *528*

Calzaturficio S.C.A.R.P.A. s.p.a. v. Fabiano Shoe Co., Inc., 201 F.R.D. 33 (D.Mass.2001), *497, 556*

Caplan v. Fellheimer Eichen Braverman & Kaskey, 161 F.R.D. 29 (E.D.Pa.1995), *129, 307, 538, 551*

Cisneros–Gutierrez, United States v., 517 F.3d 751 (5th Cir. 2008), *532*

Claar v. Burlington Northern R. Co., 29 F.3d 499 (9th Cir.1994), *415*

Cobell v. Norton, 213 F.R.D. 16 (D.D.C.2003), *291*

Coleman v. Keebler Co., 997 F.Supp. 1102 (N.D.Ind.1998), *581*

Conderback, Inc. v. Standard Oil Co. of Cal., Western Operations, 239 Cal.App.2d 664, 48 Cal.Rptr. 901 (Cal.App. 1 Dist. 1966), *118*

Condit v. Dunne, 225 F.R.D. 100 (S.D.N.Y.2004), *245, 364, 575*

Cornell Research Foundation, Inc. v. Hewlett Packard Co., 223 F.R.D. 55 (N.D.N.Y.2003), *418*

Coryn Group II, LLC v. O.C. Seacrets, Inc., 265 F.R.D. 235 (D.Md.2010), *262, 503, 504*

Craig v. St. Anthony's Medical Center, 2009 WL 690210 (E.D.Mo. 2009), *321, 323, 547*

Cunningham v. Heard, 667 A.2d 537 (R.I.1995), *215*

D

Daubert v. Merrell Dow Pharmaceuticals, Inc., 43 F.3d 1311 (9th Cir.1995), *415*

Daubert v. Merrell Dow Pharmaceuticals, Inc., 509 U.S. 579, 113 S.Ct. 2786, 125 L.Ed.2d 469 (1993), *414*

Derderian v. Polaroid Corp., 121 F.R.D. 13 (D.Mass.1988), *263, 504*

Detoy v. City and County of San Francisco, 196 F.R.D. 362 (N.D.Cal.2000), *389*

Disability Rights Council of Greater Washington v. Washington Metropolitan Transit Authority, 242 F.R.D. 139 (D.D.C.2007), *263*

Dow Chemical Co. v. Reinhard, 2008 WL 1735295 (E.D.Mich. 2008), *245, 365, 367, 575*

E

Eckert v. Hurley Chicago Co., Inc., 638 F.Supp. 699 (N.D.Ill. 1986), *552*

Eggleston v. Chicago Journeymen Plumbers' Local Union No. 130, U. A., 657 F.2d 890 (7th Cir.1981), *291, 525*

Eli Lilly and Co. v. Actavis Elizabeth LLC, 2010 WL 1849913 (D.N.J.2010), *581*

Ellis v. City of Chicago, 667 F.2d 606 (7th Cir.1981), *15, 73, 302, 532*

Elm Grove Coal Co. v. Director, O.W.C.P, 480 F.3d 278 (4th Cir.2007), *418*

Emerson Electric Co. v. Superior Court, 68 Cal.Rptr.2d 883, 946 P.2d 841 (Cal.1997), *215, 481*

Encore Entertainment, LLC v. KIDdesigns, Inc., 2005 WL 2249897 (M.D.Tenn.2005), *580*

Equal Employment Opportunity Comm'n v. American Intern. Group, Inc., 1994 WL 376052 (S.D.N.Y.1994), *548*

Exxon Research and Engineering Co. v. United States, 44 Fed. Cl. 597, 1999 WL 711422 (1999), *351, 392*

F

F.C.C. v. Mizuho Medy Co. Ltd., 257 F.R.D. 679 (S.D.Cal.2009), *561*

Federal Deposit Ins. Corp. v. Butcher, 116 F.R.D. 196 (E.D.Tenn. 1986), *382, 383*

Fidelity Nat. Title Ins. Co. of New York v. Intercounty Nat. Title Ins. Co., 412 F.3d 745 (7th Cir.2005), *418*

First Tennessee Bank v. Federal Deposit Ins. Corp., 108 F.R.D. 640 (E.D.Tenn.1985), *129, 307, 538*

Frazier v. Ford Motor Co., 2008 WL 4809130 (W.D.Ark.2008), *503*

G

Gell v. Town of Aulander, 252 F.R.D. 297 (E.D.N.C.2008), *532*

General Elec. Co. v. Joiner, 522 U.S. 136, 118 S.Ct. 512, 139 L.Ed.2d 508 (1997), *415*

Glenwood Farms, Inc. v. Ivey, 229 F.R.D. 34 (D.Me.2005), *579*

GMAC Bank v. HTFC Corp., 248 F.R.D. 182 (E.D.Pa.2008), *317, 320*

H

Hall v. Clifton Precision, a Div. of Litton Systems, Inc., 150 F.R.D. 525 (E.D.Pa.1993), *323, 496, 547, 557*

Hambleton Bros. Lumber Co. v. Balkin Enterprises, Inc., 397 F.3d 1217 (9th Cir.2005), *269, 579*

Hammond v. Air Line Pilots Ass'n, 1987 WL 20421 (N.D.Ill. 1987), *351, 392*

Haney v. Mizell Memorial Hosp., 744 F.2d 1467 (11th Cir.1984), *15, 73, 301, 532*

Hanlin v. Mitchelson, 623 F.Supp. 452 (S.D.N.Y.1985), *551*

Hearst/ABC–Viacom Entertainment Services v. Goodway Marketing, Inc., 145 F.R.D. 59 (E.D.Pa.1992), *551*

Henry v. Champlain Enterprises, Inc., 212 F.R.D. 73 (N.D.N.Y. 2003), *559*

Herman v. Marine Midland Bank, 207 F.R.D. 26 (W.D.N.Y.2002), *418*

Heron Interact, Inc. v. Guidelines, Inc., 244 F.R.D. 75 (D.Mass. 2007), *261, 503, 504*

Howard v. Michalek, 249 F.R.D. 288 (N.D.Ill.2008), *481*

I

Ierardi v. Lorillard, Inc., 1991 WL 158911 (E.D.Pa.1991), *381, 382*

Independent Service Organizations Antitrust Litigation, In re, 168 F.R.D. 651 (D.Kan.1996), *352, 392*

In re (see name of party)

Intermedics, Inc. v. Cardiac Pacemakers, Inc., 1998 WL 35253493 (D.Minn.1998), *580*

International Business Machines Corp., United States v., 66 F.R.D. 180 (S.D.N.Y.1974), *291, 526*

Iris Corp. Berhad v. United States, 84 Fed. Cl. 489, 2008 WL 4885120 (2008), *351*

J

James Julian, Inc. v. Raytheon Co., 93 F.R.D. 138 (D.Del.1982), *261, 503*

Johnson v. Manitowoc Boom Trucks, Inc., 484 F.3d 426 (6th Cir.2007), *415*

Jones v. Moore, 95 Cal.Rptr.2d 216 (Cal.App. 2 Dist.2000), *413, 422*

K

Kansas Wastewater, Inc. v. Alliant Techsystems, Inc., 217 F.R.D. 525 (D.Kan.2003), *307, 528, 539*

Karn v. Ingersoll–Rand Co., 168 F.R.D. 633 (N.D.Ind.1996), *418*

Kendrick v. Heckler, 778 F.2d 253 (5th Cir.1985), *290*

Kennett–Murray Corp. v. Bone, 622 F.2d 887 (5th Cir.1980), *114*

King v. Pratt & Whitney, a Div. of United Technologies Corp., 161 F.R.D. 475 (S.D.Fla.1995), *389, 390*

Kirschner v. Broadhead, 671 F.2d 1034 (7th Cir.1982), *540*

Krisa v. Equitable Life Assur. Soc., 196 F.R.D. 254 (M.D.Pa. 2000), *418*

Kumho Tire Co., Ltd. v. Carmichael, 526 U.S. 137, 119 S.Ct. 1167, 143 L.Ed.2d 238 (1999), *414*

Kymissis v. Rozzi, 1997 WL 278055 (S.D.N.Y.1997), *319*

L

Landers v. Kevin Gros Offshore, L.L.C., 2009 WL 2046587 (E.D.La.2009), *552*

Lapenna v. Upjohn Co., 110 F.R.D. 15 (E.D.Pa.1986), *552*

M

Magee v. Paul Revere Life Ins. Co., 172 F.R.D. 627 (E.D.N.Y. 1997), *261, 503*

Managed Care Litigation, In re, 415 F.Supp.2d 1378 (S.D.Fla. 2006), *264, 504*

Marker v. Union Fidelity Life Ins. Co., 125 F.R.D. 121 (M.D.N.C. 1989), *380, 382*

Mattocks v. Daylin, Inc., 78 F.R.D. 663 (W.D.Pa.1978), *118*

McCormick–Morgan, Inc. v. Teledyne Industries, Inc., 134 F.R.D. 275 (N.D.Cal.1991), *351, 392*

McKinley Infuser, Inc. v. Zdeb, 200 F.R.D. 648 (D.Colo.2001), *328*

Medtronic Xomed, Inc. v. Gyrus ENT LLC, 2006 WL 786425 (M.D.Fla.2006), *503*

Miller v. Holzmann, 238 F.R.D. 30 (D.D.C.2006), *263*

Miller v. Waseca Medical Center, 205 F.R.D. 537 (D.Minn.2002), *245, 365, 575*

Mitsui & Co. (U.S.A.), Inc. v. Puerto Rico Water Resources Authority, 93 F.R.D. 62 (D.Puerto Rico 1981), *382, 389*

Mora–Higuera, United States v., 269 F.3d 905 (8th Cir.2001), *532*

Morales v. Zondo, Inc., 204 F.R.D. 50 (S.D.N.Y.2001), *320, 323, 547, 559*

Morris Stulsaft Foundation v. Superior Court In and For City and County of San Francisco, 245 Cal.App.2d 409, 54 Cal. Rptr. 12 (Cal.App. 1 Dist.1966), *571*

N

National R.R. Passenger Corp. v. Certain Temporary Easements Above Railroad Right Of Way In Providence, Rhode Island, 357 F.3d 36 (1st Cir.2004), *532*

Nexxus Products Co. v. CVS New York, Inc., 188 F.R.D. 7 (D.Mass.1999), *418*

Ngai v. Old Navy, 2009 WL 2391282 (D.N.J.2009), *328*

O

O'Brien v. Amtrak, 163 F.R.D. 232 (E.D.Pa.1995), *321*

Odone v. Croda Intern. PLC., 170 F.R.D. 66 (D.D.C.1997), *272, 329, 332*

Ortho Pharmaceutical Corp. v. Smith, 1990 WL 10011 (E.D.Pa. 1990), *351, 392*

Overseas Private Inv. Corp. v. Mandelbaum, 185 F.R.D. 67 (D.D.C.1999), *389*

P

Paparelli v. Prudential Ins. Co. of America, 108 F.R.D. 727 (D.Mass.1985), *389*

Parry v. Highlight Industries, Inc., 125 F.R.D. 449 (W.D.Mich. 1989), *261, 503*

Perma Research & Development Co. v. Singer Co., 410 F.2d 572 (2nd Cir.1969), *114*

Philip Morris Inc., United States v., 212 F.R.D. 418 (D.D.C.2002), *496, 556*

Pilates, Inc. v. Georgetown Bodyworks Deep Muscle Massage Centers, Inc., 201 F.R.D. 261 (D.D.C.2000), *291, 525*

Pioneer Hi–Bred Intern., Inc., In re, 238 F.3d 1370 (Fed.Cir. 2001), *417*

Plaisted v. Geisinger Medical Center, 210 F.R.D. 527 (M.D.Pa. 2002), *245, 324, 328, 365, 496, 538, 556, 575*

Potashnick v. Port City Const. Co., 609 F.2d 1101 (5th Cir.1980), *329*

Precisionflow Technologies, Inc. v. CVD Equipment Corp., 140 F.Supp.2d 195 (N.D.N.Y.2001), *373*

Prucha v. M & N Modern Hydraulic Press Co., 76 F.R.D. 207 (W.D.Wis.1977), *263, 504*

Q

Quantachrome Corp. v. Micromeritics Instrument Corp., 189 F.R.D. 697 (S.D.Fla.1999), *324*

R

Ralston Purina Co. v. McFarland, 550 F.2d 967 (4th Cir.1977), *291, 526*

Ransdell v. Berrie, 1996 WL 242961 (N.D.Ill.1996), *581*

Rappy, United States v., 157 F.2d 964 (2nd Cir.1946), *193*

Redwood v. Dobson, 476 F.3d 462 (7th Cir.2007), *291, 525, 551, 552*

Regional Airport Authority of Louisville v. LFG, LLC, 460 F.3d 697 (6th Cir.2006), *418*

Reilly v. TXU Corp., 230 F.R.D. 486 (N.D.Tex.2005), *269, 579*

Rifkind v. Superior Court, 27 Cal.Rptr.2d 822 (Cal.App. 2 Dist. 1994), *351, 391, 392*

Roper v. Exxon Corp., 1998 WL 341838 (E.D.La.1998), *278, 548*

Rossano v. Blue Plate Foods, Inc., 314 F.2d 174 (5th Cir.1963), *15, 74, 302*

Roy v. Austin Co., 194 F.3d 840 (7th Cir.1999), *528*

S

S & A Painting Co., Inc. v. O.W.B. Corp., 103 F.R.D. 407 (W.D.Pa.1984), *263, 503*

Scanlon v. Bricklayers and Allied Craftworkers, Local No. 3, 242 F.R.D. 238 (W.D.N.Y.2007), *262, 263, 504*

S.E.C. v. Buntrock, 217 F.R.D. 441 (N.D.Ill.2003), *278, 548*

S.E.C. v. Morelli, 143 F.R.D. 42 (S.D.N.Y.1992), *548*

S.E.C. v. Nacchio, 614 F.Supp.2d 1164 (D.Colo.2009), *278, 548*

S.E.C. v. World Information Technology, Inc., 250 F.R.D. 149 (S.D.N.Y.2008), *532*

Security Ins. Co. of Hartford v. Trustmark Ins. Co., 218 F.R.D. 29 (D.Conn.2003), *351*

Sigmund v. Starwood Urban Retail VI, LLC, 236 F.R.D. 43 (D.D.C.2006), *351*

Singh v. Wackenhut Corp., 252 F.R.D. 308 (M.D.La.2008), *373*

Smith v. Logansport Community School Corp., 139 F.R.D. 637 (N.D.Ind.1991), *551, 561*

South Yuba River Citizens League v. National Marine Fisheries Service, 257 F.R.D. 607 (E.D.Cal.2009), *418*

Sperling v. City of Kennesaw Dept., 202 F.R.D. 325 (N.D.Ga. 2001), *263, 504*

Sporck v. Peil, 759 F.2d 312 (3rd Cir.1985), *261, 503*

Stahl v. Sun Microsystems, Inc., 775 F.Supp. 1397 (D.Colo.1991), *15, 73, 302, 532*

State Farm Mut. Auto. Ins. Co. v. Dowdy ex rel. Dowdy, 445 F.Supp.2d 1289 (N.D.Okla.2006), *307, 311, 317, 321, 528, 539, 559*

Stewart v. Colonial Western Agency, Inc., 105 Cal.Rptr.2d 115 (Cal.App. 2 Dist.2001), *551*

Stone Container Corp. v. Arkwright Mut. Ins. Co., 1995 WL 88902 (N.D.Ill.1995), *261, 503*

Stratosphere Corp. Securities Litigation, In re, 182 F.R.D. 614 (D.Nev.1998), *496, 556, 559*

Sulfuric Acid Antitrust Litigation, In re, 230 F.R.D. 527 (N.D.Ill. 2005), *290*

Suntrust Bank v. Blue Water Fiber, L.P., 210 F.R.D. 196 (E.D.Mich.2002), *290*

Suss v. MSX Intern. Engineering Services, Inc., 212 F.R.D. 159 (S.D.N.Y.2002), *263, 504*

T

Taylor, United States v., 166 F.R.D. 356 (M.D.N.C.1996), *381, 383*

Teleglobe Communications Corp., In re, 392 B.R. 561 (Bkrtcy. D.Del.2008), *264, 418, 504*

Thomas v. Cardwell, 626 F.2d 1375 (9th Cir.1980), *15, 74, 302, 532*

Thomas v. Euro RSCG Life, 264 F.R.D. 120 (S.D.N.Y.2010), *504*

TRW, Inc., United States ex rel. Bagley v., 212 F.R.D. 554 (C.D.Cal.2003), *263, 504*

Tsesmelys v. Dublin Truck Leasing Corp., 78 F.R.D. 181 (E.D.Tenn.1976), *486*

Tuerkes–Beckers, Inc. v. New Castle Associates, 158 F.R.D. 573 (D.Del.1993), *278, 496, 548, 557*

TV–3, Inc. v. Royal Ins. Co. of America, 194 F.R.D. 585 (S.D.Miss.2000), *418*

U

Udkoff v. Hiett By and Through Hiett, 676 So.2d 522 (Fla.App. 2 Dist.1996), *215*

United States v. _____ (see opposing party)

TABLE OF CASES

United States E.E.O.C. v. Caesars Entertainment, Inc., 237 F.R.D. 428 (D.Nev.2006), *351*

United States E.E.O.C. v. Continental Airlines, Inc., 395 F.Supp.2d 738 (N.D.Ill.2005), *264, 504*

United States ex rel. v. _____ (see opposing party and relator)

V

Van Pilsum v. Iowa State University of Science and Technology, 152 F.R.D. 179 (S.D.Iowa 1993), *320, 547*

VMP Intern. Corp. v. Yushkevich, 1993 WL 33463 (S.D.N.Y. 1993), *178*

W

Wanke v. Lynn's Transp. Co., 836 F.Supp. 587 (N.D.Ind.1993), *269, 579*

Western Gas Const. Co. v. Danner, 97 F. 882 (9th Cir.1899), *215*

White, United States v., 846 F.2d 678 (11th Cir.1988), *319*

Wilson v. Kautex, A Textron Co., 2008 WL 189568 (N.D.Ind. 2008), *245, 365, 367, 575*

DEPOSITIONS
IN A NUTSHELL

PART ONE

DEPOSING ADVERSE WITNESSES

This part (Chapters 1 through 15) illustrates common questioning strategies and techniques you might employ in the context of the most common type of deposition, the deposition of an adverse percipient witness. This part discusses strategies and techniques for obtaining complete information, encouraging deponents to provide your desired answer, responding to incomplete, evasive or non-responsive answers, undermining harmful testimony and responding to inconsistent or implausible statements. This part concludes with a discussion of how to respond to objections, instructions not to answer and obstructionist behavior of opposing counsel.

CHAPTER 1

THREE PRIMARY DEPOSITION GOALS

This Chapter focuses on three primary deposition goals you commonly pursue when deposing an adverse witness. These goals are: (1) obtaining a deponent's version of significant events; (2) searching for and confirming helpful evidence; and (3) uncovering and undermining harmful evidence.[1] The questioning strategies and techniques discussed throughout this book help you pursue these three goals.

The Chapter concludes with a brief discussion of the typical goals you pursue when deposing a "neutral" witness.

1. Goal #1—Obtain an Adverse Witness' Version of Significant Events

For the reasons discussed below, you typically want to obtain a deponent's version of significant events. Of course, you cannot pursue every detail about every event about which the deponent has

1. These are, of course, not the only goals you will pursue. In addition, for example, you may want to obtain the names of other possible deponents, assess the credibility of the deponent, determine the capability of opposing counsel, convince your opposition that your client is reluctant to settle, shift the blame from your client to another party, etc.

knowledge. Instead, you have to use your judgment to decide which events are significant enough to inquire into. And to the extent possible, you want to elicit testimony about these events in chronological order. Consider the following examples of "versions of significant events":

 * In an auto accident case, a deponent's version of significant events might consist of the events leading up to the accident, the accident itself, and the events following the accident (e.g., treatment for physical injuries, car repairs, etc.).

 * In a product liability case, a company engineer's version of significant events might describe the company's design, development, marketing and risk assessment for an allegedly defective product.

 * In a wrongful termination case, the plaintiff's supervisor's version of significant events might describe problems with the plaintiff's work as a computer programmer, steps the supervisor took to remedy those problems, the supervisor's decision to fire the plaintiff, and the termination itself.

 * In a breach of contract case, if a deponent is competent to testify only about mitigation of damages, deponent's version would consist of the steps a party took to investigate and purchase substitute goods.

In some cases a deponent's version of what happened may not be a series of discrete, one-time occurrences. Instead, you may get a deponent's version of a common or typical practice or procedure. For example, in a civil rights case challenging a governmental agency's procedures for determining who is eligible for welfare benefits, a deponent's version of what happened might concentrate on the steps the agency usually takes when making eligibility decisions.

Of course, with some deponents you may decide not to pursue a deponent's version of significant events. A deponent may, for example, have knowledge only of a company's organizational structure and therefore have no meaningful version of events to relate.

A. The Benefits of Obtaining an Adverse Witness' Version of Events

There are several benefits to obtaining a deponent's version of significant events:

* <u>Surface critical factual disputes.</u> You typically put together your client's version of what happened as you interview the client and other friendly witnesses. As you position a case for settlement, contemplate a motion for summary judgment, or prepare for trial, you need to know where your client's version differs from your opposition's. The differences in the two versions help to define the important facts admitted by your opponent and the factual disputes you will try to resolve in your client's favor.

* <u>Prepare to undermine your opponent's version.</u> During settlement negotiations and at trial you typically try to convince opposing counsel or the

factfinder that your client's version of what happened is correct. You can do that both by showing that your client's version of what happened is credible, and by showing that the opposition's version of the important events is not credible (e.g., it is implausible and/or internally inconsistent). Obtaining individual deponents' versions of significant events prepares you to attack the credibility of the opposition's overall version of what happened.

* Anticipate trial testimony. At trial, your adversary will frequently elicit testimony from friendly witnesses in chronological story form. By obtaining an adverse witness' version of events, you can anticipate direct examination and have a useful basis from which to prepare for cross.

* Obtain helpful evidence. When you obtain a deponent's version of what happened, a deponent may mention helpful information you would not otherwise have thought to ask about. After all, when you prepare for deposition, you cannot think of every topic that might uncover helpful evidence.

B. The Risks of Obtaining an Adverse Witness' Version of Events

Despite these very real advantages, putting a deponent's version of events on the record at deposition does entail some risks. The chief ones are these:

* Preserve trial testimony. Evidence rules allow attorneys to offer depositions of unavailable wit-

nesses into evidence at trial. (FRCP 32.) If you elicit a deponent's version of significant events, and the deponent is unavailable at trial, your opponent may offer the deposition against you to establish his client's version of what happened.

* <u>Assist careless adversaries.</u> Your adversary's lawyer may be a near-incompetent who neglects to obtain versions of events from friendly witnesses. Your deposition, then, may provide a useful service for opposing counsel.

In most cases, neither of these risks justifies forgoing the advantages of eliciting deponents' versions of what happened. Statistically, most cases settle before trial, and most deponents are available to testify at trial. Thus, the likelihood that an adversary will offer a deposition you take into evidence at trial is quite low. And in those cases in which an important adverse witness is likely to be unavailable for trial, your adversary would probably elicit a deponent's version of events to perpetuate the testimony for use at trial if you fail to do so. As to the risk of helping an adversary's incompetent lawyer, such a lawyer will probably not greatly benefit from and may not even recognize your generosity.

2. Goal #2—Searching for and Confirming Helpful Evidence

You will not simply be satisfied with obtaining the information an adverse deponent is willing to disclose as you ask questions pursuing the deponent's version of events. You routinely inquire into the specific topics and events that you identified during deposition preparation (or that occur to you as the deposition unfolds) that might produce helpful evidence to support your client's case. For example, in a wrongful termination case, assume that you have no information about whether or not the supervisor who discharged your client ever received compliments about your client's work. As this would constitute helpful evidence, you might ask the deponent questions such as, "Are you aware, from any source whatsoever, that anyone ever complimented my client's work?"

You also frequently want to ask a deponent to confirm the accuracy of significant helpful evidence even if you already have a source for the helpful evidence. For example, again assume that you represent a plaintiff in a wrongful termination case. Your client has told you that he exceeded his sales quota in the two months prior to his termination. You are deposing the client's supervisor. You might question the supervisor to determine if he will confirm that your client exceeded the sales quotas. Doing so helps you determine whether helpful evidence is disputed or admitted.

3. Goal #3—Uncovering and Undermining Harmful Evidence

A third goal is to uncover and undermine harmful evidence. Of course, much of an adverse deponent's version of what happened will constitute harmful evidence. However, you'll typically want to ferret out any additional harmful evidence of which a deponent is aware.

Trying to uncover additional harmful evidence is not a product of masochistic tendencies. You need to be aware of the harmful evidence available to your adversary so as not to be blind-sided by the information during settlement negotiations or at trial. Only if you have a complete picture of the evidence and arguments your opponent may make can you prepare to meet them.

For example, assume that you represent Danny Jackson, the plaintiff in a wrongful termination suit. The defendant claims that your client was discharged in part because of customer complaints. At the deposition of your client's supervisor, you might ask the following questions to ferret out potential harmful evidence:

Q: Mr. Jackson worked on the Johnson and Frank account for over three years, correct?

A: That's right.

Q: Are you aware of information from any source that indicates that any of the customers at Johnson and Frank ever complained about anything that Mr. Jackson did on that account?

A: No, I don't know of anything on that account.

Q: Mr. Jackson worked on the Pittsfield account for over a year, correct?

A: For at least a year.

Q: Are you aware of information from any source that indicates that any of the customers at

Pittsfield ever complained about anything that my client did on that account?

A: Yes. Mark Herman, the marketing director for Pittsfield, complained that Jackson was late developing the marketing plan for one of their major housing developments, the one in Riverdale county.

Q: Other than Herman's complaint about the development in Riverdale, are you aware of any information from any source that indicates that any of the customers at Pittsfield ever complained about anything else that my client did on that account?

A: No, I'm not.

Knowing that the company claims that it received a complaint from Herman allows you to think about how you might respond to the claim. For example, either later in this deposition or through subsequent discovery, you might try to show that Herman never in fact made such a complaint, or that the complaint was unknown to the people who made the decision to fire Jackson.

Despite the advantages of identifying harmful evidence, you may choose in a particular situation to forego a search for additional harmful evidence. For instance, you might choose to forego a search when:

* Inquiring into a particular topic might surface damaging evidence or highlight a legal theory, affirmative defense, or argument that opposing

counsel probably would not have otherwise uncovered.

* A deponent is likely to be unavailable at trial, and you do not want the harmful evidence to be read in at trial from the deposition.

4. The Order of Inquiry

You typically do not pursue the three goals described above in sequential order. That is, rarely does it make sense to seek a version of events, then go back in an effort to confirm and search for helpful evidence that failed to emerge earlier, and then go back again and search for and try to undermine harmful evidence. Instead, you typically shift from one goal to another throughout a deposition. For example, assume that a deponent has testified to his version of what took place during an important meeting. That version did not mention a topic that your client has told you was raised at the meeting and that constitutes helpful evidence. Thus, before continuing with the deponent's version of events, you might well ask the deponent to confirm that the topic was raised at the meeting. You might also probe for and seek to undermine harmful evidence that did not emerge during the deponent's initial version of what occurred at the meeting.

5. Goals When Deposing "Neutral" Witnesses

Your goals may change when you depose a neutral witness, i.e. someone who is not associated with any party in the case.

You may have talked to a neutral witness prior to deposition and believe that the witness' testimony will be favorable for your case. If so, you may take the deposition only to preserve the witness' helpful testimony for later use at trial or in connection with a pre-trial motion or settlement. Chapter 21 discusses how to conduct such a deposition.

If a neutral witness will not talk to you, you will not know whether a neutral witness' testimony will be favorable. You may nevertheless decide to depose the witness. If so, you want to search for and confirm helpful evidence and obtain the deponent's version of significant events. You may well decide, however, not to actively pursue the goal of uncovering and undermining harmful evidence. If such evidence does not surface at the deposition, your opponent may remain unaware of it throughout the case.

CHAPTER 2

OBTAINING COMPLETE INFOR-MATION: THE T–FUNNEL QUESTIONING PATTERN

As you probably know, adverse parties and witnesses are frequently reluctant to provide you with complete information. This natural tendency to withhold information may be reinforced by instructions from deponent's counsel to answer questions as narrowly as possible and to refrain from volunteering. This Chapter and Chapter 3 describe and illustrate two questioning patterns that you can routinely use throughout a deposition to obtain complete information from an adverse deponent.

This Chapter discusses the T–Funnel questioning pattern. You can use a T–Funnel pattern to systematically explore everything that a deponent knows about any topic, subject or event. You can use this pattern when you are searching for helpful evidence, obtaining a deponent's version of significant events, or uncovering and undermining harmful evidence.

1. The T–Funnel Questioning Pattern

The T–Funnel pattern has two basic components:

*A series of two or more open questions seeking a narrative response concerning a topic or event.

*A series of closed or leading questions seeking "yes" or "no" answers related to the topic or event.

This pattern is called a T–Funnel because the questions are broader or more open at the top and narrower or more closed at the bottom. This pattern can be depicted graphically as follows:

OPEN

OPEN

OPEN

OPEN

CLOSED/
LEADING

CLOSED/
LEADING

CLOSED/
LEADING

CLOSED/
LEADING

A. An Illustration of the T–Funnel Pattern

The following sequence illustrates the use of the T–Funnel pattern for the topic "people who reported directly to the deponent":

1. Q: Who are the people that reported directly to you?

2. A: Paul Blasi, Jack Carlson and Ann Freeman.

3. Q: Who else reported directly to you?

4. A: Well, I guess you could say that Dave Moore did also.

5. Q: Who else?

6. A: That's it; just those four people.

7. Q: Al Bergman reported to you, didn't he?

8. A: Yes, sometimes he reported to me.

9. Q: Did Melinda Johnson report to you?

10. A: No, she did not report directly to me.

11. Q: Shari Binder reported directly to you, correct?

12. A: Once in awhile, yes.

13. Q: Have you now told me about everyone who reported to you?

14. A: Yes.

In this example, the questioner first asks a series of open questions (Nos. 1, 3 and 5). These questions are "open" because they call for a narrative response, rather than a "yes" or "no" answer.

Then, when the open questions appear to have exhausted the deponent's independent recollection (No. 6), the questioner turns to closed/leading questions (Nos. 7, 9, 11 and 13) seeking additional information that the deponent may have omitted. Closed questions typically seek a "yes" or "no" answer (Nos. 9 and 13). Leading questions are closed questions that suggest the desired "yes" or "no" answer (Nos. 7 and 11). At the deposition of an adverse witness, you are entitled to ask closed/leading questions at any time.[1]

You may develop the closed/leading questions at the bottom of the T–Funnel as you prepare for deposition and identify information that might help your client's case. Alternatively, you might develop these closed/leading questions during the deposition, based on your instinct and intuition, either in an effort to obtain helpful testimony or to simply find out everything a deponent knows about a topic or event.

B. Using a Series of T–Funnels

When a topic is very narrow or specific, you can sometimes exhaust the deponent's knowledge with

1. See FRE 611 9 (c). See also Wright & Gold, Federal Practice and Procedure: Evidence § 6168; see also Haney v. Mizell Memorial Hosp., 744 F.2d 1467 (11th Cir. 1984); Ellis v. City of Chicago, 667 F.2d 606 (7th Cir. 1981); Stahl v. Sun Microsystems, Inc., 775 F.Supp. 1397 (D. Colo. 1991). For a discussion of the meaning of "hostile" witness, see Wright & Gold, Federal Practice and Procedure: Evidence § 6168; Thomas v. Cardwell, 626 F.2d 1375 (9th Cir. 1980); United States v. Brown, 603 F.2d 1022 (1st Cir. 1979); Rossano v. Blue Plate Foods, Inc., 314 F.2d 174 (5th Cir. 1963).

a single T–Funnel. This was the case in the immediately preceding example. It is far more common, however, to use a **series of T–Funnels** to exhaust the deponent's knowledge about a subject, topic or event.

> **Example**: You represent the plaintiff in a wrongful termination case and are deposing your client's former supervisor. You want to find out the deponent's version of everything that happened at the meeting when the deponent and your client reviewed your client's last performance report.

<u>**Initial T–Funnel**</u>—What happened at the meeting to review the last performance report.

1. Q: Mr. Gillig, you said that you met with my client to review his last performance report, I'd like you to tell me everything you can recall about that meeting.

2. A: Well, we discussed the **contents of the report** and I told him that he'd **have to improve**.

3. Q: Other than going over the report, and telling him he'd have to improve, what else happened?

4. A: Nothing.

5. Q: Did you discuss any documents other than his performance report?

6. A: Yes, we briefly went over the **written response that he had made** to the performance report.

7.   Q: Did you discuss any other documents?

8.   A: No.

9.   Q: Did you discuss anything other than his performance report and the fact that he would have to improve or be let go?

10.   A: I don't really remember.

11.   Q: Take your time and think about it. Can you remember discussing anything in this meeting other than his performance report and the fact that he would have to improve or be let go?

12.   A: I can't remember anything else.

13.   Q: Did you talk about **what might happen if my client did not improve**?

14.   A: Yes, we did discuss that.

15.   Q: Okay, and you talked about a **time table for evaluating my client's performance,** correct?

16.   A: Yes, we did. I told him that I'd be giving him another review in a month.

17.   Q: Did you talk about any changes in my client's responsibilities?

18.   A: No, we didn't talk about that.

19.   Q: Did you discuss anything else at the meeting other than what you have told me about?

20.   A: No.

As you completed your **Initial T–Funnel** on "what happened at the meeting to discuss the performance report,'' you identified the following topics that were discussed at the meeting.

(1) The contents of the performance report.

(2) The need for your client to improve.

(3) Your client's written response to the performance report.

(4) What might happen if your client did not improve.

(5) A time table for evaluating your client's performance.

To obtain the deponent's complete version of what happened at this meeting you might want to do secondary T–Funnels of some or all of these five topics. For example, a secondary T–Funnel of (1) above might begin as follows:

Secondary T–Funnel—What was discussed when your client and the deponent reviewed the **contents of his performance report**.

21. I'm showing you what has been marked as Exhibit 27. Is this the performance report you went over with my client during the March 2nd meeting?

22. A: Yes.

23. Q: Could you go through each section of the report and tell me what was said with respect to that section?

24. A: Well, we went over section 3 first and I said....

This **Secondary T–Funnel** might well produce answers that identify yet additional topics that you might inquire into with additional T–Funnels.

After using multiple T–Funnels to get the deponent's version of what was discussed about the **contents of the performance report**, you could then turn to (2) above, the topic of the **need for your client to improve**. You might need another series of T–Funnels to obtain the deponent's complete version of what was discussed on this topic. For example, assume that when asking a question about the need for your client to show improvement, the deponent mentions that your client was told that he must show improvement within a three month period. You might then T–Funnel all the reasons the deponent had for selecting this three month period.

How many T–Funnels you use to probe a particular topic or event is a matter of judgment. Generally speaking, the more significant a topic or event, the more extensively you will question.

C.   *T–Funnels and Note Taking*

Taking notes will help you to complete your T–Funnel questioning. Thus, in the above example, as you complete you **Initial T–Funnel** about what happened in the meeting to review your client's performance report, you will want to make a note of the topics or subjects the deponent mentions so that you can follow up with **Secondary T–Funnels**. Your notes for the **Initial T–Funnel** on the meeting to review the performance report might look like the following:

-contents of report

-need to improve

-client's written response

-what happens if no improvement.

-time table for evaluating performance.

If you fail to take notes, you will almost certainly have great difficulty remembering all the topics on which you want to complete **Secondary T–Funnels**. You could, of course, ask the court reporter to read back the testimony. But reading back testimony will dramatically slow the pace of the deposition.

2.   Benefits of the T–Funnel Pattern

You realize several benefits from using T–Funnels at deposition.

* T–Funnels promote thoroughness. The open questions at the beginning of a T–Funnel exhaust a deponent's independent **recall** (relying on a deponent's own paths of association). When responding to such open questions, a deponent may volunteer information about which you would not otherwise have specifically thought to ask. The closed/leading questions at the bottom of the T attempt to stimulate a deponent's **recognition** memory by suggesting information that a deponent may have overlooked. This recognition phenomenon is reflected in the common expression,

"Now that you mention that, I do remember something about...."

* The open questions at the beginning of a T–Funnel tend to **minimize a deponent's ability to hide evidence** that helps your client's case. The open questions at the top of the T typically ask the deponent to relate everything the deponent knows about a particular subject or event. These open questions give no hint as to the exact information you are seeking. Hence, the open questions at the top of the T may increase your chances of obtaining evidence that a disingenuous or mendacious deponent might hide or slant if you asked a direct question.

* The closed/leading questions at the bottom of a T–Funnel likewise minimize a wily deponent's opportunity to "conveniently forget" or hide information by claiming that you never specifically asked for that particular data.[2]

* A T–Funnel is flexible enough to cover any **topic, subject** or **event** you deem important. For example, you can use a T–Funnel to inquire into each of the following:

*The reasons an employer fired an employee

*The risks known to a manufacturer when a product was first placed on the market.

2. For an interesting example of the importance of asking specific as well as general questions, see R. Posner, An Affair Of State: The Investigation, Impeachment, and Trial of President Clinton 44 (1999).

*What happened at a meeting between the plaintiff and the defendant.

*The actions taken by the plaintiff in reliance on the alleged false statements of the defendant.

*The reasons a plaintiff believed she was terminated because of her race.

*The basis for a deponent's opinion that your client was "unhappy" at his job.

3. Avoiding Problems in T-Funnel Questioning

This section addresses two common problems that may interfere with your ability to use T-Funnels and suggests approaches for overcoming them.

A. *Problem #1: Failure to Go to the Bottom of a T-Funnel*

You need not slavishly complete every T-Funnel you start during a deposition. For many reasons you might **consciously** choose to temporarily or permanently abandon a T-Funnel before completing it. For example, as questioning proceeds, you might temporarily abandon a T-Funnel to refresh a deponent's recollection with a document. Similarly, you might decide to permanently abandon a topic without bothering to ask closed questions at the bottom of the T-Funnel if you conclude that a deponent has little or no knowledge about that topic. But you need to guard against **inadvertently** failing to complete a T-Funnel, especially when inquiring about an important topic. This typically occurs when a deponent mentions something about which you are particularly interested. Instead of completing the T–Funnel, you may inadvertently abandon it and turn immediately to the new topic that interests you.

For example, assume that you represent Ms. Romero, who was allegedly defrauded into executing a note and deed of trust on her home in favor of Carl Smith. Smith subsequently sold the note and deed of trust to Hammer, who wants to enforce it against your client. You contend that Hammer cannot enforce the note because she should have known that Smith defrauded your client and therefore is not a purchaser in good faith. You are deposing Hammer and are T–Funneling the topic "all the aliases used by Carl Smith" when dealing with Hammer.

1. Q: In your dealings with Mr. Smith, did he ever use names other than Carl Smith?

2. A: A couple of times.

3. Q: What names did he use besides Carl Smith?

4. A: Once he used the name Ralph Schmidt and once Bill Sharp.

5. Q: What other names did he use?

6. A: I guess once he used the name Bob Snyder.

7. Q: What other names did he use?

8.   A: Well around the middle of last year, it was at the same time that I bought the note and deed of Ms. Romero, he was still going by Bob Snyder.

9.   Q: You purchased both the note and deed of trust at the same time?

10.   A: That's right.

11.   Q: Did Smith tell you why he was also using the name Snyder around the time you purchased the note?

12.   A: I didn't ask him.

13.   Q: But did he say anything about why he was using the name Snyder?

14.   A: Yes, but I can't remember what he said.

15.   Q: Where were you when you had this conversation?

16.   A: It was in my office when Smith first brought over the note and deed of trust from Ms. Romero.

17.   Q: Okay, start at the beginning and tell me everything that happened when Smith came over.

18.   A: Well it was around 5:00 in the afternoon. . . .

Here, you start out to learn all the aliases Smith used when dealing with Hammer. However, at No. 9 you leave the initial T–Funnel about aliases and ask about the purchase of a note and deed of trust. Then in Nos. 11 and 13, you make a second switch and take up the subject of what Smith said about why he was using the alias of Snyder. And by No.

17, you are well into an inquiry about what happened when Smith purchased a note and deed of trust executed by Ms. Romero. The original T–Funnel of "all aliases used by Smith" will probably never be completed and you may not learn whether Smith used other aliases in addition to Schmidt, Sharp and Snyder.[3]

Solution—"Park" References to Subjects or Events that Interest You So that You Can Inquire About Them Later

In the above example, you should have "parked" interesting topics until you completed the inquiry about all aliases used by Smith. To "park," simply make an indication in your notes to explore a parked topic later in the deposition. For example, here you might have made a quick reference in your notes that "Smith using the name Snyder" was a matter for later inquiry.

The need to park information is particularly important with hostile, evasive deponents. Such deponents often do not want to tell you all they know about a potentially damaging subject or event. As a result, when you start your T–Funnel inquiry into such a subject or event, these deponents may consciously provide an answer that mentions new and interesting subjects outside the scope of the T–Funnel. If you grab the lure and abandon your initial T–Funnel, you allow the deponent to successfully hide information you would otherwise have

3. While use of many aliases in a situation such as this may sound far-fetched, this example is based on an actual case in which the defendant used at least 9 aliases.

gotten at the bottom of the T–Funnel. In addition, the deponent will also escape a legal dilemma. Your switch from the initial T–Funnel to a new subject allows the deponent to avoid choosing between revealing damaging information and committing perjury.

B. *Problem #2: The T–Funnel Is Too Vague or Too Broad*

If you try to T–Funnel an ill-defined subject or a long period of time, the information that results is likely to be vague and conclusory.

For example, assume that you try to use T–Funnel questioning on the subject of "my client's performance as a sales representative during his 3 years at Oren Corp." The topic is extremely broad, covering both a substantial period of time and numerous relevant subtopics (e.g., plaintiff's sales, work habits, ethics, etc.). As a result, T–Funnel questioning is unlikely to be thorough:

* Open questions (e.g., "Tell me about the plaintiff's performance as a sales representative.") are unlikely to be productive. The scientific theorem that "the angle of incidence equals the angle of reflection" is usually matched by the practical reality that overly broad questions produce overly broad, vague answers. For instance, a deponent is likely to respond to the question above with an answer such as, "Your client was never very good. He just didn't have the drive or the right attitude and he had lots of problems."

* When the answers to open questions are vague, the only way you can develop information is to rely entirely on closed/leading questions. Such questions are unlikely to exhaust a deponent's knowledge because you lose the benefit of the deponent's independent recall.

Solution—Narrow Your Focus to More Discrete Subjects or Events

T–Funnel questioning promotes thoroughness so long as you focus on discrete subjects or events. Thus, to use T–Funnel questioning effectively you'll usually need to break long periods of time into shorter ones, and general subjects into discrete subtopics. Simply put, try to chop big chunks of information into smaller chips. For example, instead of asking broadly about "my client's job performance over 3 years," consider narrower topics such as:

* The client's participation in staff meetings.

* The client's strengths as a sales person.

* The client's weaknesses as a sales person.

* What was said in the client's last performance evaluation.

* Changes in the client's work responsibilities during the last year.

4. Consciously Omitting Closed Questions at the Bottom of the T to Limit Damaging Testimony

As discussed above, for many reasons you may consciously decide to refrain from completing a T–Funnel. You will be particularly likely to avoid closed questions at the bottom of a T when inquiring into potentially harmful topics or events. For example, assume that you represent the plaintiff in a wrongful termination case. Your client says that on his last day at work he was told by his **supervisor** that he was being discharged for alleged insubordination, having unexcused absences from work and making inappropriate sexual advances to one of his co-workers. You are now deposing the **vice president** who decided to discharge your client and you are T–Funneling the "reasons why your client was fired":

1. Q: Ms. Rosen, are you the person who decided to discharge my client?

2. A: Yes I did, after talking to his supervisor and reviewing his personnel file.

3. Q: I'd like you to tell me all the reasons that you decided to discharge my client, Mr. Duffy.

4. A: Well, Duffy had been absent from work on several occasions without authorization and he was repeatedly insubordinate to his supervisor after being warned not to be.

5. Q: Are there any other reasons that you decided to discharge my client?

6. A: No. That's it.

7. Q: So you decided to discharge my client because you thought he had been absent from work on several occasions without authorization and he was repeatedly insubordinate to his supervisor after being warned not to be, is that correct?

8.   A: That's correct.

9.   Q: And as far as you were concerned, Duffy's being absent from work on several occasions without authorization and being repeatedly insubordinate to his supervisor after being warned not to be were the only reasons he was discharged, is that correct?

10.   A: Well, he may have had some other problems with his work—I don't know—but those were the only reasons that I decided to discharge him.

In this example, you ask no closed/leading questions at the bottom of the T–Funnel. If you had asked questions such as, "Did you decide to fire Mr. Duffy in part because of any allegations that he had made inappropriate advances to a co-worker?" you would run the risk of either reminding the deponent of harmful testimony she had forgotten or suggesting harmful testimony to a mendacious deponent and opposing counsel.

Deciding whether to omit closed/leading questions when inquiring into matters that are potentially damaging is a strategic judgment. The risks must be weighed against the potential benefits of asking such closed questions. One benefit of asking closed questions is that you may obtain a favorable answer and strengthen your impeachment should a deponent later change his testimony. For instance, in the above example, assume that you did ask the following closed question: "Did you decide to fire Mr. Duffy in part because of any allegations that he

had made inappropriate advances to a co-worker?''
An explicit ''No'' answer would help your case and
allow you to more effectively impeach the deponent
should he later change his testimony. A second
benefit is that if the harmful evidence exists you
will learn about it at the deposition rather than
being surprised by it later. If the evidence exists,
you may be able to undermine it during the deposition or through subsequent discovery. You must
weigh such potential benefits against the risk of
unearthing additional harmful evidence.

5. Inverted T–Funnels

Another way to use a T–Funnel pattern is to turn
it upside down and ask closed/leading questions
first, followed by open questions. In a child custody
case, for example, you might invert the T–Funnel
about the information the deponent has indicating
your client was a good father. For example:

1. Q: Did you ever see Mr. Yeazell help his
    children with their homework?

2. A: No.

3. Q: Did you ever see Mr. Yeazell cook dinner
    for the children?

4. A: A couple of times.

5. Q: Do you know if Mr. Yeazell ever took his
    children to sporting events?

6. A: Yes. He took them to soccer games and
    baseball games.

7. Q: Did you ever see him watching television with his children?

8. A: Sure, but he would often yell at the kids to be quiet so he could hear the T.V.

9. Q: And you saw Mr. Yeazell put the children to bed, correct?

10. A: No.

11. Q: Tell me about any other things you observed that you thought were positive interactions between Mr. Yeazell and his children.

12. A: Well he would sometimes....

In this example, you invert the T–Funnel by asking closed/leading questions first (Questions 1–9) and following up with an open question (Question 11) to find out about information your closed questions may have missed. This pattern may sometimes work better than the normal T–Funnel pattern because it avoids people's psychological tendencies to conform specific data to previously-expressed opinions.[4] If you begin by asking a deponent for an opinion (e.g. "Did you ever see Mr. Yeazell have what you thought were positive interactions with his children?") and the adverse deponent gives a harmful answer, the deponent may then be inclined to conform answers to subsequent questions to the harmful opinion. The inverted T–

4. See R. Kahn and C. Cannell, The Dynamics of Interviewing; Theory, Technique, and Cases 160 (1957).

Funnel seeks to avoid the potential biasing effect of asking for the opinion first.

6. Common T–Funnels

The precise topics and events you will T–Funnel obviously depend on the legal and factual issues in an individual case. There are, however, certain T–Funnels that you will routinely use during depositions. These T–Funnels are illustrated below.

A. *"Everything That Happened During a Given Event" T–Funnels*

You will frequently use a T–Funnel or a series of T–Funnels to learn what happened during an event or on a specific occasion.

Example 1

"Tell me everything that occurred during the meeting in Mr. Hobbs' office."

"Did X occur?"

"Did Y occur?"

Example 2

"Tell me everything that occurred from the time the police arrived until the ambulance got there."

"Did X occur?"

"Did Y occur?"

When T–Funneling an event, you will frequently want to get the **"event essentials"** either before or after doing your T–Funnel. The event essentials are typically the following: who was present, where and when did it take place, how long did it last, why did the event take place, and did anyone record or memorialize information about what happened during the event. This information may identify potential witnesses and will often help you assess the credibility of the deponent's testimony about what happened at the event. For example, if a meeting lasted two hours but the deponent remembers almost nothing about what happened, you may be able to argue that the deponent's testimony is implausible and therefore undermines her credibility.

B. *"Clumped Events" T–Funnels*

Frequently, you will want to know what happened during each event in a series of events. If a deponent can separate the series into individual events, a T–Funnel pattern such as that in "A" above should prove useful in learning what occurred during each separate instance. Unfortunately, however, deponents often cannot separate a series of events into individual discrete events. For example, a deponent may know that the environmental ramifications of a proposed project were discussed at several meetings but be unable to remember precisely what was said about the environmental considerations at each meeting. Or a deponent may know that she received various physical therapy treatments for a shoulder injury on several occasions but not recall what precise treatment she received during any particular visit to the therapist.

When a deponent knows generally what happened during a series of events, but cannot recall exactly what happened during any individual event, you have a "clumped event." However, you can still use a T–Funnel pattern. As the following example illustrates, you T–Funnel a clumped event by treating all the events as a single unit.

1.   Q: Ms. Shaw, before Mr. Grubb contacted you about the Hanley Avenue apartment building, had you ever discussed the building's vacancy factor with any other prospective buyers?

2.   A: Yes.

3.   Q: When was the first time you had such a discussion?

4.   A: I don't recall. I had discussions about this property on and off for almost a year before Mr. Grubb contacted me.

5.   Q: Can you recall the names of any of these prospective buyers?

6.   A: Well, I believe there was a Ms. Wu and a Mr. Osterreich. Oh yes, there was also a Mr. Pretty.

7.   Q: Can you recall the names of any other possible buyers?

8.   A: No.

9.   Q: Did you discuss the vacancy factor with Ms. Wu?

10.   A: I probably did, but I can't say for sure.

11.   Q: How about with Mr. Osterreich and Mr. Pretty?

12.   A: I'm sure I did.

13.   Q: Well, let's start with Mr. Pretty. What did you tell Mr. Pretty about the vacancy factor in the Hanley Avenue apartments?

14.   A: I don't know. I talked with all these people on several occasions. I can't remember what happened specifically with any one of them.

15.   Q: Okay. Tell me everything that you discussed with Ms. Wu, Mr. Pretty or Mr. Osterreich regarding the vacancy factor in the Hanley Avenue apartments.

16.   A: We talked about how the vacancy factor was seasonal and that it varied from ten to twenty percent.

17.   Q: What else was talked about with regard to vacancies?

18.   A: That vacancies also varied depending upon whether the empty units were one or two bedroom units.

19.   Q: Besides vacancies varying because of the season, or whether the empty units had one or two bedrooms and the percent of vacancies, what else was discussed regarding vacancies with these prospective buyers?

20.   A: That's all I can recall.

21.   Q: Did you discuss whether vacancies varied depending on a given apartment's location?

22. A: Yes.

23. Q: Did you discuss whether the vacancy factor depended in any way on who was managing the apartment?

24. A: Yes.

25. Q: How about vacancies in competing apartment buildings? Did you discuss whether competing vacancies influenced the vacancy rate at Hanley Avenue?

26. A: No.

27. Q: Can you recall anything else that was discussed with prospective buyers regarding vacancies in the Hanley Avenue apartments that you have not told me about?

28. A: No.

29. Q: Okay, let's go back to your discussions about how the season of the year affected the vacancy rate. What was said about that?

30. A: Well....

Questions 1 through 11 reflect several attempts to identify prospective buyers with whom the deponent discussed vacancy factors. Question 13 attempts to have the deponent describe what was said about the vacancy factor with an individual prospective buyer. When it becomes obvious that the deponent is unable to do so, No. 15 begins a T–Funnel to examine the various conversations that the deponent had with the prospective buyers as a single unit. Nos. 15, 17 and 19 start the T–Funnel with open ended questions. In No. 20 the deponent indicates that she cannot recall anything else in response to open questions. Then Nos. 21, 23, and 25 use closed questions to ask about specific possibilities that lawyer has identified. Finally, in No. 28 the deponent states that she can recall nothing else that was discussed with regard to vacancies. The questioning then shifts to secondary T–Funnels. No. 29 starts a secondary T–Funnel on the topic of seasonal vacancies, a topic which the deponent mentioned in No. 16.

C. *"Everything That You Did or Said" T–Funnels*

You may also use T–Funnels to investigate all that a deponent did or said.

<u>Example 1</u>

"Tell me everything that you did to investigate my client's claim that she was being treated unfairly."

"Did you ...?"

"Did you ...?"

<u>Example 2</u>

"Tell me everything that you did to try to obtain construction financing between the time of the initial meeting and the meeting on the fourth of February."

"Did you ...?"

"Did you ...?"

<u>Example 3</u>

"Tell me everything you told Ms. Jones about the stock before she agreed to purchase the 2500 shares."

"Did you . . .?"

"Did you . . .?"

D. "All the Reasons" T–Funnels

Frequently, you will want to learn all the reasons **why** a deponent undertook (or failed to undertake) a particular action. A T–Funnel or a series of T–Funnels will prove useful in gaining the information you seek.

Example 1

"Tell me all the reasons that you denied my client's request for a transfer to another department."

"Was another reason . . .?"

"Was another reason . . .?"

Example 2

"Tell me all the reasons that you decided not to include the language on Exhibit 12 in the final report."

"Was another reason . . .?"

"Was another reason . . .?"

E. "Basis for a Conclusion, Opinion or Belief" T–Funnels

Conclusions and opinions are often liberally sprinkled throughout deposition testimony. Sometimes you will specifically ask for a conclusion, opinion or belief. For example, in a breach of contract case involving a software program, defense counsel might ask a plaintiff's employee if the employee believed that the defendant's program "functioned properly." Moreover, whether or not you ask for a conclusion or opinion, a deponent will often give you one:

"Q: Mr. Shahriari, why do you think Wonderful Mortgage rejected my client's loan application?

A: Because Mr. Grubb was not financially qualified."

Whenever a deponent testifies to an opinion, conclusion or belief regarding an important matter, a T–Funnel typically will prove useful in learning all the bases for the conclusion, opinion or belief. Such T–Funnels usually begin with questions such as:

Q: Please tell me all the reasons why you concluded that Mr. Grubb was not financially qualified.

Q: Please tell me everything you observed that led you to conclude the software program was defective.

F.   *"Reactions to an Occurrence or Event" T–Funnels*

A deponent's reactions to a significant event or occurrence can often provide you with useful information. Consequently, you will frequently use a "tell me your reactions to" T–Funnel. Such T–Funnels usually begin with question such as:

<u>Example 1</u>

Q: You testified that Johnson yelled at Mr. Smith when going over Smith's employee evaluation, what were your reactions when Johnson yelled at Smith?

A: I thought Johnson was a bit out of line.

Q: Did you have any other reactions?

A: I also thought that . . . .

Example 2

Q: You previously testified that the plaintiff called you and told you that the software delivery would be two weeks late, what were your reactions when the plaintiff told you that?

A: My first reaction was that we'd probably miss our deadline for delivery of the computer program to State Line Bank, one of our biggest customers.

Q: Did you have any other reactions to Plaintiff's telephone call saying the software would be two weeks late?

A: I was concerned that . . . .

G. "Do You Have Information to Help Prove My Case" T–Funnels

Even when deposing an adverse witness, you can sometimes use a T–Funnel pattern to obtain information that will help you prove your case.[5] For example, assume that your client is a software developer who provided computer software to Big Bank. Big Bank claims that the software is defective

---

5. For a discussion of how to identify topics that you might inquire into to help you prove your case, see Chapter 16.

and sues for rescission, seeking to recover the entire contract price. Your client admits that there were minor problems with the software program. But you contend that the program worked well and thus there was no material breach justifying rescission and return of the entire contract price. You are deposing an employee of Big Bank who worked in their computer department. To help prove your case, you might T–Funnel the topic of "the functions the program performed well" as follows:

1. Q: You've told me about the various problems you had with the software. I'd like you to tell me all the functions or tasks that the program performed without problems.

2. A: Well, it did work fine on some of the things. It allowed us to do our monthly earnings reports and loss control checks just fine.

3. Q: What other functions or tasks did the program perform without problems?

4. A: Well, there were lots of database searches that we performed from time to time that were fine. But we didn't do those kinds of searches very often.

5. Q: What other functions or tasks did the program perform without problems?

6. A: That's about it.

7. Q: What about generating monthly statements to be mailed to the customers, was that function performing well?

8. A: We had a problem with that the first week the software was installed.

9. Q: After the first week, you didn't have any problems generating monthly statements to be mailed to the customers, did you?

10. A: Not really.

11. Q: What about delinquent loan reports, were you able to produce those without any problems?

12. A: Well....

This is only one example of how you might use a T–Funnel to obtain evidence to support your case. You might, for instance, use such a T–Funnel in the following cases:

*Wrongful Termination Cases: You represent the plaintiff, who was terminated from her employment allegedly for poor work performance and insubordination. You contend that the plaintiff performed satisfactorily and was terminated because of a non-work related argument with her supervisor. When deposing the plaintiff's supervisor, you could T–Funnel the topic of "tasks the plaintiff performed satisfactorily."

*Child Custody Cases: You represent a father in a divorce and child custody case. The wife contends that she should be awarded exclusive custody of the children and your client seeks joint custody. You contend that your client is a devoted father. You are deposing a neighbor who is a close, supportive friend of the wife and has spent a substantial amount of time in the family home. You might T–Funnel "all the positive interactions she observed between the father and his children."

H.   *"All the Documents" T–Funnels*

A final area where a T–Funnel pattern commonly proves useful is in uncovering documents. This sort of T–Funnel commonly begins with questions such as:

"Can you identify all the files containing documents that relate in any way to the police department's investigation into the events surrounding the arrest of my client?"

"What documents does your department have that in any way describe the duties of an admissions counselor?"

CHAPTER 3

OBTAINING COMPLETE INFOR-MATION: THE TIMELINE QUES-TIONING PATTERN

This Chapter describes the Timeline questioning pattern, a second questioning pattern that you use repeatedly throughout a deposition, whether you are obtaining a deponent's version of significant events, searching for helpful evidence, or uncovering and undermining harmful evidence.

The Chapter concludes by illustrating how you might obtain complete information by combining Timeline questioning with the T–Funnel technique described in Chapter 2.

1. What Are Timelines?

A Timeline is a chronologically-ordered series of events or occurrences relating to a particular topic or subject matter. For example, a Timeline might cover subjects such as:

* A plaintiff's activities up to and following a traffic accident.

* The process followed in creating or designing an allegedly defective product.

* The actions a defendant took to mitigate damages after an alleged breach of contract.

44

* The steps that an agency usually follows when processing an application for welfare benefits.

* Instances when a plaintiff allegedly was insubordinate in the six months prior to termination.

* Everything that happened when a health inspector visited a restaurant.

* Everything that happened during a prospective buyer's visit to a sheet metal plant.

2.   The Basic Timeline Questioning Pattern

*Seek the earliest Timeline event.

You begin by establishing the first event in the Timeline.

Example 1: Q: On the morning that the accident occurred, what was the first thing that happened after you left the warehouse?

Example 2: Q: When was the first time that my client was insubordinate?

Example 3: Q: You said that you informed my client about the risks involved in purchasing the building. When was the first time you discussed those risks with my client?

*Move the Timeline forward to the next event in the sequence.

Once you have established the first event in the sequence, move the Timeline forward to the next event in the chronological sequence.

Example 1: Q: After you met with him in his home sometime around March, when was the next time anything happened with respect to the balloon payment on my client's loan?

Example 2: Q: After you review an application for completeness, what is the next thing that the agency does with the application?

Example 3: Q: After you talked with the building contractor, what was the next thing that occurred that was in any way related to estimating the damages to the foundation of your house?

*Identify (even if only approximately) the dates of events or the time intervals between events.

To clarify testimony, you frequently need to determine when an event took place. Although it is often difficult to get exact times or dates from a deponent, you can often get approximate dates or times.

Example 1: Q: Approximately how long after the treatment from the acupuncturist did you talk to Dr. Jones about the pain in your back?

Example 2: Q: How long was it between the second meeting with your supervisor and the meeting when you were told that you were on probation?

Example 3: Q: Do you remember the approximate date when you first thought that you had been misled by my client in connection with the purchase of the stock?

*Check for Gaps (possible omitted events) in the Timeline.

Since deponents may (consciously or unconsciously) skip over important events, you will often need to ask focused questions to minimize the likelihood of gaps in a Timeline.

Example 1: Q: Between the time you were told that you were on probation and the time that you were fired, did anything else happen that led you to believe you were being discriminated against because of your race?

Example 2: Q: Between the incident in January when you couldn't go to work for three days and the incident at work when you had to leave early to go to the doctor, did you have any trouble with your back?

Example 3: Q: Between the time you completed the loan application and the funding of the loan by the Business Bank, did you seek funding from any other source?

3.   An Illustrative Example of a Timeline Pattern

The following example illustrates the Timeline questioning pattern.

1.   Q: You said earlier in your testimony that at some point you began to feel that you were **being forced out**. When did you first feel that you were being forced out?

2.   A: When I learned that Smith was being placed in charge of the outside sales force.

3. Q: When did you learn about this?

4. A: When I had a meeting with Harold and Arlene.

5. Q: When was that?

6. A: It was in the afternoon, sometime in early September.

7. Q: Okay. After the meeting with Harold and Arlene when you were told that Smith was being placed in charge of the outside sales force, what was the next thing that happened that led you to think you were **being forced out**?

8. A: About two weeks later, I got a call from Arthur Rosett telling me that productivity in my department was not what it might be and that he'd like to discuss some changes that might help increase production.

9. Q: Between the time of the meeting with Harold and Arlene and the call from Rosett, did anything else happen that led you to think you were **being forced out**?

10. A: No.

11. Between the time of the meeting with Harold and Arlene and the call from Rosett, did you receive any memos from anyone that led you to think you were **being forced out**?

12. No.

13. Q: After the call from Rosett, what was the next thing that led you to believe that you were **being forced out**?

14. A: I didn't receive a discretionary bonus at the end of the year.

15. Q: Between the time you got the call from Rosett and the failure to receive a discretionary bonus at the end of the year, did anything else happen that led you to think that you were **being forced out**?

16. A: No.

17. Q: What was the next thing that happened after the failure to receive a bonus at the end of the year that led you to think you were **being forced out**?

18. A: Well....

In this example, the first question identifies the subject matter of the Timeline, the deponent's feeling of **being forced out**, and asks for the first event. Questions 3 and 5 identify the approximate time when a particular event took place. Questions 7, 13, and 17 move the Timeline forward to the next event, while Questions 9, 11 and 15 check for gaps in the Timeline.

4. Benefits of Eliciting a Timeline

You are likely to realize several benefits by obtaining Timelines.

* A Timeline provides a chronology which promotes your understanding of the significance of a deponent's testimony. The chronological order of events often dictates the inferences that may be drawn, either at trial or during settlement negotiations, from their occurrence.

Example: "Harry left the office, drove down Third Ave., swerved into a telephone pole, went into a bar, and had two martinis" versus "Harry left the office, went into a bar, had two martinis, drove down Third Ave., and swerved into a telephone pole."

* A Timeline pattern simply seeks to identify all events relating to a particular subject matter. As a result, the pattern may shield from the deponent how certain testimony helps your case. Hence Timeline questioning may increase your chances of obtaining evidence that a disingenuous or mendacious deponent might hide or slant if you simply asked a direct question.

Example: Assume that you represent the plaintiff in an automobile accident case where the major dispute concerns whether the defendant was drunk when the accident occurred. You are deposing an adverse witness who was a passenger in the defendant's car. You could just ask the deponent, "Did the defendant have anything to eat before the accident?" But the deponent may realize that a "No" or "Not very much" answer will help your case, and may therefore give an evasive answer such as, "I don't really remember." However, if you instead elicit a Timeline of pre-accident activities the deponent may strengthen your case by describing a series of events that makes no reference to eating.

* Timelines promote thoroughness. Even the most rigorous preparation typically cannot identify every item of potentially helpful or harmful evidence. A Timeline will often help you unearth important evidence that you did not specifically think to ask about when preparing for a deposition.

> Example: Assume that you represent the plaintiff in a wrongful termination case and you are deposing an employee who is sympathetic toward the company. You decide to obtain a Timeline of all conversations the deponent had regarding your client's replacement. The deponent reveals a conversation in which your client's supervisor mentioned that the supervisor's wife and your client's replacement are former business associates. During preparation, you might not have specifically thought to ask about business relationships between your client's replacement and the supervisor's wife.

* At trial, an adverse witness' direct examination testimony is frequently elicited primarily in chronological order. When you obtain a Timeline at deposition, you often get a preview of a witness' direct examination and can assess its credibility and decide how to attack it.

5. Refining Your Timeline Techniques

This section addresses problems that may interfere with your ability to elicit Timelines and suggests approaches for overcoming them.

A. <u>Problem:</u> The Subject of Your Timeline Is Vague or Too Broad

Assume that you represent the plaintiff in a wrongful termination case and at deposition you seek to elicit from the defendant a Timeline of "all the problems he had with your client while he worked for the defendant." This subject may be too broad or vague to produce a sufficiently complete Timeline. For example, the deponent might respond: "Slaughter worked for me for over three years and from time to time he had several problems. But I can't possibly remember what happened for all of them."

Solution—Refine the Definition of the Subject of Your Timeline

In the example above, you may have greater success if you seek <u>multiple</u>, more narrowly defined Timelines, such as:

(1) All the conversations the deponent had with Slaughter regarding the failure to promptly file invoices.

(2) All disagreements the deponent had with Slaughter about the Campbell account.

(3) Instances when Slaughter failed to report to work on time in the six months prior to termination.

These three narrowly defined Timelines will likely enhance thoroughness.

B. <u>Problem:</u> *The Deponent Does Not Understand That You Want a Timeline (i.e. A Chronology About a Specific Subject)*

Deponents are unlikely to be familiar with the concept of a Timeline when they come to a deposition. As a result, they may not immediately give responsive answers to Timeline questions. For example, instead of focusing on the subject you are interested in and proceeding event by event in chronological order, deponents may respond to Timeline questions by describing all the events that they think are important or all the evidence that seems to help their side without regard to chronology. When you think a deponent is having difficulty understanding how to respond to your Timeline questions, you can try one or more of the following techniques.

Solution #1—Specify that You Want Chronological Order

Explicitly tell a deponent that you want to proceed in chronological order. If a deponent seems unfamiliar with the word "chronological," you can replace it or define it with phrases such as "step by step" or "event by event."

<u>Example</u>: "I'd like you to tell me everything that happened that relates to the loan your company ultimately made to Mrs. Romero. <u>Please start at the beginning and go chronologically, event by event</u>. Can you try to do that?"

Solution #2—Continue to Use Your Timeline Definition

Once a deponent starts responding appropriately to your Timeline questions, moving the Timeline forward will often require continued identification of the subject matter. If your questions do not do so, a deponent (often with the encouragement of opposing counsel) will frequently become evasive with a response along the lines of, "Lots of things happened next. What do you want to know about?" To overcome such responses, continue to use your Timeline definition when asking what happened next.

Example:

1. Q: After you talked with Mrs. Romero about coming over to her house on Saturday, what happened next?

2. A: What do you mean, what happened next? Lots of things happened next. Ask me a specific question and I'll answer it.

3. [Opposing lawyer] The deponent is correct counsel, you're just asking for a narrative. I object. What do you mean, what happened next? Do you want him to talk about where he went to dinner that night? Be specific.

4. Q: After you talked with Mrs. Romero about coming over to her house on Saturday, **what is the *next thing that happened which in any way relates to the loan Federal Mortgage ultimately made to Mrs. Romero*?**

Solution #3—Use "The Very Next Thing" Signposts to Overcome "Quickie" Timelines

Sometimes a deponent will give you a "run on" or "quickie" Timeline rather than a step-by-step narration. Consider this example.

1. Q: Okay, please tell me step by step the events leading up to Mr. Phillips' resignation?

2. A: Well, I talked with him about why he hadn't been promoted and later so did Bob Davis. Then Phillips' wife called Bob, and right after that Phillips said he was leaving. The next thing we knew was that we were being sued.

You can often obtain a more detailed Timeline by taking the deponent back to the beginning and asking the deponent to identify the "very next" occurrence in the sequence.

Example:

1. Q: Let's slow down a bit. I'd like to go through this step by step. You said you had a conversation with Phillips about why he hadn't been promoted. When was this conversation?

2. A: Sometime around June.

3. Q: After this conversation in June, what is the **very next thing** that happened with regard to the denial of Phillips' promotion?

4. A: Well, I talked to Bob Davis about the meeting I had with Phillips and Bob said he'd talk to Phillips.

5. Q: Good. Now after this conversation between you and Davis, what is the **very next thing** that happened?

6. A: I think Davis met with Sherrill Johnson, the head of our department, to talk about Phillips and . . . .

C. <u>Problem</u>: *Creating Timeline Gaps When a Deponent Mentions a Future Event*

When in response to a Timeline question, a deponent refers to a future occurrence, you may assume that the future occurrence is the "very next thing" that happened. If so, you may inadvertently create a gap in a Timeline. For example, in a wrongful termination case, assume that the deponent responds to a "what happened next" question as follows:

A: Well, we got together and went over Ms. Boxer's report. We went over the report line by line trying to figure out how accurate the report was. We were probably there an hour. We had several questions about the costs for the addition and also about the projections regarding the supplemental work. We decided we'd do some research **and get together the following week.**

Q: Tell me what happened when you **got together the following week**?

In this example, the deponent's response alludes to a future occurrence. You immediately proceed to inquire about that event. By assuming that the "get together" was the next relevant event, you may overlook intervening events. Some deponents will purposely include references to future events, hoping that you will immediately proceed to that event without checking for gaps. If you do, you permit the deponent to hide information by omitting an event in the Timeline.

Solution—Check for gaps

When deponents refer to future events you may want to check for gaps to be sure you get complete information.

Example Q: Between the time you decided to do some research and the time you got together the next week, what happened with respect to Ms. Boxer's termination?

D. *Problem: Becoming Sidetracked into Non–Timeline Subjects*

As Timeline questioning proceeds, deponents invariably mention topics or events which are unrelated to the subject of inquiry. For example, assume that you represent Ms. Carlson, a plaintiff in a wrongful termination case. You are deposing Ms. Carlson's supervisor, seeking a Timeline of all the conversations the supervisor had with the plaintiff relating to the Campbell account. The questioning proceeds as follows:

1. Q: After the conversation when you talked about the need for Ms. Carlson to pay special attention to the Campbell account, when was the next time you spoke with Ms. Carlson about the Campbell account?

2. A: I'm not real sure when the next time was. But I know that shortly after that I told her that her year-end sales reports contained several serious mistakes.

3.   Q: And what were these mistakes in the year end sales reports?

4.   A: Well there were two important ones. . . .

In this example the deponent takes you off the subject of the Timeline by mentioning what appears to be an important topic unrelated to the Campbell account. Deponents may make such references innocently or in a calculated attempt to lure you off the subject to avoid revealing damaging information that would come up if the Timeline questioning on the Campbell account continued. In either event, if you allow yourself to be drawn off your Timeline, it will often be difficult for you to return to the Campbell account later in the deposition without confusing yourself and the deponent about what has already been covered.

Solution—"Park" References to Subjects or Events Unrelated to Your Timeline

Instead of being lured off the Timeline, in the above example you should have "parked" the new topic. Parking requires little more than a reference in your notes about "problems with the year end sales report." This "parked" topic could then be examined later in the deposition after completing the Timeline on the Campbell account.

Example:

1.   Q: After the conversation when you talked about the need for Ms. Carlson to pay special attention to the Campbell account, when was the

next time you spoke with Ms. Carlson about the Campbell account?

2. A: I'm not real sure when the next time was. But I know that shortly after that I told her that her year-end sales reports contained several serious mistakes.

3. Q: I'll ask you about the problems with the year-end sales reports later on. For the moment, let's continue with the Campbell account. Even if you can't remember exactly when it occurred, can you tell me about the next conversation you had with Ms. Carlson about the Campbell account?

4. A: Well, I had a discussion with her where I mentioned that Mr. Campbell had said that he was happy with the way we had responded to his concerns about the need to develop a sales strategy for the next five years.

5. Q: And after this conversation about Mr. Campbell being happy with your response to his concerns, when was the next. . . .

E. *Problem:* *Uncertainty About a Timeline's Beginning*

Deponents sometimes (consciously or unconsciously) start a Timeline at some point other than the beginning. For example:

1. Q: When was the first time that you learned Ms. Suh might be interested in the apartment?

2. A: I received Ms. Suh's written application in May and I talked about it with Mark, the other manager in the office.

The deponent's answer at least implicitly suggests that nothing happened prior to the receipt of the application in May. To determine if this is really the first event in the Timeline, you might proceed as follows:

1. Q: Prior to receiving the application in May, did anything happen that indicated Ms. Suh might be interested in the apartment?

2. A: Well, I had a conversation with my supervisor about Suh about a week before I received Suh's application.

F. *Problem: Uncertainty About a Timeline's End*

Deponents may also suggest a premature ending to a Timeline. For example:

1. Q: After you informed Ms. Suh that you felt she was not financially qualified to rent the apartment, when was the next time you had a conversation with anyone relating to Ms. Suh?

2. A: Well, after I told her that we didn't consider her financially qualified, the next thing that happened was we were served with a complaint alleging that we refused to rent her the apartment because of her race. Then we contacted our lawyer.

The deponent's answer implicitly suggests that there were no more relevant events. But again, you may probe to determine if other relevant events occurred. For example:

1. Q: After you talked to your lawyer, did you have any conversations with anyone other than your lawyer that were in any way related to Ms. Suh?

2. A: Well, I did talk to one of the other tenants about Suh but that occurred after I had met with the lawyer to discuss the case.

3. Q: When did you talk to the tenant?

4. A: It was just last week.

5. Q: Let's talk about that conversation with the tenant. Can you tell me everything that was discussed in that conversation?

As this example illustrates, you often want to continue to probe for events that may have occurred right up until the date of the deposition.

6. Eliciting the Details of Timeline Events—Combining Timelines and T–Funnels

The Timeline questioning pattern allows you to obtain a chronological series of events from a deponent. To obtain complete information from a deponent, you need to elicit the details of what occurred during each significant event. Typically, you will flesh out details with the T–Funnel pattern described in Chapter 2. In other words, you use the Timeline pattern to identify an initial event and then use the T–Funnel pattern to flesh out the details of the initial event. You then return to the Timeline pattern to identify the second event, and use T–Funnels to obtain the details of what happened during the second event. You can repeat this process until you reach the end of the Timeline.

The following example illustrates how you might combine Timeline and T–Funnel questioning to obtain as complete a picture as possible of a deponent's version of significant events.

Illustrative Example—Combining Timelines and T–Funnels to Obtain a Deponent's Version of Case Specific Events

An opposing party's version of significant events will routinely focus on what happened in a particular case. For example, assume that you represent the defendant in the case of Terry v. Biderman Construction Co. Biderman Construction built a concrete processing plant in the city of Lyte. Ann Terry, a homeowner living near the plant, has sued Biderman alleging that the plant is a nuisance and that Biderman made numerous misrepresentations to the Lyte City Council when applying for the permit to build the plant. The suit seeks compensatory and punitive damages for Biderman's knowing and willful maintenance of a nuisance and for intentional infliction of emotional distress. You are deposing plaintiff Terry.

You would undoubtedly have to develop a number of Timelines to elicit Terry's complete version of significant events. For example, you would want to try to obtain Timelines for each of the following: the misrepresentations allegedly made by the defendant to the City Council, the property damage suffered as a result of the operation of the plant, the manifestations of emotional distress by the plaintiff. For illustrative purposes, the following example focuses on only one subject: complaints that Terry allegedly made about the plant.

1.   Q: Ms. Terry, you mentioned earlier that you complained about the plant and what was going on there. So I'd like to ask you about any complaints you made to anyone in any way related to the plant. If possible, I'd like to start at the beginning and go through each complaint one by one. Could you tell me when was the first time you complained to someone about the plant?

[This question begins the Timeline.]

2.   A: Do you want to know about the complaints I made to the people at the city or the times I called Biderman and told him about the problems?

3.   Q: I want to know about both. In fact, I want to know about any complaints you made to anyone: the people with the city, Mr. Biderman or anyone else. So when was the first time that you made a complaint to anyone that related to the plant?

4.   A: I don't remember the exact date but the first time was when I called my councilman, Mr. Stevenson.

5.   Q: Okay, I know it's hard to remember exact dates sometimes, but could you tell me approximately when that occurred?

6. A: It was about a month or so after they opened that plant.

7. Q: All right, I'd like you to tell me everything that you can recall that you talked about with Mr. Stevenson when you first talked to him about the plant.

[This question shifts from Timeline to T–Funnel questioning about what happened during the first event, the complaint to Stevenson.]

8. A: Well, I told him that there were trucks delivering stuff to the plant at all hours of the day and night and that the noise was too much, and they'd have to get them to stop taking deliveries and making so much noise, especially late at night because it was making it hard to sleep.

9. Q: Other than saying that the plant was making too much noise and taking deliveries at all hours of the night, did you say anything else to Mr. Stevenson in this first call?

10. A: That was pretty much it in the first call, because we hadn't started to have any problems with the dust at that time. So I was just complaining about the noise. But later, I called Stevenson two other times to complain about the dust and to complain about the noise again.

11. Q: For right now, I'd like to stick to the first call. We'll talk about what happened in the other calls later. You said that you complained about the noise and taking deliveries at all hours of the

night and that was pretty much it. When you say pretty much it, I'm not sure if you mean that's all you talked about. So just to be clear, did you talk to Mr. Stevenson about anything other than the noise and taking deliveries at all hours of the night in that first call?

[Here, examining counsel "parks" the reference to other calls and continues with the T–Funnel on the first telephone call to Stevenson.]

12.   A: No, that was all in the first call.

13.   Q: Now, I'd like you to tell me as best you can recall everything you and Mr. Stevenson discussed in this first call about the noise at the plant.

[T–Funnel questioning about what was said by the deponent and Mr. Stevenson in the first telephone call regarding noise at the plant omitted.][1]

23.   Q: After this first call to Mr. Stevenson, when was the next time you complained to someone about the plant?

[Timeline questioning resumes to identify the next event.]

24.   A: Well a few weeks after I called Mr. Stevenson, I hadn't heard back from him so I decided I'd call Biderman, the guy who owned the plant,

1.   The T–Funnel about what was said about the topic "noise at the plant" is technically a secondary T–Funnel. For a discussion of secondary T–Funnels, see Chapter 2.

and tell him that he had to stop taking deliveries at night because they were making too much noise.

25.   Q: And did you get in touch with the owner?

26.   A: Yes, I called the plant and he was there.

27.   Q: Between the time you first talked to Mr. Stevenson and the time you talked with Mr. Biderman, did you make any complaints about the plant to anyone else?

28.   A: No, not at that time.

29.   Q: All right, I'd like to go over this first conversation with Mr. Biderman just like we did with the first conversation with Mr. Stevenson. Why don't you tell me everything you said to him and everything he said to you?

30.   A: Well, I told him that . . . .

[T–Funnel questioning about what was said by the deponent and Mr. Biderman during this call omitted.]

7.   Abandoning the Timeline When the Deponent Can Not Remember the Order in Which Events Occurred

In the example above, the deponent is able to recall the order in which her complaints occurred, and can therefore provide a Timeline of the complaints. Of course, deponents sometimes are unable, or claim to be unable, to remember the chronological order in which events occurred. In such situations, you may abandon the Timeline pattern and switch to a series of T–Funnels to obtain complete information. In other words, you use T–Funnels to elicit testimony about events without regard to the order in which the events occurred.

The transcript below illustrates how you might use a series of T–Funnels to question Ms. Terry about her complaints in the <u>Terry v. Biderman Construction Co</u>, case if she did **not remember the order in which her complaints were made**.

1.   Q: Ms. Terry, you mentioned earlier that you complained about the plant and what was going on there. So I'd like to ask you about any complaints you made to anyone in any way related to the plant. If possible, I'd like to start at the beginning and go through each complaint one by one. So could you tell me when was the first time you complained to someone about the plant?

2.   A: I made lots of complaints to people. I don't really remember which one I made first or second or whatever.

3.   Q: I realize it's hard to remember the order of all the complaints that you made but can you remember the first complaint you made?

4.   A: I don't remember who I complained to first or when I did it. It was a long time ago and I just can't remember when things happened.

5.   Q: Okay, I know it's hard to remember dates but do you remember approximately how long after the plant started operation that you made your first complaint?

6. A: It was about a month or so after they opened that plant.

7. Q: And can you remember to whom you made the first complaint?

8. A: I'm not sure. It may have been my city councilman, Mr. Stevenson, or the owner of the plant that I talked to first. I just can't recall.

9. Q: All right. Ms. Terry let's try this, maybe it will work easier for you. Just tell me all the things that you complained about at any time that were in any way related to the plant.

   [Since the deponent is unable to provide a Timeline, you turn to T–Funnel questions. The topic of this first T–Funnel is "Things the Deponent Complained About."]

10. A: The biggest problem was the dust. It was everywhere. I couldn't keep it out of my house even when I kept all the windows closed.

11. Q: So the dust is one thing. Did you make any other complaints related in any way to the plant?

12. A: The noise. There were trucks parked on the streets at all hours of the night, there were deliveries at night and the trucks made all sorts of noise. And the owner of the plant was supposed to put up a screen to control the dust, but it was always falling apart and he wouldn't do anything about it for weeks at a time. I told Mr. Stevenson, my city councilman, that I couldn't keep my house clean because of all the dust, that I had to

keep all my windows closed or my house would be a mess from the dust.

13.   Q: Did you make any other complaints, other than about dust and noise, related in any way to the plant?

14.   A: I had to go see the doctor several times because I was having breathing difficulties from all the dust in the air and in my house. And I complained to Mr. Stevenson that the city should never have let them build that plant.

15.   Q: Did you ever complain about anything else?

16.   A: No, that's about it.

17.   Q: So the complaints you've told me about are the only significant ones that you had about the plant, is that right?

18.   A: That's right.[2]

19.   Q: Now Ms. Terry, I'd like you to tell me everyone that you complained to about the problems you had as a result of the operation of the plant.

[Having gotten a list of the deponent's complaints, you now begin a new T–Funnel of "People To Whom the Deponent Complained."]

2.   Note that in this example, examining counsel does not ask any closed questions at the bottom of the T–Funnel to suggest additional problems the deponent might have had. Whether or not to suggest additional damaging testimony by asking such questions at the bottom of the T–Funnel is a matter of judgment, see Chapter 2.

20.   A: I complained to my city councilman, Mr. Stevenson, the owner of the plant, Mr. Biderman, my lawyer and the local newspaper.

21.   Q: Other than those four, did you complain to anyone else?

22.   A: I don't think so.

23.   Q: Did you complain to any of your neighbors?

24.   A: Well, we talked about the problems all the time. But they were complaining to me as much as I was complaining to them.

25.   Q: Did you ever complain to a homeowners' association?

26.   A: Yes, I did. I sent a letter to the homeowners' association asking them to do something about the noise and the dust.

27.   Q: Other than your city councilman, Mr. Stevenson, the owner of the plant Mr. Biderman, your lawyer, the local newspaper, your neighbors and the homeowners association, did you complain about the plant to anyone else?

28.   A: Well, I complained to my children about it all the time. Do you want to know about that?

29.   Q: Sure. Maybe we can talk about that in a little while. Did you complain to anyone else?

30.   A: No. That's it.

[T–Funnel #3—What Deponent said to Councilman Stevenson]

31. Q: Now Ms. Terry, I'd like to find out what you and Mr. Stevenson, your city councilman, discussed regarding the problems you were having. So please tell me everything that you can recall that you said to Mr. Stevenson about the plant or the problems you were having with it.

32 A: I know I told Mr. Stevenson about. . . .

[Questioning continues to determine what the deponent said to Stevenson, and then goes on to explore her conversations with other people.]

Note that you may be able to obtain Timelines in some areas and not in others. For example, Ms. Terry may be unable to remember the order of her complaints about problems with the plant. However, Ms. Terry may have made three visits to the doctor for illnesses allegedly caused by the dust from the plant and, perhaps with the aid of the medical records obtained prior to the deposition, she may remember what happened during each visit. If so, you would be able to obtain a Timeline in that area.

CHAPTER 4

OBTAINING HELPFUL ANSWERS

Even when deposing adverse witnesses, you routinely seek helpful answers. An adverse witness' deposition testimony may be helpful for several reasons. For example, it might be helpful because it:

- Provides evidence that helps to satisfy a legal element of a claim or affirmative defense;

- Creates an inconsistency between the testimony of two adverse witnesses;

- Creates an implausibility in the deponent's version of events;

- Calls into question the credibility of the deponent or another adverse witness; or

- Undermines an adversary's version of events.

This Chapter describes questioning strategies and techniques for encouraging adverse witnesses to provide helpful answers. Some of these questioning strategies can help you <u>overcome</u> bias by encouraging adverse witnesses to give truthful and helpful testimony. Some of these same strategies can help you <u>capitalize</u> on a biased deponent's willingness to fabricate testimony.

At the outset, recognize that no questioning strategy or technique can guarantee that an adverse deponent will give you a helpful answer. Whatever the persuasive force of your questioning, you cannot compel deponents to provide your desired answers. The approaches discussed below are intended to increase the <u>probability</u> of getting answers you desire.

1. Leading Questions

As discussed in Chapter 2, leading questions are those that typically can be answered "yes" or "no" and suggest the answer you desire.

Examples:

Q: You never told the plaintiff that you were dissatisfied with his work on the Campbell account, correct?

Q: Isn't it true that my client told you that the Hines Co. was in default on its loan before you decided to purchase the company?

Leading questions are probably the most commonly used technique for encouraging helpful testimony. By their very nature, they suggest your desired response, and thus such questions tend to encourage an adverse deponent to provide helpful answers. You can use leading questions throughout the deposition of an adverse witness,[1] as your judgment and intuition dictate.

[1] See FRE 6119(c); see also Wright & Gold, Federal Practice and Procedure: Evidence § 6168; <u>Haney v. Mizell Memorial Hosp.</u>, 744 F.2d 1467 (11th Cir. 1984); <u>Ellis v. City of Chicago,</u> 667 F.2d 606 (7th Cir. 1981); <u>Stahl v. Sun Microsystems, Inc.,</u>

2. Plausibility Chains

Plausibility chains are also a commonly used technique for overcoming deponents' bias and increasing the likelihood of obtaining helpful answers. A plausibility chain begins with a series of preliminary questions that elicit answers that provide circumstantial evidence supporting the accuracy of your desired admission. When you complete the chain by seeking to elicit the helpful admission, you put deponents between "a rock and a hard place." Deponents who recognize the link between their preliminary answers and your desired admission must either: (1) provide the admission, or (2) risk damaging their credibility with implausible testimony.

A. An Illustrative Example

The following example demonstrates how a series of questions that elicit circumstantial evidence of the admission that you seek to elicit encourages deponents to provide the admission.

Assume that you represent Sam Older, a 72 year old retiree living on a pension. Older executed a promissory note and second deed of trust on his home to secure a loan made to Older by Robert Smith. Smith subsequently sold the note and second deed of trust to Bob Badd. Claiming that Older is in

775 F.Supp. 1397 (D. Colo. 1991). For a discussion of the meaning of "hostile" witness, see Wright & Gold, Federal Practice and Procedure: Evidence § 6168; Thomas v. Cardwell, 626 F.2d 1375 (9th Cir. 1980); United States v. Brown, 603 F.2d 1022 (1st Cir. 1979); Rossano v. Blue Plate Foods, Inc., 314 F.2d 174 (5th Cir. 1963).

default on the loan, Badd has begun to foreclose on Older's home.

You have sued to enjoin the foreclosure and rescind the loan transaction. You contend that Smith defrauded Older into executing the deed of trust and promissory note, and that because Badd is not a bona fide purchaser in good faith, he cannot enforce the note. (Applicable law provides that a purchaser of a deed of trust cannot claim to be a bona fide purchaser if he or she possessed knowledge of facts which would cause a prudent buyer to undertake an inquiry that would uncover underlying fraud.) The handwriting on Older's loan application appears to be from two different people, and the application indicates that Older is 72 years old and employed as a construction worker.

At deposition, you want Badd to admit that **he read Older's loan application before he purchased Older's note from Smith**. Based on this admission, you plan to argue that Badd is not a bona fide purchaser because he should have inquired into the handwriting on the application and Older's employment status. Such an inquiry would have led Badd to contact Older and discover that the note and deed of trust were obtained by false representations.

Your plausibility chain questioning of Badd might proceed as follows:

1. Q: In your experience, a person who borrows money through a second deed of trust is usually in greater need of money than someone who

borrows through a first deed of trust, isn't that right?

2. A: I suppose that's usually the case, but not always.

3. Q: And generally speaking, you'd say that loaning money to someone on a second deed of trust is somewhat more risky than loaning on a first deed of trust, right?

4. A: Generally speaking, that's true.

5. Q: And in your experience when someone buys a second deed of trust, they want to be careful to make sure that the borrower has the ability to repay the loan, correct?

6. A: Sure.

7. Q: And one way of being careful is to make sure that the borrower has filled out a loan application in which the borrower accurately lists his or her assets, liabilities, income, job history and other matters relating to the borrower's credit history, isn't that true?

8. A: That's one way.

9. Q: So in your experience, people purchasing a second deed of trust often review the borrower's loan application, isn't that right?

10. A: That's typically done, yes.

11. Q: And you generally want to be careful when purchasing notes secured by second deeds, right?

12. A: Yes, I do.

13. Q: And you tried to be careful when purchasing Mr. Older's note and deed of trust, correct?

14. A: I tried to be.

15. Q: So in this case, in order to be careful, you looked at the initial loan application filled out by Mr. Older, correct?

16. A: I did.

17. Q: And, of course you looked at Mr. Older's loan application before you agreed to purchase the second deed of trust on his property, correct?

18. A: That's right.

In this example, Nos. 1–15 elicit circumstantial evidence of the ultimate admission you want Badd to provide. By first eliciting this evidence, you encourage Badd to provide the admission you seek (Nos. 17 and 18). Once Badd has admitted the circumstantial evidence tending to prove the accuracy of the admission, he is likely to realize that he is between "a rock and a hard place." A refusal to provide the admission would tend to make his testimony implausible in the light of ordinary experience.

B. *Common Features of Questions in a Plausibility Chain*

Questions in a plausibility chain frequently have the following features:

*As in the example above, the questions are either leading or call for yes/no answers. Such questions tend to increase the chances that a deponent will give the desired response.

*Each question asks for affirmation of a single piece of circumstantial evidence that suggests the ultimate desired admission is true. By not including multiple facts in each question, you likely avoid evoking a "compound" objection that might disrupt the momentum of your plausibility chain. In addition, it is usually harder for the deponent to quibble with a question that asks for a single admission than a question that incorporates several items of evidence.

*Ideally, each of your questions should not be subject to legitimate objections at deposition.[2] If you questions are objectionable, you invite opposing counsel to disrupt momentum with a valid objection. For example, try not to ask questions about what "generally happens" as such questions are objectionable as "calling for speculation". Instead ask for the deponent's own state of mind or belief. For example, ask questions such as: "Don't you believe that—is generally what happens?" or "Isn't it your experience that—generally occurs?" See, for example, Nos. 1, 3, 5 and 9 above.

*The plausibility chain typically ends with "payoff" questions asking the deponent to make your desired admission. See, for example, Nos. 15 and 17 above.

2. Generally, only objections as to form of the question are proper at deposition. See Chapter 15.

C. Accepting Less Than Perfect Answers

No matter how carefully you frame plausibility chain questions, adverse deponents often wiggle in one way or another and give you an evasive response. Rather than try to pin the witness down to a specific answer, usually your best tactic is to accept the evasive response and continue with other questions in the chain. For example, assume that the dialogue in the Badd deposition had gone as follows:

1. Q: In your experience, a person who borrows money through a second deed of trust is usually in greater need of money than someone who borrows through a first deed of trust, isn't that right?

2. A: That's usually the case, yes.

3. Q: So generally speaking, you'd say that loaning money to someone on a second deed of trust is somewhat more risky than loaning on a first deed of trust, right?

4. A: Not necessarily, it depends on the amount of equity in the property.

5. Q: <u>But regardless of the equity in the property, you ultimately want the borrower to be able to repay the loan, correct?</u>

6. A: That's true.

7. Q: And in your experience when someone buys a second deed of trust, they want to be careful to make sure that the borrower has the ability to repay the loan, correct?

8.   A: Sure.

9.   Q: And one way of being careful is to have the borrower fill out a loan application in which the borrower lists his or her assets, liabilities, income, job history and other matters relating to the borrower's credit history, isn't that true?

10.   That's one way, but....

In this example, Badd wiggles a bit in response to No. 3. However, rather than digressing to questions about riskiness, in No. 5 you accept the answer and move on to other questions in the chain. Questions pursuing the topic of how the amount of equity affects riskiness might well have obscured the connection between the preliminary questions and your desired admission.[3] As a result, the plausibility chain might have lost some of its force, and Badd might be less likely to have provided the desired admission.

D. Plausibility Chains and Prior Statements

This section illustrates the use of plausibility chains to encourage deponents to admit the accuracy of prior statements. Although you can use plausibility chains to try to obtain **any** admission, establishing the accuracy of prior statements is a common use of plausibility chains. The prior statement may have been made either by the deponent or by some other person.

3. You could, of course, return to the issue of how the amount of equity affects risk after completing your plausibility chain.

1. Deponents' Prior Written Statements

This section illustrates the use of a plausibility chain to encourage a deponent to admit that the deponent's own pre-deposition written statement is accurate.[4] Assume that you are deposing Mr. O'Malley, a defendant real estate developer. You want O'Malley to admit that as of a certain date, he did not have solid financing for a proposed real estate development. Assume also that you have a May 23 memo from O'Malley to one of his partners, Mr. Lloyd, in which O'Malley stated, among other things, "Our sources of financing appear very shaky at this point." Your plausibility chain questioning might go something like this:

Example A

1. Q: Mr. O'Malley, let's go back to the document that has been marked as Exhibit 27 that you testified was a memo from you to Mr. Lloyd dated May 23rd. In May of last year, Mr. Lloyd was one of your partners, correct?

2. A: Yes.

3. Q: Those are your initials by your typewritten name on Exhibit 27, correct?

4. A: Yes.

5. Q: And you wrote Exhibit 27 at that time because you had been involved in discussions about financing for the development, correct?

6. A: Yes.

---

4. Obviously you will not always want a deponent to reaffirm the accuracy of a prior statement.

7. Q: And when you wrote Exhibit 27 to Mr. Lloyd, you weren't trying to deceive him or mislead him, were you?

8. A: No.

9. Q: Please read Exhibit 27 to yourself—it is only a couple of paragraphs long—and tell me when you have done that.

10. A: (Pause) I have read it.

11. Q: Do you see the last sentence at the bottom of the second paragraph of Exhibit 27 which reads, "Our sources of financing for this development appear very shaky at this point."

12. A: Yes.

13. Q: So at the time you wrote Exhibit 27, you thought your sources of financing for the development were very shaky, correct?

14. A: I suppose that's true.

In this plausibility chain, Nos. 1 through 7 establish that the pre-deposition statement was probably accurate; Nos. 9 and 11 confront the deponent with his pre-deposition statement; and No. 13 asks the deponent to repeat the crucial admission under oath at the deposition. Your use of the plausibility chain makes it more likely that the deponent will reaffirm the pre-deposition statement than if you had asked No. 13 "cold."

You can use this same type of plausibility chain questioning when a deponent's written statement is contained in pleadings or responses to discovery.

For example, assume that a plaintiff, Ms. Gillig, files an action against a real estate broker and a seller for fraud in connection with the sale of real property and for conversion of Gillig's deposit given to the real estate broker. You represent the seller, and are deposing Gillig. You want Gillig to admit that she instructed the broker about what to do with her deposit. This admission supports your argument that the broker was Gillig's agent, not your client's agent. At deposition, your plausibility chain questioning to obtain this crucial admission might go as follows:

Example B

1. Q: Ms. Gillig, please look at the complaint that you have filed in this action, which has been marked as Exhibit 3. Did you read the complaint before it was filed?

2. A: Yes.[5]

3. Q: At the time you read the complaint, did you believe it was inaccurate in any way?

4. A: No.

5. Q: And you knew that the complaint was a document that would be submitted to the court, correct?

6. A: Yes.

[5] The answer to this question may be "No. I never read the complaint." If so, you can still use the plausibility chain to establish that the statement in the complaint is accurate. Your plausibility chain would be based on the statement of a third person. See discussion infra at section D (3).

7.   Q: You understood that when this complaint was filed that, among other things, you were suing the broker to recover the deposit moneys which the broker had received from you, correct?

8.   A: Yes.

9.   Q: Please look at paragraph 32 of the complaint, at page 8, which reads "By signing the deposit receipt, the broker assumed a duty to safely care for the plaintiff's deposit pursuant to plaintiff's instructions." Do you see that paragraph?

10.   A: Yes.

11.   Q: And you read paragraph 32 when you read the complaint, correct?

12.   A: Yes, I suppose I did.

13.   Q: So you gave instructions to the broker about how to handle your deposit, correct?

14.   A: Well, yes.

15.   Q: And you gave instructions to the broker about how to handle your deposit before the sale was final, correct?

16.   A: That's true.

In this plausibility pattern, Nos. 1 through 7 tend to establish that the deponent believed that the pre-deposition statement was probably accurate; No. 9 confronts Gillig with the pre-deposition statement in the complaint; and Nos. 11 and 15 ask Gillig to reaffirm the pre-deposition statement.

2. Deponents' Prior Oral Statements

The plausibility chains in the **Examples A** and **B above** were based on a deponent's prior written statement. You can create similar chains when seeking to establish the accuracy of deponents' pre-deposition oral statements.

For example, assume that you represent the plaintiff, Mr. Pine, in a wrongful termination case. You are deposing Ms. Dent, Pine's former supervisor. You want Dent to admit that she thought that Pine had done a good job on the "Korobkin" account. This admission supports your argument that Pine was fired not for poor work performance, but because he was an active union organizer. Your investigator has talked with Korobkin and Korobkin told your investigator that three months before Pine was fired, Dent had told Korobkin that Pine had done a good job on the Korobkin account. Your plausibility chain questioning at Dent's deposition might go as follows:

1. Q: Ms. Dent, Mr. Pine worked on the Korobkin account for about two years prior to his termination, correct?

2. A: That's right.

3. Q: And you talked with Mr. Korobkin about his account from time to time, during the two years prior to Mr. Pine's termination, correct?

4. A: Yes, I routinely talk with our clients about their accounts.

5. Q: And you generally don't lie to your clients when you talk about their accounts, do you?

6.   A: No. Of course not.

7.   Q: And you didn't lie to Mr. Korobkin when you talked about his account with him, did you?

8.   A: No, I didn't.

9.   Q: Ms. Dent, did you know that Mr. Korobkin told my investigator that approximately three months before plaintiff's termination you said that Mr. Pine had done a good job on the Korobkin account?

10.   A: I didn't even know that your investigator had talked to Mr. Korobkin.

11.   Q: You believe that Mr. Korobkin is an honest person, don't you?

12.   A: I've always found him to be.

13.   Q: Didn't you say to Mr. Korobkin that Mr. Pine had done a good job on the Korobkin account?[6]

14.   A: I suppose I did.

15.   Q: And did you say to Mr. Korobkin that Mr. Pine had done a good job on the Korobkin account approximately three months before Mr. Pine was terminated?

16.   A: Sometime around then, I don't recall the exact date.

6. If you had already taken Korobkin's deposition, you could ask Dent to read the portion of the deposition transcript where Korobkin had testified that Dent had said Pine had done a good job on the Korobkin account.

17. Q: And you weren't lying to Mr. Korobkin when you said that Mr. Pine had done a good job on the Korobkin account, were you?

18. A: No.

19. Q: So when you spoke to Mr. Korobkin about this matter you thought that Mr. Pine had done a good job on the Korobkin account, correct?

20. A: Yes, I suppose I did.

This chain based on Dent's prior oral statement follows the same format as the earlier chains based on prior written statements. All of them (1) elicit circumstantial evidence in support of the accuracy of a pre-deposition statement,[7] (2) confront the deponent with the pre-deposition statement, and (3) ask the deponent to repeat the pre-deposition statement under oath at the deposition.

3. Statements of Third Persons

This section illustrates the use of a plausibility chain to encourage a deponent to admit that a prior statement of a third person is accurate.

Assume again that you represent Mr. Pine in his wrongful termination case and you are deposing Ms. Dent, Pine's former supervisor. As before, based on information given to your investigator by Mr. Korobkin, you want Dent to admit that she thought

---

7. In some cases, of course, you may have little or no circumstantial evidence indicating that the prior statement by the deponent is probably accurate. In such cases, you may still decide to confront the deponent with the prior statement before asking for the crucial admission, but your plausibility pattern will not be as strong.

Pine had done a good job on the Korobkin account. This time, however, the statement on which you base the chain was made by Korobkin rather than by the deponent Dent. Your plausibility chain might look something like the following:

1. Q: You know a Mr. Korobkin, don't you Ms. Dent?

2. A: Yes, he's one of our clients.

3. Q: And you think that Mr. Korobkin pays attention to what your firm does on his account, don't you?

4. A: I think he pays attention to what we do, yes.

5. Q: And if Mr. Korobkin thought that someone at your firm was doing a bad job on his account, you think Mr. Korobkin would probably tell you about that, correct?

6. A: I suppose he probably would. I'd hope he would.

7. Q: You've found Mr. Korobkin to be an honest man, haven't you?

8. A: Yes.

9. Q: Ms. Dent, did you know that Mr. Korobkin told my investigator that he thought Mr. Pine had done a good job on his account?

10. A: I was not aware of that.

11. Q: Well, Mr. Korobkin never told you that he thought Mr. Pine was doing a <u>bad</u> job on his account, did he?

12. A: No.

13. Q: And you thought that Mr. Pine did a good job on the Korobkin account, isn't that right?

14. A: On that account Pine did a pretty good job, but there were other problems with his job performance.

15. Q: I'm only asking you about the Korobkin account right now, Ms. Dent. You thought that Mr. Pine did a good job on the Korobkin account, isn't that right?

16. A: On that account, yes.

In this example, Nos. 1–7 attempt to elicit evidence that Korobkin's pre-deposition statement was probably accurate. Nos. 9 and 11 confront Dent with the Korobkin's pre-deposition statement, and Nos. 13 and 15 ask her to provide the answer your desire.[8]

3. Exploiting Bias

Exploiting bias is another strategy for eliciting a desired admission. Exploiting bias involves suggest-

---

8. When a witness other than the deponent has made a pre-deposition statement that helps your case, you may use a plausibility pattern something like that one in the text because you want the deponent to testify to the helpful evidence under oath at the deposition. Once again, however, this is not the only strategic decision you might make when you have such a pre-deposition statement from a witness other than the deponent. You might, for example, decide that you want the deponent to contradict the other witness' pre-deposition statement. See Chapter 7 for a discussion of strategies and techniques for exploiting inconsistencies between a statements by the deponent and that of another adverse witness.

ing that an answer helps the deponent's case, when in fact the answer helps your case. This technique takes advantage of biased deponents' natural inclination to testify falsely or slant, consciously or unconsciously, testimony in a way that helps the deponent (or the party the deponent identifies with) to prevail in the litigation.

For example, assume that you represent a plaintiff, Mr. Pepper, who is suing to recover on a promissory note that the defendant, Mr. Williams, signed in connection with plaintiff's sale of her business to the defendant four years ago. Williams admits to signing the note but counterclaims for fraud, alleging that Pepper misrepresented the income of the business at the time of the sale. You believe that a reasonable examination of the financial records of Pepper's business at the time of the sale would have disclosed any of the alleged errors, thus triggering your statute of limitations defense and barring Williams' fraud claim. Thus, you want Williams to admit that he closely examined the financial records prior to the sale. To encourage Williams to make this admission, you may ask questions in a way that suggests that this admission would actually help Williams' own case. Your questioning might proceed as follows:

1.   Q: Mr. Williams, you didn't inform my client, Mr. Pepper, about the alleged inaccuracies in the financial records until about four months ago, right?

2.   A: Yes.

3. Q: So you first informed my client of the alleged inaccuracies in the financial records <u>after</u> my client had contacted you about paying on your note, correct?

4. A: That's true.

5. Q: So you really didn't do anything to investigate the accuracy of the financials until recently when you decided you needed to fabricate a reason for not paying on the note, isn't that right?

6. A: That is not true.

7. Q: Well, you certainly didn't do anything to investigate the accuracy of the financial records around the time you acquired the business, did you?

8. A: We most certainly did. We just didn't discover the inaccuracies until after we began operating the business.

9. Q: Mr. Williams, are you saying that you did do an investigation of the accuracy of the financial records around the time you acquired the business?

10. A: Absolutely.

11. Q: Please tell me everything you did to investigate the accuracy of the financials at the time you acquired the business.

12. A: Well . . .

In this example, questions 5, 7 and 9 suggest that you plan to argue that Williams' claim that financial records were misleading or false is just an eleventh hour excuse concocted when he became unable to make payments on the note. When your questions make this argument apparent to the deponent, he may realize that he can rebut this argument, and thereby help his case, by testifying that he thoroughly investigated the financials at the time of purchase. Of course, this is exactly the answer you are seeking.[9] Once Williams gives you the answer you want, No. 11 you proceed to cement it by asking him to describe the investigation.[10]

Consider another example. Assume that you represent the plaintiff in a personal injury case. You are trying to prove that your client was struck by the defendant's car while crossing the street in a crosswalk. The defendant truck driver claims that your client was struck when she suddenly darted out from between two parked cars. You know from interviewing a witness that three young children were standing on the corner where the accident occurred. You want to argue that the defendant was distracted by the young children and consequently did not see your client in the crosswalk. At the defendant's deposition, you want the defendant to admit that he saw the children on the corner just prior to the accident. Your questioning proceeds as follows:

9. If you are familiar with the Uncle Remus stories, you will recognize the questioning pattern as an example of B'rer Rabbit's "don't throw me in that briar patch" ploy.

10. For a discussion of cementing helpful evidence, see Chapter 5.

1. Q: As you began to make your left hand turn just before the accident, you weren't paying close attention to the road, were you?

2. A: That's not true.

3. Q: Well, you didn't notice the three children standing on the northeast corner of the intersection where the accident occurred, did you?

4. Objection: Assumes facts not in evidence.

5. Q: Let me rephrase. Shortly before the accident occurred, did you notice any children standing on the northeast corner of the intersection where the accident occurred?

6. A: Yes.

7. Q: How many children did you notice?

8. A: Three.

9. Q: What were the approximate ages of the children?

10. A: They were all young, about ten to twelve years old.

11. Q: Could you tell us where these children were standing?

12. A: Yes. . . .

In this example, you imply to the defendant that you will argue that he was inattentive because he did not see the children on the corner. The defendant may then admit to having seen the children to undercut your suggested argument.

4. Risks of Plausibility Chains and Exploiting Bias

One risk of plausibility chain questioning is that a deponent may recognize that you are trying to encourage or "force" a specific answer, and that you are doing so because the answer would help your case. As a result, an adverse deponent who is willing to lie may choose to give an implausible answer rather than provide your desired admission.

You run a similar risk when you exploit bias. Deponents, especially sophisticated ones, may recognize that you are attempting to manipulate them into thinking that answers are harmful to your case when in reality they are helpful. If such deponents are willing to lie, they may refuse to provide your desired admission.

Since both of these techniques entail potential benefits and risks, you must make strategic judgments on an admission-by-admission and case by case basis about when to employ them. When you decide to forgo these techniques, you may still be able to employ the masking technique discussed below.

5. Masking—Obscuring the Significance of Questions

Masking the significance of questions is another technique for overcoming bias and obtaining important admissions. Masking consists of obscuring the link between the information you seek and the point you ultimately want to prove. You typically mask through over inclusive questioning. That is, you mask by burying an important inquiry among a series of unimportant ones. You adopt this strategy to hide the importance of a specific inquiry and minimize a deponent's proclivity to withhold or slant helpful evidence.

For example, consider again the case in which you represent Sam Older, the 72 year old retiree living on a pension. Older executed a promissory note and second deed of trust on his home to secure a loan made to Older by Robert Smith. Smith subsequently sold the note and second deed of trust to Bob Badd. You want Badd to admit that he read Older's loan application before he purchased Older's note from Smith. You will then argue that Badd is not a bona fide purchaser because he would have known there were two different handwritings on Older's application and that a 72 year-old man was claiming to be employed as a construction worker. These facts would arguably cause a prudent buyer to undertake an inquiry about the reasons for the two different handwritings and the implausibility of a 72 year old being employed as a construction worker. Such an inquiry would arguably have revealed that the note and deed of trust were obtained by false representations. Your deposition questioning proceeds as follows:

1. Q: When you purchase a note secured by a second deed of trust you typically want to examine the file on the loan to make sure there are no problems, correct?

2. A: I'm not sure what you mean.

3. Q: Maybe I can be more specific. Before you bought Mr. Older's note did you check over the appraisal on the property?

4. A: Yes

5. Q: Before you bought Mr. Older's note did you ask the seller about Mr. Older's payment history?

6. A: Sure. He assured me the note was current.

7. Q: Before you bought Mr. Older's note, did you look at the note to see if it was properly signed?

8. A: No. I didn't need to because I had a copy of the seller's title policy and I was going to have that policy changed into my name as a part of the escrow.

9. Q: Before you bought Mr. Older's note did you look at Mr. Older's loan application?

10. A: Yes.

11. Q: Did you also run a TRW or other credit history on Mr. Older before you bought his note?

12. A: I ran a TRW, yes.

13. Q: Other than the things that you've mentioned, what else did you do to examine the file on the loan to make sure there were no problems?

14. A: That's it.

In this example, you are interested only in encouraging Badd to admit that he read the loan application. You do so with a broadened focus that masks your interest in that specific admission. The masking questions make it appear that you are mechanically going through everything Badd did prior to purchasing the note.

The above example demonstrates the use of T–Funnel questioning to mask.[11] You can also mask through Timeline questioning.[12] Recall that Timeline questioning simply seeks to identify all events in chronological order relating to a particular topic. As a result, you can use the pattern to hide the importance of a specific inquiry and minimize a deponent's proclivity to hide or slant helpful evidence.

For example, assume that you represent the plaintiff in an automobile accident case where the major dispute concerns whether the defendant was under the influence of alcohol when the accident occurred. You want to argue that the defendant was more likely to be under the influence because he had had a few drinks and nothing to eat prior to the accident. You are deposing an adverse witness who was a passenger in the defendant's car. You ask the deponent, "Did the defendant have anything to eat before the accident?" The deponent may realize that a "No" or "Not very much" answer helps your case, and may therefore either lie or give an evasive

11.   For a description of T–Funnel questioning, see Chapter 2.

12.   For a description of Timeline questioning, see Chapter 3.

answer such as, "I don't really remember." However, if you elicit a Timeline consisting of "all pre-accident activities on the day of the accident," the deponent may strengthen your case by describing a series of events that makes no reference to eating.

A. Masking During Background Questioning

At the inception of depositions, deponents are frequently asked general background questions regarding such matters as their education, training and experience and the employment practices and procedures they routinely follow. Typically deponents see little connection between such topics and the major factual disputes in a case. As a consequence, background questioning often furnishes an ideal opportunity to mask inquiries directed at obtaining circumstantial evidence related to arguments you would like to advance.

For example, assume that you represent a Spanish-speaking plaintiff who is suing a Ford dealer, First Ford, to rescind his lease of a new Ford SUV. Your client claims that he negotiated his lease in Spanish with a Spanish-speaking salesperson. State law provides that contracts for the sale or lease of vehicles must be written in Spanish if the lessee primarily speaks Spanish. First Ford admits that the lease signed by your client is in English. However, First Ford claims that there was no need to give your client a Spanish language lease because your client spoke English. You expect the salesperson, Mr. Solis, to testify that your client spoke only in

English. In deposing the salesperson, you would like to use background questioning to develop circumstantial evidence that the deal with your client was so routine that the salesperson would have no basis for recalling whether or not the lease with your client was negotiated in English or Spanish. Your client has given you the salesperson's card which has on it, "Se Habla Espanol." The following example illustrates how you might use background questioning to mask your search for evidence that the salesperson's dealings with your client were so routine he has no basis for recalling what language was primarily spoken by your client:

1.   Q: Mr. Solis, in what city did you grow up?'

2.   A: Los Angeles

3.   Q: Did you go to school in Los Angeles?

4.   A: Yes. I went to Garfield high school in East Los Angeles.

5.   Q. I'd like to ask you a few questions about your education and experience. What is the highest grade of education that you received?

6.   A: I spent two years at Pasadena Community College.

7.   Q: Did you get a degree from that school?

8.   A: No. I was one course short of receiving an AA degree but I had to go to work.

9.   Q: Did you take any language courses while you were in either high school or at Pasadena Community College?

10.   A: No.

11.   Q: Do you speak Spanish?

12.   A: Yes.

13.   Q: Where did you learn Spanish?

14.   A: I grew up in a bilingual home; both my parents speak Spanish.

15.   Q: Do you consider yourself to be fluent in Spanish?

16.   A: Yes.

17.   Q: Are you employed at this time?

18.   A: I work at Tom's Toyota.

19.   [Questions regarding employment at Tom's Toyota omitted]

20.   Q: Before you worked at Tom's Toyota, did you have other jobs that involved the sale or leasing of cars?

21.   A: Yes, I worked First Ford in Alhambra.

22.   Q: How long were you at First Ford?

23.   A: About two and one-half years.

24.   Q: What was your job at First Ford?

25.   A: I was a sales representative

26.   Q: What were your duties as a sales representative?

27.   A: I'd meet and greet customers, show them cars, answer their questions, take them on test drives; negotiate sales and lease agreements.

28. Q: What other duties did you have as a sales representative?

29. A: I'd run appropriate credit checks, help them fill out the necessary paper work to complete the transaction, acquaint customers with their car once the transaction closed and follow-up with them once they took their cars home.

30. Q: Did most of the customers you dealt with at First Ford purchase their cars for cash?

31. A: I'd say ninety percent of the customers did not pay cash. They purchased cars on an installment basis or leased their cars.

32. Q: So would it be fair to say that the vast majority of most of First Ford's customers were middle income people?

33. A: Absolutely.

34. Q: Did First Ford customers speak languages other than English?

35. A: Yes. We had a large number of Spanish-speaking and Chinese-speaking customers.

36. Q: What percentage of the First Ford customers that you dealt with spoke Spanish?

37. A: Maybe forty to fifty percent.

38. Q: Do you speak Chinese?

39. A: No.

40. Q: Given that you speak Spanish, did you sometimes use Spanish in dealing with Spanish-speaking customers?

41.   A: Sure, that often happened.

42.   [Questions regarding Spanish speaking customers omitted]

43.   Q: Were there standard agreements that First Ford customers signed when they purchased or leased vehicles?

44.   A: They were all pretty standard. The specific terms, of course, varied but we had standard sales and lease agreements.

45.   Q: Were the lease agreements for cars different from the lease agreements for SUV's?

46.   A: No.

47.   Q: While you were at First Ford, did more customers buy cars or lease them?

48.   A: It was about fifty-fifty; half bought and half leased.

49.   Q: As sales representative on what basis were you paid?

50.   A: Hourly plus commission.

51.   Q: Did your commission vary depending on whether a customer purchased or leased a vehicle?

52.   A: No.

53.   Q: And while you were at First Ford how many customers did you typically talk to in a week?

54.   A: Thirty to forty; something like that.

55.   Q: And of those thirty to forty persons that you talked to each week, how many did typically end up buying or leasing a car?

56.   A: Three or four in a slow week and seven or eight in a good week.

57.   Q: Does that estimate cover the two and one-half years you worked for First Ford?

58.   A: I'd say that's correct. Perhaps it was a bit higher in the year that I left.

59.   Q: Why did you leave First Ford?

60.   [Remainder omitted.]

Your background questioning hopefully has masked the fact that you are seeking circumstantial evidence indicating that the leasing of an SUV to a Spanish-speaking person was a routine event. Thus, the following inquiries, while never mentioning the salesman's dealings with your client, uncover evidence supporting an argument that the salesman would have no special reason to recall that he spoke English when dealing with your client:

Most customers did not pay cash

[No. 34 et seq.]

The substantial percentage of Spanish-speaking customers.

[No. 34 et seq.]

The frequency of speaking Spanish with customers.

[No. 40 et seq.]

The standard nature of lease agreements and the fact that the leases did not vary depending on the type of vehicle involved.

[No. 43 et seq.]

Half of the customers leased their vehicles.

[No. 47 et seq.]

Commissions did not vary depending on whether customers leased or purchased.

[No 49 et. seq.]

The substantial number of customers with whom the deponent dealt in a given week.

[No. 53 et seq.]

B. Combining Masking and Plausibility Chains

You can sometimes use a masking strategy to obtain helpful answers and then later in the deposition use those helpful answers to create a plausibility chain. In the dispute regarding the auto lease in the immediately preceding example, for instance, masking during background questioning produced admissions that would allow you to argue that the deponent would be unable to remember whether he spoke English or Spanish when he reviewed the terms of the auto lease with your client. Later in the deposition those same admissions might be used to construct a plausibility chain to encourage the deponent to admit that he does not remember whether he spoke English or Spanish when he reviewed the lease with your client. Consider the following example:

61.   Q: You testified earlier that First Ford had a large number of Spanish-speaking customers, correct?

62.   A: Yes.

63.   Q: In fact, about forty to fifty percent of the customers you worked with at First Ford were Spanish-speaking customers, correct?

64.   A: That's about right.

65.   Q: And you typically talked to thirty or forty customers in a week when you worked at First Ford?

66.   A: About that.

67.   Q: So you spoke Spanish with several customers each week that you worked at First Ford, right?

68.   A: That's right.

69.   Q: In fact, you believe that you spoke Spanish with as many as twenty customers during some weeks, isn't that right?

70.   A: Possibly.

71.   Q: So during a two or three month period you believe you spoke Spanish with dozens of customers, correct?

72.   A: That's possible.

73.   Q: And some of these customers with whom you spoke Spanish leased rather than purchased a vehicle, correct?

74.   A: Some of them, sure.

75.   Q: Well, you testified earlier that about half the customers purchased and half the customers leased, correct?

76.   A: That's about right.

77.   Q: So you frequently went over the terms of a standard lease agreement with a customer in Spanish, correct?

78.   A: Yes.

79.   Q: And you frequently went over the terms of a standard lease agreement with a customer in English, correct?

80.   A: That's true.

81.   Q: Just by looking at the name of a customer with whom you negotiated a lease at First Ford, you couldn't remember whether you spoke Spanish or English with that customer, could you?

82.   Objection: Calls for speculation. I'll let him answer if he can.

83.   A: Just by looking at the name, no I probably couldn't do that.

84.   Q: And isn't it true that as you sit here today, you don't remember whether you spoke

Spanish or English with my client when you went over the lease terms with him?

85.   A: Your client's lease was in English, so I must have spoken English when I went over the terms of the lease. I always give the customer a copy of the lease in the same language that I use to review it.

86.   Q: I understand about your usual practice, and we'll talk about that some more later on. But what I am asking you now is this. Isn't it true that as you sit here today, you do not remember the language you used when you went over the terms of the lease with my client?

87.   A: No, I don't remember that specific transaction. It was quite a while back.[13]

C. *Masking to Create an Opportunity for Impeachment*

To set up possible impeachment, you may also mask to hide the fact that you are aware of information that a deponent may not want to reveal. A deponent who does not know that you are already aware of such information may be more willing to lie to try to conceal it. Thus this strategy allows you to test a deponent's willingness to lie at deposition.

---

13. If the deponent answered "Yes" to this question, you could follow up by asking him to explain how he could remember the transaction with your client given that he had engaged in so many similar transactions. If the deponent has no explanation, his testimony would hopefully appear implausible to a judge or jury. If the deponent does have an explanation, you can investigate its veracity with additional questioning at the deposition or during subsequent discovery.

If the deponent does lie, you may then be able to impeach the deponent in subsequent proceedings.

For example, assume that you represent a police officer who has been sued for using excessive force during an arrest. You are deposing Tim Treemont, a witness to the arrest. You know from prior discovery that Treemont is likely to give testimony damaging to your client's case. You also know from your independent investigation that two years prior to the arrest giving rise to the complaint, Treemont's application to the police academy was rejected.

You could make a strategic decision to confront Treemont with the fact that his application was rejected and then try to get Treemont to admit that he was upset or angry about being rejected.[14] Alternatively, you might make a strategic decision to test Treemont's willingness to testify untruthfully about his rejection by the police academy. A masking technique may help you to do so:

1. Q: Mr. Treemont, since this case involves a police officer, I need to ask you some questions about your and your family's interactions with the police. Have you ever been arrested?

2. A: No.

3. Q: Have you ever been stopped for a traffic ticket?

4. A: Yes, several times.

14. If you made this strategic decision, you could use the plausibility chain technique described earlier in this Chapter.

5. Q: I'd like to ask you some questions about how you were treated by the police when you were stopped on these occasions.... [Questions about traffic stops omitted]

6. Q: Do you have any personal friends who are police officers?

7. A: No.

8. Q: Do you have any personal friends who were in the past police officers?

9. A: No

10. Q: Are any members of your family police officers?

11. A: No.

12. Q: Were any members of your family ever police officers?

13. A: No.

14. Q: Did any member of your family ever apply for any sort of employment with the police department?

15. A: No.

16. Q: Did you ever apply for employment with the police department?

17. A: ?

In this example, you mask your knowledge with questions designed to make your inquiries about police contacts look routine (Nos.1–14). As a result, if Treemont is willing to lie under oath (something that the factfinder is entitled to consider when evaluating credibility), he will be more likely to answer question 16 untruthfully.[15] And if Treemont is untruthful, you can "have your cake and eat it too." That is, you can show that Treemont was rejected by the police academy and therefore might be biased, and you can undercut his credibility by showing that he is willing to lie under oath about the rejection.

6. Preparation Versus Seeking Admissions on the Fly

Deposition preparation is an opportunity to make strategic decisions about how and whether to use the strategies and techniques described in this Chapter. Making such decisions in the relative calm of your office is easier than utilizing the techniques "on the fly" in mid-deposition.

Nevertheless, recognize that during depositions unanticipated facts often surface. Thus, you may

15. You are prohibited from encouraging or assisting your own witness from giving knowingly false testimony. See Restatement (Third) Of The Law Governing Lawyers, § 120 (2000) This prohibition, however, does not apply when examining an adverse witness.

"It is not a violation to elicit from an adversary witness evidence known by the lawyer to be false and apparently adverse to the lawyer's client. The lawyer may have sound tactical reasons for doing so, such as eliciting false testimony for the purpose of later demonstrating its falsity to discredit the witness. Requiring premature disclosure could, under some circumstances, aid the witness in explaining away false testimony or recasting it into a more plausible form." Id. at cmt. e.

realize for the first time at deposition that you have an opportunity to obtain an important admission by using the strategies and techniques discussed in this Chapter. You will then have to do your best to adjust your questioning "on the fly" or during a break in the deposition.

CHAPTER 5

CEMENTING HELPFUL ANSWERS

This Chapter focuses on strategies for cementing helpful answers. Cementing makes it difficult for deponents to later disavow helpful answers.

1. Cementing Defined

Cementing (aka pinning down) consists of having a deponent repeat or reaffirm helpful testimony at least once during a deposition. For example, assume that you represent Seth Altman in an action against Four Star Mortgage Company based on a theory of fraudulent misrepresentation. Among other things, you seek to prove that Altman relied on a broker's misrepresentations. During your deposition of the Four Star broker who dealt with Seth, the following occurs:

Q: When you first called Mr. Altman on the 14th, what happened?

A: Not very much in this first call. I just said that Four Star had been in the mortgage business for a long time, that I had handled many loans for people who were in Mr. Altman's situation and that I would like to meet with him at his home to discuss a possible loan. Mr. Altman said he already had appointments to talk to some other brokers but that he would be willing to meet with me and we arranged to meet later in the week.

Q: What else happened at that time?

A: Nothing else. We just set up an appointment; I believe it was for the following Friday.

Given your desire to establish that Altman relied on the broker's representations, the testimony that the broker told Altman that (1) "Four Star had been in the mortgage business for a long time" and that (2) "I have handled many loans for people in Mr. Altman's situation," constitutes helpful evidence. Borrowers are likely to rely on the statements of brokers who have been in business for a long time and who have handled loans for similarly situated borrowers.

To cement these items of helpful evidence, you might have the deponent repeat the helpful evidence:

Q: So when you first called Mr. Altman, you told him that Four Star had been in the mortgage business for a long time, correct?

A: Yes.

Q: And in this initial call to Mr. Altman, you also said you had handled many loans for people who were in Mr. Altman's situation, is that right?

A: Yes.

2. Benefits of Cementing

By cementing helpful evidence, you generally realize two significant benefits:

* **Reduce the Risk of Future Disavowal**

One reason to cement helpful deposition evidence is to reduce the chances that a deponent will subsequently seek to retract a helpful answer. As you probably know, deponents often seek to disavow such deposition answers. They may do so when they review and sign their depositions, by filing inconsistent declarations in connection with pretrial motions[1] and/or when testifying at trial.

By cementing, you make it less likely that deponents will subsequently seek to disavow helpful evidence. Deponents generally recognize that a judge or juror may be suspicious of a changed answer. And a deponent who has repeated helpful evidence is likely to be doubly reticent to recant. After all, even under oath, people sometimes make mistakes. But plausible reasons for making an error the first time often won't have much credence if an answer has been re-affirmed. For example, a deponent's explanation that "I was confused" will be less believable if the testimony has been given more than once.

* **Improve Your Ability to Impeach Deponents Who Disavow.**

1. In general, a party may not defeat a motion for summary judgment by filing an affidavit contradicting the party's deposition testimony. Perma Research & Dev. Co. v. Singer Co., 410 F.2d 572, 577 (2d Cir. 1969). However, if the party's affidavit shows that the party genuinely made a mistake or was confused in the party's deposition testimony, some courts allow a party to defeat a motion for summary judgment with an affidavit that contradicts the party's deposition testimony. See e.g., Kennett–Murray Corp. v. Bone, 622 F.2d 887, 893 (5th Cir. 1980).

No matter how well you cement evidence at deposition, a deponent can still disavow or recant the helpful evidence later in a case. However, when a deponent does so you typically want to impeach by showing that the deponent has contradicted his deposition testimony. The cementing techniques discussed in this Chapter sharpen the force of any post-deposition impeachment.

3.   Potential Risks of Cementing

Cementing is not risk-free. Your attempt to cement may make the deponent aware that testimony helps your case. As a result, the deponent might immediately recant or qualify a helpful answer. Cementing may also educate opposing counsel as to your trial strategy and the evidence on which you will rely, thus allowing opposing counsel to prepare to counter it.

You, of course, always have to weigh the risks and benefits before deciding to cement helpful testimony.

4.   Basic Cementing Techniques

The following subsections explore several techniques for cementing helpful evidence, which you can often use in combination.

A.   *Isolate Cemented Testimony*

One key to effective cementing is isolating the helpful evidence in a discrete question-answer sequence. If helpful evidence is simply part of a longer answer, any later impeachment is likely to lose much of its impact.

The following example suggests how failure to isolate cemented testimony can obfuscate its impeachment value. Assume that you represent Julie Park, who has brought a sexual harassment action against First Rate Bank and one of its vice-presidents, Bob Delaney. Ms. Park contends that Mr. Delaney asked her to engage in sexual relations in exchange for favorable job evaluations. Prior to trial you took the deposition of Lorena Guzek, Delaney's supervisor. During Ms. Guzek's deposition, Ms. Guzek testified as follows:

Q: What happened next with respect to Ms. Park?

A: On the 14th, Mr. Delaney told me that two weeks earlier he had asked Ms. Park to prepare a report for him on the tellers in the Southwest branch and that she had just handed in a 20 page report. He said that since Ms. Park had had trouble in the past getting her work done on time he was surprised that Ms. Park had submitted the report on time but that he would review the report the next day and give me his evaluation of the situation. He said he hoped her report would be a sound one because despite the shortcomings in her work performance he had become quite fond of her. He said that within a week he would forward Ms. Park's report along with his own evaluation to me and that we could then get together and go over the situation. About two weeks later, we met to discuss Ms. Park's report and to review the situation at the Southwest branch.

This narrative answer contains an item of helpful evidence: According to Ms. Guzek, Mr. Delaney said that he had become quite fond of Ms. Park. This testimony would constitute circumstantial evidence that Mr. Delaney made sexual advances toward Ms. Park.

Assume now that you <u>fail</u> to cement this bit of helpful evidence. The case proceeds to trial, and First Rate calls Ms. Guzek as a defense witness. When testifying to the meeting on the 14th, Ms. Guzek says nothing about Mr. Delaney's "fond of Ms. Park" remark. Your cross examination of Ms. Guzek goes as follows:

Q: On the 14th, Mr. Delaney talked to you about Ms. Park, correct?

A: Yes.

Q: And on the 14th Mr. Delaney told you that he had become quite fond of Ms. Park, correct?

A: I don't think that is right. I'm pretty sure he didn't say that.

Q: Ms. Guzek, you remember that your deposition was taken in this case, do you not?

A: Yes.

Q: And you understood that at that time you were testifying under oath didn't you?

A: Yes.

Q: Your Honor, I'd like to read into evidence line 6 from pg. 43 of Ms. Guzek's deposition transcript.

Defense Counsel: Objection your honor. Counsel is asking to read only part of the witness' answer. If counsel wants to use the deposition answer to impeach the deponent, counsel needs to put in the entire answer.

The Court: Objection sustained. Counsel, if you want to proceed, use the deponent's entire prior answer.[2]

Q: Very well Your Honor. [reading from the deposition] "Question: What happened next with respect to Ms. Park? Answer: On the 14th, Mr. Delaney told me that two weeks earlier he had asked Ms. Park to prepare a report for him on the tellers in the Southwest branch and that she had

2. This requirement stems from rules such as FRCP 32(a)(4). This provision and others like it are commonly denominated "the rule of completeness." The rule is designed to preclude the selective use of deposition testimony. Such use would allow testimony to be taken out of context and perhaps convey a misleading impression. Therefore, if a party offers part of a deponent's answer into the record, a court will usually allow an opposing party to insist that the complete answer be read into the record. By way of example, see Mattocks v. Daylin, Inc., 78 F.R.D. 663, 669 (W.D. Pa. 1978), overruling a party's effort to introduce a partial deposition answer. See also FRE 106. State law is generally in accord with Federal law. See Cal. Evid. Code § 356; Fla. Stat. Ann. § 90.108; Ill. S. Ct. R. 212 (c); Iowa R. Evid. 106; N.Y. Civ. Prac. L & R. 3117 (b); Tex. R. Evid. 106; Pa. R. Civ. P. 4020 (a) (4). For a state case upholding a trial court's ruling that a complete deposition answer must be read into the record, see Conderback, Inc. v. Standard Oil Co. 239 Cal.App.2d 664, 686; 48 Cal.Rptr. 901, 916 (1966).

just handed in a 20 page report. He said that since Ms. Park had had trouble in the past getting her work done on time he was surprised that Ms. Park had submitted the report on time but that he would review the report the next day and give me his evaluation of the situation. He said he hoped her report would be a sound one because despite the shortcomings in her work performance he had become quite fond of her. He said that within a week he would forward Ms. Park's report along with his own evaluation to me and that we could then get together and go over the situation. About two weeks later, we met to discuss Ms. Park's report and to review the situation at the Southwest branch.

Q: And you told the truth at your deposition, didn't you.

A: Yes.

You have managed to impeach Ms. Guzek's trial testimony that Mr. Delaney said nothing about being fond of Ms. Park. However, the helpful impeachment is part of a lengthy, narrative-style answer. As a result, the inconsistency between the in-court testimony and the deposition testimony may be difficult for the factfinder to appreciate. In addition, because you were required to read in the long narrative answer to impeach, you were forced to repeat testimony harmful to your case (e.g. the fact that Mr. Delaney said Ms. Park had had trouble getting her work done on time.)

By contrast, assume that during Ms. Guzek's deposition you had isolated and cemented the helpful evidence as follows:

Q: What happened next with respect to Ms. Park?

A: On the 14th, Mr. Delaney told me that two weeks earlier he had asked Ms. Park to prepare a report for him on the tellers in the Southwest branch and that she had just handed in a 20 page report. He said that since Ms. Park had had trouble in the past getting her work done on time he was surprised that Ms. Park had submitted the report on time but that he would review the report the next day and give me his evaluation of the situation. He said he hoped her report would be a sound one because despite the shortcomings in her work performance he had become quite fond of her. He said that within a week he would forward Ms. Park's report along with his own evaluation to me and that we could then get together and go over the situation. About two weeks later, we met to discuss Ms. Park's report and to review the situation at the Southwest branch.

Q: So on the 14th, Mr. Delaney told you he was quite fond of Ms. Park, is that correct?

A: That's what he said, yes.

Having isolated the helpful evidence in its own question-answer sequence, at trial your impeachment of Ms. Guzek could proceed as follows:

Q: On the morning of the 14th, Mr. Delaney talked to you about Ms. Park correct?

A: Yes.

Q: And on the 14th, Mr. Delaney told you that he had become quite fond of Ms. Park, correct?

A: I don't think that is right. I'm pretty sure he didn't say that.

Q: Ms. Guzek, you remember that your deposition was taken in this case, do you not?

A: Yes.

Q: And you understood that at that time you were testifying under oath, didn't you?

A: Yes.

Q: Your Honor, I'd like to read into evidence lines18–20 from pg. 43 of Ms. Guzek's deposition transcript. [reading from the deposition] "Question: So on the 14th Mr. Delaney told you he was quite fond of Ms. Park, is that correct? Answer: That's what he said, yes." And Ms. Guzek, when you gave that deposition testimony, you told the truth, didn't you?

A: Yes.

Isolating cemented evidence makes the inconsistency between in-court and deposition testimony easy for a factfinder to recognize and eliminates the need to repeat harmful or irrelevant deposition testimony during cross examination.

B. Occasionally Use Non–Leading Questions

In the example above, you consistently cement with leading questions. However, cementing repeatedly with leading questions sends strong signals that an answer helps your case. To prevent cementing from becoming more transparent than necessary, sprinkle in non-leading questions such as the following:

* Q: So on the 14th, did Mr. Delaney tell you that he was quite fond of Ms. Park? (In "yes-no" rather than leading form, this question may be less likely to alert a deponent to the fact that the deponent has helped your case.)

* Q: In this meeting on the 14th, what was it Mr. Delaney said about being fond of Ms. Park? (This cannot be answered "yes" or "no" so it is an open question.)

C. Obscure Your Purpose by Cementing "Surrounding Evidence"

As you know, the usual risks of cementing are educating your adversary and perhaps encouraging a deponent to recant helpful evidence. A method of minimizing these risks and camouflaging a helpful answer is to cement "the surroundings" in addition to the key item of helpful evidence. Like a magician, you hope the verbal "slight of hand" deflects attention from your real goal.

For example, return to Ms. Guzek's overview concerning the meeting on the 14th in the sexual harassment case of Park vs. First Rate Bank. Recall that Ms. Guzek testified as follows:

Q: What happened next with respect to Ms. Park?

A: On the 14th, Mr. Delaney told me that two weeks earlier he had asked Ms. Park to prepare a report for him on the tellers in the Southwest branch and that she had just handed in a 20 page report. He said that since Ms. Park had had trouble in the past getting her work done on time he was surprised that Ms. Park had submitted the report on time but that he would review the report the next day and give me his evaluation of the situation. He said he hoped her report would be a sound one because despite the shortcomings in her work performance he had become quite fond of her. He said that within a week he would forward Ms. Park's report along with his own evaluation to me and that we could then get together and go over the situation. About two weeks later, we met to discuss Ms. Park's report and to review the situation at the Southwest branch.

To cement both the helpful evidence and the surroundings, isolate a number of remarks the deponent made:

Q: Let me make sure I understand. On the 14th Mr. Delaney told you that two weeks earlier he had asked Ms. Park to prepare a report for him on the tellers in the Southwest branch and that she had just handed in a 20 page report, is that correct?

Q: Also on the 14th, Mr. Delaney told you that he was surprised that Ms. Park had submitted the report on time, am I right about that?

Q: And he also said that he would review the report the next day and give you his evaluation of the situation, is that right?

Q: And also on the 14th, Mr. Delaney said he had become quite fond of Ms. Park, correct?

Q: Additionally, he mentioned that he hoped Ms. Park's report would be a sound one, am I correct about that?

Q: And on the 14th Mr. Delaney also said that within a week he would forward Ms. Park's report along with his own evaluation to you and that you and he could then get together and go over the situation, is that right?

Note that you can cement more than the helpful "fond of Ms. Park" answer, without asking a deponent to repeat all the surrounding testimony. You need only cement enough to deflect the deponent's attention from the key item. To further allay the deponent's suspicions you may even repeat potentially harmful evidence (e.g. that Mr. Delaney was surprised that Ms. Park's report was handed in on time). Cementing harmful evidence will not prevent you from attacking it later in the deposition.[3]

D. Obscure Your Purpose by Delaying Cementing

You need not routinely cement as soon as a deponent provides a helpful answer. Immediate ce-

3. For a discussion of techniques to undercut harmful answers, see Chapter 6.

menting helps deponents and opposing lawyers recognize that a deponent has helped your cause, and may lead a deponent to wiggle away from a helpful answer. Instead, consider delaying cementing until you've finished probing an event or even a series of events, and then cement the helpful (and a few nonhelpful) evidentiary items. Your hoped-for impression is that you are doing nothing more than briefly recapping a portion of a story, especially if you cement periodically even when a deponent has not given helpful evidence.

E.   Cement in the Deponent's Own Words

You can further reduce a deponent's suspicions by cementing in a deponent's own words. This practice avoids any intimation that you are trying to put words into a deponent's mouth. Taking notes during depositions will probably be necessary if you are to use this technique.

F.   Offer a Neutral Explanation for Cementing

Another way to obscure the fact that you regard evidence as helpful is to offer a neutral reason for repeating the evidence. Common reasons you can offer include:

* Clarifying chronology. Example: "Ms. Guzek, so that we're clear on time, it was the meeting on the 14th that Mr. Delaney said that he was fond of Ms. Park?"

* Providing a summary. Example: "Ms. Guzek, by way of summary, let me go back for a moment to the meeting with Mr. Delaney on the 14th. One thing that Mr. Delaney said was that he was fond of Ms. Park, correct?"

G.   *Obtain a Foundation*

On some occasions, you can cement by asking for the foundation for the helpful evidence. That is, you may ask a deponent how he knows that the helpful evidence is true. You are particularly likely to ask for a foundation when the helpful evidence is a conclusion or opinion. Assume for example, that you are trying to prove that a company hired day laborers to do electrical work on a construction project. You are deposing the defendant's office manager. The questioning proceeds as follows:

Q: Did the company hire any day laborers to do electrical work on the Valley View construction project?

A: Yes.

To cement this testimony you might proceed as follows:

Q: How do you know that the company hired day laborers to do electrical work on the Valley View construction project?

A: I could tell from looking at the pay records and from talking to the foreman on that project.

Q: Other than the pay records and the conversations with the foreman, what else led you to conclude that the company hired day laborers to do electrical work on the Valley View construction project?

A: Well, I knew what the practice of the company had been on other projects of this sort.

Q: Was there anything else that led you to conclude that the company hired day laborers to do electrical work on the Valley View construction project?

A: No, not that I can think of.

Q: All right. Let's talk about your conversation with the foreman, then we'll go to the pay records and the company's practices on other projects. Tell me everything you can recall that the foreman said to you that indicated the company hired day laborers to do electrical work on the Valley View construction project?

A: Well I remember that when we discussed the completion deadline the foreman, Frank, told me that. . . .

By asking for the foundation for a deponent's testimony, you determine whether helpful information is based on direct perception or on hearsay. If you uncover a solid foundation for helpful testimony, you minimize the ability of the deponent to later recant.

5. Cementing "That's All"

Answers such as "that's all" or "I don't remember anything else" are often helpful, and can be cemented like any other helpful answer.

Example: You represent Orin in a wrongful termination case, and are deposing Orin's supervisor. The deponent testifies to basing Orin's termination on two reasons—excessive tardiness and preparing sloppy reports. You then proceed as follows:

1. Q: Did you have any other reasons for the termination?

2. A: No, that's it, just the two I've told you about.

You might well regard "that's it" as helpful evidence, especially if you suspect that the supervisor could have had other work-related reasons for terminating Orin. In these circumstances, you would generally not search for other possible reasons. Instead, cement the helpful evidence:

3. Q: So the two reasons you fired Orin were excessive tardiness and preparing sloppy reports, correct?

4. A: Yes.

5. Q: And these are the only reasons that you fired Orin, right?

6. A: Yes.

6. Responding to an "Asked and Answered" Objection

When you cement helpful evidence, opposing counsel may object on the ground of "Asked and Answered." The objection is improper so long as your cementing does not amount to witness harassment.[4] Therefore, treat such an objection as you would any other improper objection to form: ignore the objection and ask the deponent to answer your question.[5]

4. See e.g. Caplan v. Fellheimer, Eichen, Braverman, & Kaskey, 161 F.R.D. 29, 32 (E.D. Pa.1995) ("During the course of a routine deposition, a lawyer is free to revisit areas already examined, so long as that does not become oppressive or harassing"); see also Applied Telematics, Inc.v. Sprint Corp, No. 94–CV–4603, 1995 WL 79237, at *2 (E.D. Pa. Feb. 22,1995); First Tennessee Bank v. Federal Deposit Ins. Corp., 108 F.R.D. 640, 641 (D.C. Tenn.1985).

5. For a discussion of how to handle objections to form, see Chapter 15.

CHAPTER 6

UNDERMINING HARMFUL ANSWERS

Adverse witnesses routinely testify to harmful evidence during a deposition. Whether you want to try to undermine harmful evidence depends in large part on its probative value. The more damaging the evidence, the more time and effort you will likely spend at deposition trying to undermine it. This Chapter explains three questioning strategies for undermining harmful answers. They are:

* Challenge the accuracy of harmful answers.

* Undermine the inference to be drawn from harmful answers.

* Employ an "aggrandize the lie" strategy.

At the Chapter's conclusion is a Checklist reflecting these three strategies. You can use the Checklist both during a deposition and as you prepare for a deposition when you anticipate harmful testimony.

1. Strategy #1—Challenge Accuracy

One way to potentially undermine a harmful answer is to elicit evidence suggesting that it is inaccurate. Below are seven factors that may lead you to evidence that undermines harmful testimony. You may decide to inquire into one or more of them.

A. *Inconsistent Behavior*

You can argue that a harmful answer is inaccurate by showing that it is inconsistent with **subsequent** or **prior** behavior. To employ this strategy, simply ask yourself questions such as:

  * If the deponent's answer is accurate, what else would I also expect to have taken place?

  * If an event took place as the deponent claims, what kinds of activities, conversations or documentation are likely to have preceded the event, taken place during the event, or occurred subsequently?

Such questions alert you to topics you can inquire into as you search for inconsistent behavior.

For example, assume that in a wrongful termination case, a supervisor's harmful answer is that one basis for terminating your client is that the client failed to return a customer's important phone call. "Inconsistency" questions you might ask include:

  * "Did you make a written notation of this failure in my client's personnel file?"

  * "Did you report the incident to anyone else in the company?"

  * "Did you personally call the customer to apologize?"

If the deponent answers "no" to such questions, you have a basis for arguing that the claimed failure to return a phone call is a fiction. However, you may want to also search for possible explanations that might explain away the apparent inconsistency. Questions that begin with "why" or "can you explain" are common ways of unearthing explanations. For example:

Q: Ms. Supervisor, if my client failed to return an important call, why is it that you made no note of that fact in my client's personnel file?

Q: Ms. Supervisor, can you explain why you did not speak to the customer after my client failed to return the customer's call?

While you hope that adverse deponents will be unable to credibly explain away apparent inconsistencies, it is generally better to uncover any explanations at deposition. You then have an opportunity to challenge the accuracy of the explanation, using one or more of the strategies suggested in this Chapter and through further discovery. If you do not ask for explanations during the deposition, you may be surprised by a credible explanation later in the case.

B. *Absence of Corroborative Evidence*

Another way to challenge the accuracy of harmful testimony is to demonstrate that it is not corroborated by documents or other witnesses. Consequently, when faced with harmful testimony, you may routinely ask questions such as:

* "Are you aware of any documents that pertain to what you discussed at the meeting?"

* "Do you know of any documents that can corroborate what you've told me?"

* "Are you aware of any witnesses who can confirm what you've told me?"

* "Are you aware of any witnesses who you believe would disagree with what you've told me?"

Inquiries such as these can help you determine if the harmful answer can be corroborated and may also identify additional areas of inquiry or potential additional witnesses and documents.

C. Inability to Recall

You might also undermine the accuracy of a harmful answer by eliciting evidence that a deponent lacks a reasonable basis for being able to recall the harmful event. Below are two areas of inquiry that can help you establish that a deponent lacks a credible reason for recalling an event.

1. Routine or Fungible Events

Every day we observe and participate in numerous events, most of which are routine. We have no expectation of being called upon to remember routine events at a later time and therefore are likely to have difficulty recalling them accurately. As a result, the absence of a particular reason to recall tends to cast doubt on the accuracy of a deponent's testimony. In other words, unless what a deponent did or observed was for some reason unique or unusual, the deponent's claim to be able to recall it is questionable.[1] Examples:

1. Memorable characteristics of an event typically enhance a person's ability to recall. Thus, it is to be expected that someone

* A purchasing agent's recollection of the events surrounding a purchase order.

* A secretary's receipt of a telephone call for the boss.

* A tow truck operator's discussion with a driver involved in an automobile accident.

Questions that seek to establish that a harmful event was routine or fungible typically focus on how frequently a deponent engages in the behavior or makes the sort of observation that you want to undermine. After all, the greater the number of similar occurrences, the less plausible it is that a deponent can accurately recall the details of any particular occurrence.

For example, assume that you represent the plaintiff in an auto accident case. A waitress who served the defendant on the night of the accident testifies at deposition that the defendant did not have any alcohol to drink at dinner. You might seek to undermine this harmful testimony as follows:

1. Q: Ms. Munger, you first heard about the accident in this case approximately a month after it occurred, correct?

would have a greater ability to remember unique events, as opposed to routine or mundane happenings. See G. Cohen, Memory in the Real World 120 (1989) ("Unique occasions are usually better remembered than repeated events which blend into each other."); S. Engel, Context Is Everything: The Nature of Memory 8 (1999) ("[Y]ou are more likely to recall things that stand out (climbing to the top of a mountain) and will find it difficult to remember events that were one of many (Christmas dinner when you were 7).").

2. A: That's right. That's when I was called by the insurance company.

3. Q: How many customers do you usually wait on in an average night?

4. Well, I usually have 4 tables a night and they turn over at least twice, so I probably have about 10 to 12 parties a night.

5. Q: And approximately how many nights per week did you work during the month between the time of the accident and the time you were called by the insurance company?

6. A: I worked five nights a week.

7. Q: So you served approximately 200 parties between the night of the accident and the time you talked to the insurance company, correct?

8. A: That sounds about right.

9. Q: And some people have alcohol with their meal and some do not, correct?

10. A: That's true.

11. Q: And generally you have no reason to remember whether a particular person you waited on had alcohol with their meal, correct?

12. A: Not usually no.

13. Q: So how is it that you are able to recall that Mr. Walker did not have any alcohol to drink with his meal on the night of the accident?

14. A: ?

Here, you lay the groundwork for an argument that because the deponent routinely observed customers both drinking or not drinking alcohol with their meals, the deponent's ability to recall what happened with any single customer is dubious. You then ask the deponent to explain why she is able to do so (No. 13). Of course, you hope that the deponent will be unable to give a credible explanation. Even if the explanation is believable, however, as usual you're better off surfacing it at deposition, and possibly undermining it, rather than being blind-sided by it later in the case.

2. *"Ancient" Occurrences*

Just as we tend not to remember the commonplace, so too do we tend to forget the ancient. This is especially true if we've had no occasion to recall an event since it occurred. Thus, if you can elicit evidence not only that an event happened in the distant past, but also that a deponent has had no occasion to recall it since, you may be able to cast doubt on the accuracy of the deponent's harmful answer.[2] Consider this questioning of a tow truck driver:

Q: This accident happened about 18 months ago, right?

A: That's true.

---

2. The longer the interval between the event and the time a person attempts to recall, the greater the chance that the person's memory will become somewhat distorted. See E. Loftus & J. Doyle, Eyewitness Testimony: Civil and Criminal 60 (3d ed. 1997) ("[C]hanges in recollection appear to be more likely as the original memory fades with the passage of time.").

Q: Between the time of the accident and today, have you had any other occasion to talk about what happened on the day of the accident?

A: Well, just with that other lawyer yesterday.

Q: After the accident, did you write down what you remembered about the accident?

A: No.

While such answers may enable you to cast doubt on the accuracy of the tow truck driver's recollection, you may again want to prevent surprises by probing for a possible explanation:

Q: Given that the accident happened 18 months ago and you've never talked about it since that day, can you explain how it is that you can now remember what my client said on that day?

If the deponent testifies to intervening events which have supposedly "kept the matter fresh in my mind," you may want to probe those events. For example, how often and why did the deponent talk about what happened? Who did the deponent talk to about the accident?[3]

3. Even if no one tries to influence a deponent's memory of an event, it is quite possible that subsequent conversations and/or occurrences subconsciously distort the deponent's recollection of the event. For more discussion on the effect of this kind of interference, see E. Loftus & J. Doyle, Eyewitness Testimony: Civil and Criminal 60 (3d ed. 1997) ("[M]isinformation is casually or unintentionally assimilated into the witness's memory.").

3. No Reason to Recall

Testimony is frequently more credible if the deponent has a reason for recalling it. Therefore, you can sometimes undermine an item of harmful evidence by showing that a deponent has no specific reason for recalling it. Consequently, when faced with harmful testimony, you may routinely ask questions such as:

* "Why is it that you remember that you mailed the letter on the 16th of May?"

* "Is there any specific reason why you remember that my client arrived late to the meeting?"

* "How is it that you remember that there were three drafts of the lease prior to the signing of final agreement in Exhibit 27?

D. Unable to Provide the Details of Unique Occurrences

"Accurate recall" generally includes the salient details of non-routine or unique events. Therefore, if a deponent is unable to provide details about such events, you have a basis for attacking the accuracy of the deponent's answer. For example, assume that you are deposing a supervisor who testifies that your client insulted her at work. You might ask the supervisor to testify to your client's exact words, where the incident occurred, what time of day the incident occurred, what else was said during the conversation, and the like. The supervisor's inability to recall a number of details might cast doubt on the accuracy of the supervisor's testimony.

E.   *Inability to Perceive*

Another way to attack accuracy is to elicit evidence that a deponent lacked an adequate ability to perceive. For example, most people are likely to disbelieve a deponent's account of a conversation that the deponent overheard from a distance of fifty feet through a closed door.

Consider both external and internal obstacles when probing for evidence undermining a deponent's ability to perceive. In terms of external obstacles, ask "scene-setting" questions. That is, ask deponents to describe the scenes of important events or ask the deponent to draw a diagram or sketch of the scene. Then, picturing the scene in your mind's eye, try to identify anything that might have interfered with the deponent's ability to make an accurate observation. For example, if the scene is a room, might there have been physical obstructions such as walls or people that hindered or impaired the deponent's view? Might noises have interfered with accurate hearing? The point is to identify circumstances that could undermine an ability to perceive accurately, and then to question the deponent as to the presence of those circumstances.

As for internal obstacles, these pertain to a deponent's mental and emotional state. For example, might a deponent have been feeling ill when the observation was made? Does the deponent have permanent physical impairments, such as poor hearing or eyesight? Was the deponent taking medications or drugs which might have affected perception? Was the deponent so stressed about a professional or personal problem that the deponent couldn't readily attend to an outside event?

If you do develop evidence to support an argument based on inability to perceive, you should as usual check to see whether a deponent has an explanation that might vitiate any such argument.

F. No Reason or Motive for Behavior

Another type of argument you can make to challenge accuracy is to show that a deponent cannot provide a reasonable motive for his/her behavior. Obviously, not all behavior is predicated by a conscious motive. For example, a deponent who testifies that she was on her way to work when she saw an accident does not need to supply a reason for her seeing the accident. In other situations, however, evidence of lack of motive can support an argument that harmful testimony is inaccurate.

Example 1

The deponent testifies, "I explained to your client the general risks of investing in small startup companies before she decided to invest in this particular company." To search for evidence undermining this testimony, you might ask the deponent questions such as: "Why did you talk about the general risks of investing in small start-up companies?" "What was it about the company that led you to talk about the risks?" If the deponent cannot offer a credible explanation, you have a basis for arguing that the testimony is inaccurate.

Example 2

The deponent testifies, "I was present when Ms. Michaels explained to your client the general risks of investing in small startup companies." To search for evidence undermining this testimony, you might probe both the deponent's and Ms. Michaels' motives. For example, you might ask the deponent questions such as" "Why were you present at the meeting between Ms. Michaels and my client?" "Can you explain why Ms. Michaels talked about the general risks of investing in small startup companies?" If the deponent cannot offer a credible explanation for either the deponent's or Ms. Michaels' behavior, you again have a basis for arguing that the testimony is inaccurate.

If a deponent testifies to a reason or motive, you still have an opportunity to undermine it through additional discovery. For instance, the deponent in the example above may testify that: "I talked to your client about the risks of investing in small startup companies because that's our company policy." Through further investigation, you might be able to establish that no such policy existed.

G.   *Special Bias*

By definition, almost all adverse witnesses are likely to be predisposed in favor of your adversary. As the same slant is likely to be true for witnesses testifying on your client's behalf, general charges of bias are easy to make and often of little value. However, you might be able to undermine the credibility of harmful testimony if you can develop evidence of a deponent's "particularized bias" that goes beyond mere party association. Three ways of probing for particularized bias include:

* Special gain or loss: Does the deponent stand to gain financial or social benefits by testifying for your adversary? For example, are the deponent and your adversary in related industries such that testimony in your adversary's interest is also in the deponent's interest?

* Closeness of relationship with the adversary: Does the deponent have a particularly strong bond with your adversary? For example, do the deponent and your adversary have a long social or professional relationship?

* Hostility toward your client: Does the deponent have reason to dislike your client or anyone else on your side of the case?

For example, assume that your client Tim Malloy seeks damages against his former company after having allegedly been fired for blowing the whistle to authorities on improper company activity. The deponent has testified to an occasion on which Malloy was angry and insubordinate to the deponent's boss, Arlene Shafer. To search for particularized bias, you might ask questions such as:

Q: How long have you worked for Ms. Shafer?

Q: Do you see Ms. Shafer socially?

Q: Has Ms. Shafer recommended that you receive raises?

Q: Has Mr. Malloy ever bothered you?

Q: Do you believe that Mr. Malloy has ever complained to anyone about you?

H.   Conclusion

You can probe into the seven areas of inquiry discussed above whether or not you anticipated the harmful testimony prior to the deposition. As you do so, you also realize the following advantages:

* If a deponent gives false testimony in an effort to bolster the credibility of the harmful testimony you are trying to undermine, you may then be able to establish that the deponent has testified falsely, either through further questioning or additional investigation.

* You may learn that an attack on the accuracy of harmful evidence is unlikely to succeed. One alternative then is to modify your arguments or theory of the case to minimize the significance of the harmful evidence. A second alternative is to attempt to undercut the inference to be drawn from the harmful answer, an approach described in the next section.

2.   Strategy #2—Attack the Inference

A second method of undermining harmful evidence (which you may use either in lieu of or in addition to challenging accuracy) is to attack the inference your adversary is likely to want to draw from the evidence. This approach is potentially available whenever the harmful answer constitutes circumstantial evidence. To use this approach:

* First, decide what inference or conclusion your adversary wants the factfinder to draw from the harmful evidence.

* Second, identify the circumstances that would make your adversary's inference or conclusion <u>less likely</u> to be true. You can often do this quickly by simply saying to yourself: "My adversary's inference or conclusion is likely to be true, **except when** . . . ." As you complete this sentence you identify potential evidence to undermine your adversary's inference.

For example, assume that you represent the plaintiff in a wrongful termination case. You contend that your client was terminated because of her gender; the defendant contends that the termination was for poor work performance. At deposition, your client's supervisor testifies that one reason for your client's termination was her failure to meet her sales quota in the six month period immediately prior to her termination. You want to undermine your adversary's inference that the failure to meet the sales quota led to termination for poor work performance.

To identify topics you might ask about to try to undermine your adversary's inference, simply say to yourself:

An employee is likely to be terminated for failing to meet a sales quota, **except when:**

-Other employees failed to meet the quota but were not terminated.

-The employee misses the quota by a small margin.

-The employee has met sales quotas on all prior occasions.

-Missing the sales quota was not mentioned in the employee's evaluation.

-The person who made the ultimate decision to terminate the employee did not know of the failure to meet the quota.

You would then inquire about these potential exceptions. Testimony that these exceptions exist would tend to undermine the inference your adversary seeks to draw from the harmful evidence.

3.   Strategy #3—Aggrandize the Lie

Rather than attempting to attack the accuracy of a harmful answer or the inference to be drawn from it, you may want to encourage a deponent to affirm and expand upon the harmful answer. This approach makes sense when you can convincingly contradict the deponent's answer through a more credible witness or document. In taking this approach, you operate on the assumption that if a deponent is willing to embellish an answer that you can later clearly show is false, you can argue that the deponent has consciously lied, rather than made an innocent mistake. And, as we all recognize, factfinders and settlement conference judges tend to view much more harshly witnesses they perceive to be lying rather than merely mistaken.

To aggrandize a lie, encourage a deponent to expand or elaborate on a harmful answer. You might do so by asking questions that invite a deponent to <u>enhance</u> the credibility of a harmful answer. For instance, encourage a deponent to provide you with reasons for recalling the harmful answer. These aggrandizing questions make it difficult for a deponent to later claim that, "I made an innocent misstatement at deposition."

By way of illustration, assume that you represent the plaintiff in a breach of contract action. The deponent has testified that a Notice of Rescission dated July 13 was mailed on that date, and you contend that the Notice was mailed after that date. Moreover, you have reliable evidence that the deponent was on vacation from July 12th through July 20th, and therefore could not have mailed the Notice on the 13th. Rather than attempting to challenge the accuracy of the deponent's testimony, you might aggrandize the lie as follows:

1. Q: How is it you can remember that you mailed Exhibit 27, the Notice of Rescission, on July 13th, the date it was signed?

2. A: Because my boss told me to be sure to put the notice in the mail immediately.

3. Q: Is there any other reason that you can recall mailing Exhibit 27 on July 13th?

4. A: No. I just remember that right after my boss signed it, she told me to have it mailed immediately.

5. Q: Showing you this calendar-July 13th of that year was a Wednesday, correct?

6. A: Yes.

7. Q: So there were two more days in your work week after July 13th?

8. A: Yes.

9. Q: So you were not trying to get Exhibit 27 in the mail just before the weekend began, is that correct?

10. A: That's right.

11. Q: And because your boss told you that it was important to mail the notice right away, you mailed the notice yourself?

12. A: Yes. I put it in an envelope addressed to Phil Mueller at Plastics Inc., put a stamp on the envelope and put it directly into the mail chute that is on our floor.

13. Q: Did you have to leave your office in order to put mail into the mail chute?

14. A: Yes. You have to leave the office and walk down the hall to the elevators.

15. Q: Where is that mail chute?

16. A: It is right by the elevators.

17. Q: And you recall actually walking to the mail chute to mail Exhibit 27, the Notice of Rescission, correct?

18. A: Yes.

19. Q: So another reason that you recall mail-
         ing Exhibit 27 on the day it was signed is
         that you recall going to the mail chute be-
         cause that is something that you don't nor-
         mally do?

20. A: That's right.

Note that your questioning utilizes some of the
same categories you might use to challenge the
accuracy of the harmful testimony. For example,
No. 3 asks about a reason to recall and No. 11
elicits a motive for engaging in the behavior. When
you aggrandize a lie, however, you accept a deponent's answers at face value. Thus, for example, you
do not try to show that the deponent's stated reasons for recalling the harmful testimony are incorrect. By aggrandizing, you firmly lock the deponent
into the harmful testimony. If and when you subsequently offer evidence that the deponent was on
vacation on the date the Notice was supposedly
mailed, you can argue that the deponent consciously
lied at deposition and therefore should not be believed.

4. Undermining Opinions and Conclusions

A deponent's harmful testimony may consist of a
conclusion or an opinion rather than a concrete
perception or event.

Example 1

Describing how a driver looked after an accident,
a deponent may testify to a conclusion that a
driver was "drunk" rather than to the concrete

observations that led the deponent to conclude that the driver was drunk.

<u>Example 2</u>

Describing how an employee reacted to being fired, a deponent might state that the employee "became enraged" rather than explaining in what ways the employee manifested rage.

To try to undermine a harmful opinion or conclusion, determine first whether it is based on concrete perceptions. Sample questions seeking perceptions underlying a conclusion or opinion include:

* <u>Tell me all the reasons you concluded that</u> the driver was intoxicated?

* <u>What did you observe that led you to conclude that</u> the driver was intoxicated?

* <u>Why do you think</u> the driver was intoxicated?

* <u>What is your basis</u> for saying that the employee was enraged?

Usually, deponents respond with one or more foundational observations. You should normally continue probing until you have exhausted a deponent's recollection. Your questioning might go as follows:

1. Q: You say that Mr. Kama became irate when Mr. Singer told him that he was fired. What happened that led you to conclude Mr. Kama became irate?

2. A: It was just the way he acted.

3. Q: What else happened that led you to conclude Mr. Kama was irate?

4. A: He got very red in the face and started shouting.

5. Q: Beside getting red and shouting, what else happened that made you think that Mr. Kama was irate?

6. A: He started pounding his fist on Mr. Singer's desk.

7. Q: In addition to getting red, shouting and pounding his fist on Mr. Singer's desk, did Mr. Kama do anything else to indicate that he was irate?

8. A: No.

Having uncovered the observations underlying a deponent's harmful conclusion or opinion, you can proceed along one of two paths. If your probing indicates that a deponent has little or no concrete support for a harmful conclusion, you may later argue that the conclusion is either inadmissible[4] or not credible. If on the other hand a deponent can provide concrete observations in support of a harmful conclusion (as in the example involving Mr. Kama), you may then attempt to undercut the observation, by challenging the accuracy of the testimony or undercutting the inference that your adversary will try to draw from it.

5. Undermining Conclusions About Conditions or Behavior Over Time

A deponent's harmful conclusion or opinion may pertain not to what happened on a single occasion

4. See FRE 701.

but rather to what occurred on many occasions. For example, in a wrongful termination case, a supervisor of the defendant company might assert that the plaintiff was "always late for work" or "almost never finished an assignment on time."

To try to undermine harmful conclusions regarding conditions or behavior over time, you might proceed as follows:

* **Ask for specific instances.** Begin by asking deponents for specific instances of the behavior or condition. Example: "Mr. Supervisor, please give me a specific instance in which the plaintiff failed to finish his work assignment on time." Again, if a deponent has few or no concrete instances to support an opinion concerning a harmful behavior or condition over time, you may later argue that the conclusion is either inadmissible[5] or not credible.

* **Exhaust the deponent's memory.** Continue pressing deponents for specific instances until you have exhausted a deponent's recall. Example: "Mr. Supervisor, can you recall any other instances in which the plaintiff failed to finish his work assignment on time?"

* **Undermine the specific instances.** Once a deponent has testified to all the specific instances, you may decide to try to undermine them using any of the three strategies described earlier in

5. See FRE 701.

this Chapter. For example, to challenge accuracy you might ask questions such as: "Supervisor, what did you do after my client failed to turn in the August sales report on time?" *[probing for inconsistent behavior]* or "How is it that you can now remember that my client failed to complete the August sales report on time?" *[probing for inability to recall]*.

6. Delaying Attempts to Undermine Harmful Evidence

When a deponent testifies to harmful evidence, you may not want to immediately try to challenge its accuracy or attack the inference your opponent will likely draw from the evidence. Delaying your attempt to undermine has at least two potential advantages.

First, deponents often recognize that questions tending to undermine the evidence call their credibility into doubt and, as a consequence, may become quite antagonistic. Therefore, if harmful evidence arises at a time when you still hope that a friendly relationship with the deponent may produce evidence helpful to your case, you may put undermining questions on a back burner. Second, delay may mask the significance of your questions, increasing the chance that a deponent will not realize that you are attempting to undermine a harmful answer.

7. Undermining With Conflicting Witnesses and Documents

You will sometimes be aware of a witness or document that directly contradicts a deponent's harmful testimony. Should you disclose the existence of your conflicting witness or document at the deposition? If so, how might you go about doing so? The following Chapter (No.7) addresses several strategies and techniques related to these issues.

A Checklist for Undermining Harmful Answers

Below you will find a Checklist that summarizes the various approaches you might pursue to undermine a harmful answer. You can take this Checklist (or a customized version of it) with you to depositions to help you quickly come up with topics and questions for undermining harmful testimony. Additionally, you can use the Checklist during deposition preparation when you intend to question a deponent about harmful evidence of which you are already aware.

Of course this Checklist cannot be used like a cookie cutter to respond to all harmful testimony. You have to use your judgment to decide when to try to undermine harmful testimony and which strategies to use.

Checklist for Undermining Harmful Evidence

Strategy #1—Challenge the Accuracy of the Evidence

1. **Inconsistent Behavior**

   -Prior or Subsequent behavior

2. **Absence of Corroborative Evidence**

3. **Inability to Recall**

   - Routine or fungible event

   - Ancient event

   - No reason to recall

4. **Unable to Provide Details of the Occurrence**

5. **Inability to Perceive**

6. **No Reason or Motive for Behavior**

7. **Special Bias**

Strategy #2—Attack the Inference from the Harmful Evidence

-What inference would the other side like to draw?

-Are there circumstances that might make the other side's inference unlikely to be true in this particular case?

Strategy #3—Aggrandize the Lie

-Have the deponent repeat and expand on the harmful evidence.

Special Concerns About Opinions and Conclusions

-Obtain reasons for or perceptions on which the opinion or conclusion is based.

-Undermine the bases for the opinion or conclusion.

Special Concerns About Conditions or Behavior Over Time

-Exhaust the deponent's memory for examples.

-Undermine each example.

CHAPTER 7

RESPONDING TO INCONSISTENT STATEMENTS

A deponent's testimony is sometimes inconsistent with either:

(1) A prior statement, either oral or written, of the deponent; or

(2) A prior statement, either oral or written, of another witness.

When either of these situations arises during a deposition you potentially have the following options:

* Ask the deponent for explanations for the inconsistency.

* Ignore the inconsistency.

* Employ an "aggrandize the lie" strategy.

* Encourage the deponent to affirm the more helpful statement and recant the other one.

This Chapter explains these options and describes their risks and benefits.

1. A Deponent's Testimony Conflicts With the Deponent's Prior Statement

A. Option #1—Ask the Deponent for an Explanation

During settlement negotiations or at trial, you may use a deponent's inconsistent statements to attack the deponent's credibility. When you make such an attack, the deponent or opposing counsel may respond by explaining away the inconsistency. If the explanation is credible, your attack is likely to be ineffective. Consequently, at deposition you will typically want to ask deponents for explanations for inconsistencies between deposition testimony and prior statements. Pursuing this option typically requires only a few straightforward questions at the deposition. Consider the following example:

Q: Mr. Klee, when was the first time that you received notice of the alleged breach of warranty?

A: Mr. Henderson wrote to us in September and said that they were having problems with the equipment.

Q: Was that the first time you received notice of the breach of warranty?

A: Yes.

Q: I am showing you a document marked as Exhibit 14. Could you read the first two paragraphs on page one to yourself please?

A: Sure.

Q: Exhibit 14 is a copy of a memo you wrote on or about July 30, correct?

A: Yes.

Q: The second paragraph of Exhibit 14 states: "Yesterday Henderson called and said they were unable to use the equipment we installed due to mechanical failure. Johnson was sent to look at the problem." Is that correct?

A: Yes.

Q: Can you explain why on July 30 you wrote that Henderson said that they were unable to use the equipment because of mechanical failure, whereas now you say that the first time you received notice of breach of warranty was in September?

A: I didn't consider the conversation in July to constitute notice of a breach of warranty.

Q: I'd like you to tell me all the reasons you didn't consider the conversation in July to constitute a notice of a breach of warranty.

A: Well. . . .

You could continue your questioning until you exhausted the deponent's explanations for the inconsistency.

The benefits of seeking explanations include:

* You will be better able to assess whether you can use an inconsistency to effectively attack a deponent's credibility when you know whether a deponent has a credible explanation.

* You commit a deponent to an explanation at the deposition. As a result, opposing counsel has less opportunity to suggest (or even craft) a credible explanation after a deposition is completed.

* You gain an opportunity to undermine any explanation either later during the deposition or in further discovery. You may not have time to do so if you learn of an explanation for the first time in the middle of settlement negotiations or trial.

This option is not risk free. Asking for explanations almost surely brings an inconsistency to the attention of a deponent and opposing counsel. Accordingly, you incur the following risks:

* The deponent may immediately qualify or back away from the testimony creating the inconsistency. This may significantly limit your ability to use the inconsistency to attack the deponent's credibility.

* You give up any chance of surprising opposing counsel and the deponent by confronting the deponent with the inconsistency for the first time during settlement negotiations or at trial.

When you decide that the risks of this option outweigh the benefits, you may employ Option #2.

B.   Option #2—Ignore the Inconsistency

A second response to conflicting statements is to ignore the inconsistency. This option avoids bringing the inconsistency to the attention of a deponent or opposing counsel. As a result, a deponent is less likely to immediately qualify or back away from the testimony creating the inconsistency, and you may be able to surprise a deponent when you raise the inconsistency for the first time later in the case. Of course, if you believe that opposing counsel and the deponent are already aware of the inconsistency, this option makes little sense. In addition, when you pursue this option, you forego the benefits of Option #1—asking for explanations.

C. Option #3—Aggrandize the Lie

In lieu of Options 1 and 2, you may "aggrandize the lie" by encouraging a deponent to repeat and expand upon deposition testimony creating an inconsistency.[1] This third option is useful when you believe that you can clearly prove that deposition testimony is false. This approach firmly commits a deponent to what you think you can prove is false deposition testimony, and prevents the deponent from later claiming that the deposition testimony was an innocent misstatement. As a result, the factfinder may well conclude that deponent has given knowingly false testimony.

By way of illustration, return to the breach of warranty case above. Assume that you have the deponent's memo indicating that he talked with Henderson about problems with the equipment in July, and that you believe this conversation constituted notice of breach of warranty. If you are pursuing this option the deposition might proceed as follows:

1. Q: Mr. Klee, when was the first time that you received notice of the alleged breach of warranty?

[1] For a further discussion of the technique of "aggrandizing the lie," see Chapter 6.

2. A: The first time was when I received a letter in late September that said that they were having problems with the equipment.

3. Q: Was that the first time you received notice of the breach of warranty?

4. A: Yes.

5. Q: So it was after Labor Day that you first received notice of the breach of warranty?

6. A: That's right.

7. Q: Since this first notice was in writing, is it accurate to say that you did not have any oral discussions about breach of warranty prior to receiving the letter in September?

8. A: That is correct.

9. Q: What did you do in response to this September letter?

10. A: I called Henderson to discuss the matter.

11. Q: So the first time you talked to Henderson was after you received the letter in September?

12. A: That's right.

13. Q: Tell me what was said in this initial conversation with Henderson.

14. A: I asked Henderson....

In this example, Nos. 5, 7, 9 & 11 encourage the deponent to repeat and expand upon the deposition testimony. Note that when you employ this technique, you never mention the contradictory prior statement. If you mention the prior inconsistent statement the deponent might immediately recant the deposition testimony you want to aggrandize.

D.   *Option #4—Encourage the Deponent to Affirm the Helpful Statement and Recant the Other One*

Instead of using an inconsistency to attack credibility, you may encourage a deponent to affirm one statement and recant the other one. You pursue this option when you conclude that the deponent's admission that one of two inconsistent statements is true helps your case more than using the inconsistency to attack credibility.

The following example illustrates the "affirm and recant" option. Assume that in a wrongful termination case you represent Mike Porter and are deposing Mr. Porter's former supervisor. Prior to your client's termination, the supervisor had given your client a written year end work evaluation in which he concluded that your client's work was above average. At his deposition, the supervisor testifies that your client's work during the year prior to his termination was below average. You might try to have the deponent admit that the "above average" statement in the year end evaluation is accurate, and recant his inconsistent deposition testimony. To do so, you might proceed as follows:

1. Q: I'd like to turn to the year end evaluation you gave Mr. Porter shortly before his employment was terminated. Is Exhibit 212, the

document I'm now showing you, the year end evaluation you gave Mr. Porter shortly before he was terminated from his employment?

2. A: Yes it is.

3. Q: And is this your signature on the line that says "Supervisor?"

4. A: Yes it is.

5. Q: You completed Exhibit 212, correct?

6. A: Yes.

7. Q: A year end evaluation can be an important document, correct?

8. A: It can be.

9. Q: You thought that other people might rely on the information you included in the evaluation, correct?

10. A: They might, yes.

11. Q: Do you see this box in Exhibit 212 labeled "Overall Evaluation?"

12. A: Yes I do.

13. Q: And, you checked the square in the Overall Evaluation box that reads, "Above Average", isn't that correct?

14. A: Yes; that's correct.

15. Q: And you checked the "Above Average" square because you wanted to be honest, isn't that right?

16. A: Yes.

17. Q: So in the year prior to the time Mr. Porter was terminated, you thought his

work was better than average, isn't that correct?

18. A: Yes it is.

19. Q: So your earlier testimony today that Mr. Porter's work was below average during that period was mistaken, am I correct?

20. A: Well, if I said that, I made a mistake, yes.

In this example, you begin by enhancing the credibility of the statement that you want the deponent to accept as true (Nos. 1–15).[2] The more you can enhance the credibility of the statement you want the deponent to accept, the more likely he is to do so. You typically want to use leading questions in this portion of your examination. As in the above example, such questions allow you to confront the deponent with an uninterrupted list of evidence tending to enhance the credibility of the statement you want the deponent to accept. After completing the enhancement questions, you then ask the deponent to reaffirm that the statement is true (No. 17).

You conclude by suggesting that the deponent recant the inconsistent statement because it was the result of a mistake. When you attempt to obtain a retraction, you may want to be sensitive to deponents' understandable reluctance to admit to an erroneous statement. People don't like to publicly admit that they have been wrong and they certainly don't want to admit that they've lied. Suggesting a

2. This enhancement involves the use of a plausibility chain, discussed in Chapter 4.

mistake provides the deponent with an acceptable explanation for recanting previous testimony. Lawyers use a variety of euphemistic phrases when articulating the mistake notion. The following are illustrative.

* Q: Since in the year prior to the time Mr. Porter was terminated, his work was better than average, <u>did I fail to make my question clear this morning when you answered that that Mr. Porter's work during that time period was below average?</u>

* Q: Since in the year prior to the time Mr. Porter was terminated, his work was above average, <u>did you perhaps not understand my question this morning when you answered that Mr. Porter's work during that time period was below average?</u>

The "affirm and recant" option will, of course, not always be successful. You may not be able to enhance the credibility of the statement you want the deponent to accept as true. And even when you can enhance the credibility of one statement, a deponent can always refuse to recant a conflicting statement. When this option is unsuccessful, you may then fall back on option number one above, i.e. ask the deponent for explanations.

2. Deponent's Deposition Testimony Conflicts With Another Witness' Statement

When a deponent's answer at deposition conflicts with a statement of another witness, you usually have the same four options discussed above.

You could ask the deponent for any explanations for the conflict between the deponent and the other witness. For example:

Q: Mr. Klee, when was the first time that you received notice of the alleged breach of warranty?

A: Mr. Henderson wrote to us in September and said that they were having problems with the equipment.

Q: Was that the first time you received notice of the breach of warranty?

A: Yes.

Q: Do you know someone named Steve Derian?

A: Yes. He's my administrative assistant.

Q: I am showing you what has been marked as Exhibit 27. Would you read it to yourself please. Is that Mr. Derian's signature at the bottom of Exhibit 27?

A: Yes.

Q: Am I correct that Exhibit 27 is dated July 30 and addressed to Mr. Henderson and says in the second paragraph: "This is to confirm that, pursuant to your conversation on this date with Mr. Klee, one of our representatives will be at you facilities within 48 hours to remedy any problems you are having with our Hydro Boiler. If you have any additional problems with the operation of the boiler, please contact me directly"?

A: You are correct.

Q: Did you have a conversation on or about July 30 with Mr. Klee about problems Mr. Henderson was having with the Hydro Boiler?

A: Yes.

Q: Since you talked about these problems with the boiler in July, could you explain why you felt that you first received notice or breach of warranty in September?

A: I didn't consider the conversation with Mr. Henderson in July to constitute notice of a breach of warranty.

Q: I'd like you to tell me all the reasons you didn't consider the conversation in July to constitute a notice of a breach of warranty.

A: Well. . . .

Instead of asking for an explanation, you could have ignored the conflict and not mentioned the other witness' statement. In the above example, you could have said nothing about Derian's letter and raised the issue for the first time at trial or during settlement. Alternatively, you could have used the aggrandize the lie technique and had Klee expand on his deposition testimony indicating that he first received notice of breach of warranty in September.

Finally, you can use the conflicting statement of another witness to try to have a deponent affirm the accuracy of the other witness' statement and recant his own deposition testimony. The following example illustrates this option:

Q: In the meeting when you were let go from your job, what did your supervisor tell you were the reasons you were being let go?

A: He said it was because I had been late to work and I had dressed inappropriately at work.

Q: Do you know a woman named Ruth Goldway?

A: Yes. She is a secretary who worked with me before I was let go.

Q: Did you find Ms. Goldway to be honest in your dealings with her?

A: Yes.

Q: Do you think Ms. Goldway dislikes you?

A: Not as far as I know.

Q: Did you and she have any arguments at work?

A: Not that I recall.

Q: Do you think Ms. Goldway bears you any ill will?

A: Not as far as I know.

Q: You talked to Ms. Goldway right after the meeting where you were let go from work, correct?

A: That's true.

Q: And you talked about why you had been terminated, correct?

A: Yes.

Q: Didn't you tell Ms. Goldway the *only* reason you were terminated was for repeated tardiness?

A: I never said that to Ruth.

Q: Do you know of any reason why Ms. Goldway might be mistaken about what you told her?

A: Well, when I talked to her about what happened in my termination meeting Ruth was on the phone so she might not have been paying attention to what I said.

Q: Do you know of any other reason why Ms. Goldway might be mistaken about what you told her?

A: Well, she . . . .

Again, you begin by enhancing the credibility of the third person whose statement you want the deponent to accept as true. You then confront the deponent with the statement of the third person and then ask the deponent to affirm that the other witness' statement is true. In this example, however, your attempt at affirmation is unsuccessful. As a result, you begin to explore any explanations for the inconsistency.

CHAPTER 8

RESPONDING TO IMPLAUSIBILITIES

Implausible deposition testimony is a frequent source of attacks on a deponents' credibility during settlement negotiations or on cross examination at trial. This Chapter offers questioning techniques you can employ to try to magnify implausible testimony.

1. What Makes Testimony Implausible?

Testimony is arguably implausible when it juxtaposes two or more facts that in light of ordinary experience usually do not go together. Assume, for example that a plaintiff in a wrongful termination case testifies at deposition as follows:

Q: You contend that when you were fired you did not have a chance to explain that the charges against you were false, is that correct?

A: That's correct.

Q: Did being fired without being given a chance to explain upset you in any way?

A: No, it didn't.

Most listeners would find this testimony implausible. People sometimes do get fired without being given a chance to explain that the charges against them are false. Similarly, sometimes people get fired without becoming upset. But usually the two don't go together. Indeed in our society the opposite is typically true. People who are fired without being given a chance to explain that the charges against them are false are typically very upset. A contrary story just isn't likely to be believed.

Sometimes a single deposition answer creates an implausibility. That is, two facts that don't mesh with ordinary experience may emerge together. For example, a deponent says: "I was fired without being given a chance to explain. But it really didn't bother me." Other times, an implausibility arises when a deposition answer does not jive with a deponent's earlier deposition testimony or pre-deposition statement. For instance, at one point the deponent testifies he was fired without being given a chance to explain the charges against him were false and at a much later point the deponent testifies he was not upset when he was fired. Regardless of how an implausibility arises, you may respond to it by: (1) Trying to magnify the implausibility and/or (2) Determining whether a deponent can explain it away.

2. Magnifying Implausibilities Through the "Especially When" Technique

A judgment that testimony is implausible implicitly rests on a generalization about how people generally behave or how events generally unfold. Consequently, a technique for quickly identifying topics that might magnify an implausibility is to surface an underlying generalization and identify circumstances in which it is particularly likely to be true. In the above example, this technique might produce the following:

Generalization: "People who are fired without being given an opportunity to explain that the charges against them are false are generally upset, **especially when** they:

—need the money from their job to make ends meet

—don't have another job available

—have a poor chance of getting another job

—also lose their pension

—have no money to hire a lawyer

—have no savings to fall back on

You could potentially magnify the implausibility with further questions inquiring into these "especially whens." If, for example, further questions establish that the deponent had no savings to fall back on when he was terminated, his testimony becomes more implausible.

3. Defer Inquiries into Topics That Might Magnify an Implausibility

When you identify potential topics that might enable you to magnify an implausibility, consider delaying your inquiry into those topics. Immediate inquiry may alert a deponent to the implausibility. Once alerted, the deponent may try to minimize the implausibility by giving less than honest answers as you question about your "especially whens." Return to the example of the plaintiff who testified that he was fired without being given a chance to establish that the charges against him were false. If you at once launch into questions based on your "especially whens" (e.g., did he need the money from the job to make ends meet) the deponent may answer dishonestly so as to avoid heightening the implausibility. Consequently, you may want to delay any inquiry into topics that might magnify an implausibility.

4. Checking for Explanations

Since an implausibility is just an <u>apparent</u> conflict with common beliefs about how things <u>generally</u> happen, there is always a possibility that an implausibility can be explained away. Therefore, before deciding to rely on an apparent implausibility during settlement negotiations or at trial, consider searching for explanations. In the above example, to surface explanations you might ask questions such as the following:

<u>Example #1</u>

Q: Can you explain why you were not upset when you were discharged without being given an opportunity to explain that the charges against you were false?

<u>Example #2</u>

Q: You didn't have another job lined up when you were terminated, correct?

A: Yes.

Q: And, you had little savings at that point, correct?

A: That's true.

Q: And you were not given a chance to prove that the charges against you were false, right?

A: Yes.

Q: Then can you explain to me why you were not upset at the time of your discharge?

A: Well. . . .

Asking deponents for explanations has the following benefits:

* A deponent who fails to offer an explanation at deposition probably will be unable to credibly explain away an implausibility later in the case (after his lawyer may have suggested potential explanations).

* By determining if a deponent has an explanation at deposition, you avoid being surprised by one later at trial or in settlement negotiations.

* If you uncover an explanation at deposition, you have time prior to trial to determine if the explanation is true. If the explanation comes out for the first time at trial, you may not have time to gather the evidence to disprove it.

Asking for an explanation, however, does have a downside. You inevitably bring an implausibility to the attention of a deponent and opposing counsel when you ask for explanations. Had you not inquired about explanations, you might have been able to surprise the deponent at trial. However, most cases settle prior to trial and if you wait until trial to surface an implausibility, it may be you who is surprised by a plausible explanation which in mid-trial you do not have time to investigate.

If a deponent does offer an explanation, your follow up, if any, will be dictated by how you evaluate the explanation. If you conclude that the explanation vitiates the implausibility, you may decide to treat the explanation as a harmful answer and try to undermine it.[1] If an explanation creates a new implausibility, you may want to try to magnify it. Finally, if an explanation is credible, you may decide to simply move on.

1. For a discussion of undermining harmful answers, see Chapter 6.

CHAPTER 9

RESPONDING TO EVASIVE, FORGETFUL OR UNCER-TAIN DEPONENTS

Deponents are sometimes evasive, forgetful and/or uncertain. This Chapter explores strategies and techniques for responding to each of these situations.

1. Evasive Deponents

Deponents may be evasive because they want to avoid hurting a party with whom they identify, because they fear that a fully responsive answer may make them look bad or prove embarrassing, or because they want to give you a "hard time." This section discusses techniques for responding to evasive deponents.

A. *Non–Responsive Answers*

Deponents may evade questions by being non-responsive, i.e., by answering a question other than the one you've asked. To get a responsive answer into the record, politely indicate that you have heard the deponent's answer, and then re-ask your original question.

Consider the following examples:

Example #1

Q: Were you concerned about having the computers networked when they were installed?

A: I was concerned about getting them installed before our January push.

Q: I understand that you were concerned about getting the computers installed before the January push, and we'll talk about that in a few minutes. But first I'd like to know whether you were concerned about having the computers networked when they were installed?

Example #2

Q: Did you review Exhibit 27, the third draft of the Environmental Impact Report, with your supervisor?

A: That's what I typically do.

Q: Okay, so you typically review these reports with your supervisor. But my question is: did you review Exhibit 27 with your supervisor?

B. *"Hints" in Lieu of Complete Answers*

Rather than giving complete answers, deponents sometimes give partial answers accompanied by hints. For example, a deponent asked about what took place during a meeting may provide partial information and also say something like:

* That was the **substance** of the discussion.

* Those are the **main things** we talked about.

* That was **about it**.

All of these responses hint at possible further goings-on during the meeting. Deponent's who give such answers may tell themselves that they have done nothing wrong. They may reason that "My answer was honest because I told the lawyer there was something more. If the lawyer failed to follow up, that's her problem."

When you receive this type of answer, you may refer to the hint and then probe for the hidden information. For example:

1. Q: What did you discuss at the meeting early in June?

2: A: We talked about the acceptability of the specifications, the price per unit and the delivery date.

3: Q: Did you discuss anything else at this meeting?

4. A: Those were the main things we discussed.

5. Q: Well, when you say the "main things" it suggests that you talked about some other things. I understand that you may not consider them significant, but I would like to know everything else that you discussed at this meeting.

6. A: I remember we talked very briefly about what to do if delivery was late.

7. Q: So you discussed acceptability of the specifications, the price per unit, the delivery date, and what to do if delivery was late. Did you discuss anything else at this meeting?

8.   A: No.

9.   Q: Did you discuss subcontracting some of your work?

10.   A: No.

11.   Q: How about changing specifications as the job developed. Was that discussed?

12.   A: Now that you mention it, that was discussed.

Here, you pursue the "hint" (No. 5), and question further to pursue possible additional subjects of conversation (Nos. 9–12).

C.   *"What Do You Mean By* . . . *" Answers*

Combative deponents, sometimes encouraged by opposing counsel, may try to give you a "hard time" by "word fencing," i.e., claiming not to understand even everyday words in your questions.[1] For example,

1.   Deponents who repeatedly use this tactic may be subject to sanctions. See VMP Int'l Corp. v. Yushkevich, No.92 Civ.7573, 1993 WL 33463 (S.D.N.Y. Feb 3, 1993); (The deposition featured numerous instances of plaintiff's counsel niggling over definitions, e.g., demanding that defendants' counsel define words such as "lived" when asked if a former employee "lived in the former Soviet Union," "do" when asked "what does VMP do" and "travel" when asked if an employee "travel[ed] on business for [VMP]." The party was sanctioned.); see also Justice Eugene A. Cook, *Professionalism and the Practice of Law*, 23 Tex. Tech L. Rev. 955, 973 (1992) (Describing hardball litigators who, "in a series of depositions that stretched out over 15 days, asked the opposing attorney to define 'when,' 'where,' 'own,' and 'describe'."); Dana Rubin, *The Rambo Boys*, Dallas Morning News, February 25, 1990 at 6; (describing an occasion where attorneys opposing a Dallas law firm in depositions would bring dictionar-

Q: After you were hired as an appraiser, did anyone provide you with any training to help you do your job?

A: What do you mean by training?

You might respond by asking for the deponent's understanding of the term and then adopt it as your own. For instance, in the above example, you might respond as follows:

Q: Mr. Jones, do you have an understanding of what the word "training" means?

A: Yes, but I don't know what you mean when you say training.

Q: What do you understand the word to mean?

A: I think it means giving me instructions or materials on how to do my job.

Q: All right. When I use the word training I mean exactly what you understand the term to mean. So let me ask you again, after you were hired as an appraiser did the company give you any training to help you do your job?

This approach hopefully discourages the deponent from engaging in this tactic. Of course, if the deponent's definition of a term is particularly narrow or highly idiosyncratic, you may have to follow up with additional questions to obtain complete information. For example:

ies so they could look up the meanings of words that fell into dispute, e.g. "What do you mean by experience?" "What do you mean by manage?")

Q: Mr. Jones, do you have an understanding of what the word "training" means?

A: Yes, but I don't know what you mean when you say training.

Q: What do you understand the word to mean?

A: I think it means giving me formal classroom instruction to help me learn how to do my job.

Q: Let's use your definition for the moment. After you were hired as an appraiser did anyone give you any training to help you learn how to do your job?

A: No.

Q: Now let's assume that training means anything that anyone did to help you learn your job. Did you receive any of this type of training?

A: Well, I talked to a couple of my supervisors about....

D. *Overly Literal or Hyper–Technical Deponents*

Another form of evasion consists of a highly technical or overly literal interpretation of a question. Deponents may use this interpretive ploy because they want to provide as little information as possible and this ploy allows them to withhold information while at the same time telling themselves that their response is honest. For example, assume that a deponent once saw a report in which a defendant wrote that the plaintiff was lazy. When asked at deposition, "Did the defendant ever say the plaintiff was lazy?" the deponent responds either, "No" or "I don't know." A hyper-technical deponent may interpret the "say" in your question to mean "say orally," thereby justifying the "No" or "I don't know" response.[2]

When you think that a deponent might be using this kind of interpretive ploy to withhold important, helpful information, you may employ one or more of the following questioning techniques.

1. Use a Series of Questions Containing Synonyms

Defining important topics with a single word encourages some deponents to withhold information by interpreting that word very narrowly. To combat this ploy, you may ask a series of questions containing synonyms for a particular topic. For example, assume that you represent the plaintiff Spillenger in a wrongful termination case. Spillenger was terminated by his supervisor, Ms. Freeman, allegedly for being insubordinate. Your client said he was terminated because Freeman personally disliked him. You are deposing Freeman's secretary, Ms. Lester. Assume that a month before your client was discharged Lester heard Freeman say "I'd be happy if I never had to talk to Spillenger again." Lester knows that this information is damaging to Free-

---

2. A deponent's use of this sort of narrow definition may constitute giving knowingly false testimony. However, the narrow definition interpretive ploy may become more common now that it has been used by a President of the United States in a deposition in a Federal lawsuit. See R. Posner, An Affair Of State: The Investigation, Impeachment, and Trial of President Clinton 44 et. seq. (1999).

man and does not want to reveal it to you at deposition. At Lester's deposition, the following exchange occurs:

Q: Ms. Lester, did Ms. Freeman ever say anything indicating that she disliked working with Mr. Spillenger?

A: No.

Lester could convince herself that her answer is honest. Lester's reasoning might go as follows: Freeman only said she didn't want to talk to Spillenger. Freeman might still be perfectly happy working with Spillenger as long as they communicated by e-mail or written memo.

You are more likely to uncover the information you are looking for if you follow up the question above with a series of questions such as the following:

1. Q: Ms. Lester, did Ms. Freeman ever say anything indicating that she did not want to **work with** Mr. Spillenger?

2. Q: Ms. Lester, did Ms. Freeman ever say anything indicating that she **personally disliked** Mr. Spillenger?

3. Q: Ms. Lester, did Ms. Freeman ever say anything indicating that she did not want **to be around** with Mr. Spillenger?

4. Q: Ms. Lester, did Ms. Freeman ever say anything indicating that she did **not like communicating** with Mr. Spillenger?

5. Q: Ms. Lester, did Ms. Freeman ever say anything indicating that she did not **want to be in a meeting** with Mr. Spillenger?

6. Q: Ms. Lester, did Ms. Freeman ever say **anything negative** about Mr. Spillenger?

By asking such a series of questions containing synonyms for "disliked working with" you make it harder for Lester to withhold the information and still convince herself that she is being honest.

2. Ask for Information From All Sources

Deponents sometimes withhold information by drawing a distinction between information they perceive directly and information based on hearsay. For example, assume that Lester was **told by a colleague** that Freeman had said "I'd be happy if I never had to talk to Spillenger again." Lester might convince herself that she could honestly withhold that information in response to the above questions. Her reasoning might be something like: "I didn't hear it directly, so I don't really know it. So I can say 'No.' "

Such deponents may also withhold information by making a distinction between what another person "said," and what another person "wrote" or "did." For an example, in the above wrongful termination case, assume that Ms. Lester did not hear Freeman **say** "I'd be happy if I never had to talk to Spillenger again." Instead, assume that Lester saw a note Freeman wrote to a colleague that said "I'd be happy if I never had to talk to Spillenger again." Lester might convince herself that she could honestly answer "No" to all of the questions above because they refer to what Freeman said, and what Freeman wrote is different than what she said. Similarly, assume that Lester saw Freeman make an obscene gesture toward Spillenger when his back was turned. Lester might convince herself that she could honestly withhold this information in response to questions about what Freeman said.

The subsections below explore techniques for uncovering information by expanding possible sources.

a. Ask "Are You Aware of Any Information From Any Source That Might Indicate..."

You may thwart a hyper-technical deponent by combining synonyms with broad questions that call for any information the deponent has from any source. For example, in the above hypothetical you might ask the deponent questions such as:

Q: Ms. Lester, are you aware of any information from any source whatsoever that might indicate that Ms. Freeman disliked working with Mr. Spillenger?

Q: Ms. Lester, are you aware of any information from any source whatsoever that might indicate that Ms. Freeman did not want to work with Mr. Spillenger?

Q: Ms. Lester, are you aware of any information from any source whatsoever that might indicate that Ms. Freeman personally disliked Mr. Spillenger?

These broad questions make it more difficult for the deponent to convince herself that a "No" answer is truthful, when she has not directly heard a statement by Freeman saying "I'd be happy if I never had to talk to Spillenger again."

b.   Ask Separately About "See" and "Hear"

Another technique for obtaining information from a hyper-technical deponent is to ask separate questions about what the deponent has seen or heard. For instance, in the example above, you could ask a series of questions that distinguish between what Lester might have seen or heard.

* **Have You Seen Questions**

1.   Q: Ms. Lester, have you ever seen anything indicating that Ms. Freeman did not want to work with Mr. Spillenger?

2.   Q: Ms. Lester, have you ever seen anything indicating that Ms. Freeman may have personally disliked Mr. Spillenger?

3.   Q: Ms. Lester, have you ever seen anything indicating that Ms. Freeman did not want to be around Mr. Spillenger?

4.   Q: Ms. Lester, have you ever seen anything indicating that Ms. Freeman did not like communicating with Mr. Spillenger?

* **Have You Heard Questions**

1.   Q: Ms. Lester, have you ever heard anything indicating that Ms. Freeman did not want to work with Mr. Spillenger?

2.   Q: Ms. Lester, have you ever heard anything indicating that Ms. Freeman may have personally disliked Mr. Spillenger?

3.   Q: Ms. Lester, have you ever heard anything indicating that Ms. Freeman did not want to be around Mr. Spillenger?

4.   Q: Ms. Lester, have you ever heard anything indicating that Ms. Freeman did not like communicating with Mr. Spillenger?

c.   Potential Risks of Asking for Information From All Sources

Using these techniques to seek information from all sources has a potential downside. Questions distinguishing between directly perceived and second hand information may well encourage deponents to make such distinctions throughout a deposition. As a result, once you start making distinctions between what a deponent saw or heard, you may have to continue to make those distinctions throughout the deposition. This can make for a long deposition.

2.   Forgetful and Uncertain Deponents

Deponents often testify to a partial or complete failure of memory. For example, deponents give answers such as the following:

"I don't remember"

"I don't recall."

"That's all I can remember."

"I can't remember everything we talked about."

Deponents also frequently qualify answers through statements reflecting less than one-hundred percent certainty. Examples of this common type of response include:

"I think that Carl was at the meeting but I can't be sure."

"I'm pretty sure that Carl was at the meeting."

"I don't believe that Carl was at the meeting."

"I'm not sure if Carl was at the meeting."

When a deponent's answer reflects a lack of memory or uncertainty, you may opt not to probe further. For example, you may decide not to probe further when such answers relate to unimportant topics. Alternatively, if an "I don't remember" response helps your case, you may want to commit the deponent to that response. For example, assume that a deponent testifies that, "I don't remember whether I told your client about the earnings potential of the company during that meeting." Your client says that earnings potential was discussed at the meeting. In such a situation, the deponent's "I don't remember" answer would prove helpful. It would open the door for you to argue that your client's version of what was said should be accepted as true because the deponent cannot contradict your client. In such a situation, you may pin the deponent down to the "I don't remember" answer with a question such as, "So at the present time you have no recollection of whether you told my client about the earnings potential of the company during that meeting, correct?"[3]

On the other hand, you may decide to probe failure of memory responses in ways that encourage deponents to search their memory banks and provide as much information as they can. You might conduct such probing for at least two reasons. First, probing may uncover helpful information a deponent is trying to withhold. Second, probing may reduce deponents' opportunities to provide explanations for testifying at trial to damaging evidence that they could not recall at deposition. For example, assume that your probe of an "I don't remember" response indicates that a deponent knows of no documents that would refresh the deponent's recollection. This response minimizes the credibility of a potential explanation for improved memory at trial, such as, "I looked at my day planner after my deposition and it refreshed my recollection."

When you do decide to probe claims of inability to recall, you may employ one or more of the following techniques.

A. *Probing for Recall*

1. *Convey an Expectation That Recall Is Possible*

Indicating that you will not readily accept an "I don't recall" kind of answer is one way to encourage deponents to probe their memories and perhaps provide additional information. If you convey an

3. For a discussion of additional techniques for "cementing" helpful answers, see Chapter 5.

expectation that recall is possible and that you are prepared to push for it, deponents may dig deeper and provide information. Consider the following examples:

Q: Tell me everything you talked about at the August 15th meeting.

A: I don't remember what we talked about.

Example #1

Q: I understand that you may not be able to remember everything that was discussed at the August 15th meeting, but please tell me as much as you can remember about what was discussed at that meeting.

Example #2

Q: What do you remember about what was discussed at the August 15th meeting?

Example #3

Q: Are you saying that you recall nothing at all about what was discussed the August 15th meeting?

By suggesting that you believe that the deponent is capable of providing at least some information about the August 15 meeting, each of these questions encourages the deponent to try to recall overlooked information.

2. *Bracket to Obtain a Best Estimate*

At deposition, you often seek precise numbers or dates. For example, you might ask a deponent to state "the distance between the two cars after the collision," or "the date you first met Ms. Kekorian." Such requests often make deponents uncomfortable, because the questions ask for more certainty than the deponents feel they can provide. They may find "I don't remember" or "I'm not sure" an easy refuge. With a few additional probes, however, you can often elicit useful information.

1. Q: What was the distance between the two cars after the collision?

2. A: I don't remember.

3. Q: Would you say the distance was at least 10 feet?

4. A: I'm sorry, I'm just not sure.

5. Q: Would you say it was at least 5 feet, that's about the distance between you and me?

6. A: Yes, I'd have to say they were at least that far apart.

7. Q: All right. Could they have been more than 25 feet apart, that's probably a few feet longer than the length of this room?

8. A: No, they weren't that far apart.

9. Q: Well, how about 20 feet?

10. A: Probably they were closer than that.

11. Q: So after the accident the cars were somewhere between 5 and 20 feet apart, is that correct?

12. A: Yes, I'd agree with that.

This example illustrates "bracketing." Bracketing tends to encourage deponents who are unwilling or unable to provide exact numbers to offer estimates of the upper and lower limits of a range within which their answers lie. Since many deponents find numerical estimates alone too abstract, you can often enhance memory by relating the numbers to a visual space, such as the distance between you and the deponent. (No. 5)

The "bracketing" technique works for most kinds of estimates, not just distances. For example, you can use the technique to elicit information such as how many people were present at a location, how much money was in a bank account, the duration of an event, etc. Here is an example of the use of bracketing to find out the date of a "first meeting:"

Q: Ms. Freed, when did you first meet Mr. Partman?

A: I don't remember.

Q: Was it during April of last year?

A: I don't think so.

Q: Could it have been during May?

A: That's possible.

Q: Could it have been as late as August?

A: No, it would have been before that.

Q: So your first meeting with Mr. Partman took place sometime between May and July?

A: I'd say that's right.

Q: And can you estimate whether it was towards the beginning or the end of this time frame?

A: More towards the beginning.

Q: You'd say May, perhaps into June?

A: Right.

Just as visual references can help deponents estimate distances, so can events known to a deponent help a deponent estimate dates. For instance, assume that one event in Ms. Freed's version of events is "sale of the Hanley house." You might help Ms. Freed more precisely estimate the date of her first meeting with Mr. Partman by relating the meeting to the sale of the house:

Q: Ms. Freed, you've told us that you sold the Hanley house on July 10 of last year, correct?

A: That's right.

Q: All right, can you recall whether you met Mr. Partman before you sold the house?

A: Yes, I'm sure I met him before that.

Q: Approximately how long before the sale of your house did you meet Mr. Partman?

A: At least a month, I'd say.

Q: So that puts your first meeting with Mr. Partman sometime before June 10, correct?

A: Yes.

3. *Use Documents*

Documents often enable deponents to recall information that they cannot remember in their absence.

Thus, you can probe a lack of recollection or uncertainty with documents which refer to the topic you are pursuing.[4] For example:

Q: Can you recall who chaired the first meeting with the university representatives on the design specifications?

A: I really couldn't tell you, it was so long ago.

Q: I am now showing you Exhibit 23 titled "Report of Design Subcommittee." Please look at the second paragraph on page 1 of the report and read it over to yourself.

A: Ok, I've read it.

Q: Does looking at that paragraph help to refresh your recollection as to who chaired the first meeting with the university representatives on the design specifications?

A: Yes, I can remember now that it was John Wiley who chaired the meeting.

4. Use Closed or Leading Questions

When you question adverse deponents, closed or leading questions are permissible and may remind a deponent of forgotten information. For example:

Q: Who was present at the meeting on design specifications?

---

4. You can, of course, show a deponent any tangible object to try to refresh recollection. You can even play a song or a tape to do so. See United States v. Rappy, 157 F.2d 964, 967 (2d Cir. 1946) (Learned Hand stated: "Anything may in fact revive a memory: a song, a scent, a photograph, an allusion, even a past statement known to be false."). But recollection is most commonly refreshed with a document.

A: I was there along with Gomez. And Browning and Prager were there from the university. I'm not sure if anyone else was there.

Q: Jerry Kang was also there, wasn't he?

A: That's right he was.

Q: How about Ken Karst, was he there?

A: Yes, he was there too. I'd forgotten.

B. *Probing for Alternative Sources of Information*

Even after probing using one or more of the techniques above, deponents may remain adamant about their inability to recall. In such situations, you may try to use the deponent as a lead for uncovering alternative sources of information. To do so, you might ask about what the deponent might do if she wanted to find out the information. For example, you might proceed as follows:

1. Q: Approximately when did that meeting take place?

2. A: I really couldn't tell you, it was so long ago.

3. Q: What might you do if you wanted to find out when the meeting took place?

4. A: I guess I could call Ms. Liu over at Beta Corp. and ask her.

5. Q: Why is that?

6. A: They sent someone to the meeting, so she might have a record of when it took place.

7. Q: Okay, anything else you might do to check the date of the meeting?

8. A: Not that I can think of.

9. Q: Other than Ms. Liu, who might you talk to if you wanted to find out when the meeting took place?

10. A: Well I might talk to Bill Warren, he set the meeting up and he might know.

11. Q: Other than Ms. Liu and Mr. Warren, who else might you talk to if you wanted to find out when the meeting took place?

12. A: No one else that I can think of.

13. Q: Can you think of any document that might you might look at if you wanted to find out when the meeting took place?

14. A: Not really.

15. Q: Do you keep an appointment book that might indicate the date?

16. A: No, I didn't keep an appointment book back then.

17. Q: Might you have kept any letters that you wrote before or after the meeting that might refer to its date?

18. A: No

19. Q: Do you know of any reports made by anyone about what happened at the meeting?

20. A: Someone wrote a report about it but. . .

In this example, you begin with broad questions about what the deponent might do to find out the information (Nos. 3 and 7). You then exhaust the deponent's knowledge about people who might help (Nos. 9 and 11), and conclude by asking for documents the deponent might consult (Nos. 13–19). This approach often leads to documents or people that might provide the information that the deponent cannot recall.

3. Responding to "I Don't Know" Answers

Deponents often respond with answers such as "I don't know" or "not to my knowledge". Such an answer is sometimes a synonym for "I don't remember." For example, assume that a deponent asked to estimate the speed of a car responds, "I don't know." The deponent may mean, "I once could have estimated the speed, but I no longer remember." When you receive an "I don't know" answer you may want to probe to determine if it is a substitute for "I don't remember." For example:

1. Q: Ms. Manion, what time did your husband arrive at the trailer park?

2. A: I don't know.

3. Q: When you say you don't know the time he arrived at the trailer park, do you mean that you have never known this fact?

4. A: I mean I don't know right now.

5. Q: You say you don't know now, does that mean that at one time you knew when he arrived at the trailer park, but you have since forgotten?

6. A: Yes, you could put it that way.

When the deponent uses an "I don't know" response to mean "I don't remember" you can use the techniques described in the previous section if you decide to probe further.

When an "I don't know" answer means just that, you may still decide to probe further to determine all the things the deponent might do if she wanted to find out the information you seek. For example:

1. Q: Ms. Manion, what time did your husband arrive at the trailer park?

2. A: I don't know.

3. Q: When you say you don't know the time he arrived at the trailer park, do you mean that you have never known this fact?

4. A: Yes, that's what I mean.

5. Q: Just so we all understand, you don't mean that you at one time knew when he arrived at the trailer park, but have since forgotten?

6. A: No, I haven't forgotten. When I said "I don't know," I meant just that.

7. Q: Ms. Manion, tell me all the things you would do if you wanted to find out what time your husband arrived at the trailer park?

8. A: Well I don't know. I suppose I could ask at the front desk if anyone saw him drive in.

9. Q: What else would you do if you wanted to find out what time your husband arrived at the trailer park?

10 A: I might talk to . . . .

CHAPTER 10

USING DOCUMENTS
AND DIAGRAMS

You routinely use documents when questioning deponents. For example, you may want to authenticate a document so that you can use it as part of a pre-trial motion or at trial, to refresh a deponent's recollection with a document, or to question a deponent about a document's contents. This Chapter describes techniques for maintaining a clear record when referring to documents, and explains how to use documents effectively during deposition questioning. The Chapter concludes with a short discussion of a closely-related topic, the use of diagrams.

1. Maintaining a Clear Record

A. *Use Exhibit Numbers and Precise Segment References*

Before showing a document to a deponent, ask the court reporter to mark it with an exhibit number.[1] Thereafter, **always** refer to a document by its exhibit number. This practice prevents confusion

---

1. You should also instruct the court reporter that all the documents marked as exhibits should be attached to the deposition transcript. You typically save the originals of documents in your file, and give copies to the court reporter for marking as exhibits. See FRCP 30(f)(1).

about the precise document to which a question or answer refers.

When questioning a deponent about a document, identify both the document and any specific portion of the document you are inquiring about. Your identification should be precise enough to allow a reader of a transcript to identify the document and recognize the portion to which you referred.[2] Avoid vague, ambiguous references such as, "Please look at this document and tell me what this paragraph means to you."

The example below illustrates how to mark and refer to documents:

1. Q: [Hands document to court reporter] Please mark this document as Exhibit 6. [Reporter marks document.] Mr. Winston, I am showing you what has been marked as Defendant's Exhibit 6, a five page document with "Commercial Lease" and the date of "December 10" written on the top of the first page. Counsel, here's a copy of Exhibit 6 for you. Do you recognize Exhibit 6, Mr. Winston?

2. A: Yes, it's a draft of a lease between Menning Co. and your client, Mr. Prince.

3. Q: Directing your attention to the third paragraph on the first page of Exhibit 6, do you see

2. You are not required to describe the exhibit when you show it to the witness. But when you review a transcript of the deposition, such a description may help you to identify more easily than an exhibit number exactly which document is being shown to the deponent.

where it says that the "Percentage Rent" will be calculated on the basis of the gross sales for the first six months of the lease?

4. A: Yes.

5. Q: Why did you include the language on "Percentage Rent" in the third paragraph of page one of Exhibit 6?

6. A: Well... [witness explains.]

7. Q: [Hands a second document to court reporter.] Please mark this document as Defendant's Exhibit 7. [Reporter marks document; copy of exhibit given to opposing counsel.] Mr. Winston, I am showing you what has been marked as Defendant's Exhibit 7, a six page document with "Commercial Lease" and the date of "January 15" written on the top of the first page. Do you recognize it?

8. A: Yes, this is a later draft of a lease between Menning Co. and Mr. Prince.

9. Q: Directing your attention to the fifth paragraph on the first page of Exhibit 7, do you see where it says that the "Percentage Rent" will be calculated on the basis of the gross sales for the first month of the lease?

10. A: Yes.

11. Q: Why did you include the language on "Percentage Rent" in the fifth paragraph of page one of Exhibit 7?

12. A: Well... [witness explains.]

Here, you maintain a clear record by giving each document a separate exhibit number, and by precisely referring to portions of each document. Precise references are often essential when you want to use deposition testimony in support of pre-trial motions or to impeach deponents who subsequently change their testimony.

When questions pertain to several pages of a multi-page document, you can often further promote clarity by marking each page separately. For example, if a document consists of three pages, you might have them marked as "Exhibit 17–A, 17–B and 17–C." If a document's pages are already numbered, you might retain those numbers for marking purposes: e.g., "Exhibit 17–1, 17–2, 17–3." In general, and subject to requirements of local rules of court, use any marking system that promotes clarity.

B. *Provide Copies of Documents to Opposing Counsel*

Before showing documents to deponents, hand separate copies to opposing counsel. The practice is courteous and efficient since rules generally give opposing counsel the right to look at documents before you refer to them.[3] Nevertheless, opposing counsel does <u>not</u> have the right to confer with a deponent before you begin questioning with respect

3. At trial, opposing counsel is generally allowed to look at a document before you examine a witness about it in order to make timely objections. The same procedure should be followed at deposition. See FRCP 30(c).

to a document.[4]

2. Common Uses of Documents

A. *Laying a Foundation for Later Use of Documents in Pre–Trial Motions or at Trial*

Unless opposing counsel is willing to stipulate to a document's admissibility, you'll need proper foundational evidence to use a document in a pre-trial motion or at trial. Depositions often afford you a chance to elicit a foundation, which typically consists of evidence showing that a document is (1) authentic and (2) satisfies document-specific evidentiary requirements. The sections below address these requirements.

1. Authentication

To authenticate a document is to elicit testimony tending to prove that the document is what you contend it is. For example, assume that you claim that a photograph depicts a living room as it looked just after its ceiling collapsed. To authenticate the photograph, you might conduct the following examination:

1. Q: I am handing you what has been marked as Exhibit 3. Do you recognize Exhibit 3?

2. A: Yes.

3. Q: Exhibit #3 is a photograph depicting the living room of your house as it looked after the ceiling collapsed on December 8th, correct?

4. A: Yes, that's right.

4. See Chapter 15.

5. Q: And how do you know that?

6. A: I came home later that day and saw what had happened to the ceiling.

This testimony authenticates the photograph by establishing that it is what you contend it is.

Showing that a deponent has personal knowledge may require more extensive foundational questioning than in the example above. For example, assume that you want to authenticate the signature of a notary public on a deed. Your questioning may proceed as follows:

1. Q: Mr. Korobkin, I'm showing you what has been marked Exhibit 6. Please examine it and let me know when you have done so.

2. A: I've finished.

3. Q: Do you see the notary seal on the bottom left hand side of Exhibit 6?

4. A: Yes.

5. Q: And do you see a signature above the notary seal on Exhibit 6?

6. A: Yes.

7. Q: Is the signature above the notary seal on Exhibit 6 that of Susan Neistadt?

8. Opposing counsel: Objection lack of foundation.

9. Q: Mr. Korobkin, do you know Susan Neistadt?

10.   A: Sure. She has worked in my office for me for five years as a loan processor and notary.

11.   Q: During that five year period have you ever seen Ms. Neistadt sign her name?

12.   A: I've seen her sign her name on dozens of documents.

13.   Q: Is the signature above the notary seal on Exhibit 6 that of Susan Neistadt?

14.   A: Yes.

Authentication through familiarity with a signature is of course only one method of establishing sufficient personal knowledge to authenticate a document. There are a host of other ways of authenticating such documents as business records, computer records, e-mails, and faxes.[5] As you prepare for a deposition, you need to familiarize yourself with the authentication method that is appropriate for any document you intend to use.

2.   *Satisfying Evidentiary Requirements*

A document's ultimate admissibility may require more than a showing of authenticity. In addition, you may have to satisfy other evidentiary requirements, such as the hearsay rule. For example, you

5.   For a discussion of authenticating business records and other electronic documents, see Thomas A. Mauet & Warren D. Wolfson, Trial Evidence § 10.6, 10.11 (4th ed. 2009); Jack B. Weinstein & Margaret A. Berger, Weinstein's Federal Evidence, § 901.8 (Joseph M. McLaughlin, ed., Matthew Bender 2d ed. 1997).

may have to elicit evidence showing that a document meets the definition of a business record.[6]

B. Memory Stimulation

Documents are a common method of stimulating the recollection of forgetful witnesses.[7] The following example is illustrative.

1. Q: Who did you meet with to discuss a possible sale of the Barrington property?

2. A: I don't recall.

3. Q: Mr. Kang, I'm showing you Exhibit 55, a one page memorandum dated November 15th of last year which in the top left hand column says "From L. LoPucki to Robert Varat re: proposed sale of 1242 Barrington". I've shown a copy of Exhibit 55 to your attorney. Will you please read Exhibit 55 to yourself?

4. A: I've read it.

5. Q: The second paragraph of Exhibit 55 states, "Prior to the time I met with Bainbridge, I met with Klein and Sklanski to review the proposed sale of the Barrington property to Gulati?" is that correct?

6. A: Yes.

7. Q: So at one point you met with Klein and Sklanski to discuss a possible sale of the Barrington property to Gulati, is that correct?

8. A: Yes.

6. See FRE 803(6).

7. See FRE 612.

9. Q: Who was present at that meeting?

10. A: Just Klein, Sklanski and myself.

11. Q: Okay, please tell me everything that occurred at that meeting.

12. A: Well. . . .

If you want to use a document only to stimulate a deponent's recall and don't plan to rely on it later in the case, you needn't authenticate it or satisfy other evidentiary requirements. Note that the deponent need not have prepared a document; you can use any writing to stimulate a deponent's memory.[8]

C. *Develop a Deponent's Version of Events*

You may also use documents to help you elicit a deponent's overall version of significant events. For example, assume that in a wrongful termination case, you represent the plaintiff, Warren, who is suing Tri–Star Copiers for wrongful termination. The deponent is Joy Nauman, the head of the department in which Warren used to work. Among the documents you have obtained during discovery are the following:

* An employee evaluation of Warren written by Nauman and dated 2/9

* A letter of complaint from Warren to Tri–Star's president dated 4/12

* A memo from Tri–Star's president to Phyllis McCoy, the head of Warren's department, dated 5/1

8. See <u>McCormick On Evidence</u> § 9 (4th ed. 1992).

* A memo from McCoy to Warren's immediate supervisor, Nauman, dated 5/10

You might use these documents as chronological markers to help you to develop at least a rough chronology of events leading up to and following Warren's termination.

1. Q: Ms. Nauman, what I'd like to do at this point is have you give me a step by step account of the events that led up to Mr. Warren's termination. When did you first come to believe that Mr. Warren's work was in any way less than satisfactory?

2. A: I can't remember.

3. Q: Well, can you remember the first thing that happened that made you feel in any way that Mr. Warren's performance was less than satisfactory?

4. A: When he failed to get the Asimow report done on time.

5. Q: When did that failure occur?

6. A: Again, I don't remember.

7. Q: Ms. Nauman, I'm showing you Exhibit 12, a three page document entitled Employee Evaluation and bearing a date of February 9th of last year. I've shown a copy to your counsel. Is this an employee evaluation that you prepared regarding Mr. Warren?

8. A: Yes it is.

9. Q: And as far as you know is Exhibit 12 correctly dated?

10. A: Yes it is.

11. Q: Now, did Mr. Warren's failure to get the Asimow report done on time occur prior to February 9th of last year?

12. A: Yes it did.

13. Q: How long before February 9th did it occur?

14. A: About three weeks I'd say.

15. Q: Okay, can you please tell me about that failure?

16. [Answer omitted]

17. Prior to the incident involving the Asimow report, had you observed anything indicating that Mr. Warren's performance was unsatisfactory?

18. A: No.

19. Q: After the incident involving the Asimow report, what is the next thing that happened that in any way indicated an unsatisfactory performance on the part of Mr. Warren?

20. A: I'm not sure.

21. Q: Well, between the time that the Asimow report was not completed on time and the time you wrote Exhibit 12, Mr. Warren's February 9th evaluation, were there any oc-

currences that involved any kind of poor performance on Mr. Warren's part?

22. A: No.

23. Q: Okay. Can you now look at Exhibit 13. Is Exhibit 13 a letter of April 12th of last year written by Mr. Warren to Bob Freeze, Tri–Star's president?

24. A: Yes.

25. Q: When did you first see Exhibit 13?

26. A: When Mr. Freeze called me into his office to talk about it.

27. Q: And when was that?

28. A: Probably about a week after April 12th.

29. Q: Okay, please tell me what occurred when you went to Mr. Freeze's office to discuss Exhibit 13.

30. [Answer omitted]

31. Q: Now between February 9th of last year when you wrote Exhibit 12, Mr. Warren's employee evaluation, and the time you went to Mr. Freeze's office around the 19th of April of last year, did anything occur that in any way related to poor performance on Mr. Warren's part?

32. A: Well... [remainder omitted]

In this example, the dates in the exhibits establish <u>chronological markers</u>. For example, after establishing that Exhibit 12's date of February 9th is correct (No. 9), you use it as a signpost to ferret out the date of an event that preceded February 9th (Nos. 11 and 12). Such markers often help you to establish at least rough chronologies of deponents' versions of events.

D. *Explanations of Words and Phrases*

Full understanding of a document's role in a dispute often requires you to probe its language. For example, documents may contain ambiguous or unfamiliar words and phrases, or a deponent may attach an unusual meaning to what you think of as a familiar phrase. In such circumstances, questions about a document's language and the preparer's reasons for using that language may uncover important information.

For example, assume that you represent the Codells, borrowers who claims to have been defrauded by a broker in connection with the purchase of a house. A document prepared by the broker refers to a "Loan Origination Fee." Here, you seek the broker's interpretation of that term and its role in the transaction:

1. Q: Ms. Fairchild, I'm showing you Exhibit 23, a 12 page document entitled "Conditions of Loan, Loan No. 99–002054." I've given a copy to your counsel. Please look over Exhibit 23.

2. A: Okay.

3. Q: Exhibit 23 is a loan document that you prepared on behalf of Mr. and Mrs. Codell, is that correct?

4. A: Yes.

5. Q: On the left hand side of page one of Exhibit 23, the term "Loan Origination Fee to Lender" is typed in, right?

6. A: Yes.

7. Q: What is meant by the term Loan Origination Fee to Lender?

8. A: [Deponent explains]

9. Q: So, as far as you were concerned, the term Loan Origination Fee as used on page one of Exhibit 23 meant . . ., correct?

10. A: Yes.

11. Q: The amount of the loan origination fee set forth in Exhibit 23 is $8,876.59, correct?

12. A: Yes.

13. Q: Why were the Codells charged a loan origination fee of $8,876.59?

14. A: [Deponent explains]

15. Q: So the reason that a loan fee of $8,876.59 appears on page one of Exhibit 23 is . . ., correct?

16. A: Yes.

E. *Preparation and Distribution History*

Questions about a document's "footprints" often uncover helpful evidence. Such questions may pertain to such matters as a document's possible ancestry (e.g., prior drafts), the identity of its preparer or preparers, and the identities of the persons to whom it was distributed. The helpful evidence may include leads to the identities of persons other than a deponent who may have helpful information about the matters a document sets forth.

The following are examples of "footprint" questions with respect to an "Exhibit 77":

* Did you prepare Exhibit 77?

* Did you prepare any drafts of Exhibit 77?

* Where are those drafts?

* Why did you prepare drafts?

* To whom, if anyone, did you show those drafts?

* Why?

* With whom, if anyone, did you discuss those drafts?

* Why?

* Who, if anyone, helped you prepare Exhibit 77?

* Why did you get help?

* Why did you prepare Exhibit 77?

* Did you talk to anyone about any of the matters mentioned in Exhibit 77 before you prepared it?

* Did you talk to anyone after you prepared Exhibit 77?

*Did you send copies of Exhibit 77 to anyone?

    If yes, to whom?

    (for each recipient) Why did you send a copy of Exhibit 77 to .....?

* Did you receive any oral or written comments with respect to Exhibit 77?

(if written) Where are those comments?

F. *Obtaining Helpful Answers*

Confronting a deponent with a document is often an effective method of obtaining a clear admission of the accuracy of helpful information referred to in the document.[9] Of course, deponents may testify that a document's language is incorrect. However, deponents are often hesitant to contradict the contents of documents, especially when they or an associate have prepared them.[10]

For example, assume that you want a deponent employed by your adversary to admit that no employee of the adversary spoke to a loan applicant to verify the information in a loan application. You might use the application to elicit this admission, as follows:

1. Q: Mr. Iorillo, I'm showing you Exhibit 44. Is Exhibit 44 an accurate copy of the loan application that Mr. Alvarez submitted to your company on that date?

2. A: Yes it is.

9. Alternatively, you might have asked for the information without showing the document to the deponent and then used the document to impeach the deponent should the deponent not have provided the admission you wanted. The issue of which strategy to follow is one calling for judgment under the circumstances.

10. For a more detailed discussion of using a document prepared by a third person to obtain an admission, see Chapter 4.

3. Q: Please turn your attention to the box on the top right hand side of page four of Exhibit 44. It's headed "Information Verified By," and below that heading are two lines, one that states "Face-to-Face Interview" and the other that states "Telephone Interview." To the left of each line is a box that can be checked, correct?

4. A: Yes.

5. Q: Finally, at the bottom of the box, below the two lines, is a line below which are the words, "Signature of Loan Officer," correct?

6. A: Yes.

7. Q: In this box on page four of Exhibit 44, the line above "Signature of Loan Officer" is blank, correct?

8. A: Yes.

9. Q: Its being blank means that nobody signed the line on page four of Exhibit 44, is that correct?

10. A: Yes.

11. Q: So before the loan was made to Mr. Alverez, as far as you know, no one from the company talked to him to verify the information in the loan application, right?

12. A: Yes, that's correct.

3. Diagrams

Pictures are often said to be worth a thousand words. In depositions, diagrams' value typically stems from their ability to clarify testimony and tie deponents to stories visually as well as verbally.[11] Diagrams are flexible tools. You can prepare diagrams before depositions begin, or ask deponents to do so as questioning unfolds. You may mark locations on diagrams as directed by deponents' testimony, or you may ask deponents to make the markings. No matter which procedures you follow, however, the record should be clear enough to enable one looking at a diagram and reading a transcript to understand what the markings mean. Like any other document to which a deponent testifies, a diagram should be marked as an exhibit and referred to by its exhibit number.

In the example that follows, you've asked the deponent to draw a diagram of a room where a particular conversation took place:

1. Q: OK, let's mark the diagram of the living room you just drew as Exhibit 24. Ms. Smith, was there any furniture in the living room during your conversation with Ms. Jones?

2. A: Yes there was.

3. Q: What furniture was there?

---

11. Under FRCP 30(c) examination at deposition may proceed as at trial, and at trial a witness can be required to draw a diagram. See e.g. Western Gas Const. v. Danner, 97 F. 882 (9th Cir. 1899). Courts have also expressly held that a deponent may be required to draw a diagram and or engage in a re-enactment at deposition. See e.g. Emerson Elec. Co. v. Superior Court, 16 Cal.4th 1101, 68 Cal.Rptr.2d 883, 946 P.2d 841 (1997); Cunningham v. Heard, 667 A.2d 537 (R.I.1995); but see Udkoff v. Hiett, 676 So.2d 522 (Fla. Dist. Ct.App.1996).

4. A: Oh, a sofa, a few chairs, a coffee table, and a shelf with a television set.

5. Q: On Exhibit 24, please draw the rough outline of the sofa, the chairs, the coffee table and shelf. [deponent draws] Now, would you please label the sofa "S," the chairs "C," the table "T," and please put "TV" on the shelf where the television set was. [deponent labels]

6. Q: Where were you during your conversation with Ms. Jones?

7. A: I was sitting on the sofa.

8. Q: Please write in "Smith" on Exhibit 24 to indicate where you were sitting on the sofa. [Deponent complies.] And where was Ms. Jones during your conversation?

9. A: She was sitting in one of the chairs.

10. Q: Will you please write "Jones" on Exhibit 24 next to the chair where she was sitting?

11. Q: How far was it from where you were sitting to where Ms. Jones was sitting?

12. A: About twelve feet.

13. Q: Will you please draw a line from where you were sitting to where Ms. Jones was sitting and place the number twelve just above that line.

14. A: Like this?

15. Q: You've written the number 12 just above a line that runs from where you were sitting to where Ms. Jones was sitting, is that correct?

16. A: Yes.

Diagrams are also a technique for "masking." To "mask" is to ask questions in a context that doesn't indicate their purpose in the hope that a deponent will provide an honest, unbiased answer.[12] In the case of diagrams, the process of drawing and labeling tends to obscure the purpose of specific inquiries. For example, perhaps the testimony above that Jones and Smith were 12 feet apart is significant because it detracts from either one's ability to have overheard correctly a remark made by the other. If so, the diagramming process tends to obscure the purpose of that particular inquiry.

A deponent may try to avoid composing a diagram, perhaps by saying something like, "I'm really no good as an artist." If so, impress on the deponent that you're "not looking for anything artistic, just some shapes and a few labels." If a deponent persists in refusing, you may elicit testimony verbally and compose a diagram yourself based on a deponent's answers. If you follow this approach, be sure that the record clearly indicates that a diagram represents a deponent's version of events and not yours. After each marking, ask whether it is accurate and if not, what should be changed. (Some reluctant deponents might at this point take over drawing to speed things along!) Such questioning may go as follows:

12. For a discussion of other masking techniques, see Chapter 4.

1. Q: Ms. Jones approximately how big was the living room?

2. A: Maybe twelve by twenty.

3. Q: Okay, let me mark this piece of paper as Exhibit 25. I've placed a rectangle on Exhibit 25 and written the number 20 along the left side of the rectangle and the number 12 along the bottom side of the rectangle. Now where were you sitting at the time of the conversation with Ms. Jones?

4. A: Here.

5. Q: I'm putting the letter "S" at the spot you've indicated. Does the letter "S" correctly indicate where you were seated?

6. A: Yes.

7. Now let's turn to where Ms. Jones was seated. . . .

CHAPTER 11

QUESTIONING TIPS

This Chapter describes a variety of specific suggestions that will help you implement and enhance the questioning strategies and techniques discussed in the prior chapters.

1. Ask for Hearsay

Adverse deponents may try to hide important information by making a mental distinction between what they have observed (their personal knowledge) and what they have been told about or read (hearsay). For example, assume that you ask a deponent who is a company's vice-president what was discussed during a August 26 meeting of the company's Executive Committee. The vice-president replies, "I'm sorry. I missed that meeting, so I don't know."

Here, it may well be that the vice-president has heard or read about what was discussed during that meeting, but prefers to take refuge in lack of first hand knowledge in an attempt to avoid disclosing information that is helpful to you. Thus, if your judgment is that what took place during the August 26 meeting could be important, you might follow up the answer by asking for hearsay. Your questioning might go as follows:

* Q: Did you ever hear anything from anyone as to what took place during the August 26 meeting?

* Q: Have you ever read any document describing what took place during the August 26 meeting?

2. Ask "Why" Questions Concerning Deponents' Own Behavior

You may be able to uncover important evidence by asking not only about <u>what</u> events took place but also <u>why</u> those events took place. "Why" questions tend to promote thoroughness by ferreting out evidence about motivations that affect the inferences that may be drawn from events.

Example 1

In an automobile accident case, a deponent testifies that "At the time of the accident, I was on my way to meet with my wife and children." You then ask the deponent, "Why were you going to meet with your wife and children?" Certainly the inferences that might be drawn about the deponent's attentiveness to the road are likely to be affected by whether the answer is, "It was my daughter's birthday and we were going to eat and then see a movie," or "I was going to take them to dinner and break the news that I had been transferred and we were going to have to move to a different state."

Example 2

In an action to rescind a loan on real property, the deponent is the bank's loan officer who testifies that, "Prior to agreeing to make the loan, I ran a background check on the broker who represented the borrower." You then ask, "Why did you run a background check on the broker?" Again, the inferences that might be drawn from the running of the background check are likely to differ depending on whether the answer is "I did so because I had heard about allegations of fraud on the broker's part," or "I did so as a matter of routine."

As a general rule, you should ask "why" questions whenever deponents' testimony relates to what they did or did not do in connection with an important factual contention in a case. For instance, in the automobile action above plaintiff's counsel's "why" question might surface evidence that the defendant was not paying attention to the road because defendant was thinking about how to tell his family that he was being transferred. Similarly, in the loan officer example, the bank officer's knowledge of the broker's background might constitute evidence of whether the bank engaged in actual or negligent fraud in making the loan.

Finally, deponents sometimes testify to acting in a way that is contrary to the way that you would have expected most people to have acted in similar circumstances. Asking "why" in such situations can help you learn whether a deponent has a reasonable explanation for seemingly implausible conduct. If a deponent lacks a reasonable explanation, you will almost always have surfaced evidence suggesting that the deponent's testimony lacks credibility.

Assume for instance that a deponent who is a remodeling contractor testifies that "I agreed with the homeowner to do the remodeling job for $115,000, even though at the time of agreement I had not yet had time to take measurements and had not priced out each individual room that would be involved in the remodeling job." This testimony appears to be implausible, since few contractors can give a fixed price without knowing the costs that a remodeling job entails. Therefore, you should ask, "Why did you agree to a price of $115,000 if you hadn't taken measurements or priced out each individual room?" If the contractor has no satisfactory explanation for the seeming incongruity, you have developed circumstantial evidence that the deponent's testimony may not be true.

3. Ask "Why" Questions Concerning a Third Person's Behavior

"Why" questions can be equally valuable when you ask deponents to explain the behavior of third persons. Of course, a deponent's testimony about the motivations behind another's behavior almost always involves speculation, and therefore the deposition testimony is unlikely to be admitted into evidence at trial.[1] However, for discovery purpose, such questions are legitimate so long as they are "calculated to lead to the discovery of admissible evidence." And questions seeking reasons for a third person's behavior are often proper because after a deponent testifies to an opinion about why a third person behaved in a certain way, you can

1. See FRE 701.

follow-up with questions seeking the basis for that opinion. Often, that basis will consist of circumstantial evidence that is admissible at trial. Consider this example.

1. Q: Ms. Heiser, why did Molina Insurance Company instruct employees such as yourself that it was not necessary to keep notes of all phone conversations with claimants?

2. Objection: Speculation; there is no way this witness can tell you what reasons lay behind the company's policy.

3. Q: Ms. Heiser, do you have an opinion about why Molina Insurance had a "limited notes" policy?

4. A: Yes.

5. Q: What is your opinion?

6. A: The company wanted to avoid leaving paper trails that might reveal errors had been made.

7. Q: Do you have any reasons for thinking that the company's "limited notes" policy was based on a desire not to leave paper trails that might reveal errors?

8. A: Yes.

9. Q: And what are those reasons?

10. A: Because of what my supervisor, Ms. Watry, told me.

11. Q: Do you have any other reasons for believing that Molina wanted to avoid having notes that might reveal that errors had been made?

12. A: No.

13. Q: Okay, let's talk about what Ms. Watry told you. What did she say to you?

A: Well, she....

In this example, No. 3 asks if the deponent has an opinion about the reasons for a third person's behavior, and No. 7 asks for the basis of the opinion that the deponent gives. Of course, there is no single, "correct" way to phrase questions such as Nos. 3 and 7. For instance, you might have phrased these questions as follows:

* No. 3: Ms. Heiser, do you have any belief about why Molina Insurance had a "limited notes" policy?

* No. 7: Ms. Heiser, did you ever read anything indicating why Molina Insurance had a "limited notes" policy?

4. Ask "Have You Now Told Me Everything?"

Before leaving an important topic, consider asking a question such as, "Have you now told me everything you can recall?"

<u>Examples</u>

Before moving on from an important meeting, you might ask, "Have you now told me everything you can recall about that meeting?"

After having asked a deponent for "all the reasons you decided to terminate my client," you may ask, "Have you now told me everything you can recall about why you decided to terminate my client?''

Whether you're seeking to elicit a deponent's version of events or probing for harmful or helpful evidence, wrap up questions such as these both promote thoroughness and help to tie deponents down to their deposition testimony.

5. Elicit the Bases of Conclusions and Opinions

Deponents frequently respond with conclusions or opinions.

Examples

Q: How did Ms. Oshima reply?

A: She said that it didn't happen that way and got very angry.

Q: Please describe everything that happened at the meeting?

A: It was a debacle. They basically forced me out of my job.

Q: Did you look at the company's disclosure statement before making the investment?

A: Yes, but the disclosure statement was inadequate.

The key to thoroughness when deponents testify to such opinions and conclusions is to realize that they conceal more information than they provide. That is, the conclusion that "they forced me out of my job" omits the concrete happenings on which the conclusion is based. To uncover missing detail, follow up conclusions and opinions with questions seeking their bases. For example, you might ask questions such as:

Q: Tell me everything that you observed that led you to conclude that Ms. Oshima was angry.

Q: What happened that made you think you were being forced out of your job?

Q: Tell me all the reasons that you believe the disclosure statement was inadequate.

Asking for the bases of opinions and conclusions may be useful regardless of whether the opinion is harmful or helpful. If an opinion is harmful, follow up questions can help to determine whether a deponent has sufficient personal knowledge to provide the opinion in the first place. In addition, eliciting the bases of harmful opinions can help you undermine them.[2] And when conclusions are helpful, obtaining their bases helps you to establish their admissibility and bolster their probative value.

6. Seek Out Opinions

Independently of whether a deponent volunteers an opinion, you may actively seek opinions. You may tend to shy away from affirmatively asking for opinions because they may be inadmissible at trial under FRE 701. However, the ultimate admissibility of an opinion is beside the point at deposition. Deposition questions seeking opinions are appropriate as long as they are "reasonably calculated to

2. For a discussion of probing harmful conclusions, see Chapter 6.

lead to the discovery of admissible evidence." More-over, after eliciting an opinion, you may obtain admissible evidence by eliciting an opinion's bases. Thus, beliefs and opinions are useful windows for uncovering either helpful or harmful evidence.[3]

Example

Deposing the manager of a large apartment build-ing that your clients claim was uninhabitable, you are probing the building owner's defense that the owner made a "good faith effort" to remedy the building code violations listed in an Inspection Report prepared by a building inspector.

1. Q: Ms. Manager, you are familiar with the building code violations listed in Exhibit 27, the March 9 Inspection Report?

2. A: Yes, when the owner received it in the mail we reviewed it together.

3. Q: Do you believe that the owner made a good faith effort to remedy the violations listed in Exhibit 27?

4. Objection: Improper opinion.

5. Q: You can answer the question.

6. A: If I go by what I understand the term to mean, I'd say definitely yes, the owner did make a

---

3. In the example below, the opinion and its bases constitute harmful evidence. However, eliciting harmful evidence at deposi-tion allows you to assess the strength of an adversary's case and to possibly develop evidence undermining harmful testimony. See Chapter 1.

good faith effort to take care of the problems listed in the Report.

7. Q: What is your basis for saying that the owner made a good faith effort to remedy the violations?

8. A: We had new screens installed on the windows of each apartment. We attached metal trim to the bottom of each apartment's front door to remedy gaps that existed between the bottoms of some of the apartment doors and the hallway floors.

9. Q: Can you give me any other examples?

10. A: Well. . . .

7. Elicit the "Details" Rather Than the "Substance" of Occurrences

As you know, the "devil is often in the details." Therefore, when a deponent refers to an important occurrence such as a significant conversation or a meeting, resist the temptation to ask for the "substance" or the "gist" of what happened. Terms such as these invite deponents to characterize what happened and to choose which details to mention and which to omit. If a conversation or meeting is important, ask deponents something like, "Tell me everything that was said in that conversation." Then you may ask follow up questions to fully probe deponents' recollections.[4]

---

4. See Chapter 2 for a discussion of the T–Funnel pattern used to exhaust a deponent's recollection.

8. Don't Conflate Discrete Occurrences

Deponents frequently incorporate several occurrences into a single answer.

Examples

Q: Did you ever visit the Stork Club?

A: I went there a few times.

Q: Did you tell Johnson that oral conversations had to be followed up with written notes?

A: Several times.

Such responses may lure you into also treating several occurrences as a single one. For example, after a deponent testifies to having gone to the Stork Club "a few times," you may ask something like, "Tell me what happened when you went there?" This broad question conflates multiple occurrences and risks your failing to uncover important details that relate to a single occurrence.

To avoid conflating discrete important occurrences, ask deponents to focus separately on each occurrence. Doing so enhances the likelihood that deponents will recall the details of individual occurrences rather than resort to general statements about the events as a group. For example, your questioning may go as follows:

1.   Q: Did you ever talk with Ms. Gilbert about her getting reports done on time?

2.   A: Several times.

3.   Q: What do you mean by several?

4. A: Four or five times.

5. Q: Okay, tell me about the first time you recall talking with Ms. Gilbert about getting reports done on time.

6. A: Well....

If a deponent simply is unable to break a series of occurrences into individual instances, you have no choice other than to treat the multiple occurrences as a single unit.

9. Seek Examples of Behavior Over Time

Deponents frequently provide conclusions that include descriptions of behavior over time.

Examples

Mr. Wyzinski <u>routinely</u> gave us pep talks about being consistent in what we said to prospective borrowers.

Ms. Wich was <u>always</u> making excuses for why she couldn't provide me with that information.

Mr. Gibney <u>constantly</u> criticized me more harshly than the other salespeople for failing to reach my sales quotas.

When you encounter conclusions relating to behavior over time, in order to determine both their foundational basis and probative value you typically focus deponents on discrete instances when the behavior occurred. For example, you might ask follow up questions such as:

Can you recall a specific instance in which Mr. Wyzinski gave you a pep talk about being consistent in what you said to prospective borrowers?

Tell me about the first instance that you can recall in which Ms. Wich made excuses for why she couldn't provide you with that information.

Can you give me an example of a time when Mr. Gibney criticized you more harshly than other salespeople for failing to reach your sales quota?

Typically, you will want to follow up to obtain as many examples as you can.

10. Clarify Ambiguous References and Physical Gestures

Deponent's sometimes use ambiguous references to aspects of the deposition environment to explain their testimony. For example, if a deponent says that two people "were about as close as I am to you" you need to ask the deponent on the record to estimate the distance between you and the deponent. Similarly if deponents use physical gestures to explain their testimony, you need to clarify the gestures for the record. For example, if a deponent testifies that in a physical altercation the defendant struck the plaintiff "like this," and demonstrates how the plaintiff was struck, you need to get a verbal description of the deponent's demonstration in the record. You can either ask the deponent to provide the verbal description or provide such a description yourself and ask the deponent to confirm that your description is accurate.

11. Be Solicitous of the Court Reporter

Simple courtesy as well as the need for an accurate transcript suggest that you be solicitous of the court reporter. Steps you can take include:

* Periodically ask if the court reporter needs or wants a break.

* Speak at a reasonable rate of speed and ask the court reporter to tell you if you are speaking to quickly.

* Give the reporter an opportunity to mark exhibits before you start asking questions about them.

* At the end of the deposition, help make sure that all exhibits have been returned to the reporter.

CHAPTER 12

COMMUNICATING ARGUMENTS

As you examine a deponent, some of the arguments you are likely to make at a settlement conference or at trial may become obvious to the deponent and opposing counsel. Some of your arguments, however, may be based on evidence scattered throughout the deposition and the documents in a case and therefore may not be obvious to the deponent or opposing counsel. As a result, you may want to intentionally structure your deposition questioning to maximize the possibility of communicating your arguments to opposing counsel and the deponent. Communicating your arguments at deposition has the following potential advantages:

- **Allows you to assess the likely credibility of the deponent under cross examination.** When you communicate arguments at deposition, you primary goals is not to obtain information from a deponent. Instead, you typically use leading questions to marshal evidence illustrating your arguments. These leading questions often mimic one type of trial cross examination. As a result, you are able to assess the likely demeanor of the deponent when under cross examination at trial.

- **Increases the likelihood of settlement.** Especially if the deponent is an adverse party, or a person likely to be involved in a decision to settle, you may enhance the possibility of a favorable settlement by communicating your persuasive arguments at deposition. While you can, of course, communicate your arguments to opposing counsel after depositions, it often makes sense to communicate them through your deposition questions. One reason is that, either intentionally or unintentionally, opposing counsel may not accurately convey your arguments to adverse decision makers. In addition, your arguments may make a greater impact when you advance them directly in the question-answer format of depositions than when you refer to them during settlement negotiations.

Communicating arguments may also facilitate settlement because the cross examination style of questioning you typically use to communicate arguments may be unpleasant for a deponent. Consequently, this type of examination may make an adverse party, or a person likely to be involved in a decision to settle, more likely to settle in order to avoid an unpleasant reprise at trial.

1. Communicating Arguments by Marshaling Evidence With Leading Questions

The basic strategy for communicating an argument to a deponent involves marshaling the evidence supporting the argument. That is, group together through a series of leading questions the evidence pertaining to a single argument. The following example illustrates this marshaling technique.

Assume that you represent the plaintiff Norma Rae in a wrongful termination case. The defendant employer contends that Rae was properly terminated because of customer complaints relating to Rae's job performance. The deponent is Sherrill Franklin, the assistant vice president who made the decision to terminate Rae. The argument that you want to communicate to Ms. Franklin is that the inadequacy of her investigation of alleged customer complaints demonstrates that her alleged reliance on customer complaints was merely a pretext, and that Rae was terminated improperly because she was a union organizer.

1. Q: Ms. Franklin, you testified earlier that Mr. Woods was Ms. Rae's immediate supervisor, correct?

2. A: That's right.

3. Q: And when you decided to terminate Rae you were relying, at least in part, on Wood's recommendation that Rae should be terminated because customers had repeatedly complained about her work, correct?

4. A: Yes.

5. Q: You wouldn't have terminated Rae if these customer complaints were totally unfounded, would you?

6. Opposing counsel: Objection assumes facts not in evidence and an improper hypothetical.

7. You: I'll rephrase my question. You are concerned about how your employees interact with your important customers, correct?

8. A: Yes.

9. Q: And Sloan Brothers is one of your largest customers, isn't that true?

10. A: That's true.

11. Q: Ms. Rae worked on the Sloan Brothers account, correct?

12. A: That's right.

13. Q: You never personally checked with anyone at Sloan Brothers to see if they were unhappy with Ms. Rae's work, did you?

14. A: Not personally, no.

15. Q: And you never saw anything in writing indicating that the people at Sloan Brothers were unhappy about Ms. Rae's work, did you?

16. A: Not in writing, no.

17. Q: So when you decided to terminate Ms. Rae's employment you didn't know whether or not the people at one of your largest customers liked or disliked her work, isn't that true?

18. A: Not specifically, but I was relying on Mr. Woods' evaluation of Rae's work.

19. Q: But the ultimate decision to terminate Ms. Rae was yours, correct?

20.   A: That's true.

21.   Q: And you didn't personally determine whether or not one of your largest customers loved Ms.Rae's work before making that decision, did you?

22.   Opposing counsel: Objection asked and answered and argumentative.

23.   I'll withdraw the question.

24.   Q: At the time you terminated Ms. Rae, you knew she had been involved in an effort to organize a union at the company, correct?

25.   A: I knew she had been trying to organize a union, yes.

26.   Q: In fact, you and Mr. Woods had discussed Ms. Rae's union organizing efforts, isn't that true?

27.   A: Yes, but just as regular discussions about the business.

28.   Q: And you had heard that Mr. Woods and Ms. Rae had argued about Ms. Rae's organizing activities, right?

29.   A: Everyone in the company had heard about that.

30.   Q: So at the time you decided to terminate Ms. Rae, you knew Mr. Woods was unhappy about her efforts to organize a union, correct?

31.   A: That's true.

As this example illustrates, when marshaling evidence you use leading questions that call for one word or brief answers from the deponent. Such questions are a staple when communicating arguments since they both highlight or pinpoint the evidence on which your argument is based and minimize extraneous narrative answers by a deponent.

You may also ask an occasional argumentative question to stress a point you would make to a factfinder. For example, question No. 21 suggests that an important customer might have thought highly of your client's performance, but the deponent would not have this information because of her shoddy investigation. When you ask an argumentative question, you typically will not insist on an answer.[1] Your primary goal when using this technique is not to obtain information **from** the deponent but to convey information **to** the deponent.

2.   Deciding Which Arguments to Communicate

Rarely will you have the time or desire to communicate all the arguments you may rely on during settlement negotiations. This section describes factors that can help you decide whether to communicate an argument through deposition questioning.

Perhaps the most significant factor is an argument's strength. Marshaling evidence for a weak

---

1.   Technically you are usually entitled to insist on an answer to an objectionable question. See Chapter 15.

argument is unlikely to enhance your settlement posture. Similarly, if at the time of deposition an argument is still in its formative stages, you may decide not to convey it.

A second factor is whether an argument suggests that a deponent's behavior was negligent or ill advised. A deponent who fears that his own conduct will be viewed unfavorably if a case goes to trial, may be more likely to settle the case to prevent his shortcomings from being made public and/or being called to the attention of superiors.[2] The "Norma Rae" example above illustrates such an argument.

Finally, you may also want to convey an argument that provides you an opportunity to confront a decision maker with helpful evidence from third parties of which the deponent may be unaware. Typically this situation arises because opposing counsel fails or refuses to convey such information to an adverse party.

For an example of how you might confront an adverse party with helpful evidence from third parties, assume that you represent defendant Big Bank in a breach of contract action. The plaintiff contends Big Bank breached an agreement to provide construction financing for a shopping center. In

2. Of course, communicating this sort of argument may backfire. A deponent may feel he has to refuse a settlement and proceed to trial to vindicate his actions and show that he was not at fault. Whether this sort of argument will facilitate or impede settlement will depend on the circumstances of an individual case and the personalities of the people deciding whether or not to settle.

addition to trying to prove that your client did not breach the contract, you will also argue that plaintiff failed to mitigate damages because plaintiff did not make a reasonable effort to obtain construction financing from other sources. Your questioning of the plaintiff may proceed as follows:

1. Q: Mr. Cardona, you knew in approximately December that you would not be able to obtain construction financing from my client, correct?

2. A: It was either in November or December, that's right.

3. Q: Larry Nelson is one of the people you dealt with at Big Bank, correct?

4. A: Yes.

5. Q: I am showing you the deposition transcript of Larry Nelson at page 45 lines 2–15. It says here that Mr. Nelson called Tom Bourne at Federal Financial in early January and told Mr. Bourne that Big Bank had been unable to provide you with construction financing on the project, and that Mr. Nelson suggested to Mr. Bourne that he might want to call you and discuss possibly providing financing for you, correct?

6. A: That's what it says.

7. Q: Mr. Bourne talked to you about construction financing, correct?

8. A: I don't recall.

9. Q: Perhaps I can refresh your recollection. I am showing you Mr. Bourne's deposition tran-

script and what was marked as Exhibit 12 to Mr. Bourne's deposition in this case. Mr. Bourne testified at page 32 lines 16–30 of his deposition that Exhibit 12 were his calendar notes from January, correct?

10.   A: Yes.

11.   Q: Your name and telephone number appear on Exhibit 12 for the dates of January 12, 15 and 18, correct?

12.   A: Yes.

13.   Q: The telephone number on the Exhibit 12 is your business phone, is it not?

14.   A: Yes.

15.   Q: Drawing your attention to page 35 lines 17–26 of Mr. Bourne's deposition transcript, it says there that Mr. Bourne called you on those three dates and left a message indicating that he wanted to talk to you about providing construction financing for this project, correct?

16.   A: That's what it says, yes.

17.   Q: You recall receiving those messages, correct?

18.   A.: No, I don't.

19.   Q: And prior to this deposition, you never saw anything indicating that Mr. Bourne telephoned you, did you?

20.   A: I don't recall seeing anything like that.

21.   Q: But you did talk to Mr. Bourne about this project, correct?

22.   A: I don't recall.

23.   Q: Drawing your attention to page 40 lines 18–30 of Mr. Bourne's deposition transcript, Mr. Bourne testified that, in his opinion, his company would probably have provided you with construction financing for this project if you had sought it, correct?

24.   A: That's what it says.

25.   Q: You never applied to Federal Financial for construction financing on this project, did you?

26.   A: I did not. But I've already told you what we did to try to find financing after your client breached the contract.

27.   Q: You have no reason to believe that Mr. Bourne would testify untruthfully in this case, do you?

28.   A: I do not know Mr. Bourne so I don't know whether he is testifying truthfully or not.

29.   Q: I understand that you don't know Mr. Bourne personally, but you don't have any reason to believe from what you know about Federal Financial's reputation or Mr. Bourne's reputation that Mr. Bourne would testify untruthfully in this case, do you?

30.   [Opposing counsel.] Objection compound.

31.   Q: I'll rephrase. You believe that Federal Financial was in a position to provide you with construction financing on this project, correct?

32.   I'm not sure.

By bringing the helpful testimony relating to the failure to mitigate damages to the adverse party's attention during the deposition, you ensure that this testimony will be available to the plaintiff when considering any offer of settlement.[3]

3.   When to Communicate Arguments

As a general rule, the time to communicate arguments is when you are about to conclude a deposition. The typical advantages of waiting until late in a deposition to convey your arguments are these:

* You have had an opportunity earlier in the deposition to uncover all the evidence supporting any argument you want to communicate.

* Early communication of arguments may educate the deponent about your theories, allowing a crafty deponent to try to shape later testimony so as to avoid providing you with additional helpful evidence.

* Communicating arguments may be unpleasant for the deponent. As a result, you risk damaging rapport with a deponent. If you must damage rapport, you may want to do so late in the deposition.

3.   In this example, the helpful information related to the failure to mitigate damages was revealed at a previous deposition and therefore already available to opposing counsel. Consequently, by mentioning this information at deposition you may communicate an argument to the adverse party using this information without educating opposing counsel. In some cases, however, you may decide not to reveal information that might facilitate settlement to avoid educating opposing counsel.

CHAPTER 13

BEGINNING AND CONCLUDING DEPOSITIONS

This Chapter explores effective strategies for the beginning and ending phases of depositions.

1. Beginning Depositions

Depositions typically begin with a court officer, usually a court reporter, putting on the record the officer's name and business address; the date, time and place of deposition; and the deponent's name.[1] The officer then administers the oath to the deponent, and identifies on the record all of the persons present.[2]

After the court officer concludes these housekeeping details, the officer turns the deposition over to you.

A. Stipulations

At the outset, one issue that you might want to address through stipulation concerns the time limits imposed by FRCP 30(d)(2).[3] FRCP 30(d)(2) lim-

1. FRCP 30(b)(5)(a).

2. Id. Although court officers have a statutory obligation to begin depositions in this fashion, be sure that the officer properly carries it out. Otherwise, you create a risk that your adversary will use the officer's failure to begin a deposition properly to prevent your using favorable testimony later in a case.

3. FRCP 30(d)(1) applies to all depositions. Therefore, you or any other party have the statutory right to terminate a deposi-

its depositions to "one day of seven hours."[4] Thus, you or any other party may terminate a deposition when it exceeds <u>either</u> one day or seven hours.[5]

tion which exceeds the time limits of FRCP 30(d)(2), whether the deponent is an adverse party, a witness associated with an adverse party, an expert, a neutral third party witness, your client or a witness associated with your client.

4. Breaks during the deposition do not count toward the 7 hours. The FRCP advisory committee's notes (2000) indicate that the "only time to be counted is the time occupied by the actual deposition." See Also Condit v. Dunne, 225 F.R.D. 100, 112 (S.D. N.Y. 2004) ("[T]he 2000 Advisory Committee notes to Rule 30(d) clearly state that only the time taken for the actual deposition, not breaks, counts toward the 7 hours..."); Dow Chemical Co. v. Reinhard, 2008 WL 1735295 (E.D.Mich. 2008); Wilson v. Kautex, A Textron Co., 2008 WL 189568 (N.D.Ind. 2008). Tmie taken by objections by opposing counsel do count, unless the objections are in bad faith. FRCP 30(d)(1) states that "the court must allow additional time consistent with Rule 26(b)(2) if needed for a fair examination of the deponent or if the deponent or another person, or other circumstance, impedes or delays the examination." See Plaisted v. Geisinger Medical Center, 210 F.R.D. 527, 533 (M.D. Pa. 2002) (holding that the administrators' counsel could re-depose witnesses because the medical center's counsel did not state objections concisely in a non-argumentative and non-suggestive manner and the objections went on for pages); Miller v. Waseca Medical Center, 205 F.R.D. 537, 538 (D. Minn. 2002) (allowing additional time for the completion of depositions that were impeded by objections inconsistent with Rule 30(d); Armstrong v. Hussmann Corp., 163 F.R.D. 299, 303 (E.D. Mo. 1995) (granting the defendant's motion to re-depose witnesses because the plaintiff's attorneys violated Rule 30(d)(1) when they made constant interruptions and objections in bad faith during the depositions).

5. The FRCP advisory committee's notes (2000) provide: "The limitation is phrased in terms of a single day on the assumption that ordinarily a single day would be preferable [to more than one day]; if alternative arrangements would better

The FRCP 30(d)(2) time limits can be extended by a stipulation entered into by all parties,[6] or by a court order.[7] Therefore, if you anticipate questioning a deponent for longer than "one day of seven hours" and haven't previously done so, you may at the outset of a deposition ask opposing counsel to stipulate to a waiver of the limitations of FRCP 30(d)(2).[8] You can tailor stipulations to the circumstances of each case. For example, a stipulation may state that you have up to "one day of 10 hours" to complete a deposition, or that your deposition "is not subject to fixed time limits, but any party has the right to terminate the deposition and move the court for a protective order if the time of deposition

suit the parties, they _may_ agree to them" (emphasis added). The FRCP advisory committee's notes (2000) also indicate that "[t]he court may also _order_ that a deposition be taken for limited periods on several days" (emphasis added). This language would seem to indicate that, absent an agreement by the parties or a court order, a deposition would be limited to one day.

6. If the deponent is not a party, the deponent's consent is not required to extend the length of a deposition. See FRCP 30(d)(1).

7. The court must generally grant additional time if it is needed for a fair examination of the deponent or if the deponent or any other person has impeded the examination of the deponent. See FRCP 26(b)(2)(A) and 30(d)(1). According to the FRCP advisory committee's notes (2000), the party seeking the court order to extend the time is "expected to show good cause to justify such an order."

8. Obviously, if you have obtained an agreement regarding a waiver before the deposition, you should put the terms of that agreement on the record at the beginning of the deposition, or attach any written agreement to the deposition transcript as an exhibit.

is unduly prolonged in bad faith." Of course, be sure to read any such stipulation into the record.

If your adversary does not agree to waive the one day/seven hour time limit set forth in FRCP 30(d)(2), one alternative is to modify your questioning so as to fit within the limit. A second alternative is to use all of your allotted time, and then seek a court order extending the time limit if the opposing party continues to refuse to stipulate to an extension and you have not completed your questioning.

As a deposition proceeds, you or opposing counsel might propose a variety of stipulations. Such stipulations may relate to housekeeping matters such as the numbering of exhibits, or to more substantive matters such as the admissibility of documents. You are under no obligation to enter into stipulations at any point in a deposition, and of course should never do so if you are uncertain of what you are stipulating to. If you do agree to enter into a stipulation, better practice is to first go off the record, hash out the exact terms of the stipulation, and then read the terms into the record.

B. *Admonitions*

After a deponent has been sworn and stipulations (if any) have been entered into the record, admonitions are the typical next phase of depositions. Admonitions are questions which review basic deposition procedures and inquire into a deponent's capacity to respond fully and accurately to your questions.

Admonitions serve a variety of purposes:

* Admonitions provide you with a basis for undermining common justifications that deponents tend to give for making changes in their deposition testimony or later giving testimony that conflicts with their deposition testimony.

* Admonitions help to put deponents at ease, thereby perhaps improving a deponent's ability to recall important events and details.

* Deponents may infer from your explanations of deposition procedures that you are fair and reasonable, and if so may respond more fully and cooperatively to your questions.

Set out below is a typical set of admonitions, followed by a discussion of their contents.

1. Q: Ms. Strauss, my name is Orin Parrent and I am the attorney for Mr. Flowers. I assume that your attorney has reviewed with you what will take place here today, but just so there won't be any misunderstanding, let me briefly describe what will happen. John Flowers has filed a lawsuit concerning the loan secured by a deed of trust for the property at 9412 E. 88th Street. Today I will be asking you questions to learn information that might be relevant to that lawsuit. My questions and your answers will be taken down by the court reporter on this machine that you see in front of you. At the conclusion of the questioning, the court reporter will transcribe my questions and your answers into a booklet that will be known as your

deposition transcript and it will contain my questions and your answers. Do you understand that?

2. A: Yes.

3. Q: The court reporter can't take down nods or shakes of the head so it's necessary for you to answer my questions audibly, all right?

4. A: I'll try.

5. Q: When I begin a question you may know what I'm going to ask before I finish my question, but it's easier for the court reporter to get everything down correctly if you let me finish my question before you start to answer. Will you try to do that?

6. A: Sure.

7. Q: Have you ever been deposed before, Ms. Strauss?

8. A: No, this is my first time.

9. Q: Do you understand that you were administered an oath by the court reporter and are testifying today under penalty of perjury?

10. A: Yes, I do.

11. Q: And do you understand that your deposition testimony has the same importance and significance it would have if you were testifying in court before a judge and a jury?

12. A: Yes.

13. Q: And you'll do your best to tell the complete truth at this deposition, won't you Ms. Strauss?

14. A: I will.

15. Q: If you don't understand a question I ask you, you shouldn't answer it. Instead of answering a question you don't understand, please just tell me that you don't understand the question. Will you agree to do that?

16. A: Sure.

17. Q: So if you do answer a question, I will assume that you have understood the question and that you were giving me your best possible answer. Do you understand that?

18. A: Yes.

19. Q: Sometimes you will understand my question perfectly well, but you're not sure you know the answer because your answer is a guess or an estimate. When your answer is a guess or an estimate, you should tell me that you're guessing or giving an estimate. Will you agree to tell me when your answer is a guess or an estimate?

20. A: All right.

21. Q: If you answer a question and don't tell me that you are guessing at the answer, I'll assume that you are not guessing. Will that be a fair assumption on my part?

22. A: Yes.

23. Q: After you have answered a question,
you may realize that for one reason or another you need to change an answer that
you have previously given. If this happens,
just tell me that you need to change an
earlier answer and I'll give you an opportunity to do so. If you want to change an
answer to an earlier question, will you tell
me that you want to do so?

24. A: Yes.

25. Q: Also, after you've given your best complete answer to a question, you may sometimes later in the deposition remember additional information that responds to the
question. If this happens, just tell me that
you've remembered additional information
that relates to an earlier question and you
can tell me about the additional information.
If after you have answered a question, you
recall additional information will you tell me
that?

26. A: Yes.

27. Q: If you find yourself getting tired at any
time during the deposition, please let me
know and we'll talk about taking a break. Is
that all right?

28. A: That's fine.

29. Q: After the deposition is over, the court
reporter will prepare a written transcript of
my questions and your answers. You may

have an opportunity to review and sign the transcript under penalty of perjury. If you review your transcript you may change answers that you believe are inaccurate. You should know, however, that if you make changes in the sworn testimony in your transcript after you review it, I and other lawyers in the case will be entitled at trial to ask you why you've made changes in your sworn testimony and to point out to the judge or jury at trial that you made changes. Do you understand that?

30. A: Yes.

31. Q: So it's important today to give me your most complete answers to my questions and to avoid any need to make changes in your testimony. Do you understand that?

32. A: Yes.

33. Q: You should also know that if you testify at trial differently than you testify here today, the lawyers in this case may have an opportunity to ask you why there were changes in your sworn testimony. Do you understand that?

34. A: Yes.

35. Q: I'm going to ask you a few questions about how you're feeling today. I am not trying to pry into your medical situation, but I need to make sure anyone reading the transcript of this deposition will understand

that you are feeling fine and are able to testify today. Are you ill today?

36. A: No.

37. Q: Do you feel fine physically?

38. A: Yes.

39. Q: Are you under any medication?

40. A: No

41. Q: Are you currently under a doctor's care for any illness?

42. A: Not now.

43. Q: Have you had any alcohol today?

44. A: No.

45. Q: Is there anything at all preventing you in any way from giving accurate testimony today?

46. A: No.

47. Q: Do you have any questions about what we've covered so far?

48. A: No.

49. Q: Do you have any questions of any kind before I begin the questioning?

50. A: No.

Transcript Analysis

<u>A Lawsuit Has Been Filed</u> (No. 1)—Here, you introduce yourself and explain briefly why the deposition is taking place. A statement such as

this reflects common courtesy and may help to put a deponent at ease.

<u>Answer Audibly</u> (No. 3) and <u>Let Me Finish My Questions</u> (No.5)—These admonitions seek to make life easier for the court reporter and hopefully improve a transcript's accuracy.

<u>Prior Deposition Experience</u> (No. 7)—Evidence that a deponent has prior deposition experience can undercut a deponent's explanation that confusion about deposition procedures caused the deponent to give erroneous testimony.[9] Moreover, knowing that a deponent has prior experience can also help you evaluate the likelihood that the deponent will try to "play games" with you, such as by interpreting questions narrowly so as to conceal information. Even if a deponent has been deposed previously, you would complete the admonitions. Before doing so, you might say something along the lines of, "I realize that you are familiar with what happens at deposition, but just

9. When a deponent has had prior deposition experience, consider following up with questions pursuing such matters as how many times the deponent has previously been deposed and the types of cases in which the testimony was given. If the prior cases involved personal matters unrelated to your case (e.g., divorce proceedings or child custody matters), your questioning typically should cease. Prying into irrelevant personal matters may offend a deponent and lead your adversary to adjourn a deposition under FRCP 26(c) to seek a protective order that discovery not be had with respect to irrelevant, embarrassing matters. Of course, if a prior case seems relevant to the case at hand, you may probe further into the facts and claims of the prior case.

to make sure that there is no confusion let me explain what will happen here today."

Testifying Under Penalty of Perjury (Nos. 9, 11 and 13)—The answer to No. 9 undermines potential explanations for changed testimony based on a deponent's claim that "I wasn't that careful at deposition because I didn't think that I was under oath or testifying under penalty of perjury."[10] Nos. 11 and 13 reinforce the point by establishing that a deponent knew that deposition testimony was as important as trial testimony and that the deponent agreed to try to tell the "complete" truth.

If You Don't Understand, Don't Answer (Nos. 15 and 17)—These admonitions undermine potential explanations by a deponent that changes in testimony resulted from misunderstanding deposition questions.

Tell Me When You're Guessing (Nos. 19 and 21)—These admonitions focus on the situation in which a deponent tries to justify a subsequent change in testimony based upon a claim that what seemed to be a definite deposition answer was in reality only a guess or an estimate.

You may choose to omit admonitions such as Nos. 19 and 21 in an effort to prevent deponents from guessing. Indeed, you may prefer to give an admonition which asks deponents not to answer at all if their only answer would be a guess. This alter-

10. Indeed, some lawyers repeat question 9 after any significant break in the deposition (lunch for example).

native form of admonition may strengthen your attack on a deponent who later tries to justify a change in testimony by claiming that a deposition answer was only a guess. A potential downside, however, is that discouraging deponents from guessing may prevent you from obtaining leads to other potential evidence.

For example, assume that you represent tenants who have sued the owner of an apartment building, claiming that the owner is a slumlord who deliberately refused to make repairs. The deponent is a city building inspector who mailed a written Order to Comply to the owner requiring the owner to make listed repairs. You ask the inspector whether the owner ever considered making the repairs. If your admonitions have invited the inspector to guess, the inspector may respond by testifying, "I don't know, but my guess is that he didn't." You might then ask follow-up questions such as:

Q: What is the basis for your guess about whether the owner considered making the repairs listed in the Order?

Q: Why do you believe that the owner considered making the repairs listed in the Order?

Questions such as these might produce a helpful response such as, "Later on, a plumbing subcontractor told me that the owner had complained about the cost of redoing all the pipes in the apartment house." You might then follow up with the plumbing subcontractor to develop further evidence of the owner's neglect of the building. Had you admonished the deponent not to guess, the information may not have emerged.

Changing an Answer (No. 23)—This admonition undermines a post-deposition explanation for changed testimony that runs along the lines of, "I would have provided the changed testimony during the deposition if I had known that I could change an incorrect answer during the deposition."

Again, you may prefer to omit an admonition similar to No. 23, in the belief that such an admonition may encourage a deponent to re-think helpful answers. Or, you may give an admonition along the lines of No. 23, but not until near a deposition's end. An admonition asking deponents whether they want to change answers already given may more strongly undermine post-deposition changes than a pre-questioning admonition such as No. 23. That is, a deponent may credibly be able to claim that "By the time we got to that answer, I'd forgotten that the attorney told me that I could change my answers during the deposition." On the other hand, that excuse has little credibility when you give the admonition just before a deposition concludes.

Additional Information (No. 25)—This admonition tends to encourage deponents to give complete responses. It recognizes that especially under the stress of a deposition, even the most forthcoming deponent will not always be able to remember all the information that responds to a question immediately after the question is asked. The admonition also makes it difficult for deponents to explain subsequent changes in deposition testimony by saying something like, "I didn't think of the additional information until later on in the deposition, and by that time it was too late to mention it because we were on a whole different topic."

Taking a Break (No. 27)—This admonition tends to undermine an explanation for changed testimony along the lines of "When I gave that testimony at deposition, I was tired and not thinking clearly." Note that the question does not indicate that the deponent can take a break on demand. If you want a deponent to answer a question without consulting with opposing counsel, you may not want to immediately honor a request for a break.[11] However, delaying a break will be more difficult if you commit at the outset to allowing deponents to take a break on demand.

Effect of Changed Deposition Testimony (Nos. 29, 31 and 33)—These admonitions encourage complete answers. They also diminish the likelihood that a deponent who changes an answer can effectively explain away the change by testifying that "I didn't think it was important to testify correctly during the deposition because I knew I'd

---

11. Under the FRCP a deponent is arguably required to answer a pending question without conferring with counsel. See Chapter 15.

have a chance to correct misstatements or omissions when I got the deposition transcript.''

Mental and Physical Health (Nos. 35–45)—These admonitions undermine explanations along the lines of, ''My deposition testimony was inaccurate (or, I couldn't remember very much) because I was ill (or, taking medication) on the day I was deposed.''[12]

If answers reveal that a deponent is ill, is taking medication or is under the influence of alcohol or other drugs, inquire into the nature of the illness, or the effects of the medications and drugs. If you're going to continue with the deposition, the record should reflect the deponent's acknowledgement that the deponent can testify fully and recall accurately notwithstanding the illness or medications. If you cannot secure such an acknowledgement, you may decide to postpone a deposition to a later date when the deponent may be better able to testify, stating for the record that the deponent's condition is the reason for the postponement.

Any Questions (Nos. 47 and 49)—These admonitions cut off justifications for changes of testimo-

12. You may also want to ask questions about medications and alcohol use when you return from a lunch break, or any other long break in the deposition. Similarly, in instances where a deposition carries over to the next day, you will want to begin the renewed deposition by repeating these questions as well as Nos. 35–45. And when there is a long break between sessions of a deposition, perhaps several days or weeks, you may want to repeat all or selected portions of the admonition at the start of the session.

ny based a deponent's lack of understanding of your admonitions or your failure to give a deponent a chance to ask about an important concern that your admonitions failed to cover.

If you'll refer back to the admonitions, you'll notice that following many of them, the lawyer asks the deponent to explicitly agree that the deponent understands what the lawyer has said. For example, in No. 1 the lawyer asks the deponent to affirm the deponent's understanding that the oral dialogue will become a written deposition transcript. By placing deponent's understanding explicitly on the record, you make it difficult for deponents to explain changes in testimony by saying, "I didn't understand the admonition in the first place."

C. Questions Regarding a Deponent's Preparation

After the admonitions, the next phase of depositions commonly concerns what a deponent did to prepare for a deposition. This section describes two common areas of inquiry relating to a deponent's preparation.

1. Documents a Deponent Used to Refresh Recollection

Q: Ms. Jones did you review any documents when you were preparing for your deposition?

A: Yes.

Q: Reviewing those documents helped to refresh your memory about some of the facts of this case, is that correct?

A: I suppose that's true.

Q: Could you please identify for me the documents you reviewed to prepare for your deposition?

Opposing Counsel: I think I can speed this up. This folder contains all the documents my client reviewed in preparation for testifying here today.

Q: I am showing you documents from the folder that your lawyer just gave me. The court reporter has marked these documents as Exhibits 750 through 810. Can you look at them please and tell me if these are the documents you reviewed in preparation for your deposition?

A: Yes, these are the documents I looked at.

Q: Did you review any other documents in preparation for your deposition?

A: No, just these.

FRE 612 provides that if prior to testifying, witnesses use a writing to refresh their memory for the purpose of testifying, adverse parties are generally entitled to have the writings produced at the hearing. While FRE 612 pertains to testimony at trial, the rule also applies to testimony at deposition.[13]

To use FRE 612 to gain access to documents which you may not have previously seen, at the

13. See FRCP 30(c)(1); Sporck v. Peil, 759 F.2d 312, 317 (3rd Cir. 1985); Magee v. Paul Revere Life Ins. Co., 172 F.R.D. 627 (E.D.N.Y. 1997); Stone Container Corp. v. Arkwright Mutual Ins. Co., No.93 C 6626, 1995 WL 88902 (N.D. Ill. Feb 28, 1995); Auto Owners Ins. Co. v. Totaltape, Inc., 135 F.R.D. 199, 202 (M.D. Fla. 1990); Parry v. Highlight Indus., 125 F.R.D. 449, 452 (W.D. Mich. 1989); James Julian, Inc. v. Raytheon Co., 93 F.R.D. 138, 144 (D.C. Del. 1982); Heron Interact, Inc. v. Guidelines, Inc., 244

outset of depositions ask deponents to identify the documents they reviewed to prepare for deposition, and whether those documents refreshed their memory about the facts of a case. Often, as above, opposing counsel will willingly provide such documents at deposition.[14] Doing so speeds up depositions and may eliminate the need for additional sessions to examine deponents regarding documents that you are entitled to see but were not provided at deposition. Also as above, ask deponents if they reviewed any documents besides those provided to you by opposing counsel.

Opposing counsel may object to the production of some or all of the documents used to refresh a deponent's recollection, usually on the grounds of attorney-client or work product privilege. This objection may be raised on the ground that documents themselves constitute attorney work product or refer to attorney-client communications. Alternatively, the privilege claim may rest on the ground that

F.R.D. 75 (D. Mass. 2007); Scanlon v. Bricklayers and Allied Craftworkers, Local No. 3, 242 F.R.D. 238 (W.D. N.Y. 2007); Coryn Group II, LLC v. O. C. Seacrets, Inc., 265 F.R.D. 235, 244 n.5 (D. Md. 2010) at note 5.

14. Opposing counsel may be willing to produce these documents but may not have brought them to the deposition. In that case, counsel may be willing to agree on the record to provide the documents at a later session. If the deposition lasts less than a full day, you may want to agree on the record with opposing counsel that after you have received and reviewed the documents used by the deponent to refresh recollection, you will have the option to resume the deposition to examine the deponent about such documents.

the selection of documents used to refresh recollection might itself reveal opposing counsel's analysis of legal or factual issues.[15] If opposing counsel refuses to produce the documents, you typically go forward with your questioning without them and then decide whether you want to adjourn the deposition and move for an order compelling their production. At the hearing on the motion, the court decides whether the interests of justice require production of the documents.[16] If the order is granted

15. See, e.g., Sporck, 759 F.2d at 317; James Julian, Inc., 93 F.R.D. at 144; Disability Rights Council of Greater Washington v. Washington Metropolitan Transit Authority, 242 F.R.D. 139, 142 (D.D.C. Jun 01, 2007); U.S. ex rel. Bagley v. TRW, Inc., 212 F.R.D. 554, 564 (C.D. Cal. 2003). *But See* Miller v. Holzmann, 238 F.R.D. 30 (D.D.C. 2006) (where the number of documents selected by the attorney is large, and the selection does not reveal a trial strategy any more than other forms of discovery would, then the selection is not protected work product)

16. The extent to which courts have found that the interest of justice requires that privileged documents used to refresh the deponent's recollection prior to the deposition be turned over to an adversary varies greatly. For examples of cases requiring disclosure of privileged documents, see S & A Painting Co., Inc. v. O.W.B. Corp., 103 F.R.D. 407, 409 (D.C. Pa. 1984); James Julian, Inc., 93 F.R.D. at 145–46; Prucha v. M & N Modern Hydraulic Press Co., 76 F.R.D. 207, 209–10 (D.C. Wisc. 1977). For cases holding that privileged documents need not be disclosed even though a deponent used them to refresh memory, see Sporck, 759 F.2d at 317; Bogosian v. Gulf Oil Corp., 738 F.2d 587 (3rd Cir. 1984); Derderian v. Polaroid Corp., 121 F.R.D. 13 (D. Mass. 1988); Al–Rowaishan Establishment Universal Trading & Agencies, Ltd. v. Beatrice Foods Co., 92 F.R.D. 779, 780 (D.C.N.Y. 1982); Sperling v. City of Kennesaw Dept., 202 F.R.D. 325 (N.D. Ga. 2001); Scanlon v. Bricklayers and Allied Craftworkers, Local No. 3, 242 F.R.D. 238 (W.D. N.Y. 2007); Suss v. MSX Intern. Engineering Services, Inc., 212 F.R.D. 159 (S.D.

and the documents are turned over, you can then complete the deposition.

When opposing counsel refuses at deposition to provide documents used by a deponent to refresh recollection on the ground that the selection of those documents is likely to reveal opposing counsel's analysis of legal or factual issues, you may still be able to identify and gain access to some of those documents during the deposition itself. To do so, follow up a deponent's answer with a question such as:

> Q: "Are you aware of any document which you believe supports the testimony that you have just given?"

If the answer is "yes," you might be entitled to ask for and obtain a copy of the document. Since furnishing the document in these circumstances doesn't reveal opposing counsel's selection of documents, the work product claim probably will not in this scenario block your access to a document.[17]

2. Persons With Whom a Deponent Talked

Just as you should ask about documents a deponent may have reviewed, so too should you ask

N.Y. 2002); In re Managed Care Litigation, 415 F.Supp.2d 1378 (S.D. Fla. 2006);U.S. E.E.O.C. v. Continental Airlines, Inc., 395 F.Supp.2d 738 (N.D. Ill. 2005); In re Teleglobe Communications Corp., 392 B.R. 561, 586–87 (D. Del. 2008).

17. See Sporck, 759 F.2d at 317. This approach may be of limited utility, however. A deponent may honestly be unable to answer a question like, "What documents support your assertion that X is true?" Indeed, the answer to such a question may not always be clear to a lawyer acting in good faith.

about persons a deponent may have talked to in preparation for the deposition. Conversations with persons other than the deponent's attorney may not be privileged. If so, you can examine the deponent (as well as the other persons) about the reasons for and what was said during any and all such conversations.

D. Background Questioning

A final common beginning phase of depositions concerns deponents' backgrounds. Background questions typically probe deponents' educational and employment history. Many lawyers ask "background" questions simply because they have seen other lawyers do it, without really knowing why they are asking such questions or what they are looking for. As a result, background questioning is often nothing more than a chance for a questioning attorney to "warm up" and try to build rapport with a deponent. While these goals are themselves of value,[18] background questioning may also serve more valuable functions. For example, knowing a deponent's background may help you to identify areas where the deponent's subsequent testimony seems inconsistent with his prior experience. In addition, you can sometimes obscure the significance of important inquiries by asking them in seemingly insignificant background questioning.[19]

18. See Chapter 14.

19. For a discussion of techniques for doing so, see Chapter 4.

1. Employment History

A useful approach for eliciting testimony concerning a deponent's employment history is to obtain a timeline. Your timeline may either begin with a deponent's most recent employment and move backwards, or begin at an earlier time and move forward to the present.

Employment-related questioning may uncover evidence bearing on a deponent's personal credibility. For example, a deponent who testifies on behalf of a party who formerly employed the deponent is more susceptible to a claim of bias if the deponent worked for the party for twenty years than if the deponent worked for the party for two years. Of course, the conclusion may be the opposite if the deponent worked for a party for twenty years and was terminated six months before the deponent's pension vested! For that reason, it may be important to find out not only the sequence of a deponent's past jobs, but also the circumstances under which the deponent left each job.

Employment-related questioning may also uncover evidence bearing on the reliability of a deponent's observations. For example, if a deponent testifies to an opinion that a driver involved in a lawsuit appeared to be under the influence of alcohol, evidence that the deponent worked as a part-time bartender during college tends to increase the reliability of the opinion. Similarly, if the supervisor of a plaintiff in a wrongful termination case testifies that the plaintiff was one of the least capable employees the supervisor had ever worked with, the reliability of the supervisor's assertion may depend on how many employees the supervisor has worked with and over how long a period of time.

2. *Educational Background*

A timeline of a deponent's educational background also may help you to evaluate both a deponent's credibility and the reliability of a deponent's testimony. For example, assume that you depose the defendant in a Clean Water Act case in which the magnitude of the penalty imposed for a violation depends in part on whether the defendant acted in good faith. The defendant claims ignorance of applicable environmental regulations. Evidence that the deponent had taken courses covering environmental regulations in the deponent's industry would tend to undermine this claim. Similarly, in a real estate fraud case in which the plaintiff must prove reasonable reliance on a defendant's misrepresentations, evidence concerning the plaintiff's educational background might affect the likelihood or the reasonableness of the plaintiff's reliance on the defendant's misstatements.

2. Concluding Depositions

Just before concluding your questioning, you may choose to ask questions such as:

"Are all of the answers you've given in this deposition complete and accurate?"

"Do you want to change any of the answers you've given in this deposition?"

"Do you want to add to any of the answers you've given in this deposition?"

Such questions are likely to enhance impeachment should a deponent make a change in deposition testimony or later give testimony that conflicts with deposition testimony. The possible downside of such questions is that they may encourage a deponent to change helpful answers.

After you have finished your questions, lawyers representing all other parties are entitled to question the deponent. Not surprisingly, deposition questioning typically ends when each party's lawyer says something like, "I have no further questions." At that point, any party or a deponent may request that the deponent have an opportunity to read and sign the deposition transcript.[20] In the absence of such a request, a deponent has no right to review and correct a deposition transcript.[21] The court reporter will prepare and certify the deposition transcript and send it to you as the deposing attorney.[22] You should retain the transcript unless and until it is needed later in a case.[23]

If any party or a deponent asks that the deponent have an opportunity to read and sign the deposition

20. There appears to be no requirement that non-represented deponents be told that they can request an opportunity to review and correct a deposition transcript. However, if you are deposing a non-represented deponent, you might want to inform the deponent that he or she can ask to review a transcript.

21. See FRCP 30(e).

22. See FRCP 30(f)(1).

23. See FRCP 5(d)(1).

transcript, the court reporter prepares a transcript and notifies a deponent that he or she has thirty days to review and sign the transcript.[24] After receiving the notice, the deponent normally goes to the court reporter's place of business and may make any changes in the transcript that the deponent deems necessary.[25] Simultaneously, the deponent should prepare a separate document indicating the reasons for any changes.[26] After the transcript review is complete and the deponent has signed the transcript, the court reporter certifies the transcript, including any changes and reasons for any changes, and sends the transcript to you to retain unless and until it is needed later in a case.[27]

24. Absent a stipulation to the contrary, the review and signing will take place in the reporter's office. But, as discussed below, the parties often stipulate to an alternative procedure.

25. Generally speaking, a deponent may make any change the deponent desires; but some courts have imposed limits on the types of changes allowed. For a discussion of what types of changes are permitted, see Wright, Miller, & Marcus, Federal Practice & Procedure: Civil 2d § 2118. Of course, both the original testimony and any changes may be admissible at trial. See Wanke v. Lynn's Transportation Co., 836 F.Supp. 587 (N.D. Ind. 1993). And, at trial, a deponent may be questioned about changes made in the deponent's deposition testimony.

26. See Rule 30(e). A failure to provide a reason for a change may invalidate it. See Bongiovanni v. N.V. Stoomvaart–Matts "Oostzee," 458 F.Supp. 602, 605 n.4 (D.C.N.Y. 1978); Hambleton Bros. Lumber v. Balkin Enters., 397 F.3d 1217, 1225 (9th Cir. 2005); Reilly v. TXU Corp., 230 F.R.D. 486 (N.D. Tex. 2005).

27. If a deponent fails to review or sign the transcript within 30 days, the court reporter certifies the transcript and files it together with a statement that a request was made that the deponent review and sign the transcript but that the deponent failed to do so. See FRCP 30(e).

Through stipulations, attorneys often substitute their own signing procedures for those set forth in the FRCP. For example, a common stipulation relieves deponents of the obligation to go to court reporters' offices in order to review deposition transcripts and instead allows the review to take place at the office of the deponent's attorney. However, stipulations tend to vary according to local customs and practice areas. At the end of the day, do not agree to a stipulation unless you fully understand its effect.

CHAPTER 14

PROFESSIONAL DEMEANOR
AND RAPPORT
BUILDING

1. Maintain a Professional Demeanor With Deponents and Opposing Counsel

At depositions, good faith disagreements between counsel about the legitimate scope of inquiry, the proper manner of asserting objections and the appropriateness of instructions not to answer are common. Such disagreements often make for a tense atmosphere at deposition.

Tension is not always simply the result of good faith disagreements. Unfortunately, on some occasions defending counsel may act in an aggressive, belligerent or even an insulting manner toward you. Defending counsel may have at least the following reasons for engaging in such behavior:

* They are trying to demonstrate to clients that they are "fighting" for them.

* They are trying to upset and distract you, so that you will be less thorough and probing in your questioning.

* They are modeling behavior that they have seen by other lawyers.

271

* They personally enjoy behaving in such a fashion.[1]

In the face of such behavior, it may be difficult for you to resist the temptation to respond in kind. It is often not easy to turn the other cheek in the face of belligerent and/or unethical conduct.[2] Nevertheless, throughout a deposition you should maintain a professional demeanor, with both the witness and opposing counsel. A professional demeanor requires that you:

* Use a calm, measured, respectful tone of voice throughout a deposition, whether addressing the deponent or opposing counsel.

* Allow deponents to complete answers before propounding additional questions.

* Refrain from personal invective and snide remarks.

Your ability to obtain a protective order and/or sanctions against opposing counsel who behave inappropriately may well depend on the propriety of your own deposition behavior.[3] Maintaining a pro-

1. There is a single word which describes this sort of person, but the authors prefer to adopt a professional demeanor and will therefore not use that word here.

2. If your client is present at the deposition, it may be particularly difficult not to respond in kind. You may be concerned that you will appear unwilling to "fight" for your client if you maintain a professional demeanor in response to aggressive behavior by opposing counsel. You can, however, explain to your client, either during a break in the deposition or before it starts, the benefits of not responding in kind and that your decision not to do so is in your client's best interests.

3. See e.g. Odone v. Croda Int'l PLC, 170 F.R.D. 66 (1997).

fessional demeanor can improve your chances of success should a judge have occasion to examine a visual recording or transcript of a deposition in connection with your motion for a protective order and sanctions. In addition, maintaining a professional demeanor tends to enhance respect for the legal system and the legal profession.

Maintaining a professional demeanor is fully consistent with your ethical obligations to be an advocate for your client. Just as dogs are said to realize the difference between being kicked and stumbled over, so too can most deponents recognize the difference between questioning that is thorough and questioning that is antagonistic. You can use all the questioning strategies described in this book, including pressing deponents to provide you with complete details, encouraging deponents to provide helpful evidence, undermining the credibility of harmful evidence, and communicating arguments to a deponent while maintaining a professional demeanor. Thus, you should be persistent and thorough; but antagonism or nastiness is unnecessary, often counterproductive, and inconsistent with the aspirational norms of the legal profession.

2. Building Rapport With the Deponent

In some cases, you may want to go beyond simply maintaining a professional demeanor and consciously attempt to build rapport with the deponent. You usually want deponents to volunteer information and to provide full and complete answers to your questions. But deponents often will not be naturally expansive and forthcoming in response to your questions. Many deponents are unhappy at the prospect of being deposed. They may be upset by the disturbance to their daily routine, angry about having to testify in what they consider a frivolous case, or apprehensive about having to engage in and perhaps lose a battle of wits with you. Emotions such as these tend to restrict the flow of information through the brain.

If the deponent is an adverse party, or one who is closely identified with an adverse party, the deponent is likely to be reluctant to give expansive answers out of fear that anything the deponent says will help your case. And in all likelihood, defending counsel has met with the deponent shortly before the deposition and said something along the lines of:

> "The lawyer who will be questioning you is not your friend; the lawyer will be trying to help the other side, not us. Don't give any more information than an honest answer requires. Just answer the questions that are asked and say nothing more. Don't volunteer anything."[4]

When you are able to build rapport with the deponent you can mitigate such impediments and encourage a deponent to be expansive in response to your questions. For example, being pleasant rather than antagonistic may demonstrate to an apprehensive deponent that the deposition is not as bad an experience as the deponent had feared. If so, the deponent may, consciously or unconsciously, be-

4. For a discussion of the wisdom and propriety of giving such advice, see Chapter 23.

come more relaxed and willing to provide expansive responses.

Techniques for building rapport with a deponent include:

* Show interest in deponents' answers.

    * Watch deponents as they testify.

    * If you want to defer discussion of a topic which the deponent seems to feel is important, explicitly tell the deponent that you will come back to that topic (e.g. "We'll discuss that subject in a moment.") Doing so overtly lets the deponent know that you have heard what the deponent has said.

* As your questioning leaves one subject and begins another, explicitly indicate that you are moving to a new subject.

    * "Mr. Deponent, I'd now like to turn your attention to a different matter. I want to talk about how you first learned about problems at the Sawyer Avenue job site."

Explicitly telling a deponent that you are moving to a new topic tends to help a deponent more readily understand your questions; it also tends to minimize ambiguities in the deposition transcript.

* In some instances you may build rapport by empathizing with a deponent. For instance:

    * You represent the defendant doctor in a medical malpractice case involving a claim for loss of consortium. You might empathize with the

adverse party's likely reaction to questioning about the loss of consortium aspect of the claim:

"Mr. West, we'll take a short recess. When we go back on the record I am going to have to ask you some questions about your claim for loss of consortium. I realize that these questions may be difficult for you because I have to ask you about very personal matters relating to your relationship with your wife. Please understand that it is my professional obligation to inquire into these matters and I will try not to pry unreasonably. If you'd like, we can take a longer break so you'll have time to confer with your lawyer in private about the type of information I'll be seeking when we resume the deposition."

In some cases, building rapport with the deponent can also enhance the likelihood of settlement. Fair and reasonable deposition behavior on your part may help you to reduce (or at least avoid exacerbating) any feelings of personal animosity between the parties or counsel. And personal animosity is likely to impede settlement. On the other hand, an adverse party may consider antagonistic deposition behavior to be a continuation of the harm your client has already caused. For instance, a plaintiff who is a former employee in a wrongful termination case may believe that your client, the employer, mistreated her. If so, antagonistic behavior on your part may make the plaintiff less likely to settle because she sees the deposition behavior as simply another form of mistreatment.

CHAPTER 15

RESPONDING TO OBJECTIONS AND OTHER ACTIONS OF OPPOSING COUNSEL

This Chapter reviews strategies for responding to an opposing counsel's objections and instructions not to answer under the Federal Rules of Civil Procedure. The Chapter also discusses some improper deposition tactics and strategies opposing counsel might employ and how you might respond to them.

1. Instructions Not to Answer

Lawyers can properly instruct deponents not to answer questions only in limited circumstances. This section explains those circumstances, then sets out strategies you can follow when opposing counsel's instruction not to answer is improper.

A. The Propriety of Instructions Not to Answer

Attorneys may properly instruct deponents to refuse to answer questions **only** in the following three instances:[1]

(1) The question invades a recognized privilege;[2]

1. FRCP 30(c)(2).

2. FRCP 30(c)(2) uses only the term privilege, but courts agree that work product falls within the definition of privilege as

277

(2) The question disregards a prior court-ordered limitation on discovery;

(3) The attorney instructing the deponent not to answer immediately terminates the deposition to seek a protective order on the grounds that the deposition is being conducted in bad faith or in such manner as to unreasonably annoy, embarrass, or oppress the deponent or a party.

B. *Responding to Invalid Instructions Not to Answer*

Only by going to court and obtaining an "Order to Compel Answers" can you compel an answer from a deponent who refuses to answer a question pursuant to opposing counsel's improper instruction. However, by taking the following steps you may be able to avoid the delay and expense of seeking such an order. If you nevertheless do have to make a motion to compel an answer, these steps

used in 30(d). See Roper v. Exxon Corp., No. CIV. A. 97–1971, 1998 WL 341838, *2 (E.D. La. June 25, 1998) ("If at any time during the examination of the witnesses it appears that a question calls for the disclosure of privileged communications or attorney work product, defendant is free to employ the procedure authorized by Fed. R. Civ. P. 30(d)(1) and (3) to protect such privileged information."); Tuerkes–Beckers, Inc. v. New Castle Assocs., 158 F.R.D. 573, 575 (D. Del. 1993) ("Counsel may not instruct a witness not to answer a question, unless (1) answering the question would require the disclosure of information that is protected from disclosure as privileged or work product. . . ."); Banks v. Senate Sergeant-at-Arms, 241 F.R.D. 376 (D.D.C. 2007); SEC v. Nacchio, 614 F. Supp. 2d 1164, 1176–77 (D. Colo. 2009); SEC v. Buntrock, 217 F.R.D. 441, 444–45 (N.D. Ill. 2003). For a general discussion of what privileges are recognized by Federal courts, see Wright & Graham, Federal Practice and Procedure: Evidence § 5421.

increase the likelihood that a judge will grant your motion and sanction your adversary.

1. On the Record, Ask Your Adversary to Withdraw the Instruction

The best first step to obtaining an answer is to indicate on the record why you believe that opposing counsel has no proper basis for issuing the instruction.[3] For example, if opposing counsel instructed the deponent not to answer on the ground that your question calls for privileged information, you would respond by pointing out why it does not. You should begin with this conciliatory approach for a number of reasons:

* Especially if your comments are low-key and non-threatening in tone, opposing counsel may listen and take them seriously, and perhaps withdraw the instruction.

* The FRCP require that you confer or attempt to confer in good faith with opposing counsel to try to secure answers before seeking a court order compelling an answer.[4] Your politely pointing out the error of opposing counsel's ways constitutes partial compliance with this requirement.

* If your motion seeks sanctions, your explanation can prove particularly important. A judge is more likely to award sanctions when the deposition record indicates that the questioner gave the

3. You may want to direct counsel's attention to the applicable provisions of the FRCP 30(c) and (d) to support your claim that the instruction not to answer is improper.

4. See FRCP 26(c)(1) and 37(a)(3)(B).

recalcitrant party a thorough explanation about why the instruction not to answer was improper.[5]

2. *Put the Deponent's Refusal to Answer on the Record*

If your adversary continues to instruct the deponent not to answer, place the deponent's refusal to answer on the record. One way to do this is to ask the court reporter to repeat the question and then ask the deponent, "Do you refuse to answer that question?" The record then clearly demonstrates that the deponent will not answer in the absence of a court order. Also, ask the deponent if the refusal to answer is based on the advice of counsel. Doing so may increase the likelihood that a judge will order opposing counsel to pay your attorney's fees in connection with any successful motion that you may make to compel the deponent to answer.[6]

3. *Complete Your Questioning With Respect to the Subject Matter of the Question the Deponent Refuses to Answer*

You can realize a number of benefits by completing your questioning with respect to the subject matter of the question that the deponent refuses to answer:

* You find out whether opposing counsel intends to block all your efforts to uncover the information you seek. If opposing counsel instructs the deponent not to answer the additional questions and you later seek a court order compelling an-

5. See FRCP 37(a)(5).

6. See FRCP 37(a)(5).

swers, a single motion can encompass all the questions that the deponent refused to answer.

* The additional questions indicate the scope of your inquiry, making it likely that any court order you obtain will be broad enough to elicit the information you're seeking.

* The additional questions may convey a message that you are genuinely interested in exploring the subject matter, perhaps causing opposing counsel to withdraw the instruction.

* The additional questions may allow opposing counsel to make a graceful retreat. Opposing counsel can choose not to object to the additional questions, allowing you to obtain the information you want while not causing opposing counsel to lose face in front of a client by having to withdraw a previously given instruction.

The following examples illustrate the strategies for responding when opposing counsel improperly instructs a deponent not to answer.

Example 1 (Responding to an Instruction Based on an Invalid Claim of Work Product Privilege)

In a case involving the crash of a small commuter airplane, you are counsel for plaintiff and are deposing Ms. Herman, the airline employee who investigated the accident. The deposition proceeds as follows:

1. You: Ms. Herman, after the accident, did you obtain witness statements from any of the plane's passengers?

2: Opposing Counsel: Objection. Work product privilege. I instruct her not to answer.

3. You: Counsel, my question does not go to the content of any statement or document and therefore is not within the work product rule.[7] Perhaps if my question went to the contents of a witness statement, your objection might be well taken. But since my question merely asks about the existence of a statement, work product does not apply.

4. Opposing Counsel: I'm still instructing the witness not to answer.

5. You: Counsel, can you please spell out your basis for saying that work product applies in these circumstances? That's required by FRCP 26 (b)(5).

6. Opposing Counsel: I'm instructing the witness not to answer because her investigation after the accident is covered by work product in that she was assigned to investigate the accident by the airline.

7. You: Ms. Herman, on the basis of counsel's instructions are you refusing to answer my question about whether, after the accident, you obtained witness statements from any of the plane's passengers?

8. A: Yes I am.

7. The work product privilege applies only to documents and tangible things prepared in anticipation of litigation. See FRCP 26(b)(3).

9.   You: After the accident, did you talk with any of the plane's passengers?

10.   Opposing Counsel: I instruct you not to answer on the grounds of work product.

11.   You: Ms. Herman, on the basis of counsel's instructions are you refusing to answer my question about whether, after the accident, you talked with any of the plane's passengers?

12.   A: Yes I am.

13.   You: After the accident what are the names, if any, of the plane's passengers with whom you had conversations?

14.   Opposing Counsel: Same instruction on the same ground.

15.   You: Ms. Herman on the basis of counsel's instructions are you refusing to answer my question about what are the names of any of the plane's passengers with whom you had conversations after the accident?

16.   A: Yes I am.

17.   You: While you were investigating the accident, did you see any evidence indicating that there was a fire on the plane before it crashed?

18.   Opposing Counsel: Same instruction on the same ground.

19.   You: Ms. Herman, on the basis of counsel's instructions are you refusing to answer my question about whether, while you were investigating the accident, you saw any evidence indicating

that there was a fire on the plane before it crashed?

20.   A: Yes I am.

In No. 3, you try to get the adversary to withdraw the instruction by explaining why the instruction is improper. In No. 5, you remind opposing counsel of the obligation to spell out the facts indicating that the privilege applies. In Nos. 9, 13, and 17, you ask additional questions pertaining to the subject matter you intend to pursue. In Nos. 7, 11, 15 and 19, you make sure that the record explicitly indicates that the deponent refuses to answer based on advice of counsel.

Example 2 (Responding to an Improper Instruction Based on Claim Other than Privilege)

Your adversary may issue improper instructions not to answer on grounds other than privilege. For example, opposing counsel may object and instruct a deponent not to answer on the ground that your question is "vague," "calls for information not reasonably calculated to lead to the discovery of admissible evidence," "calls for an inadmissible opinion or speculation," has been "asked and answered," etc. Even though objections on such grounds may be valid, they cannot justify an instruction not to answer if the questions don't seek privileged information or violate a court order.[8] And you may respond

8.   Opposing counsel may issue such improper instructions for a variety of reasons: ignorance of the rules, to impress a client, to intimidate or harass a deposing lawyer, or to attempt to prevent the disclosure of damaging information.

to these improper instructions just as you do to instructions based on an illegitimate claim of privilege. Consider the following illustrative example:

1. You: Mr. Foster, who owns stock in the Wiltern Corporation?

2: Opposing Counsel: Objection. That's irrelevant and not reasonably calculated to lead to the discovery of admissible evidence. This case isn't about the shareholders, it's about whether the Wiltern Corporation is liable for what you allege was a defective product. I instruct the witness not to answer.

3. You: Counsel, as I'm sure you know, you are not authorized to instruct the witness not to answer unless my question calls for privileged information or unless you are terminating the deposition to seek a protective order. That's the rule stated in 30(d)(1) of the FRCP. I have a copy of the rule right here if you and your client would like to look at it. Since my question clearly doesn't call for privileged information, I'm entitled to have an answer unless you are going to terminate the deposition to seek a protective order. Otherwise, the witness should answer and, if necessary, the court can rule later on whether your objection is well taken.

4. Opposing Counsel: That's your interpretation of the rules. I'm still instructing the witness not to answer unless you can explain to me why this information is relevant.

5. You: Counsel, I'm not obligated to explain the legal theory on which my question is based in order to get an answer. However, if Mr. Foster or any of his friends or family own a substantial amount of stock in the Wiltern, they may suffer financial loss as a result of this case, and that may go to bias.

6. Opposing Counsel: I'm still instructing the witness not to answer.

7. You [To Reporter]: Would you read back the pending question please? [Question is read back.] Mr. Foster, on the basis of counsel's instructions are you refusing to answer that question?

8. A: Yes I am.

9. You: Mr. Foster, let me make my inquiry a bit narrower. Do you own any stock in the Wiltern Corporation?

10. A: Yes. I own about 80% of the stock.

11. And does anyone in your family, other than you, own any stock in the corporation?

12 A: Yes. My brother owns about 10% and....

In this example, you first explain why the instruction is improper (No. 3). When you fail to persuade opposing counsel to withdraw the instruction, you provide a brief explanation of why the question is proper (No. 5). As you indicate, you are not <u>required</u> to provide this explanation, but doing so may persuade an opponent to withdraw the instruction.[9]

---

9. You would be particularly <u>unlikely</u> to explain why your question is legitimate if doing so would educate the witness or

When the instruction still stands (as it does in this example at No. 6), you put the deponent's refusal to answer on the record (Nos. 7 and 8). Then you go on with additional questions in the same subject area (Nos. 9–12). If, as happens in this example, the deponent is allowed to answer these questions, you've obtained the desired information while allowing opposing counsel to "save face" by not having to explicitly withdraw the instruction not to answer in front of the client.[10] Of course, had opposing counsel instructed the deponent not to answer any questions pertaining to stock ownership, you would have to either move to compel or forgo this information.

C. *Obtain an Order Compelling an Answer*

After you respond to an improper instruction not to answer as described in the previous section, opposing counsel may continue to refuse to withdraw the instruction. If you still want answers to your questions, you have two choices:[11]

opposing counsel about one of your legal theories. For example, you would not want to explain how your questions seek information that tends to establish a statute of limitations defense, especially if opposing counsel has not yet focused on that issue. Mentioning the statute of limitations defense might lead deponents to shape their testimony so as to vitiate the defense.

10. You may want to delay until later in the deposition any inquiry into the area where counsel has instructed the deponent not to answer. The delay makes it easier for opposing counsel to save face by permitting you to inquire into the subject area without having to appear to back down in front of her client.

11. You may, of course, decide to do nothing about an improper instruction not to answer. For example, you may decide that the information you might obtain from an answer is not

* Terminate a deposition immediately and move for an order to compel answers; or

* Complete your deposition questioning on all matters except those that the deponent has refused to answer, and then terminate the deposition and seek an order to compel answers.[12]

If you choose the first alternative, a deposition may proceed as follows:

1.   You [To Reporter]: Would you read back the pending question please? [Question is read back] Mr. Foster, on the basis of counsel's instructions are you refusing to answer that question?

2.   A: Yes I am.

3.   You: Counsel, if you do not withdraw the instruction not to answer, I will terminate the deposition at once and move the court for an order compelling the deponent to answer.

4:   Opposing Counsel: My instruction not to answer stands.

5.   You: Very well. I have not finished questioning your client, but at this time I am terminating the deposition to seek an order compelling your client to answer the questions he has refused to answer at this deposition.

You would follow up a with motion for an order compelling the deponent to answer and for sanc-

worth the time and trouble involved in seeking a court order to compel the deponent to answer.

12.   See FRCP 37(a)(3)(B).

tions against your opponent.[13] The advantages of this first alternative are that:

* You might cause your opponent to reconsider and withdraw the instruction not to answer.

* A successful motion to compel will probably discourage opposing counsel from issuing similar improper instructions when the deposition resumes.

* By the time the deposition resumes, you will have had additional time to prepare. In effect, you have two opportunities to depose a witness.

At the same time, this first alternative has its downsides. You commit to the time and expense of a motion to compel. You must wait until the deposition resumes to obtain the remainder of the deponent's testimony. Moreover, your motion may be unsuccessful even though it is based on grounds that are technically accurate. If so, an emboldened opposing counsel may be more aggressive when the deposition resumes.

If you decide to pursue the second alternative, you would conclude the deposition questioning on matters other than those the deponent has refused to answer. Then you would indicate on the record that you are reserving the right to move to compel with respect to questions the deponent has refused

13. You are entitled to sanctions under FRCP 30(d)(2) and (3). The advisory committee notes make clear that sanctions are appropriate under FRCP 30(d) for improper instructions not to answer. See FRCP 30 advisory committee notes on 1993 amendments, reprinted in 146 F.R.D. 665 (1993).

to answer, and necessary follow-up questions. You can then later decide if the withheld information is sufficiently important to justify the time and expense of seeking a court order.[14]

Court rules in many jurisdictions offer a third and far less costly and complicated alternative. A judge (or magistrate) may be available by telephone to resolve disputes relating to instructions not to answer. In these jurisdictions, you recess a deposition and telephone a judge (or magistrate). After the court reporter reads the questions to which the dispute pertains, both counsel can be heard on the propriety of the instructions not to answer. Typically, the judge or magistrate issues a ruling "on the spot" and the deposition can resume immediately.

2. Responding to Objections

Objections are far more common than instructions not to answer. The following subsections set forth strategies for responding to objections to questions.

14. See, e.g., <u>Armstrong v. Hussmann Corp.</u>, 163 F.R.D. 299 (E.D. Mo. 1995). The Federal Rules are silent about how much time you have to decide whether to move to compel an answer. But see <u>Kendrick v. Heckler</u>, 778 F.2d 253 (5th Cir. 1985) (granting motion to compel production of documents at deposition eight months after deposition completed); *In re Sulfuric Acid Antitrust Litigation*, 230 F.R.D. 527 (N.D. Ill. 2005) (Court denied a motion to compel further testimony because the plaintiff, after several delays, filed the motion on the last day discovery permitted); <u>Suntrust Bank v. Blue Water Fiber, L.P.</u>, 210 F.R.D. 196 (E.D. Mich. 2002) (Citing cases where motion to compel was denied because it was filed after discovery period had ended).

A. *Step One: Obtain an Answer*

Your usual initial response to an objection to your question should be to obtain an answer. Whether or not an objection is valid, **you are almost always entitled to an answer.**[15] This result follows from FRCP 30(c), which provides that when an objection is made at deposition, "the examination shall proceed, with the testimony being taken subject to the objections."[16] Because testimony is taken subject to

15. Of course, this assumes that opposing counsel does not combine an objection with an instruction not to answer. When the objection is combined with such an instruction, you will have to respond to the instruction as discussed in the previous section of this Chapter.

16. The courts have interpreted FRCP 30(c)(2) to mean what it says: questions must be answered notwithstanding an objection. See Eggleston v. Chicago Journeymen Plumbers' Local No. 130, 657 F.2d 890 (7th Cir. 1981); Ralston Purina Co. v. McFarland, 550 F.2d 967 (4th Cir. 1977); United States v. International Bus. Machines, Corp., 66 F.R.D. 180, 186 (S.D.N.Y. 1974) (relevance objections should be noted and the question answered) Cobell v. Norton, 213 F.R.D. 16, 26–27 (D.D.C. 2003); Redwood v. Dobson, 476 F.3d 462, 467–68 (7th Cir. 2007) (Even though deposing attorney was asking inappropriate and not relevant questions, court says the witness's counsel's behavior was a clear violation of FRCP 30(d)(4) "he told [the witness] not to answer, which was untenable as no claim of privilege had been advanced."); Pilates, Inc. v. Georgetown Bodyworks Deep Muscle Massage Ctrs., Inc., 201 F.R.D. 261 (D.D.C. 2000) (Most of the objections by counsel were not based on privilege, so witness was ordered re-deposed and directed to answer questions where privilege was not asserted); Amari Co. v. Burgess, 2009 WL 1269704 (N.D. Ill. 2009). You are not, however, entitled to abuse your position as examining counsel by, for example, insisting on answers to (1) highly argumentative questions; (2) questions clearly beyond the scope of discovery, especially when they seek personal information; or (3) questions which you have asked repeatedly despite having previously received a fully responsive answer from the deponent. If you engage in such tactics, oppos-

objections, the court need not rule on the validity of objections made at deposition until after the deposition is complete. This approach saves a great deal of time and money because deposing counsel does not have to run to court to get a ruling on every objection in order to obtain an answer.

When faced with an objection, you typically respond as follows:

You: Who are the people who own stock in the Wiltern Corporation?

Opposing Counsel: Objection. Irrelevant and not reasonably calculated to lead to the discovery of admissible evidence.

You: Will you answer the question please?

A: Well, I own some and. . . .

Obtaining answers to objected-to questions is usually in your best interests. If you had a good reason to ask the question in the first place, you want it answered regardless of the objection. Indeed, your adversary's primary motive in objecting might be to coax you into rewording a question that if answered honestly would reveal important information. Thus, rephrasing a question so as to obviate an evidentiary problem may alter a deponent's answer, causing you to do without information you might have otherwise obtained.

The general rule, "obtain answers even in the face of valid objections," is of course subject to

ing counsel may terminate the deposition and move for a protective order and sanctions against you. See FRCP 30(d)(2).

common sense exceptions. If you can easily reword a question without altering its meaning, or if you realize that a question is hopelessly ambiguous or confusing, you can keep the record clear by simply withdrawing the question and rephrasing it.

When you decide to obtain an answer to an objected-to question, you can proceed in at least two different ways. After the objection has been made, you can respond by asking a deponent to answer the question. Alternatively, if a deponent cannot recall the question, you can ask the court reporter to read it back and then ask a deponent to answer it. Consider the following examples:

Example 1

1. A: We left the meeting and went out to her car.

2. You: And when you left, you intended to go to the Red Rooster because it was the bar closest by, correct?

3. Opposing Counsel: Objection. Vague with respect to "you" and assumes facts not in evidence.

4. You: Would you answer the question please?

5. A: Yes; that's why we intended to go the Red Rooster.

Example 2

1. A: We left the meeting and went out to her car.

2. You: And when you left, you intended to go to the Red Rooster because it was the bar closest by, correct?

3. Opposing Counsel: Objection. Vague with respect to "you" and assumes facts not in evidence.

4. You: Would you answer the question please?

5. A: I don't remember the question.

6. You: Ms. Reporter, will you please read back the last question?

7. Reporter: And when you left, you intended to go to the Red Rooster because it was the bar closest by, correct?

8. You: Please answer the question.

9. A: Yes, that's true.

B. Step Two: Decide Whether a Valid Objection Is Curable

Since you are normally entitled to answers even in the face of valid objections, why should you ever care about deposition objections? The reason is that under FRCP 32(a), if you do not "cure" (overcome) a <u>valid</u> deposition objection, you may be unable to later use the deposition testimony to support a motion or at trial.[17] Consider the application of Rule 32(a) in the context of the following example:

17. FRCP 32(a)(1)(B) provides that deposition testimony may not be used for any purpose at trial or in connection with a motion if the deposition testimony would not be admissible under the rules of evidence if the deponent were testifying in person at trial.

You: Why was Ms. Carlson upset after the meeting you had with her?

Opposing Counsel: Objection. Calls for speculation and lack of foundation.

You: Would you answer the question please?

A: I suppose she thought that Mr. Stark would probably get the promotion and she wouldn't. She thought she was going to be passed over.

Opposing counsel's objection is well taken because, at trial, a witness generally cannot speculate or guess about the state of mind of another person. Therefore, although you are entitled to an answer at deposition, your failure to cure the problem raised by the objection probably means that Rule 32 (a) prevents you from later using the answer to support a motion or at trial.

Because failure to cure a problem raised by a valid objection can prevent your using deposition testimony later in the case, after obtaining an answer, you should generally evaluate the objection's validity. An objection is valid if it might be sustained by a judge if the deponent were testifying live in court.[18]

If you are comfortable that an objection is obviously <u>invalid</u>, you may safely ignore it and proceed with further questioning.

Often reasonable judges can disagree about whether an objection is valid. For example, one judge might find a question to be objectionable as

18. See FRCP 32(a)(1)(B).

"vague," while another judge might find the exact same question to be sufficiently clear to render a "vague" objection invalid. Therefore, if you think that a judge <u>might</u> uphold an objection, you need to think about finding a cure that can make a deposition answer available for use in support of a motion or at trial. To illustrate how you might cure an arguably valid objection, consider the following example:

Example

1. A: We left the meeting and went out to her car.

2. You: And when you left, you intended to go to the Red Rooster because it was the bar closest by, correct?

3. Opposing Counsel: Objection. Vague with respect to "you" and assumes facts not in evidence.

4. You: Would you answer the question please?

5. A: Yes; that's why we intended to go the Red Rooster.

6. You: As far as you knew at the time, the Red Rooster was the bar closest to the meeting, is that correct?

7. A. Yes, as far as I knew.

8. You: Did you intend to go to that bar when you left the meeting?

9. A: Yes.

10. You: At that time did you intend to go to the Red Rooster bar because you thought it was the bar closest to the meeting?

11.   A: Yes.

12.   You: When you left the meeting, did Ms. Boskin say anything about going to the Red Rooster bar?

13.   A: We discussed it as we left the meeting. She told me she wanted to go to the Red Rooster because it was the closest place to get a drink.

Here, you first obtain an answer to the original question (No. 5). You then use questions Nos. 6, 8, 10, and 12 to cure the arguably valid objections of "vague" and "assuming facts not in evidence."

Of course, not all answers are equally important, and deposition time may be precious. Therefore, you'll have to exercise judgment when deciding which objections to try to cure. Situations in which you may decide not to cure include the following:

* The information in a deponent's answer is insignificant.

* You are certain that you will not want to use deposition testimony later in the case for any purpose.[19]

* You ask a question only to develop leads to other sources of information, and the answer has already provided those leads. For example, as-

19.   You can rarely be certain that you will not want to use deposition testimony later in the case. It is often difficult to predict what deposition testimony would later be useful, especially when you are in the early stages of a case. And even when the deposition testimony is somewhat harmful to your case, if the

sume that you are only interested in learning the names of a company's CEO and CFO. When you ask for this information, your adversary objects that the question is "compound," and the deponent answers the question. Even if the objection is valid, having obtained the desired information you might well decide not to cure the objection.

While you may choose not to cure some valid objections, other objections you will be unable to cure. For example, you won't be able to cure a valid "lack of foundation" objection if the deponent is unable to provide the necessary foundation. For instance, assume that your adversary objects that a document identified by a deponent is hearsay. You could cure the objection by eliciting foundational evidence that the document qualifies as a business record.[20] However, if the deponent cannot personally testify to the record's "mode of preparation," you won't be able to cure the objection during the deposition of that deponent.

Section 3 below illustrates how to cure many common deposition objections, and reviews those which generally need not be cured.

3. Objections Commonly Raised at Deposition

Below are two lists of common deposition objections. Those in Section **A** are typically curable; those in Section **B** typically need not be cured.

deponent later changes his story you may decide to impeach the deponent with the inconsistent deposition testimony to attack his credibility.

20. FRE 803(6).

A. *Common Objections That Can Often Be Cured*

You can often cure the following objections with additional questioning.

—Compound

A question is compound if it is essentially two questions phrased as one.

* Example of Problem: "Who was at the party and which of them had you met previously?"

* Example of Cure: Break the question into two or more subparts: (a) "Who was at the party?" (b) "Which of them had you met previously?"

—Assumes Facts Not in Evidence

A question assumes facts not in evidence when it incorporates into a question information to which a deponent has not already testified.

* Example of Problem: A deponent who has not testified to talking to a Mr. Pell prior to a meeting is asked: "When you and Mr. Pell met before the termination meeting, what did you talk about?"

* Example of Cure: Ask a question which establishes the assumed fact: "Did you and Mr. Pell meet before the termination meeting?"

—Vague

A question is vague when a deponent cannot be reasonably certain of the information being sought.

* Example of Problem: "Before that meeting, what was going on between you and Mr. Pell?" Here, a deponent may reasonably be uncertain about the meaning of the phrase "what was going on."

* Example of Cure: "What did you and Mr. Pell talk about prior to the meeting?"

—Calls for a Narrative

A question "calls for a narrative" when it is overly broad in scope and permits a deponent to testify to inadmissible evidence before opposing counsel can object to it.

* Example of Problem: 'Please tell me everything that led up to the decision to purchase the new computer system."

* Example of Cure: Narrower, more focused questions, such as, "Did you attend any meetings in which the purchase of the new computer system was discussed?" If the answer is yes, then you might continue by saying, "Please tell me what happened at the first

meeting in which purchasing a new computer system was discussed."

—Argumentative

An argumentative question asserts counsel's argument or comment on the testimony in the form of a question.

* Examples of Problem: "Doesn't the fact that you can't remember who was present show that you never were at that meeting?" "Since Mrs. Green's report was written right after the meeting, why shouldn't we believe Mrs. Green's report rather than your testimony."

* Example of Cure: Delete any comment on the testimony and ask only for information that might support your argument. "Do you believe Mrs. Green's report is inaccurate?" "Why do you think it is inaccurate?"

—Leading

A leading question is one which typically seeks a "yes" or "no" answer and suggests the answer desired by the questioner. If you are deposing an adverse witness, you may ignore this objection since leading questions are in this situation permitted.[21] If the depo-

---

21. FRE 611(c). See Wright & Gold, Federal Practice and Procedure: Evidence § 6168; see also <u>Haney v. Mizell Memorial</u>

nent is not an adverse witness, leading questions are usually improper.

* Example of Problem: "Isn't it true that you met with Mr. Pell before the meeting?"

* Example of Cure: "Did you meet with Mr. Pell before you went to the meeting?"

—Misquotes or Mischaracterizes the Testimony

A question that misstates what a deponent said earlier in the deposition falls into this category.

* Example of Problem: You ask a deponent who had testified that your client "shouted" during a performance review, "When my client raised her voice during the performance review, do you think anyone outside your office could have heard what my client said to you at that time?"

* Examples of Cure: You may cure the problem by restating the question and correcting the mischaracterization:

Hosp., 744 F.2d 1467 (11th Cir. 1984); Ellis v. City of Chicago, 667 F.2d 606 (7th Cir. 1981); Stahl v. Sun Microsystems, Inc., 775 F.Supp. 1397 (D. Colo. 1991). For a discussion of the meaning of "hostile" witness, see Wright & Gold, Federal Practice and Procedure: Evidence § 6168; Thomas v. Cardwell, 626 F.2d 1375 (9th Cir. 1980); United States v. Brown, 603 F.2d 1022 (1st Cir. 1979); Rossano v. Blue Plate Foods, Inc., 314 F.2d 174 (5th Cir. 1963).

"When my client allegedly shouted during the performance review...." You may also simply delete the reference to the prior testimony: "During the performance review, do you think anyone outside your office could have heard what my client said to you at that time?"

—Lack of Personal Knowledge (Lack of Foundation)

These objections are appropriate when the record does not indicate that a deponent had first-hand knowledge.

* Example of Problem: You ask, "What did Ms. Julian do after she left the meeting?" However, the record doesn't indicate that the deponent was in a position to know what Ms. Julian did after she left the meeting.

* Example of Cure: Establish the deponent's personal knowledge: "Did you see Ms. Julian after she left the meeting?"

—Calls for Speculation

This objection is similar to the objection for lack of personal knowledge. The objection is appropriate when the question asks a deponent to testify about a matter which the deponent would appear to have no basis for knowing.

* Example of Problem: You ask, "Why was Ms. Julian worried about the decision to purchase computers?" The question calls for speculation because a deponent cannot perceive another's thoughts.

* Example of Cure: Establish the deponent's personal knowledge: "Did Ms. Julian tell you what she thought about the decision to purchase computers?"

—Inadmissible Opinion

This objection asserts that an opinion of a lay witness is (a) not rationally based on the deponent's perceptions or (b) not helpful to a clear understanding of the deponent's testimony.[22]

* Example of Problem: A deponent who testified that "I caught a quick glimpse of the driver" is asked, "Did the driver appear to be driving carefully?" (A "quick glimpse" may be insufficient for the opinion to be rationally based on the deponent's perceptions.)

* Example of Cure: Try to establish that the deponent has an adequate basis for the opinion: "How long did you

22. See FRE 701.

watch the driver?" "Over what distance?"

This objection can also raise the issue of whether a question calls for an expert opinion from a witness who has not been qualified as an expert. You can cure this problem if you can qualify the deponent as an expert for the opinion you seek.

—Hearsay

Whether you can cure a valid hearsay objection typically depends on whether you can elicit foundational evidence satisfying a hearsay exception or exemption.[23]

* Example of Problem: You ask a deponent who saw an automobile accident, "What did the passenger in the defendant's car say when you first went over to the car?"

* Example of Cure: Elicit foundational evidence establishing that the passenger's statement falls within the "excited utterance" exception to the hearsay rule: "How long after the collision did you speak to the passenger?" "What was the passenger's demeanor at the time you spoke to the passenger?"

23. See FRE 801, 803, 804.

—Lack of Foundation For, or Failure to Authenticate a Document

Opposing counsel may object "lack of foundation" or "failure to authenticate" when you refer to or use a document at deposition. You can cure these objections by laying the proper foundation for the document.[24]

—Violates the Best Evidence Rule

This objection may assert that you've used a copy instead of the original of a document, or that you've attempted to prove the contents of a document through oral testimony.[25]

* Example of Problem: "What did the report say about the reason for the decline in sales?"

* Example of Cure: Authenticate the report, ask the deponent to read from it and ask the court reporter to attach a copy to the deposition transcript.

B. *Objections That Usually Need Not Be Cured*

The following objections generally need not be cured at deposition.

24. For a discussion of the proper foundation for documents, see Chapter 10.

25. See FRE 1002–1007.

—Asked and Answered

This objection asserts that the same question has already been asked and answered previously in the deposition. This objection is typically inappropriate at deposition.[26] Consequently, you need only ask for an answer to your question in the face of this objection. You need do nothing to "cure" the objection.[27]

—Inadmissible Legal Conclusion

If your question asks for an improper legal conclusion, you're entitled to an answer, but you can do nothing to cure the objection.

26. See, e.g., Caplan v. Fellheimer, Eichen, Braverman, & Kaskey, 161 F.R.D. 29, 32 (E.D. Pa. 1995) ("During the course of a routine deposition, a lawyer is free to revisit areas already examined, so long as that does not become oppressive or harassing"). See also Applied Telematics, Inc. v. Sprint Corp., No. 94-CV-4603, 1995 WL 79237, at *2 (E.D. Pa. Feb. 22,1995); First Tennessee Bank v. Fed. Deposit Ins. Corp., 108 F.R.D. 640, 641 (D.C. Tenn. 1985). But Cf. State Farm Mut. Auto. Ins. Co. v. Dowdy, 445 F. Supp. 2d 1289, 1293 (N.D. Okla. 2006) (Indicating this objections is waived if not made at the deposition.); Kansas Wastewater, Inc. v. Alliant Techsystems, Inc., 217 F.R.D. 525 (D. Kan. 2003) (No objection at deposition that question was asked and answered, so it was waived because it was an issue that could have been cured).

27. You are not, of course, entitled to ask the same question an unlimited number of times. At some point, repeating the exact same question and insisting on an answer may constitute harassment. If so, opposing counsel may terminate the deposition to seek a protective order. See Chapter 24.

—Irrelevant

> Typically, you need do nothing to cure this objection; testimony is usually either relevant or it is not. However, if you think the relevance of the information you are seeking is obscure or unclear, you may decide to ask additional questions to demonstrate that the testimony sought by the objected to questions is indeed relevant.

—Not Reasonably Calculated to Lead to Admissible Evidence

> You generally need not cure this objection; testimony is usually either reasonably calculated to lead to the discovery of admissible evidence or it is not.[28]

4. Objections to Improper Answers

Thus far, the Chapter has focused on objections to questions. Of course, an adversary may object to deponents' answers as well as to your questions.

---

28. FRCP 26(b)(1) provides that <u>relevant</u> information is discoverable if it is reasonably calculated to lead to the discovery of admissible evidence. However, this same provision limits discovery, absent a court order, to information that is relevant to the claim or defense of any party; while information that is only relevant to the subject matter of the action is discoverable only if a court so orders. It is not clear how these recent amendments will effect the scope of permissible questioning at deposition. It would appear, however, that at a minimum, information that is reasonably calculated to lead to the discovery of admissible evidence with respect to a claim or defense of a party should be discoverable at deposition. For a further discussion of the effect of the 2000 amendment to FRCP 26(b)(1), see Wright, Miller & Marcus: Federal Practice and Procedure: Civil 2d. § 2008.

Most commonly, an adversary objects to an answer on the grounds that it is non-responsive.[29] An objection to an answer is usually accompanied by a motion to strike the answer from the record.

A. *The Answer Is Non–Responsive*

An objection that an answer is non-responsive is generally curable. To cure, ask a question that renders the answer responsive. You then may want to re-ask the original question that produced the non-responsive answer. Consider the following example.

1. You: When Mr. Smith came to your office on the fourth and asked to renegotiate the loan, were you suspicious about what he said regarding why he wanted to renegotiate the loan?

2. A: When Mr. Smith came in on the fourth, he was already in default.

3. Opposing Counsel: Objection; move to strike. The answer is non-responsive.

4. You: When Mr. Smith came into your office on the fourth and asked to renegotiate the loan, what was the status of his loan at that time?

5. A. His loan was in default. He was at least three months behind in his payments.

6. You: When Mr. Smith asked to renegotiate the loan on the fourth, were you suspicious about

29. Additionally, objections to answers can be simply a delayed objection to your question. As such, an objection to an answer can raise any of the objections that might have been timely raised to a question.

what he said regarding why he wanted to renegotiate the loan?

7.   A: Yes.

No. 4 is a question that renders the answer in No. 2 responsive. No. 6 is an attempt to obtain an answer to the initial question.

B. The Objection to the Answer Raises a Potential Problem With the Question

An adversary may object to an answer on the same grounds as to a question. And if the objection is valid and would have been curable if made to a question, you should cure in the same way as if the objection followed the question. Consider the following example, in which your adversary makes "lack of personal knowledge" and "lack of foundation" objections following an answer.

1.   You: What physical defects, if any, did Ms. Bird have at that time?

2.   A: She was hard of hearing.

3.   Opposing Counsel: Objection; move to strike. There is no showing that the deponent has personal knowledge that Ms. Bird was hard of hearing. There was no foundation for that question.

4.   You: At that time, did you think that Ms. Bird was hard of hearing?

5.   A: Yes I did.

6.   You: What made you think that at that time Ms. Bird was hard of hearing?

7. A: She was wearing a hearing aid in her left ear. Also prior to that day, she was always telling me to speak louder because she had trouble hearing.

8. You: Is there any other reason that you felt that at that time Ms. Bird was hard of hearing?

9. A: Only that when her husband asked her a question, she didn't answer.

5. Responding to Inappropriate Behavior by Opposing Counsel

FRCP 30(c) provides that examination and cross examination of witnesses at deposition "may proceed as permitted at trial under the Federal Rules of Evidence except Rules 103 and 615,"[30] with all objections noted for the record, but testimony taken subject to objection. Rule 30(c) has been interpreted to mean that "counsel should not engage in any conduct during a deposition that would not be allowed in the presence of a judicial officer."[31] Unfor-

---

30. FRE 103 relates to objections and offers of proof and FRE 615 relates to the exclusion of witnesses at trial.

31. FRCP 30, advisory committee notes on 1993 amendments, reprinted in 146 F.R.D. 666 (1993). See also In re Amezaga, 195 B.R. 221, 227 (Bankr. D. P. R. 1996) ("[D]eposition procedures mirror the giving of testimony at trial with the exception of objections which are only noted for the record...."); Armstrong v. Hussmann Corp., 163 F.R.D. 299 (E.D. Mo. 1995); State Farm Mut. Auto. Ins. Co. v. Dowdy, 445 F. Supp. 2d 1289, 1292 (N.D. Okla. 2006). Of course, it is not literally true that opposing counsel must always behave as they would at trial. For example, opposing counsel is authorized to unilaterally terminate the witness' examination when necessary to seek a protective order. That does not happen at trial. Never-

tunately, attorneys sometimes conduct themselves during depositions in ways that clearly would not be tolerated at trial. This section discusses how to respond to such inappropriate behavior.

A. *Disruptive Statements or Objections*

Generally, an attorney defending a deposition is limited to making objections, instructing a deponent not to answer when appropriate, and entering into stipulations (if any) with examining counsel. Furthermore, objections must be stated in a concise, non-argumentative fashion.[32] It is thus improper for a defending attorney to make argumentative or frivolous objections or other statements that clutter up the record and disrupt the flow of your examination. Consider the following examples:

Example 1

1. You: Mr. Bean, did your brother ever meet the plaintiff?

2. Opposing Counsel: Objection. Irrelevant. You're never going to use that sort of information at trial. You're just wasting our time. Focus on the facts of the case, why don't you. If you want to go on a fishing expedition, do it on your own time and not ours. We've been here too long already, and now you're going into this stuff. My client and I will only stay here one more hour, and then we're leaving. So why don't you ask

theless, to the extent possible, both counsel should generally behave at deposition as they would at trial.

32. FRCP 30(c)(2).

something having to do with the facts of this case?

Example 2

1. You: Mr. Bean, did your brother ever meet the plaintiff?

2. Opposing Counsel: Objection. Irrelevant. I don't see how this is relevant, counsel. I'll be happy to have my client answer the question if you'll just explain why this information is or might be relevant to the case.

Example 3

1. You: Mr. Bean, did your brother ever meet the plaintiff?

2. Opposing Counsel: Objection. Irrelevant, vague and ambiguous, compound, and assumes facts not in evidence.

In the first example, opposing counsel makes a "speaking objection," i.e. an objection that violates FRCP 30(d)(1) because it does not constitute a concise, non-argumentative statement of the grounds of objection. A defending attorney may make such speeches in an attempt to intimidate you into limiting your inquiries into a particular matter or rushing through a deposition. Or, a speaking objection may be a defending attorney's way of impressing a client with the defender's zeal and willingness to "fight" for the client.

In the second example, opposing counsel uses another type of improper speaking objection to try to obtain information about your legal or factual theories. You are not, however, required to explain the theory supporting any of your questions to opposing counsel.

In the third example, the objections are concise. Yet they are clearly unfounded and therefore frivolous and in violation of the FRCP.[33] A defending attorney may repeatedly make such objections in an attempt to distract or irritate you.

The following strategies may help you successfully respond to an opposing counsel who persists in disruptive objections.

1. Ignore the Improper Tactics and Obtain an Answer

Do not let opposing counsel's improper tactics distract you. Regardless of the propriety of opposing counsel's conduct, you should almost always try to obtain an answer before responding to the tactics. That may require some persistence on your part, as the following example demonstrates.

1. You: Mr. Bean, did your brother ever meet the plaintiff?

2. Opposing Counsel: Objection. Irrelevant. You're never going to use that sort of information at trial. You're just wasting our time. Focus on the facts of the case, why don't you. If you want

33. See FRCP 30(d)(1) and (2). The advisory committee notes state that making an excessive number of "unnecessary objections may itself constitute sanctionable conduct" under FRCP 30(d)(3). FRCP 30, advisory committee notes on 1993 amendments, reprinted in 146 F.R.D. 666 (1993).

an answer to that question, you're going to have to explain why it is relevant.

3. You: Mr. Bean, would you answer my question, please?

4. Opposing Counsel: Are you deaf? I just asked for an explanation of the relevance of that information; that's the least you can do.

5. You: Mr. Bean, would you answer my question, please?

6. Opposing Counsel: Are you refusing to explain why the information is relevant?

7. You [To Opposing Counsel]: Yes. [To The Deponent]: Mr. Bean, would you answer my question, please?

8. Opposing Counsel: He doesn't have to answer unless you explain why it is relevant.

9. You: Mr. Bean, would you answer my question, please?

10. Opposing Counsel: I'll let him answer, but you'd better not take too long on this area, or I will instruct my client not to answer.

11. You: Mr. Bean, would you answer my question please?

12. A: They met at least.....

Ignoring inappropriate disruptive behavior and obtaining answers can be the quickest and easiest way to discourage such behavior and keep the deposition moving. Hopefully, opposing counsel will realize that you will not be distracted or goaded into explaining your legal or factual theories. Moreover, keeping your composure in the face of such tactics may send a signal to the adverse party that the party's lawyer is foolish and ineffective.

2. *Cure a Valid Underlying Objection*

Underlying a disruptive "speaking" objection may be a valid objection. For example, your adversary's "lack of foundation" objection may be valid even if the objection is accompanied by improperly disruptive argument. In such circumstances, respond to the objection as though it were properly stated. That is, after obtaining an answer, consider curing the problem as set forth earlier in this Chapter.

3. *Cite the Rules and Threaten to Seek a Protective Order*

If opposing counsel's disruptive behavior persists despite your attempts to ignore it, you may want to refer counsel to the applicable portion of the FRCP and threaten to move for a protective order. Here is an example:

1. You: Mr. Bean, did your brother ever meet the plaintiff?

2. Opposing Counsel: Objection. Irrelevant. You're never going to use that sort of information at trial. You're just wasting our time. Focus on the facts of the case, why don't you. If you want an answer to that question, you're going to have to explain why it is relevant.

3. You [To Opposing Counsel]: Counsel, as I am sure you well know, FRCP 30(d)(1) provides that

objections are to be stated in a concise and non-argumentative manner. Furthermore, FRCP 30(c) provides that examination and cross examination at deposition may proceed as permitted at trial. I have a copy of the rules right here if you would like to examine them. You have been consistently violating both of these rules by making argumentative objections that would be clearly inappropriate at trial. I have ignored your inappropriate behavior as long as I can. If you continue to make these inappropriate objections, I will have no choice but to terminate this deposition to seek a protective order and sanctions against you and your client.[34]

If you do ultimately have to terminate the deposition and move for a protective order, your having

34. You are entitled to suspend the deposition to move for a protective order to prevent disruptive behavior by opposing counsel under FRCP 26(c) and 30(d)(3). And you are expressly entitled to sanctions, including reasonable costs and attorney's fees, against the opposing counsel and/or the deponent under FRCP 30(d)(2). The advisory committee notes clearly state that 30(d)(2) was intended to authorize sanctions when opposing counsel unreasonably prolongs a deposition and "also when an attorney engages in other practices that improperly frustrate the fair examination of the deponent, such as making improper objections." FRCP 30, advisory committee notes on 1993 amendments, reprinted in 146 F.R.D. 665 (1993). See also State Farm Mut. Auto. Ins. Co. v. Dowdy, 445 F. Supp. 2d 1289, 1292 (N.D. Okla. 2006) (Sanctioning counsel for "obstructionist" tactics at a deposition, including suggesting answers, answering questions himself, and instructing deponent not to answer.) GMAC Bank v. HTFC Corp., 248 F.R.D. 182, 186 (E.D. Pa. 2008) (Holding that an attorney's failure to intervene to stop his client's misconduct during a deposition was sanction-worthy behavior).

cited opposing counsel to the appropriate authorities helps to demonstrate that you made a good faith effort to resolve the problem before bringing your motion.[35]

Of course, a danger exists that confronting opposing counsel on the record, perhaps in front of the client, serves only to goad the attorney into even further improper behavior. Consequently, if your personal relationship with opposing counsel permits, you may first try to handle the problem in a conversation just between you and opposing counsel "off the record." Take a break and privately cite counsel to the relevant authorities. Such a conversation may go as follows:

"Terri, you've been making a lot of argumentative objections, and I've been ignoring it up to now. You may feel like you've got to show your client that you're aggressively protecting his interests. But you and I both know that your argumentative objections are inappropriate under the FRCP, and if you continue to make them, I'll have no choice but to terminate the deposition and seek a protective order and sanctions. And that's just a waste of time and money for everyone. So I'm asking you to just state the grounds of any objections, and then we can move on with the testimony."

35. FRCP 26(c) provides that you cannot obtain a protective order unless you certify that you have made a good faith effort to resolve the problem without court intervention.

4. Offer to Stipulate That "All Objections Are Preserved"

You may discourage frivolous and argumentative objections by offering to stipulate that all objections to your questions are preserved. Such a stipulation may allow opposing counsel to dispense with all objections at deposition while arguably retaining the ability to make objections if and when you attempt to use deposition testimony later in the case.[36] Your offer to stipulate may go as follows:

> You [To Opposing Counsel]: Counsel, let us stipulate that all objections are preserved and that you may raise any objections you have later at trial or in connection with a motion. This relieves you of the need to state objections on the record here and allows us to complete the deposition more quickly, which saves everyone time and money.

This approach is less confrontational than citing opposing counsel to the relevant authorities and threatening to move for a protective order. In addition, if you ultimately do have to move for a protective order, opposing counsel's argumentative objections will seem that much more inappropriate if you have proffered this stipulation.

On the downside, such a stipulation rewards opposing counsel's inappropriate behavior and may

---

36. It is not clear that such stipulations will preserve defending counsel's right to later raise an objection. See United States v. White, 846 F.2d 678, 690 (11th Cir. 1988) ("[D]efendants cannot rely on these stipulations to preserve their Fifth Amendment rights."); Kymissis v. Rozzi, No. 93CIV.8609 (JGK) RLE, 1997 WL 278055, at *3 (S.D.N.Y. May 23, 1997) ("If an attorney allows a deponent to testify concerning an area to which an alleged privilege would normally apply, the client is bound by the resulting waiver.").

encourage repetition of such behavior at future depositions. Moreover, the stipulation relieves opposing counsel of making objections to the form of your questions that you might be able to cure. Opposing counsel may then be able to raise objections to the form of your question when you later try to use the deposition transcript. Consequently, the burden is on you to avoid any objectionable questions on pain of being unable to later use deposition testimony. Therefore, this approach probably works best when you are taking only a single deposition in a relatively small case, when the costs of going to court for a protective order may be prohibitive.

5. *Terminate the Deposition and Move for a Protective Order*

You have the right to terminate a deposition and move for a protective order requiring that opposing counsel cease engaging in disruptive behavior.[37] Be-

37. See FRCP 26(c). In cases of extreme abuse by opposing counsel or the deponent, you may request a variety of sanctions, including the appointment of a magistrate or referee to attend future deposition sessions with the costs for doing so imposed on your adversary. See, e.g., Van Pilsum v. Iowa State Univ. of Science & Tech., 152 F.R.D. 179 (S.D. Iowa 1993) (The Van Pilsum court granted a protective order to prevent abusive behavior at future depositions, appointed a master to preside over future depositions, and imposed part of the cost of the master on the attorney who engaged in the disruptive behavior necessitating the master's appointment.). See also GMAC Bank v. HTFC Corp., 248 F.R.D. 182 (E.D.Pa. 2008) (Holding that the deposing party could recover costs associated with motion to compel and the failed deposition because of the deponent's abusive behavior.) Morales v. Zondo, Inc., 204 F.R.D. 50, 54 (S.D.N.Y. 2001) (Deponent's counsel made "detailed objections

fore doing so, cite opposing counsel on the record to
the appropriate authority prohibiting the behavior
and make a good faith effort to work out the problem.[38] This approach is expensive and time consum-
ing. Consequently, you typically pursue this course
only when the disruptive behavior is egregious
and/or often repeated.[39]

B. Attempts to Coach the Deponent

Opposing counsel may resort to improper "coaching" in an attempt to influence a deponent's testimony. This section discusses common coaching

... colloquies, interruptions, and ad hominem attacks." Court
granted motion for sanctions and ordered the counsel to pay the
transcript costs, the deposing counsel's fees, and the court fees
for bringing the motion.) State Farm Mut. Auto. Ins. Co. v.
Dowdy, 445 F. Supp. 2d 1289, 1292 (N.D. Okla. 2006) (Counsel
sanctioned for "obstructionist" tactics at a deposition and required to pay fees incurred from filing for a protective order and
the court referred the order to the Oklahoma bar association for
further action.); J. Cary, *Rambo Depositions: Controlling An
Ethical Cancer in Civil Litigation*, 25 Hofstra L. Rev. 561 (1996);
W. Snipes, *Problems in Dealing with the Difficult Adversary*, 507
PLI/Lit 125 (1994).

38. See FRCP 26(c) and 37(a)(1).

39. You may be able to obtain relief for disruptive behavior of
opposing counsel even after you have completed the deposition.
Some courts have granted sanctions and the right to a second
deposition of the deponent as a result of disruptive behavior of
opposing counsel. See, e.g., Armstrong v. Hussmann Corp., 163
F.R.D. 299 (E.D. Mo. 1995); O'Brien v. Amtrak, 163 F.R.D. 232
(E.D. Pa. 1995); Craig v. St. Anthony's Med. Ctr, 2009 WL
690210 (E.D. Mo. 2009): court declared a deposition "unusable"
because of the disruptive behavior of plaintiff's counsel. The
court ordered a new deposition, extended the discovery deadline,
and ordered the plaintiff to pay the defendant's reasonable
expenses, including attorney's fees.

techniques and suggests strategies for responding to them.

1. Speaking Objections

An attorney may use "speaking" objections to suggest answers to deponents. Consider the following examples.

Example 1

1. A: Bob said that he thought the sample was inadequate and that we should insist on a larger one. Ms. Fazio disagreed.

2. You: After Ms. Fazio voiced her disapproval, what's the next thing that occurred with respect to the sample?

3. Opposing Counsel: Objection. Misstates the testimony. The witness didn't say anything about Ms. Fazio having disapproved of the sample. Maybe all Ms. Fazio said was that she didn't think the sample was adequate. Maybe Ms. Fazio was commenting on the issue of insisting on a larger sample. If you want to know what happened, ask a question but don't put words in the witness' mouth.

Example 2

1. You: Did anyone else at the meeting have an opinion about Karen's performance?

2. A: Yes, Monty did.

3. You: What were Monty's thoughts?

4. Opposing Counsel: Objection. Speculation. Also, lack of personal knowledge. How can this

witness possibly testify to the thoughts of someone else? If you want to ask her what she
thought, you can certainly do that. But don't ask
her a question that calls on her to speculate about
someone else's state of mind.[40]

These "speaking" objections coach by suggesting
the attorney's desired responses. For instance, the
objection in Example 2 above suggests that the
deponent should respond by testifying, "I don't
know." Consequently, such objections violate FRCP
30(d)(1), which requires that objections be stated
"concisely and in a non-argumentative and non-
suggestive manner." In addition, such suggestive
speaking objections are not permitted at trial and
therefore violate FRCP 30(c), which provides that
examination and cross examination of witnesses at
deposition "may proceed as permitted at the trial
under the provisions of the Federal Rules of Evidence. . . ."[41]

When counsel attempts to coach the deponent
with speaking objections you must again first re-

40. Although questions calling for speculation are improper
at trial, they are proper at deposition so long as they are
calculated to lead to the discovery of admissible evidence. As a
consequence, a deponent must answer such a question unless the
question is one that the deponent can be instructed not to
answer.

41. Speaking objections have consistently been interpreted as
violating the Federal Rules of Civil Procedure. See, e.g., Armstrong, 163 F.R.D. at 303; Hall v. Clifton Precision, 150 F.R.D.
525, 530 (E.D. Pa. 1993); Morales v. Zondo, Inc., 204 F.R.D. 50,
54 (S.D.N.Y. 2001); Craig v. St. Anthony's Med. Ctr., 2009 WL
690210 (E.D. Mo. 2009); Amari Co. v. Burgess, 2009 WL 1269704
(N.D. Ill. 2009).

spond to the objection as though it were properly stated. That is, normally you'd obtain an answer and then decide whether to cure the underlying objection if it's valid. You also have the same options as above for responding to disruptive objections. However, because coaching tends to influence the substance of a deponent's testimony, you may be more likely to terminate a deposition and move for a protective order if coaching continues despite private and "on the record" requests to cease and desist and offers to stipulate.

2. Conferences With a Deponent

Unless a conference is for the purpose of deciding whether to assert a privilege, opposing counsel is generally prohibited from conferring with a deponent during your examination.[42] Thus, for example, a deponent who is unclear about the meaning of a question should not talk to opposing counsel. Instead, the deponent should indicate uncertainty to you.[43] Of course, many conferences, although tech-

---

42. See In re Amezaga, 195 B.R. 221, 228 (Bankr. D.P.R. 1996) ("Counsel for the deponent has a very limited role during the taking of a deposition and conversing with the witness is limited to discussions about whether the objection of privilege should be asserted."); Armstrong, 163 F.R.D. at 303; Hall, 150 F.R.D. at 527 ("[C]ourts have held that private conferences between deponents and their attorneys during the taking of a deposition are improper unless the conferences are for the purpose of determining whether privilege should be asserted.")

43. See Hall, 150 F.R.D. at 528–29; Plaisted v. Geisiner Med. Ctr., 210 F.R.D. 527 (M.D. Pa. 2002); Birdine v. City of Coatesville, 225 F.R.D. 157, 159 (E.D. Pa. 2004); Quantachrome Corp. v. Micromeritics Instrument Corp., 189 F.R.D. 697 (S.D. Fla. 1999).

nically violative of the FRCP, are not a matter of concern. Consider the following examples:

Example 1

1. You: What, if anything, did Sara say in response?

2. A: She said that she didn't give a damn about the stupid policy. [Deponent whispers to counsel in a voice that the reporter cannot hear.]

3. Opposing Counsel: My client has just advised me that he has an appointment at 5 P.M. and he'd like to know if the deposition will be concluded in time for him to make that appointment. If not, he'd like to take a break soon so he can call and cancel.

Example 2

1. You: Why do you think Phillips agreed with the decision to terminate the contract for failure to perform after finding out about the problems with the disks delivered in early January?

[Deponent looks totally confused and briefly whispers to counsel.]

Opposing Counsel: My client's having difficulty understanding your question. Perhaps you could rephrase it.

In these examples, you may well conclude that there was no intent to coach. Consequently, you may ignore these innocent, though technically improper, conferences or politely ask the deponent to speak directly to you in future about taking breaks or questions they do not understand.

However, mid-deposition conferences are not always so innocent. Opposing counsel may use a whispered conference as a means of suggesting answers to particular questions, or of coaching a deponent about how to respond to questions in general (e.g. by reminding a client to "just answer the question, don't volunteer information"). When such conferences occur, you typically want to object to them on the record. For example:

1. You: Mr. Biggs, company policy encouraged providing employees with notice of any unsatisfactory performance prior to discharge, correct?

2. A: Yes. That's right.

3. You: Please tell me everything that you said to Mr. Shepard, prior to his discharge, that you felt gave him notice that his performance was unsatisfactory.

[Opposing counsel begins to whisper to deponent.][44]

You: Let the record reflect that counsel is now conferring with his client off the record. Counsel, as you are aware you are not entitled to confer with your client during my examination, especially when a question is pending, unless your conference is necessary to determine whether or not to

44. In the example in the text, the conference is initiated by opposing counsel. But such conferences are prohibited regardless of whether initiated by opposing counsel or the deponent. See, e.g., Hall, 150 F.R.D. at 527.

assert a privilege. This question clearly does not call for privileged information. If your client thinks that my question is unclear, please tell him to let me know and we can try to solve that problem. But you are not entitled to confer with your client before he answers this question.

Opposing Counsel: I am conferring with my client to make sure he understands the question. I think I'm entitled to do that.

You: The FRCP prohibit you from doing that. Rule 30(c) provides that this deposition may proceed as at trial, and you are not entitled to confer with your client during my examination at trial. Furthermore, cases interpreting the FRCP have held that you are not entitled to confer with your client for that purpose. I have copies of the FRCP and the cases right here. If you think the question is unclear you can object on that ground.

Opposing Counsel: You're being hypertechnical. My job is to make sure that the record is clear and that my client understands your question before he answers it. That makes for a clear record. That's all I'm doing.

You: I disagree. I request that you do not improperly confer with your client again during my examination.

Of course, your objections and citations to applicable authorities may be to no avail. If improper conferences continue to occur, you should note them for the record, and briefly repeat your objection to them as improper. Ultimately, you have to decide if the problem is serious enough to terminate the deposition and move for a protective order prohibiting such conferences.

3. Conferences With the Deponent During a Recess

In a deposition of any length, defending counsel will routinely and properly call for recesses to allow the participants to relax and stretch their legs. Defending attorneys commonly use these recesses to review testimony with deponents and to remind them of important facts.[45]

By contrast, opposing counsel's request for a break when a question is pending, or when you are in the middle of an important line of questioning, may constitute an improper attempt at coaching. For example:

1. You: Mr. Biggs, company policy encouraged providing employees with notice of any unsatisfactory performance prior to discharge, correct?

2. A: Yes. That's right.

3. You: Please tell me everything that you said to Mr. Shepard, prior to his discharge, that you

---

45. If the deponent is opposing counsel's client, these conversations are generally protected by the attorney client privilege. See McKinley Infuser, Inc. v. Zdeb, 200 F.R.D. 648 (D. Colo. 2001); But Cf. Hall, 150 F.R.D. at 532 ("Any conferences which occur ... are a proper subject for inquiry by deposing counsel to ascertain whether there has been any witness-coaching and, if so, what."); Plaisted v. Geisinger Med. Ctr., 210 F.R.D. 527 (M.D. Pa. 2002); Ngai v. Old Navy, 2009 WL 2391282, at *5 (D.N.J. 2009). See generally A. Darby Dickerson, *The Law and Ethics of Civil Depositions*, 57 Md. L. Rev. 273, 321–22 (1998).

felt gave him notice that his performance was unsatisfactory.

4. Opposing Counsel: We'd like to take a break now. My client has been testifying for quite a while and I need to use the restroom. So let's take a ten minute break.

5. You: We can take a break in a moment, but first I'd like an answer to my question.

6. Opposing Counsel: Sorry, but my client and I are taking a break. [Opposing Counsel and Deponent get up and leave the room.]

Although you may suspect that opposing counsel's primary motive for taking the break is to discuss how a deponent should respond to your questions, your options are limited. Obviously, you cannot physically stop them from taking a break and leaving the room.[46] You can, however, note for the record your objection to the recess and indicate on the record the factors that seem to indicate that opposing counsel requested the recess in order to instruct the deponent as to how to respond to your questions.[47] For example, you might indicate for the

46. Some courts have attempted to prevent coaching by ordering counsel not to talk to his client about matters related to the deposition during recesses or breaks, and providing that if any such conferences do occur what was discussed during them may be inquired into when the deposition resumes. See, e.g., Hall, 150 F.R.D. 527–28. The enforceability of such orders is unclear. See Potashnick v. Port City Const. Co., 609 F.2d 1101 (5th.Cir. 1980); Odone v. Croda Int'l, 170 F.R.D. 66 (D.C. 1997).

47. Some jurisdictions have local rules relating to taking breaks during a deposition. You can point out any violations of

record that a question was pending at the time and that this is the third time that such a recess has been taken over objection in the past hour. In the case of serious and repeated abuse of conferences to coach the deponent, you may terminate the deposition and seek a protective order and sanctions.

C. *Resolving Disputes Via Telephone*

As discussed earlier, in many jurisdictions, judges and magistrates are willing to consider discovery disputes over the telephone. When available, this procedure typically saves considerable time, money, and inconvenience for all concerned, as compared to terminating a deposition and seeking a protective order. You should, of course, resort to a telephone call only after you have made a good faith effort to work a problem out with opposing counsel.

D. *Visually Recording Depositions*

Visually recording a deposition tends to reduce the likelihood of both disruptive behavior and improper coaching.[48] In addition, if you eventually terminate a deposition to seek a protective order, a visual recording of opposing counsel's inappropriate behavior may provide more compelling evidence of misconduct than a transcript.

such rules to try to control opposing counsel or to make a better record should you ultimately have to move for a protective order.

48. For a further discussion of visually recorded depositions, see Chapter 22.

E. *A Cautionary Note About Protective Orders*

The issuance of a protective order is within a court's nearly unfettered discretion. Even if you've fulfilled all the preconditions for a protective order (e.g., you've made a good faith effort to resolve the dispute[49]), you'll may need to demonstrate that opposing counsel's behavior is a serious, and not merely a technical, violation of the rules. Although FRCP 30(c) provides that examination at deposition should proceed generally as at trial, no judge is present at a deposition to mediate disputes between counsel. Moreover, judges recognize that disputes are common because it is natural for opposing counsel to want to appear protective of their clients, especially in the face of legitimate but sometimes damaging, uncomfortable, and arguably repetitive, cross examination. These disputes, and the understandable tension that accompanies them, often result in at least technical violations of deposition rules. Courts would be swamped if every violation resulted in a motion for a protective order. Consequently, when you seek a protective order, you should be prepared to demonstrate that opposing counsel's behavior has materially affected your legitimate discovery efforts.[50]

Finally, your ability to obtain a protective order and/or sanctions against opposing counsel may well

49. Such a good faith effort is required by FRCP 26(c) and 37(a)(1).

50. When you are beginning a series of depositions in a case, you may be more likely to move for a protective order to control inappropriate behavior of opposing counsel. A protective order early on in discovery will likely prevent similar improper behavior by opposing counsel in future depositions.

depend on the propriety of your own deposition behavior.[51] Respond to opposing counsel and question the deponent as you would if a judge were present. You can be professional and courteous and still be a zealous advocate. And maintaining a professional demeanor can improve your chances of success should a judge have occasion to examine a deposition transcript or visual recording in connection with a motion for a protective order.[52]

51.   See, e.g., <u>Odone v. Croda Int'l</u>, 170 F.R.D. 66, at 68 (D.C. 1997).

52.   For a discussion of how to maintain a professional demeanor at deposition, see Chapter 14.

PART TWO

PREPARING TO DEPOSE ADVERSE WITNESSES

This part (Chapters 16 and 17) describes techniques and strategies for preparing yourself to take a deposition. It concludes with a discussion of the rules and procedures for arranging for depositions.

CHAPTER 16

DEPOSITION PREPARATION

This Chapter describes preparation strategies and techniques to help you accomplish the three primary deposition goals of: obtaining a deponent's version of significant events; searching for and confirming helpful evidence; and uncovering and undermining harmful evidence. The preparation process can be broken down into two main steps: (1) Identify crucial factual contentions; and (2) Identify topics, events and documents you will likely explore during the deposition.

Of course, not all depositions will justify your pursuing each and every preparation technique described in this Chapter. Instead, this Chapter provides a menu of preparation techniques from which you can pick and choose, each of which may help you identify the topics, events or documents you might explore at a deposition. Which techniques you employ are likely to depend on such factors as personal preference, the preparation you've already done in connection with earlier depositions or discovery, your litigation budget, a case's value and complexity, your litigation experience, and a deposition's importance.

The strategies and techniques discussed in this Chapter can help you produce an outline that records the topics, events, and documents you plan to inquire into at a deposition.

1. **Step One**—Identify Crucial Factual Contentions

Factual contentions are the specific factual conclusions you would like the trier of fact to reach. For both plaintiffs and defendants, most cases boil down to a limited number of crucial factual contentions. Factual contentions are crucial when they are both: (1) likely to be disputed by your adversary and (2) pivotal to establish if you are to achieve a successful result. Since your ability to prove crucial factual contentions is likely to determine the outcome of a case, these contentions largely determine the evidence that you pursue during depositions and all other discovery. Therefore, before beginning to prepare for a deposition, if you haven't already done so, make a list of your crucial factual contentions. These contentions will typically fall into one of the following three categories.

* **Elements from Causes of Action or Affirmative Defenses**

Example: In a fraudulent misrepresentation case, one legal element that a plaintiff must prove is that a defendant "knowingly" made a false statement. One crucial factual contention with respect to this element for a plaintiff might be that "When the defendant told my client that XYZ Corp. had a signed contract for the distribution of a new software system, the defendant knew that the contract had not been signed." In the same case, one crucial factual contention for the defense might be "When the defendant told Plaintiff that XYZ Corp. had a signed contract for the distribution of a new software system, the defendant believed that statement to be true."

Example: In an age discrimination case, one of plaintiff's crucial factual contentions might be that "The plaintiff was discharged because the employer wanted to save money by hiring a younger, less experienced replacement at a lower salary." In the same case, one of the defendant's crucial contentions might include: "The defendant discharged the plaintiff because she was repeatedly insubordinate to her supervisor at work."[1]

* Pivotal Evidentiary Disputes

Some crucial contentions do not satisfy a legal element but instead are focused on important evidentiary disputes.

Example: In a sexual harassment case, the plaintiff claims that two months prior to her discharge she declined her supervisor's request for a date; the supervisor denies ever asking the plaintiff for a date. The crucial factual contention for plaintiff might be that "The supervisor asked plaintiff for a date prior to

---

1. In some cases you may need the help of an expert to identify the crucial contentions. For example, in a construction defect case you may need an expert to help you identify the crucial issues you will need to prove to establish that a building collapse was not the fault of your client.

discharging her." The defendant's crucial factual contention in that same case may be that "The supervisor never asked plaintiff for a date."

Example: In a breach of contract case, the defendant claims he never signed any agreement. Plaintiff argues she has a copy of an agreement that defendant did, in fact, sign. A crucial factual contention for the defendant is that "The defendant's signature on the agreement was a forgery." On the other hand, one of plaintiff's crucial factual contentions is that "The defendant's signature on the agreement was genuine."

* "Extra–Legal" Contentions

Example: A factual contention may be crucial because it improves a case's emotional appeal to a factfinder at trial or provides you with settlement leverage. Evidence that evinces sympathy for your party or witness or hostility towards an adverse party or witness can improve your case's emotional appeal. For example, in a case against police officers for using unreasonable force when effectuating an arrest, the plaintiff may seek to prove that the police initially stopped the plaintiff only because he was a young racial minority driving alone in what the police considered a "high crime area." Proving this contention may provide the plaintiff with settlement leverage with police department officials who control settlement, and increase the case's emotional appeal if it proceeds to trial.

2. Step Two—Identify the Topics, Events and Documents to Explore at the Deposition

Once you have identified your crucial factual contentions, you can use one or more of the following techniques to identify areas of inquiry that might lead to helpful or harmful evidence relating to each of your crucial contentions. Remember, you need not pursue each and every preparation technique described below in every single deposition; instead, this list of techniques is intended to provide you with a menu of alternatives, each of which may give you a structured way to identify the topics, events and documents you might explore at a deposition.

A. *Technique #1—Review Documents & Deposition Transcripts*

Even in the early stages of discovery, a case file typically contains numerous documents from a variety of sources. For example, you may have documents provided by your client and an adversary[2] as well as memos to the file, witness statements and reports from investigators and/or experts. Furthermore, often you will have transcripts from prior depositions. Time and resources permitting, review

---

2. FRCP 26(a)(1)(B) currently requires that at a case's inception, each party must voluntarily turn over documents supporting that party's claims or defenses, unless the documents are to be used solely for impeachment. Hence, often you will have documents provided by an adversary even if you have not requested them.

these documents and deposition transcripts as you prepare for a deposition to identify:

  * Helpful evidence that you want the deponent to confirm.

  * Harmful evidence that you hope to undermine.

  * Questions you have concerning such matters as how and why a document was prepared, to whom it was distributed and the significance of topics and events to which a document refers.[3]

If a case file contains thousands or even hundreds of documents, you may not have time to read each and every document before taking a deposition. Moreover, many documents may be unrelated to the deposition you are about to take. Therefore, to prepare for a given deposition, you will usually have to cull through documents to determine which ones you want to examine in detail.

If you have a computerized litigation support system that contains a database composed of an abstract for each document or deposition transcript in your file, the culling process may not prove difficult.[4] You can quickly develop a list of keywords

  3. For other suggestions for document-related inquiries, see Chapter 10, Using Documents and Diagrams.

  4. For a discussion of the function and creation of computerized litigation support databases, see D. Kartson, Designing Litigation Support Databases (Wiley Law Publications, 1997). At the present time, a number of companies market computer programs that enable you to create and maintain document management databases that allow you to keep track of documents obtained during the discovery process. For a discussion of some of the major programs presently in use in large law firms,

that you, an associate and/or a paralegal can use to search the document database. One keyword will, of course, be the name of the person to be deposed. Other keywords will be those that you believe relate to your crucial contentions. Finally, consider whether you can further cull documents by excluding those outside a certain time period.[5]

B. Technique #2—Review a Case Chronology

As discussed in Chapter 1, you routinely want to obtain a deponent's version of significant events during a deposition. Doing so allows you to anticipate the deponent's direct examination should the case proceed to trial. Perhaps more importantly, as you obtain a deponent's version of events, you may

see Bob Moss, "Putting the Pieces Together: Utilizing Technology to Educate Yourself, the Court, and the Jury," 17 The Complete Lawyer 50 (2000); David Beckman and David Hirsch, "Making a Case for CaseMap: This software organizes facts for litigators—and you don't have to refold it," 86 A.B.A.J. 80 (2000).

5. When coding documents, many firms use a designation such as "HotDoc" to indicate that the document is quite important. If your firm uses this practice, you typically will want to examine any such documents as part of your preparation. For an analysis of the legal profession's use of HotDocs, see CAROLE BASRI & IRVING KAGAN, CORP. LEGAL DEP'T. § 6:2 (2009) (discussing how HotDocs provides legal departments with a "time saving option to develop, control and distribute documents."). *See also* David Kiefer & Marc Lauritsen, *Technology and Legal Practice Symposium Issue: Recent Developments in Automating Legal Documents*, 52 SYRACUSE L. REV. 1091, 1099 (2002) (explaining why HotDocs is the industry leader in web-based data collection); Lee S. Rosen, *Tools of the Trade: Jeez, What are you, Paid by the World?*, 30 FAM. ADV. 6, 8 (2008) (describing how more and more law firms are using HotDocs to create routine documents).

uncover helpful or harmful evidence you had been unaware of prior to the deposition. You can then try to undermine the harmful evidence at the deposition or through further discovery.

1. Create a Case Chronology

To obtain a deponent's version of significant events, if you have not already done so, create a case chronology. While formats for a case chronology tend to vary from one lawyer to another, a useful case chronology typically incorporates four types of information:

* All parties versions of important events, listed as much as possible in chronological order.[6]

* The approximate or precise dates when important events occurred.

* The documents, individuals and/or other sources that provide support for the important events.

* An indication of disputes in the parties' version of events.

The following illustrative example of a small portion of a case chronology involves a lawsuit by the National Resources Defense Council ("NRDC") against a county for failing to take adequate measures to keep toxic materials at a county construction site out of storm water.

6. A case chronology often combines the stories of several different people. For example, a single chronology might reflect the stories of several corporate employees, or an injured pedestrian and the bystanders who witnessed the mishap.

Date	Event	Source	Disputes
02/10/__	NRDC letter notifies County of Toxic Dirt Problem	NRDC letter 000047	
03/14/__	Depart Road Maint refers NRDC notice letter to Benson	County Memo 00104	
04/25/__	Smith of NRDC calls County Engineer, Helms, re: no response to Tox dirt letter	Smith memo 00023	Helms says Smith never called. Helms deposition Page 42 line 5
Late April	Benson tells Carson that NRDC is being unreasonable	Anders statement 04673	
05/14/__	Benson prepares memo on construct site visits. County inspectors are requiring the contractor to put down appropriate matting	Benson memo 01435	
06/10/__	Higgins tells Carson that Benson said sometimes county inspectors prepare reports without actually visiting the site	Carson memo 02234	

In a straightforward case with one or two crucial contentions, a single case chronology of important events may provide an adequate overall perspective. In complex cases, however, you may want to supplement an overall chronology with sub-chronologies. For example, you may have separate chronologies for each crucial contention in a case, or a separate chronology for each significant witness in a case.

7. This number, and the similar ones below, identify the document in which the information is found. Numbering documents and recording the number in the chronology facilitates retrieval as you prepare for a deposition. Some numbering system is essential when you have a substantial number of documents in a case.

2. Review Your Case Chronology

Review your case chronology and identify:

* Topics, events and documents you would like to inquire into to flesh out the deponent's version of significant events. For example, as the NRDC's lawyer preparing to depose Benson, you would want to seek Benson's version of what happened during visits to the construction site. You also want to try to fill in any gaps in your chronology. For example, the chronology above might remind you as the NRDC's lawyer to probe the gap between 03/14/___ (when a letter was referred to Benson), and late April (when Benson spoke to Carson) when deposing Benson.

* Helpful evidence that you want the deponent to confirm.

* Harmful evidence that you hope to undermine.

A case chronology can also come in handy during a deposition. Comparing the deponent's testimony to your case chronology may disclose a conflict between the parties' versions of events of which you had been previously unaware. You can then make a decision at the deposition about whether you want to question the deponent about such a conflict. If you do not have a written chronology with you at the deposition, you will be required to hold the entire chronology of the case in your head as you listen to the deponent's testimony. This is, to say the least, a difficult task.

C. Technique #3—Brainstorming

You can brainstorm for topics, events and documents that might uncover evidence supporting or refuting a crucial contention. Common brainstorming methods include: (1) Historical Reconstruction and (2) Generalizations.

1. Brainstorming With Historical Reconstruction

Historical reconstruction is a reasoning method which allows you to use your experience and intuition to identify potentially valuable areas of inquiry. To engage in historical reconstruction, assume that your crucial factual contention is accurate. Then ask yourself, in essence, "If this contention is true, what else also might have occurred?" The topics, events and documents you identify when answering this question will become areas of inquiry to explore with the deponent.

As an illustration of historical reconstruction, assume that you represent Perfect Properties Inc. in a rescission action against Moonshine Management. Perfect seeks to rescind its purchase of an apartment complex from Moonshine based on an allegation that Moonshine failed to disclose that laundry areas in the complex flooded when it rained. One crucial factual contention you want to prove is that "When Moonshine sold the apartment complex to Perfect, Moonshine knew that the laundry areas in the complex flooded when it rained."

To employ historical reconstruction, start from the premise that your crucial factual contention is accurate—i.e., Moonshine did know that the laundry areas flooded when it rained. Then ask yourself what actions or happenings are consistent with Moonshine having such knowledge. Using this approach, even those of us with little plumbing experience might identify at least the following events that might have occurred:

* Tenants made written and oral complaints to Moonshine's building manager about the flooding.

* Moonshine's building manager promised the tenants that the flooding in these laundry areas would be remedied.

* Moonshine's building manager requested Moonshine maintenance personnel to take steps to stop the flooding.

* Moonshine's maintenance personnel made some attempts to stop the flooding.

* The attempts to stop the flooding were inadequate and flooding continued during periods of heavy rain.

* Tenants complained to government agencies about Moonshine's failure to remedy the flooding.

* Government agencies contacted Moonshine regarding the tenants' complaints.

* Tenants started using the laundry areas outside the complex when it rained.

* Tenants started to withhold rent or move out of the complex because the flooding was not remedied.

You might then inquire into these events in the depositions of employees of Moonshine and third party witnesses, e.g. former and current tenants at the property.

a. Breaking Historical Reconstruction into Multiple Time Periods

You may further refine historical reconstruction by separately considering what might have happened "before," "during" and "after" the event to which a factual contention relates. By focusing on different time frames, you often can uncover additional topics that might yield helpful evidence. For example, refer again to the Perfect–Moonshine case above. As you see, most of the events were likely to have occurred prior to the time Moonshine entered into negotiations with Perfect. However, if you consciously think about what might have taken place during the time that sale negotiations were taking place, you might identify additional topics such as:

* Moonshine steered Perfect's inspectors and bank appraisers away from tenants and the laundry areas.

* Moonshine undertook repairs to mask evidence of water damage in the laundry areas.

2. *Brainstorming With Generalizations*

To identify areas of inquiry through the use of generalizations, again assume that your crucial factual contention is correct. Next, convert that factual contention into a generalization, i.e. a statement of what usually or generally happens. For example, assume that you represent Wallace in an age discrimination action against Papik Corp. A crucial factual contention you are trying to prove is, "The manager of Papik's accounting division fired Wallace in order to promote a younger employee."

Converted into a generalization, the crucial contention is as follows:

"Managers of accounting divisions generally fire an older employee in order to promote a younger employee."

A generalization such as this helps you to "break the frame" imposed by the facts of a specific case and encourages you to think broadly of circumstances which are likely to strengthen the generalization. To identify such circumstances, simply add "especially when" to a generalization and then generate a list of topics, events and documents that would make the generalization more likely to be true. For example, here you would say, "Managers of accounting divisions generally fire an older employee in order to promote a younger employee **especially when:**"

 * The manager is under pressure from higher ups to cut costs.[8]

 * An older employee has a higher salary and the manager's bonus depends on cutting costs.

8. Note that you may well identify many of the same topics using historical reconstruction and generalizations. Because of this overlap, you may want to select from these two techniques the one that seems to work best for you.

* The manager considers the older employee to be less deferential than a younger employee.

* The manager believes that a younger employee will be more productive.

* The manager prefers working with younger people.

Each "especially when" can suggest a topic, event or document that you might inquire about at deposition. If you obtain testimony at a deposition to support an "especially when," you help to prove the accuracy of your crucial contention. For example, if you can elicit testimony indicating that the manager was under pressure to cut costs, you have uncovered support for your factual contention that Wallace was fired because of his age.

A second way to use generalizations to identify topics that support a factual contention is to add "except when" to a generalization. Doing so encourages you to think of circumstances that make a generalization <u>less likely</u> to be accurate. For example, if you add "except when" to the generalization in Wallace's case, you might come up with the following: Managers of accounting divisions sometimes fire an older employee in order to promote a younger employee, **except when:**

* The older employee is a close friend of the manager.

* The manager has received customer complaints concerning the older employee.

Of course, an "except when" that you do uncover constitutes evidence that your factual contention is not true. Thus, what you really hope to establish is the non-existence of "except whens." If a deponent cannot provide evidence of an "except when," you have obtained evidence that supports your crucial contention. For example, in Wallace's case, evidence that the manager had not received customer complaints regarding Wallace tends to support your contention that the manager fired your client in order to promote a younger employee.[9]

D. Technique #4—Use an Expert

Even when you are preparing for a lay witness deposition, your expert can often help you identify existing helpful or harmful evidence and topics that might produce additional evidence to support a crucial factual contention. Consider this example. Your client has brought an unfair business practice case against a computer trade school that claims to train students to be computer programmers. One of your client's crucial contentions is that the classes did not cover the basic skills required to become a computer programmer. You are about to depose the school's educational director. When preparing for this deposition, you might well be able to identify helpful topics even without an expert's help. For

---

9. There's no "magic" in using the "except when" technique. In fact, were you a "perfect thinker," you'd identify exactly the same topics with the "except when" technique as you would with the "especially when" technique. However, few of us are perfect thinkers, and flipping your perspective from one technique to the other might enable you to identify topics you would have overlooked had you used only one of the techniques.

example, you probably wouldn't need an expert's help to identify a topic such as the percentage of students who got jobs as computer programmers after graduation. However, an expert's help may produce such additional topics as:

> * What computer languages are currently in wide use?
>
> * What experience and training should teachers have so as to be able to teach these subjects effectively?
>
> * What kinds of lab projects and drills should students be given in order to learn to program in these languages?
>
> * What is the average salary of teachers who work in private, for-profit computer training schools?

An expert's answers to such questions will provide you with topics that you may inquire into at deposition.

While you may automatically think of an "expert" as a hired outsider, in some situations you may be able to look to your client or to a more experienced colleague as a source of expertise.

E. Technique #5—Undermine Existing Harmful Evidence

A common deposition goal is to undermine existing harmful evidence. Existing harmful evidence includes harmful evidence of which you are already aware, as well as harmful evidence which you are reasonably sure will emerge at deposition. For example, assume that in a wrongful termination case, you believe that a deponent will testify that one reason that your client was fired is that the client was insubordinate to the deponent. Since this is harmful evidence, you might want to identify topics which might undermine it by using the approaches and the "Credibility Checklist" described in Chapter 6.

F. Technique #6—Use Direct Inquiries

A straightforward technique for eliciting helpful evidence is to use direct inquiries to ask a deponent for information supporting your factual contentions.[10]

10. You are generally entitled to ask the deponent if she has information to support a factual conclusion or contention. See. eg. Arkwright Mut. Ins. Co. v. National Union Fire Ins. Co., No.90 Civ.7811, 1993 WL 34678 (S.D.N.Y. 1993); Rifkind v. Superior Court, 22 Cal.App.4th 1255, 27 Cal.Rptr.2d 822 (1994). The cases are split, however, on whether it is appropriate at deposition to ask questions that seek facts or information supporting a legal conclusion in the pleadings or a legal theory. Some courts have upheld the use of such questions at deposition. See Ortho Pharm. Corp. v. Smith, No. 90–0242, 1990 WL 10011 (E.D.Pa.1990); Hammond v. Air Line Pilots Ass'n., No. 87 C 2792, 1987 WL 20421 (N.D. Ill. 1987); Equal Employment Opportunity Comm'n v. Caesars Entm't, Inc., 237 F.R.D. 428, 433–34 (D. Nev. 2006); Sec. Ins. Co. of Hartford v. Trustmark Ins. Co., 218 F.R.D. 29, 34 (D. Conn. 2003); Iris Corp. Berhad v. United States, 84 Fed. Cl. 489, 493 (Fed. Cl. 2008); Sigmund v. Starwood Urban Retail VI, LLC, 236 F.R.D. 43, 46–7 (D.D.C. 2006). Other cases have held that in some circumstances such questions need only be answered in response to contention interrogatories. See Rifkind v. Superior Court, 22 Cal.App.4th 1255, 27 Cal.Rptr.2d 822 (1994); Exxon Research and Eng'g Co v. United States, 44 Fed. Cl. 597 (1999); McCormick–Morgan, Inc. v. Teledyne Indus., Inc., 134 F.R.D. 275 (N.D. Cal. 1991), *rev'd on other grounds*, 765 F.Supp. 611 (N.D. Cal. 1991); In Re Independent Serv. Orgs.

Example

* <u>Crucial Contention</u>: The opposing party, a personal software company, offered rebates to customers. Questions at deposition to a manager of the software company: "Did you ever see anything indicating that the company offered rebates?" "Did you ever hear anything indicating that the company offered rebates?"

You can also use direct inquiries to determine whether the deponent knows of any evidence that would undermine your factual contentions. Similarly, when you know the crucial factual contentions your adversary will try to prove, you can use direct inquiries to assess whether the deponent is aware of evidence that would tend to prove those contentions. For example, assume that one of your adversary's contentions is that your client knew that his statement that a house was built to code was false. Direct inquiries you might identify in your preparation include:

Antitrust Litig., 168 F.R.D. 651 (D. Kan.1996); <u>BB & T Corp. v. United States</u>, 233 F.R.D. 447, 449–51 (M.D.N.C. 2006). In light of this split in authority, you may want to focus your questions on the facts supporting a legal theory or conclusion rather than on the legal theory or conclusion itself. For example, instead of asking a deponent for all the facts supporting a statute of limitations affirmative defense in an answer, you might ask questions such as: "Do you believe that my client became aware prior to [date] that your statement about the earnings growth of the stock was false?" "Tell me all the information that you are aware of that leads you to believe that my client became aware prior to [date] that your statement about the earnings growth of the stock was false?"

Q: "Do you believe that my client knew that his statement about the house being built up to code was false?"

Q: "(Following a "yes" answer) Then please tell me all the information of which you are aware that indicates that my client knew that statement was false."

A risk of identifying your factual contentions through direct inquiries is that you may educate your opponent about legal or factual theories of which the opponent is unaware. Thus, you should consider not only the likelihood that a deponent will have relevant information but also your adversary's level of preparedness when thinking about whether to employ this technique.

G. *Technique #7—Anticipate Your Cross Examination*

Another way to identify potentially useful areas of inquiry at deposition is to simply ask yourself, "What would I want to ask this deponent on cross-examination at trial?" This approach shifts your frame of reference to testimony you would hope to elicit from the deponent on cross-examination at trial. As a result, you may identify topics that you would otherwise overlook. Questions that you might ask yourself when using this approach include:

* "What evidence might I elicit on cross examination at trial to attack the deponent's credibility?"

* "Are there aspects of my adversary's version of events that seem implausible?" "If so, what evi-

dence might I be able to elicit from this deponent to heighten that implausibility?"[11]

* "What evidence would I like to bring out on cross from this deponent to support my affirmative case?"

H.   Technique #8—Anticipate Your Important Arguments

As when you identify topics by thinking of possible cross-examination, focusing on arguments you are likely to make to a neutral person such as a settlement conference judge or a factfinder at trial is another technique for identifying potentially useful areas of inquiry at deposition. Using an "important arguments" frame of reference may enable you to identify topics you would otherwise overlook. Questions that you might ask yourself when using this approach include:

* Example: "What are the strongest arguments I might present to a neutral factfinder to show reasonable reliance by my client?" "What topics might I inquire into to obtain evidence to strengthen those arguments?"

* Example: "How is my adversary likely to respond to (rebut) my arguments about reasonable reliance?" "What topics might I inquire into to obtain evidence to undermine or cut off my adversary's likely rebuttal?"

11. For a discussion of techniques to heighten an implausibility, see Chapter 8.

I.   Technique #9—Use a Pre–Fab Checklist

Another approach for identifying areas of inquiry is to use a checklist found in a practice guide or text. A number of practitioner-oriented texts set out checklists that identify topics that generally pertain to specific types of cases. Here, for example, is a partial checklist that you might use in a lawsuit growing out of an automobile accident.[12]

Pre–Accident Events

1.   Activities earlier in the day

2.   Food, alcohol, drugs

3.   Physical condition at time

Events Immediately Preceding the Collision

1.   Location and direction of the vehicles

2.   Passenger

3.   Traffic conditions

4.   Visibility

5.   Other distractions

6.   Where first saw defendant's car

7.   Marking diagram and photographs

Collision

1.   Speed before impact

2.   Traffic signals

12.   For deposition checklists for actions involving automobile accidents, see Douglas Danner, Pattern Discovery: Automobiles §§ 2:01 et seq. (Bancroft–Whitney Co., 1985); 18 Am. Jur. Trials 443 (1971); 2 Am. Jur. Trials 1 (1966); Automobile and accident case checklist, 3 Am.Jur.Pl. & Pr. Forms, frontispiece of volume; 8 Am. Jur. Trials 1 (1965).

3.   Braking and other conduct of plaintiff

4.   Braking and other conduct of defendant

5.   Marking diagram and photographs

Post–Collision Events

1.   Bystander activities

2.   Police activities

3.   What plaintiff and defendant did

4.   What plaintiff and defendant said

5.   Plaintiff's and defendant's condition after the accident

6.   Ambulance

You may also be able to obtain a checklist from a friend or colleague who has extensive experience in a particular area of substantive law. For example, if you are taking your first deposition in a wrongful termination case or a construction defect case, you may want to ask colleagues with experience in these types of litigation for their deposition outlines or checklists.

J.   Technique #10—Computer Searches to Gather Background Information About the Deponent

You may benefit from learning about a deponent's background before a deposition. Such information may alert you to topics you might inquire into or help you assess the credibility of testimony that emerges at the deposition.

In this computer age, gathering such information is often relatively easy. Through Lexis and Westlaw you can often obtain a host of pertinent information about a potential deponent. Both companies maintain a variety of specialized public information databases that help you locate assets, civil and criminal court filings, judgments and liens, professional licenses, SEC filings, etc. By running a potential deponent's name through such databases you can often uncover a substantial amount of information about a deponent. In addition, if you believe a deponent is a newsworthy person, you might uncover pertinent with more general computer searches or by running the deponent's name through the web sites of your local newspaper or national papers such as the New York Times or the Wall Street Journal.

3. Organize a Deposition Outline

The techniques described previously in this Chapter should help you to identify topics, events, and documents to explore during the deposition. Once you have identified the potential areas of inquiry, a helpful last step is to organize that information into a deposition outline. This section describes several issues you might want to consider as you finalize your outline.

A. *How Should You Organize Your Outline?*

While there are numerous ways to organize a deposition outline, one straightforward organizational scheme is to list areas of inquiry in three main categories: (1) Background; (2) Deponent's version of the significant events; and (3) Strategically reserved areas of inquiry.

Using this organizational approach, inquires relating to education, experience, training, and other matters not directly relating to the case would be included in the "Background" section. Inquiries designed to seek the deponent's version of significant events would be included in the "Version" section. You might want to list the areas of inquiry in the "Version" section chronologically, event by event. Areas of inquiry that you want to reserve for later in the deposition would be included in the "Strategically reserved" section. For example, you might choose to reserve questions that would be embarrassing or upsetting to the deponent, or questions designed to communicate arguments to the deponent and/or opposing counsel, until the end of the deposition in order to avoid disrupting rapport.

B. What Questioning Techniques Should You Use for Important Areas of Inquiry?

Not all areas of inquiry are created equal. In every deposition, some topics, events or documents will be more important than others. For particularly important areas of inquiry, consider using the questioning techniques described in Chapters 2–4 of this book. For example, if you want to be sure to obtain complete information about a topic or event, you can use the T–Funnel questioning pattern described in Chapter 2 and/or the Timeline questioning pattern described in Chapter 3. If you want to maximize the likelihood of obtaining a specific answer or admission at the deposition, consider the plausibility chain, exploiting bias or masking questioning techniques described in Chapter 4.

C. Should You Include Questioning Prompts or Specific Questions in Your Outline?

Even for important areas of inquiry, trying to "script" your precise deposition questioning rarely makes sense. Any script would have to correctly predict deponent's answers, a near impossibility. Moreover, scripted questions are likely to inhibit your ability to adjust to unexpected answers.

In lieu of specific questions, consider including questioning prompts in your outline for important areas of inquiry. To illustrate how you might incorporate questioning prompts in an outline, consider the following example. Assume that you represent John Power, a plaintiff who alleges that he was terminated from his employment due to age discrimination. You are preparing to depose Power's former supervisor, Jon Varat, who made the decision to discharge Power. A factual contention on which you want to develop evidence is: that Varat believed that a younger worker would be more productive than Power. If your outline contains nothing more than this topic, you may have difficulty thoroughly probing it at deposition. If, for example, you simply ask Varat, "Did you think a younger employee would be more productive than my client?," Varat will probably say something like: "Not necessarily. It depends on the quality of the employee, not the employee's age." You would then have to think of follow-up questions "on the fly" at deposition to thoroughly probe this important topic.

It is often easier to think of follow-up questions in the quiet of your office than it is when you are under the gun at deposition. As you think of potential follow-up questions for important topics during preparation, you can include prompts in your outline which will serve to remind you of the questions you might ask at the deposition. For example, your outline for above topic might include such prompts as the following:

<u>Varat believed that a younger worker would be more productive than Power.</u>

- approximate age of any employees recommended by Varat for termination in previous year

- approximate age of any employees supervised by Varat in previous year who have received or been recommended by Varat for

       performance bonuses

       merit raises

       promotions

       employee of the month award

- names and ages of most important or largest customers with whom Varat works.

- approximate age of employees who work on the accounts of each of these customers (may show Varat assigns younger employees to the best accounts).

- existence of time cards showing whether younger employees supervised by Varat work longer hours

. . . .

Many areas of inquiry commonly re-occur throughout a deposition. For example, as you pursue a deponent's version of events you may elicit testimony of similar events, e.g., a series of meetings or inspections. If so, you might want to develop a standard set of prompts that you can refer to each time a deponent mentions a similar event. Your standard prompts for a meeting might include:

When?

Where?

Who present?

Duration?

Purposes?

What happened?

Notes or records?

You could include a prompt like "Ask Event Essentials" for each event you include in your outline rather than repeating these questions in your outline verbatim for every single meeting. Other re-occurring areas of inquiry for which you might develop standard sets of prompts include documents, conversations and telephone calls.

D. Should You Omit Topics to Avoid Educating Your Opposition?

A common risk of deposing adverse witnesses is educating an opponent about your legal theories and factual contentions. For example:

* If you ask a deponent to explain an inconsistency between the deponent's testimony and the account of a friendly third party witness, you will reveal the conflict and perhaps encourage your adversary to seek evidence undermining the friendly witness' account.

* If your questions emphasize the importance of the time when an adverse party deponent became aware of information on which a lawsuit is based, you may prompt the deponent and opposing counsel to characterize events so as to eliminate your Statute of Limitations defense.

* Your adversary may be unaware of a document containing evidence that hurts your case. If you question a deponent with respect to such a document, you reveal the harmful information to your adversary.

In situations such as these, you have to make a strategic decision about whether the advantages of obtaining a fuller picture of and possibly undermining your adversary's case outweigh the risks of educating the opponent.

E. Should You Avoid Putting Harmful Evidence on the Record?

You ordinarily want to uncover harmful evidence at a deposition so that you can try to undermine it at the deposition or through further discovery. Nevertheless, if you think the deponent may be unavailable as a witness at trial, you may choose to omit questioning relating to harmful evidence. This strategy may prevent an adversary from reading in harmful evidence from a transcript when a deponent is unavailable at trial.

F. Might You Enhance Settlement?

The vast majority of cases settle prior to trial. Consequently, if settlement is a reasonable possibility, you may want to consider how what you do at deposition might enhance the terms or likelihood of settlement. Obviously, to the extent that you obtain evidence to support your client's case or undermine the opposition's case, you tend to enhance the terms of settlement. Other factors you may want to consider to increase the possibility of a favorable settlement include:

   * Using the strategies and techniques in Chapter 12 to illustrate the strengths of your case;

   * In multi-party cases, elicit testimony tending to shift the blame to another party. For example, if you represent one of multiple defendants, elicit testimony emphasizing the culpability or liability of a co-defendant. The deposition record may make the co-defendant recognize that its exposure at trial is greater than previously thought.

As a result, the co-defendant may be more likely to make or increase a settlement offer.[13]

* Seek information providing you with a window into an adverse party's underlying needs and concerns. To the extent that you can elicit information about such matters as an adverse party's economic circumstances and social values, you foster your ability to fashion settlement proposals that meet both parties' underlying needs. For example, if your questions reveal that an out-of-work opponent has been making earnest efforts to find employment, you may infer that the adversary has an immediate need for money and therefore might be especially anxious to settle.

G. Do You Need to Prioritize to Comply With the Seven–Hour Rule?

FRCP 30(d)(2) provides that a deposition may not exceed one day of seven hours, absent a court order or a stipulation among the parties to extend the time.[14] If you are subject to a time limitation for a

13. Bringing out information that increases a co-defendant's liability to the plaintiff is not always strategically wise. Such information may increase plaintiff's evaluation of the settlement value of the case and therefore make settlement more difficult for all defendants. As a result, you may wish to disclose such information to the co-defendant privately, when plaintiff is not present, to attempt to convince the co-defendant to contribute to a settlement. But in some cases disclosing such information during deposition may be the only way to make a reluctant co-defendant contribute a fair share toward settlement.

14. Breaks during the deposition do not count toward the 7 hours. The FRCP advisory committee's notes (2000) indicate that the "only time to be counted is the time occupied by the actual deposition." See Also <u>Condit v. Dunne</u>, 225 F.R.D. 100,

deposition, you will want to adjust your outline to make sure that you cover the most important areas of inquiry during the allotted time.

112 (S.D. N.Y. 2004) ("[T]he 2000 Advisory Committee notes to Rule 30(d) clearly state that only the time taken for the actual deposition, not breaks, counts toward the 7 hours..."); Dow Chemical Co. v. Reinhard, 2008 WL 1735295 (E.D.Mich. 2008); Wilson v. Kautex, A Textron Co., 2008 WL 189568 (N.D.Ind. 2008). Tmie taken by objections by opposing counsel do count, unless the objections are in bad faith. FRCP 30(d)(1) states that "the court must allow additional time consistent with Rule 26(b)(2) if needed for a fair examination of the deponent or if the deponent or another person, or other circumstance, impedes or delays the examination." See Also Plaisted v. Geisinger Medical Center, 210 F.R.D. 527, 533 (M.D. Pa. 2002) (holding that the administrators' counsel could re-depose witnesses because the medical center's counsel did not state objections concisely in a non-argumentative and non-suggestive manner and the objections went on for pages); Miller v. Waseca Medical Center, 205 F.R.D. 537, 538 (D. Minn. 2002) (allowing additional time for the completion of depositions that were impeded by objections inconsistent with Rule 30(d); Armstrong v. Hussmann Corp., 163 F.R.D. 299, 303 (E.D. Mo. 1995) (granting the defendant's motion to re-depose witnesses because the plaintiff's attorneys violated Rule 30(d)(1) when they made constant interruptions and objections in bad faith during the depositions).

CHAPTER 17

ARRANGING FOR DEPOSITIONS

This brief Chapter explains the basic steps involved in arranging for depositions under the Federal Rules of Civil Procedure. Following these steps is necessary both to assure a deponent's attendance and to remove possible obstacles to the subsequent use of helpful deposition testimony.

1. Who May You Depose?

You can depose anyone who may have information relevant to the claims or defenses in a lawsuit.[1] The roster of potential deponents includes:

* All parties in a case;

* Non-party individuals;

* Non-party entities such as partnerships, public or private corporations and government agencies;[2]

* Experts who an adversary may call at trial.[3]

---

1. Absent a court order, you cannot depose a prisoner. See FRCP 30(a).

2. FRCP 30(b)(6). See also J. Grenig & J. Kinsler, <u>Handbook of Federal Civil Discovery and Disclosure</u> §§ 5.20–5.21 (1998).

3. See FRCP 26(b)(4). For a discussion of when you might depose an expert who will testify on an adversary's behalf, see Wright, Miller, & Marcus, Federal Practice and Procedure: Civil 2d § 2031.1. For a discussion of when you might depose a non-

2. Number of Depositions

Absent a court order or a written stipulation among the parties, a party may take no more than ten depositions.[4] Moreover, absent court approval or a written stipulation from all adverse parties, you may not depose a person more than once in the same case.[5]

3. Length of Depositions

Absent a court order or a stipulation, a deposition is limited to a single day of no more than seven (7) hours of testimony.[6] Breaks and recesses do not count towards the seven hours.

4. Necessity of a Notice

Before you depose a party or non-party, you **must serve** every other party with "reasonable **written**

testifying expert, see Wright, Miller, & Marcus, Federal Practice and Procedure: Civil 2d § 2032.

4. See FRCP 30(a)(2)(A)(i).

5. See FRCP 30(a)(2)(a)(ii).

6. See FRCP 30(d)(1). The phrase 7 hours of questioning is a limitation added by a 2000 amendment to FRCP 30. The 2000 Advisory Committee notes to FRCP 30 state that the seven (7) hour "limitation contemplates that there will be reasonable breaks during the day for lunch and other reasons, and that the only time to be counted is the time occupied by the actual deposition." Moreover, FRCP 30(d)(2) provides that the court "must allow additional time … if needed for a fair examination of the deponent or if the deponent or another party impedes or delays the examination." Court decisions have also indicated that breaks in the deposition do not count toward the 7 hour limitation, see Dow Chemical Co. v. Reinhard, 2008 WL 1735295 (E.D.Mich. 2008); Wilson v. Kautex, A Textron Co., 2008 WL 189568 (N.D.Ind. 2008). For a further discussion of these time constraints, see Chapter 24.

notice" of your intention to take the deposition.[7] If your advance notice to a deponent is unreasonably short, the deponent can properly refuse to attend a deposition. Moreover, if you fail to provide notice to a party, or if the length of advance notice to a party is unreasonably short, you will be unable to use any deposition testimony against a party who was not present or represented at the deposition.[8] In addition, if you fail to properly notice a deposition, and as a result the deponent fails to attend but other noticed parties do attend, a judge can order you to pay the reasonable expenses incurred by the attending parties, including attorney's fees.[9]

It is both good practice and professionally courteous to clear the times and places for depositions with opposing counsel whenever possible.[10] Doing so before you send out a deposition notice typically saves time and aggravation in both the short and the long run. After all, if you do not cooperate with other parties in this way, they may well respond in like manner by scheduling their own depositions at times and places that are inconvenient for you or your client or by seeking protective orders pursuant to FRCP 26(c).[11]

7. FRCP 30(b)(1). For a discussion of what constitutes reasonable notice, see Wright, Miller, & Marcus, Federal Practice and Procedure: Civil 2d § 2111.

8. See FRCP 32(a)(1).

9. See FRCP 30(g).

10. You may also want to send a confirming letter regarding any such agreement.

11. See also FRCP 30(d)(3). For a discussion of the kinds of orders courts may make with respect to the time and place of taking depositions, see Wright, Miller, & Marcus, Federal Practice and Procedure: Civil 2d §§ 2111–2112.

5. Contents of a Notice

At a minimum, a Notice of Deposition must set forth the following information:[12]

* The date, time and place of a deposition.

* The name and address of each person to be deposed. If you are deposing an entity pursuant to FRCP 30(b)(6) and you do not know the name of the person to be deposed, you need only a general description sufficient to identify the examinee or the particular class or group to which the person belongs.[13] Thus, for example, if you are taking a deposition of an entity pursuant to FRCP 30(b)(6),[14] you might describe a deponent as "the person most knowledgeable with respect to the Health Department's June 12 inspection of the premises at 1053 Hanley Avenue."

* The method of recording the testimony.

Testimony is most commonly recorded stenographically. However, either in lieu of or addition to a stenographic record, you may specify that a deposition will be visually recorded[15] or sound recorded.[16]

12. See FRCP 30(b)(1) (2) and (3).

13. FRCP 30(b)(1).

14. See Chapter 18 for a discussion of 30 (b) (6) depositions of an entity.

15. For a further discussion of visually recorded depositions, see Chapter 22.

16. By virtue of a stipulation or a court order, depositions may also be "taken by telephone or other remote means." FRCP 30(b)(4).

* If pursuant to FRCP 30(b)(6) you intend to depose an entity such as a partnership or corporation, the notice must identify the subjects that you will explore at deposition.[17]

6. When You May Take Depositions

Absent a court order or a written stipulation, you generally cannot take a deposition until after you and your adversary have met and developed a joint discovery plan pursuant to FRCP 26(f) and the court has issued a Scheduling Order pursuant to FRCP 16(b).[18] Typically, such an order issues within 90 days after the first defendant's appearance and within 120 days after a defendant has been served with a complaint.[19]

Unless you are precluded from doing so by a Scheduling Order, and except with respect to expert

17. See FRCP 30(b)(6). If the deponent entity is a non-party, the subpoena requiring its attendance at the deposition must advise the entity to designate a person(s) who will testify on its behalf. The entity then has the responsibility to produce at the deposition a person who is competent to testify about the subjects listed in the deposition notice. If one person is not competent to testify about each subject listed in the deposition notice, the entity must produce as many competent persons as are necessary to testify about the listed topics. For a more detailed discussion of taking an entity's deposition, see Chapter 18.

18. See Wright, Miller, & Marcus, Federal Practice and Procedure: Civil 2d § 2046.1 and FRCP 26(d). A party may take a deposition prior to this time if "the deponent is expected to leave the United States and be unavailable for examination in this country after that time." FRCP 30(a)(2)(A). Also, in some instances, you may take a deposition to preserve testimony before an action is filed. FRCP 27(a). By stipulation depositions may be taken prior to the time identified in FRCP 26(d); see FRCP 29.

19. See FRCP 16(b).

witnesses, you can proceed to take depositions at whatever time and in whatever order you choose.[20] That another party may have already noticed a deposition does not deprive you of the right to notice an earlier deposition of a different deponent. In other words, the FRCP do not provide for priorities in the taking of depositions.[21]

7. Where You May Take Depositions

Typically you can depose a **party** in the district where an action has been brought.[22] However, you must normally notice a **non-party's** deposition for a location which is no more than 100 miles away from the place where the non-party deponent resides, is employed or regularly transacts business in person.[23] FRCP 45(a)(1)(C) mandates that a Subpoena recite this limitation. Agents of non-party corporations ordinarily must be deposed within the

20. Your deposition of an adversary's testifying **expert** will typically occur "late in the game." Under Rule 26(a)(2)(C), a party typically need not disclose the identity of any expert witness until ninety (90) days prior to trial. Accordingly, you usually will not depose any adverse expert prior to ninety days before trial. For a more detailed discussion on deposing an adversary's expert witnesses, see Chapter 20; J. Grenig & J. Kinsler, Handbook of Federal Civil Discovery and Disclosure § 5.31 (1998).

21. See Wright, Miller, & Marcus, Federal Practice and Procedure: Civil 2d §§ 2046 & 2046.1.

22. For a discussion of circumstances in which a plaintiff may avoid being deposed in the district where the action was brought, see Wright, Miller, & Marcus, Federal Practice and Procedure: Civil 2d § 2112.

23. This limitation is imposed by FRCP 45, which governs the subpoenaing of witnesses. See also Wright, Miller, & Marcus, Federal Practice and Procedure: Civil 2d § 2454.

district where the corporation has its principal place of business.[24]

The 100–mile limit for non-party deponents may require you to conduct a deposition in a district in other than the one in which an action is pending. In such instances, you can compel a non-party to attend the deposition only if you first obtain a Subpoena from the district court in the jurisdiction where the deposition will take place.[25]

When you are counsel taking the deposition, you ordinarily hold depositions in your office. However, you may notice a deposition for a site other than your office for such reasons as:

* Your office is not located in a proper district. For example, if you must depose a non-party deponent in a different district, the deposition may take place in the suite of a hotel located in the proper district.

* You want to videotape a deposition, and your office lacks proper video facilities. In this instance, you may notice the deposition for the office of the videographer who oversees the videotaping.

8.   Securing a Deponent's Attendance

When the deponent is a **party** (or an officer, director or managing agent of a party), the only predeposition task you must complete in order to com-

24.   See Wright, Miller, & Marcus, Federal Practice and Procedure: Civil 2d § 2112.

25.   See Wright, Miller, & Marcus, Federal Practice and Procedure: Civil 2d § 2112.

pel the party's attendance is to serve a proper Notice of Deposition.[26] For parties, mailed notice generally suffices.

You can compel a **non-party** deponent to attend a deposition only through personal service of either a Subpoena re Deposition and/or a Subpoena Duces Tecum re Deposition.[27] Use the latter if a non-party deponent is to bring documents to a deposition. To compel a non-party deponent to appear, you must also tender **witness fees**.[28]

9. Arranging for Document Production

A. *Production at a Deposition*

If you want a **party** deponent to bring documents to a deposition, identify those documents in the

26. See Wright, Miller, & Marcus, Federal Practice and Procedure: Civil 2d § 2107; see also Precisionflow Tech., Inc. v. CVD Equipment Corp., 140 F.Supp.2d 195 (N.D.N.Y. 2001) (Plaintiff could be sanctioned where its employees failed to attend a deposition after being served with a Notice of Deposition. The plaintiff had assumed the responsibility of having the employees appear, even though they weren't officers or managers.); Singh v. Wackenhut Corp., 252 F.R.D. 308 (M.D.La. 2008) (Sanctions granted against plaintiff for failure to show at deposition. Plaintiff claimed she never received notice of deposition, but court said it was sufficient that the defendant sent the notice to her last known address via certified mail, even though the notice was returned as unclaimed.)

27. See FRCP 30(a)(1). A subpoena may be issued by a court clerk or by a lawyer admitted to practice in the district where the deposition will take place. See FRCP 45(a)(3); Wright, Miller, & Marcus, Federal Practice and Procedure: Civil 2d § 2107. For a discussion of the proper service of a subpoena, see FRCP 45(b).

28. See J. Grenig & J. Kinsler, Handbook of Federal Civil Discovery and Disclosure § 5.52 (1998); FRCP 45(b)(1).

Notice of Deposition.[29] However, you must then serve the Notice of Deposition on the party at least thirty days in advance of the deposition. The reason for this is that FRCP 34 requires that parties have at least thirty days to respond to requests to produce documents.[30] Some lawyers have tried to circumvent the 30 day requirement by giving less than 30 days notice for a deposition, and then serving a party deponent with a Subpoena Duces Tecum re Deposition which identifies the documents to be produced at the deposition. Courts have tended not to look favorably on this approach.[31]

To obtain documents from a **non-party** deponent, serve the deponent with a Subpoena Duces Tecum re Deposition. The documents to be produced at the deposition should be described in the Subpoena Duces Tecum re Deposition or in a separate attachment which must be served along with the Subpoena. To compel a non-party deponent to appear, you must also tender **witness fees**.[32]

B. Production Prior to a Deposition

Questioning at deposition with respect to documents is likely to be more effective if you have

29. See FRCP 30(b)(2).

30. See FRCP 34(b).

31. For a discussion of the incongruity that exists because a non-party can be required to bring documents on less than thirty (30) days notice while a party must be given at least thirty (30) days notice, see Wright, Miller, & Marcus, Federal Practice and Procedure: Civil 2d § 2108.

32. See J. Grenig & J. Kinsler, Handbook of Federal Civil Discovery and Disclosure § 5.52 (1998); FRCP 45(b)(1).

reviewed the documents in advance of the deposition. That way, you can examine the documents without being under pressure to simultaneously pose questions.

Often, a party's "mandatory disclosures"[33] include documents that you can examine in advance of a deposition. In addition, you may secure further documents in advance of a deposition from a **party** by making a Request for Production under FRCP 34.[34]

To obtain documents prior to a deposition from a **non-party**, serve the non-party with a Subpoena Duces Tecum that simply requires the non-party to produce specified documents for inspection and copying at the time and place designated in the Subpoena.[35] You must, however, give prior written notice to all other parties regarding the time and place that the documents are to be produced.[36] After reviewing the documents, you can then decide whether or not you want to depose the non-party. Initially subpoenaing only the documents is particularly useful when a non-party is an entity whose only connection to a case seems to be that it possesses relevant documents.

33. See FRCP 26(a)(1). See also Wright, Miller, & Marcus, Federal Practice and Procedure: Civil 2d § 2053.

34. For a discussion of how to obtain documents pursuant to Rule 34, see Wright, Miller, & Marcus, Federal Practice and Procedure: Civil 2d § 2201 et seq.

35. See FRCP 45(a)(1)(A) and Wright, Miller, & Marcus, Federal Practice and Procedure: Civil 2d § 2108.

36. FRCP 45(b)(1). See also Wright, Miller, & Marcus, Federal Practice and Procedure: Civil 2d § 2108.

10. Ensuring a Presiding Officer's Attendance

If you notice a deposition, you are responsible for ensuring the attendance of a presiding officer, who is a person authorized to swear in the deponent.[37] Under FRCP 28, a person who can administer the oath is "an officer authorized to administer oaths by the laws of the United States or of the place where the examination is held, or before a person appointed by the court in which the action is pending." Typically a presiding officer is also a certified court reporter who can both administer the oath and stenographically record the deposition.

To carry out your responsibility under FRCP 28, be sure to make prior arrangements with a notary or other court officer to be present at the time and place set for the deposition. Should you fail to do so and no one is present to administer the oath, you may be sanctioned if other parties appear at the deposition ready to proceed.[38]

11. Ensuring That a Deposition Is Recorded

If you notice a deposition, you are responsible to make sure that it is recorded. As noted above, a deposition may be recorded stenographically or in a variety of other ways. If your chosen method is other than stenographic recordation, the method

37. See FRCP 28(a)(1).

38. See FRCP 30(g).

must be one from which a stenographic record can subsequently be made.[39]

12.   Waiving FRCP Requirements

FRCP 29 gives parties broad latitude to enter into stipulations modifying the FRCP provisions relating to depositions and other discovery methods. For example, you might stipulate with opposing counsel that a deposition may be taken on 2 days notice. Stipulations modifying the provisions of the FRCP should generally either be stated on the record or memorialized in writing.[40]

39.   See FRCP 26(a)(3)(A) and FRCP 32(c).

40.   See Wright, Miller, & Marcus, Federal Practice and Procedure: Civil 2d § 2091.

PART THREE

SPECIAL DEPOSITIONS

Part Three (Chapters 18 through 22) focuses on taking "special" depositions, including those of an adverse expert, a Rule 30(b)(6) deponent, and those to preserve the testimony of your own witness for trial.

CHAPTER 18

FRCP 30(b)(6) "SUBJECT MATTER" DEPOSITIONS

FRCP 30(b)(6) allows you to depose a corporation, a partnership, an association or a government agency on one or more subjects without identifying a particular person to be deposed.[1] When you notice a 30(b)(6) "subject matter" deposition, an entity must respond by designating for deposition one or more representatives who are most knowledgeable about the subjects set forth in your notice.[2] When a designee testifies, the answers are binding on an entity to the same extent that deposition testimony

1. You may depose a party or non-party entity. FRCP 30(b)(6); see also Wright, Miller & Marcus, Federal Practice and Procedure: Civil 2d Sec. 2104. Similar rules exist in most states. See e.g. Cal. Civ. Proc. § 2025(d)(6) (West 2001) (California); Ga. Code Ann. § 9–11–30(b)(6) (2000) (Georgia); Kan. Stat. Ann. § 60–230(b)(5) (2000) (Kansas); La. Civ. Code Ann. art. 1442 (West) (Louisiana); Mont. Code Ann. §§ 25–20 Rule 30(b)(6) (1999) (Montana); N.C. Gen. Stat. § 1A–1 (1999) (North Carolina); Okla. Stat. Ann. tit. 12, § 3230(C)(5) (West)n (Oklahoma); Or. Rev. State § 39(C)(6) (1999) (Oregon); SC ST RCP Rule 30(b)(6) (West 2001) (South Carolina); S.D. Codified Laws § 154–6–30(b)(6) (South Dakota); Wis. Stat. Ann § 804.05(2)(e) (West 2001) (Wisconsin).

2. The entity's obligation to produce such a designees includes a duty to "prepare them so that they may give complete, knowledgeable and binding answers on the [entity]." Marker v. Union Fidelity Life Ins. Co. 125 F.R.D. 121, 126 (M.D.N.C. 1989).

of an individual is binding on that person.[3] This Chapter explores the noticing and taking of subject matter depositions.[4]

1.　Why Take a Subject Matter Deposition?

Subject matter depositions often reduce discovery efforts and costs. You can avoid the time and expense of first sending out interrogatories to identify entity representatives who are knowledgeable about a relevant subject, and then deposing each of those people. Instead, you can simply require the entity to produce the person(s) most knowledgeable in response to a single deposition notice. Thus, for example, in litigation about a plane crash you might send a 30(b)(6) notice to the airline requiring it to produce the person(s) most knowledgeable about subjects such as the maintenance history of the plane and the electrical system on the plane.

Subject matter depositions can also help you educate yourself about an entity's organizational structure, procedures and operations. Assume for example that you want to learn about a financial entity's usual practices and procedures when initiating a

3. See <u>United States v. Taylor</u>, 166 F.R.D. 356, 362 n 6. "[J]ust as in the deposition of individuals, it is only the statement of the corporate person which, if altered, may be explained away and explored through cross-examination as to why the opinion or statement was altered. (Citations) However, the designee can make admissions against interest under FRE 804(b)(3) which are binding on the corporation. (Citations)." (Id.) (citing <u>Ierardi v. Lorillard, Inc.</u>, Civ. A. No. 90–7049, 1991 WL 158911, at *3 (E.D. Pa. Aug. 13, 1991).

4. These depositions are also sometimes referred to as "Person Most Knowledgeable" depositions.

foreclosure. You can notice a subject matter deposition on this subject and educate yourself about what usually happens, and then later take additional depositions to determine what actually happened in your client's case.

2. How Many 30(b)(6) Depositions Can You Take?

You may be limited to one 30(b)(6) deposition for a given entity. The reason is that the person being deposed is the entity, and under FRCP 30(a)(2)(B), in the absence of court permission, you can depose a person only once.[5]

3. The Importance of Comprehensive 30(b)(6) Notices

Since you may be limited to a single FRCP 30(b)(6) deposition, frame a notice comprehensively so as to include all discoverable subjects that interest you. It is not necessary that a single person within an organization be knowledgeable about all the subjects you identify. Rather, an entity is responsible for designating and producing representatives who can testify fully on each subject in a notice.[6] Therefore, if no single person within an entity is knowledgeable on all subjects in a notice,

---

5. Cf Wright, Miller & Marcus, Federal Practice and Procedure: Civil 2d, § 2104.

6. FRCP 30 advisory committee notes on 1993 amendments, reprinted in 146 F.R.D. 401, 666 (1993). See also Marker v. Union Fidelity Life Ins. Co., 125 F.R.D. 121, 126 (M.D.N.C. 1989); See also FDIC.v. Butcher, 116 F.R.D. 196 (E.D.Tenn. 1986); Mitsui & Co. v. Puerto Rico Water Res. Auth., 93 F.R.D. 62 (D.P.R.1981); Ierardi v. Lorillard, Inc., 1991 WL 158911, 1 (E.D.Pa).

the entity must designate as many persons as are necessary to produce a knowledgeable person on each subject.[7] If an entity fails to designate a person who is knowledgeable about a discoverable subject included in your notice, you are entitled to a court order requiring an entity to produce a knowledgeable person and possibly to sanctions.[8]

4.   Questioning 30(b)(6) Designees

The subsections below explore two questioning concerns that tend to be unique to 30(b)(6) depositions.

A.   *Is the Designee Knowledgeable?*

To avoid wasting time questioning a designee who in reality has little information about subjects in a 30(b)(6) notice, determine the extent of a designee's knowledge at a deposition's outset.[9] To do so, you might pursue topics such as the following:

* What makes a designee knowledgeable?

* What did the designee do to prepare to testify on each subject? For example, what documents

7. <u>FDIC v. Butcher,</u> 116 F.R.D. 196. See also Wright, Miller & Marcus, Federal Practice and Procedure: Civil 2d, § 2103. If an entity no longer employs someone knowledgeable about a designated matter, the entity must take steps to reasonably prepare a representative by using sources such as documents and former employees. <u>United States v. Taylor,</u> 166 F.R.D. 356, 362 (M.D.N.C. 1996).

8. See Wright, Miller & Marcus, Federal Practice and Procedure: Civil 2d, § 2103.

9. It often makes sense to probe a designee's knowledge immediately after giving admonitions, or perhaps after background questioning.

did a designee read and with whom did the designee talk?

* Who else within the entity might be as knowledgeable or more knowledgeable that the designee on the subject?

Exploring such topics can help you determine whether an entity has properly complied with the requirement that it produce a person who can testify fully about the subjects in your notice. You also gain an indication at the outset of the extent to which a designee will testify from personal knowledge.[10] You may also identify documents of which you were previously unaware and ask to see them before questioning the designee.[11]

In the example below, you probe the designee's knowledge by using the deposition notice and proceeding through the subjects it includes.

1. Q: Mr. Montross, I'd like to show you this four page document entitled Notice of Deposition that has been marked as Exhibit 1. Will you look at it please?

2. A: OK.

10. There is no requirement that a designee only testify from personal knowledge. Indeed, in some instances an entity may no longer have in its employ persons who are personally knowledgeable on the subjects in your notice. However, if the designee is not personally knowledgeable you want to know that such is the situation. In addition, you want to identify who is personally knowledgeable so that you can decide whether you also want to depose that person.

11. As with any other deposition, you typically try to obtain relevant documents before a 30(b)(6) deposition or require a deponent to bring documents to the deposition.

3. Q: Have you seen a copy of Exhibit 1 before coming here today?

4. A: Yes.

5. Q: When did you first see it?

6. A: About a week ago.

7. Q: Where did you see Exhibit 1?

8. A: In my lawyer's office.

9. Q: Was anyone else present when you saw Exhibit 1 other than your lawyer?

10. A: No.

11. Q: Please read to yourself paragraph one on page two of Exhibit 1.

12. Q: Are you knowledgeable about the matters described in paragraph one on page two of Exhibit 1?

13. A: Yes.

14. Q: What makes you knowledgeable about the matters described in paragraph one?

15. A: I was employed by Blue Bus Company as a chief mechanic for 10 years.

16. Q: What else makes you knowledgeable with respect to the matters described in paragraph one on page two of Exhibit 1?

17. A: I worked on and inspected brakes for the company during that time period and I supervised the work of other mechanics who worked on the brakes.

18. Q: Is there anything else that makes you knowledgeable about the matters described in paragraph one on page two of Exhibit 1?

19. A: No.

20. Q: Did you read or review any documents in preparing to testify here today about the matters described in paragraph one on page two of Exhibit 1?

21. A: No.

22. Q: Are you aware of any written materials relating to the subjects described in paragraph one on page two of Exhibit 1?

23. A: A company manual sets forth how often we should inspect the brakes of company buses and there are various manufacturers' manuals on brake maintenance and repair.

24. Q: Are there any other materials relating to the subjects described in paragraph one on page two of Exhibit 1?

25. A: Not that I can think of at this time.

26. Q: If you wanted to find out if Blue Bus Company had any other written materials relating to the subjects described in paragraph one on page two of Exhibit 1, how would you go about doing so?

27. A: I'd ask our maintenance supervisor, Robert Garcia.

28. Q: In preparing to testify today, why didn't you read the company manual that sets forth how

often the brakes of company buses should be inspected?

29. A: Because I know what it says and because we have a vehicle database that we use constantly to remind ourselves of when inspections on each company vehicle need to be done.

30. Q: Any other reason you didn't read the manual?

31. A: No.

32. Q: Please describe the vehicle database.

33. A: [Answer omitted]

34. Q: Is there anyone at the Blue Bus Company who you believe knows more than you do about the subjects described in paragraph one on page two of Exhibit 1?

35. A: Mr. Garcia may know more than I do; I'm not sure on that point.

36. Q: Anyone else beside Mr. Garcia?

37. A: Well, Marshall Fogerty, but he is no longer with the company. He retired about two months ago.

38. Q: Why do you believe that Mr. Fogerty might be more knowledgeable on the matters in paragraph one on page two of Exhibit 1?

39. A: He was the overall maintenance supervisor for more than twenty years.

40. Q: Do you know how to contact Mr. Fogerty?

41.   A: No, but I believe Mr. Garcia knows how to get hold of him.

In theory, you might go through each subject in a 30(b)(6) notice in the kind of detail as in the above example. However, you may shorten this phase of a 30(b)(6) deposition in various ways. For example, you may go through each subject, but in a more limited fashion. Alternatively, you might omit inquiries about some subjects. Or, you may explore a designee's knowledge with a question aimed at all the subjects in a notice. An example of such a question is, "What makes you knowledgeable about the subjects described in Exhibit 1?"

B.   *Inquire About an Entity's Actions Rather Than a Designee's*

When you question a designee, one of your goals is to obtain information about the entity and its operations and to bind the entity to the designee's statements about the entity. Therefore, ask about the entity and not the designee.

Example

Incorrect: How often did <u>you</u> inspect the brake systems of the buses on Route 21?

Correct: How often did the <u>Blue Bus Company</u> inspect the brake systems of the buses on Route 21?

When you find out what an entity has done, you can then inquire about who acted on the entity's behalf, what each individual (including the designee) did, and the foundation for the designee's knowledge.

5. Going Beyond the Subjects in a Notice

The scope of 30(b)(6) questioning is not necessarily limited to the subjects set forth in a deposition notice.[12] However, if it turns out that a deponent has no knowledge about matters beyond those in a notice, you cannot claim that the entity has failed to designate a knowledgeable representative.[13]

Questioning beyond the subjects in the notice of deposition may not bind the entity. An entity that has not been notified in advance that you will pursue a subject beyond those in the notice may

12. See King v.Pratt & Whitney, 161 F.R.D. 475, 476 (S.D.Fla.1995) ("If the examining party asks questions outside the scope of the matters described in the notice, the general deposition rules govern, so that relevant questions may be asked and no special protection is conferred on a deponent by virtue of the fact that the deposition was noticed under 30(b)(6).") See also Detoy v. City and County of S.F., 196 F.R.D. 362 (N.D.Cal. 2000); Mitsui & Co. v. Puerto Rico Water Resources Authority, 93 F.R.D. 62, 67 (D. P. R.1981); Overseas Private Investment Corp. v. Mandelbaum, 185 F.R.D. 67, 68 (D.D.C. 1999). But see Paparelli v. Prudential Insurance Co., 108 F.R.D. 727, 730 (D. Mass 1985) ("I rule that if a party opts to employ the procedures of Rule 30(b)(6), F.R.Civ.P., to depose the representative of a corporation, that party must confine the examination to the matters 'stated with reasonable particularity' which are contained in the Notice of Deposition.") See also, See Wright, Miller & Marcus, Federal Practice and Procedure: Civil 2d, § 2103. If you are defending a 30(b)(6) deposition, you may want to prepare the deponent on all areas that might be relevant to the case.

13. See King v. Pratt & Whitney, 161 F.R.D. 475, 476 (S.D. Fla 1995) ". . . [I]f the deponent does not know the answer to questions outside the scope of the matters described in the notice, then that is the examining party's problem.").

argue that it has not had an opportunity to designate the most knowledgeable person on the unnoticed subject, and that as a result it should not be bound by the designee's testimony.

6. Can You Depose a 30(b)(6) Designee Twice?

You must ordinarily obtain court permission to depose the same person more than once.[14] However, a 30(b)(6) designee appears on behalf of an entity and not as an individual. Therefore, the one deposition rule may not foreclose you from subsequently deposing, without court permission, an individual who has previously been designated in response to a 30(b)(6) notice.[15] In other words, you may be able to depose the same person as a designated representative and later as an individual.

For example, assume that you send a 30(b)(6) notice to the Blue Bus Company requiring it to designate a person to be deposed regarding its general practices and procedures for maintaining the brakes on its buses. The company designates a representative who both knows about the Company's general maintenance practices and who worked on the bus involved in the accident that injured your client. If you limit your questions at the 30(b)(6) deposition to the Company's general prac-

14. FRCP 30(a)(2)(B).

15. See <u>King v. Pratt & Whitney,</u> 161 F.R.D. 475, 476 (S.D. Fla 1995) ("Clearly, Plaintiff could simply re-notice a [30(b)(6) designee's deposition as an individual] under the regular notice provisions ...") See also Wright, Miller and Marcus, Federal Practice and Procedure: Civil 2d, § 2103.

tices, you may then be entitled to depose the designee a second time in his individual capacity to determine what he did with respect to the bus involved in the accident. On the other hand, assume at the 30(b)(6) deposition you ask both about the company's general practices and what the deponent did with respect to the bus involved in the accident. You would then arguably be questioning the deponent in his individual capacity and therefore you may not be able to depose him a second time without leave of court. Consequently, if you go beyond the scope of the matters stated in a 30(b)(6) deposition notice, question the deponent thoroughly; you may not have an opportunity for a second bite at the apple.

7. Using a 30(b)(6) Deposition to Obtain the Bases for an Adverse Party's Contentions

Special concerns arise when you use a 30(b)(6) deposition to obtain information about an adverse party's legal contentions. You should generally not phrase a 30(b)(6) notice in a way that asks an adversary to designate a person who is most knowledgeable about the facts supporting a legal theory or a legal conclusion in a pleading.[16] For example, in

16. You are generally entitled to ask the deponent if she has information to support a factual conclusion or contention. See e.g. Arkwright Mut. Ins. Co. v. National Union Fire Ins. Co., No.90 Civ.7811, 1993 WL 34678 (S.D.N.Y.1993); Rifkind v.Superior Court, 22 Cal.App.4th 1255, 27 Cal.Rptr.2d 822 (1994). The cases are split, however, on whether it is appropriate at deposition to ask questions that seek facts or information supporting a legal conclusion in the pleadings or a legal theory. Some courts have upheld the use of such questions at deposition, see Ortho

litigation resulting from the crash of an airliner, assume that the airline's answer asserts that the crash resulted from the negligence of air traffic controllers. You send out a 30(b)(6) notice asking the airline to designate the "representative who is most knowledgeable about the affirmative defense in your answer that the crash was due in part to the negligence of air traffic controllers." A court might well uphold the airline's request for a protective order preventing the deposition from going forward, on the ground that your deposition is an impermissible attempt to require the airline to marshal evidence supporting a legal theory.[17]

Nevertheless, by carefully phrasing a 30(b)(6) deposition notice you may be able to depose the person most knowledgeable about the information supporting an adversary's legal contentions. In the above example, for instance, you may be able to send out a 30(b)(6) notice asking the airline to designate the "representative who is most knowledgeable about the activities of the air traffic controllers on the day of the accident giving rise to this

Pharm. Corp. v. Smith, No.90–0242, 1990 WL 10011 (E.D. Pa.1990); Hammond v. Air Line Pilots Ass'n., No.87 C 2792, 1987 WL 20421 (N.D. Ill. 1987). Other cases have held that in some circumstances such questions need only be answered in response to contention interrogatories, see Rifkind v. Superior Court, 22 Cal.App.4th 1255, 27 Cal.Rptr.2d 822 (1994); Exxon Research and Eng'g Co.v.United States, 44 Fed.Cl. 597 (1999); McCormick–Morgan, Inc.v.Teledyne Indus., Inc., 134 F.R.D. 275 (N.D. Cal. 1991), *rev'd on other grounds*, 765 F.Supp. 611 (N.D. Cal. 1991); In re Independent Serv. Orgs. Antitrust Litig., 168 F.R.D. 651 (D.Kan.1996).

17. Id.

litigation." This notice does not mention any legal theory or allegation in the pleadings. It simply seeks the person most knowledgeable about what happened on the day of the accident. Therefore, the notice is less likely to be seen as an impermissible attempt to require the airline to marshal evidence supporting a legal theory.[18]

18. The determination of whether a subject matter deposition is an impermissible attempt to have the deponent marshal evidence is a question of fact in each case. If you receive a notice for a subject matter deposition that you think improperly seeks to have your client marshal evidence, you may want to go to court to obtain a protective order which either prohibits the deposition from going forward or limits the scope of the questioning.

CHAPTER 19

INQUIRING ABOUT PRACTICES AND POLICIES

This Chapter explores strategies and techniques for inquiring about an adverse organization's practices and policies.[1] You might confine a deposition to an organization's practices and policies, or you might ask about practices and policies as well as inquiring into the events of your specific case. For example, assume that you represent the plaintiff in an action to recover damages against a bank for failure to fund a loan. You might choose to devote an entire deposition to the bank's general policies for investigating and approving loans.[2] Alternatively, you might inquire into those matters during a deposition in which you also question a bank officer concerning the loan made to your client. Whichever

1. The term organization refers to any public or private corporation, partnership, association or agency. In some cases, you may inquire about the practices and policies of an individual rather than an organization. For example, you might make such an inquiry in a case involving a business operated by an individual.

2. You may follow the procedures outlined in FRCP 30(b)(6) when you want to take a "practice and policy" deposition but do not know which of an entity's representatives would be most knowledgeable. For more information about FRCP 30(b)(6), see Chapter 18.

option you choose, you can enhance the effectiveness of practice and policy inquiries by using the strategies discussed in this Chapter.

1. Distinguishing "Practices" From "Policies"

As you'll see below, questioning strategies vary somewhat depending on whether your inquiry concerns a practice or a policy. Therefore, having in mind how a practice tends to differ from a policy may help you apply the strategies described below.

A "practice" consists of the usual series of steps that an organization or individual actually takes when processing a particular type of matter. That is, a practice consists of "what's on the ground" as part of an organization's daily operations. For instance, a practice might consist of the steps that a company usually follows when moving to terminate employees, or the procedures that a government benefits office normally follows when determining whether clients remain eligible for welfare benefits.[3]

The term "policy" generally refers to a rule or a custom that an organization's representatives are supposed to follow when they handle a particular kind of matter. For example, a policy might be a company's rule defining the type of misconduct for which employees can be terminated or a policy might set forth the steps that a company's representative **should** follow when terminating employ-

---

3. As the examples suggest, the term "practice", as used here, is virtually synonymous with the terms "procedure" and "process."

ees for certain types of misconduct. Policies may be reflected either by written documents or by unwritten customs.

2. Purposes of Practice and Policy Inquiries

As stated above, the usual purpose of practice and policy inquiries is not to investigate what happened in a particular case, but rather to gather information about what usually happens in a given class of cases. You might want to undertake such an inquiry for one or more of the following purposes:

Ascertaining whether practices were adhered to. Liability may turn on whether an entity or individual adhered to its usual practices when carrying out a particular action. For example, a conclusion that an employee was "wrongfully" terminated may turn in part on whether the employer followed its usual termination practices. Thus, if you represent the employee in such a case you might make practice and policy inquiries to ascertain the employer's usual disciplinary procedures.

Ascertaining whether practices comply with industry standards. You may also decide to make practice and policy inquiries when you intend to argue that an opposing party's practice or policy conflicts with an industry standard. For example, assume that you've sued a municipality under the federal Clean Water Act, claiming that the municipality's practices for maintaining catch basins conflict with industry-wide "best management practices." You might depose a municipal official concerning the municipality's general catch basin practices.

Ascertaining whether practices comply with legal standards. Another purpose of practice and policy inquiries is to support a claim that an entity's practices violate a normative legal standard. For example, if you claim that a prison's procedures for allowing prisoners to have access to legal materials violates due process, you might depose a prison official concerning those procedures.

Identifying Witnesses and Documents. Still another purpose of practice and policy inquiries is to identify potential documents and witnesses. For instance, if you claim that a company's product was defectively designed, you might depose a company agent concerning the company's normal "R and D" practices. The information can help you identify the departments and employees who may have been involved in designing the product and documents that may have been generated during the design process.

3. Who to Depose

Especially in large organizations, knowledge of policies and practices tends to differ according to a representative's stature in the hierarchy. For example, an upper echelon employee may be quite familiar with an organization's policies, yet have much less familiarity with its actual practices and still less knowledge of the events involved in a specific case. Therefore, who you choose to depose concerning practices and policies may depend on the argument you are attempting to support.

For example, assume that one of your principal arguments is that your client should prevail because an organization failed to follow its own practices and policies in your client's specific case. Your argument may be that although a company's policies and practices called for employees to be given an opportunity to correct deficiencies in performance before being terminated, your client was given no such opportunity. In such a situation, you may want to depose an upper echelon employee concerning the company's practices and policies. Since the upper echelon employee may have little information about the events involved in your specific case, the employee may be unable to conveniently "match" testimony to your client's experience. The conflicts that may result between what is supposed to happen or generally happens and what happened in your client's case may bolster your argument.

On the other hand, assume one of your arguments on a client's behalf is that both an organization's general practices and what happened to the client conflict with the organization's policies. Here, you may want to depose a lower echelon employee concerning the organization's practices. The lower echelon employee may be less inclined to match usual practices to those called for by an organization's policies.

4. Questioning Strategies Regarding Practices

To obtain a full description of an organization's practices, you'll typically seek to obtain a chronology of the steps and an account of what happens at each step.[4] The subsections below examine strategies for confronting issues that often arise when deponents testify concerning an organization's practices.

A. *Responding to "It Depends" Answers*

Often, practices are dependent on one or more variables. Consequently, asked a question such as "what then happens," deponents may well answer, "It depends." An effective response is to identify the important and common variables that may alter the practice and then pursue the effects of each.

For example, assume that you have filed a lawsuit against a private company responsible for monitoring detainees being held at an Immigration and Naturalization Service (INS) holding facility. Your complaint alleges that the company's current procedure denies detainees due process. You are taking a "practice and policy" deposition of a security officer for the company, and want to put on the record the company's version of the current procedure that INS detainees generally have to follow to obtain access to legal materials. Your questioning about the procedure proceeds as follows:

4. Chapter 3 describes questioning strategies you can employ to identify and obtain details about each step in a practice or procedure.

1.   Q: After a detainee asks a unit officer to use the library, what happens next?

2.   A: It depends.

3.   Q: Tell me all the things it depends upon.

4.   A: It depends on whether the request is made on a weekday or weekend.

5.   Q: Does what happens after a detainee asks a unit officer to use the library depend upon anything else beside whether the request is made on a weekend or a weekday?

6.   A: Yes, whether the request is made before or after noon.

7.   Q: Does what happens after a detainee asks a unit officer to use the library, depend upon anything else beside whether the request is made on a weekend or a weekday and whether it is made before or after noon?

8.   A: No.

Here, the questioning thus far establishes that the procedure depends on the day of the week and the time of day that a request is made. You may now follow up by trying to uncover the reasons for the existence of these variables.

9.   Q: All right. Why does the day of the week make a difference?

10. A: Because if the request is made on a Saturday or Sunday, the request will not be processed until Monday. We don't have a library officer who can do unit pick-ups on the weekends.

11.   Any other reason the request can't be processed until Monday?

12.   No.

[Inquiries about why there is no library officer on weekends omitted]

17.   Q: Why does whether the request is made before noon make a difference?

18.   A: Because . . .

19.   Any other reason?

20.   No.

At this point, you may probe the effect of each important variable on an entity's practices. For example:

21.   Q: Okay. Let's assume that on a week day and before noon, a detainee asks a unit officer to use the library. What happens next?

22.   A: The unit officer would. . . .

B. *Inquire About Exceptions*

After a deponent has described a practice or policy, you may want to inquire into instances known to the deponent in which the practice was not followed. Such inquiries are likely to be particularly important if your client's claim rests on an individual's or entity's failure to follow usual practices.

Inquiries concerning exceptions might concern both: (1) specific instances in which a general practice was not followed, and (2) broad categories of cases in which a general practice was not followed.

When making these inquiries you may ask about both occasions with which a deponent is personally familiar as well as those that a deponent is aware of from the verbal or written comments of others. The following examples illustrate each of these inquiries.

Inquiring Into Specific Instances

1.   Q: Ms. Foreman, you've told me about the procedure that the company generally uses when warning employees that their performance has been deemed unsatisfactory. Do you know of any particular instances within the last five years in which this procedure was not followed?

2.   A: Yes.

3.   Q: As far as you know, on how many occasions was this procedure not followed?

4.   A: I can recall two in that period of time.

5.   Q: Can you tell me about the first instance?

[Inquiry into each instance omitted]

14.   Q: In addition to the two instances you've just told me about, have you heard of any other instances within the last five years in which the usual warning procedure was not followed?

15.   A: No.

16.   Q: In addition to the two instances you've just told me about, have you read of any other instances in which the usual warning procedure was not followed?

17.   A. . . .

Inquiring Into Categories of Cases

1. Q: Ms. Foreman, you've told me about the procedure that the company generally uses when warning employees that their performance has been deemed unsatisfactory. Were there any categories of cases within the last five years where this procedure was not used?

2. A: Yes.

3. Q: In what kinds of cases did the company not use the warning procedure you just described?

4. A: Where physical violence was involved.

5. Q: Any other type of case?

6. A: Not that I know of.

7. Q: Have you heard of any other types of cases in which the usual warning procedure was not followed other than in cases involving violence?

8. A: No.

9. Q: Have you read of any other types of cases in which the usual warning procedure was not followed other than in cases involving violence?

10. A. No.

11. Okay, let's return to situations involving physical violence. What. . . .

Of course, once you have identified situations in which the common practice was not followed, your follow up questions may focus on why a different practice was followed in those situations, and what that different practice entailed.

C. Inquire About Prior and Subsequent Changes

Both for reasons of relevance and efficiency, inquiries into practices and procedures typically focus on particular time periods. For instance, a practice and policy deposition in a products liability case may emphasize the time period when the allegedly defective product was designed and developed. Similarly, a practice and policy deposition in a case in which you claim that a prison's library practices violate due process is likely to emphasize the practices in effect at the time your clients sought access to prison library materials.

However, evidence tracing prior or subsequent changes to a practice can support a variety of arguments. For example, evidence that an entity changed its practices several times in a relatively short span of time may support an argument that the practices are in such disarray that your adversary's account of current practices is unreliable. Similarly, in a products liability case, evidence that a company changed its design procedures subsequent to the time that it developed an allegedly defective product may support an argument that the company was aware that the prior process did not meet industry standards, or may rebut an argument that alternative design procedures were not feasible.

Inquiries such as those below can help you elicit evidence of changes in an adversary's general practices. With respect to each change, you may ask:

* What was the change?

* When was the change made?

* Why was the change made?

* Who made the decision to make the change?

D. Distinguish Between the Entity's Practice and That of the Deponent

When deposing the agent of an organization, you want to distinguish between an organization's practice and the practice followed by the deponent. You can do so by not using "you" when asking about an organization's practice. Instead, ask questions such as "What is the next step the in the **company's** procedure for evaluating an employee?"

Of course, you often want to inquire into both the company's general practice, what the deponent generally does and, if applicable, what the deponent actually did in your case. But you want to keep these lines of inquiry separate.

5. Questioning Strategies Regarding Policies

Whereas "practice" inquiries focus on how organizations typically proceed when taking particular types of actions, "policy" inquiries center on rules or customs that set forth how organizations are supposed to operate in given situations. For example, a company may have written or unwritten policies regarding when employees may take "sick leave" and what steps supervisors should follow when disciplining employees.

When questioning a deponent about a <u>written policy</u>, you may begin by showing the policy to the deponent and asking the deponent to confirm that the policy was in effect at the relevant time. This strategy tends to encourage a deponent to agree that the policy was the one that was in effect at that time. Alternatively, you may question a deponent as to what policy was in effect at the relevant time without first showing the written policy to the deponent. This strategy may be advantageous if you hope to establish that the policy actually in effect was different from that set forth in written form.

<u>Examples</u>

<u>Beginning policy questioning with a written document</u>: "Please look at item number 6 in Exhibit 3, entitled "Maintaining a Productive Work Environment," and tell me whether during the time that my client was employed by Castiron Co., this exhibit accurately states the company's policy regarding employees' use of sick leave to care for family members who are ill."

<u>Beginning policy questioning without using a written document</u>: "During the time that my client was employed by Castiron Co., what was the company's policy regarding employees' use of sick leave to care for family members who are ill?

Once a deponent testifies to a policy's existence, your follow-up questions, of course, depend on the disputes in a specific case. However, in general the topics are likely to be very similar to those that apply when you make practice-focused inquiries. Thus, in flushing out a written policy you might pursue topics such as the following:

Who has copies of the document?

To what personnel, if any, was the document distributed?

Who established the policy?

Do you know of specific situations in which this policy was not applied?

Do you know of any categories of cases to which this policy was not applied?

Had the policy been the same during the preceding ___ years?

> If "no," when and why was the policy changed, and who changed the policy?

Has the policy subsequently been changed?

> If "yes," when and why was the policy changed, and who changed the policy?

If a deponent is personally unaware of policies concerning a particular subject, you may nonetheless pursue hearsay information. You might ask questions such as:

> Have you ever had discussions with anyone in the organization regarding a policy about _____?

> Have you ever heard of any discussions regarding a policy about _____?

> Have you seen any documents which refer to a policy about _____?

If a deponent testifies that an organization does not have a written policy with respect to a particular matter, you may then inquire about the possibility of <u>informal or unwritten policies</u>. For example, an organization may have an unwritten policy that employees who have been disciplined are ineligible for overtime work assignments for six months. Thus, you might ask a deponent whether the organization has an unwritten policy with respect to a particular subject. If the deponent testifies that such a policy exists, you would then pursue many of the topics suggested above. In addition, you might pursue such topics as whether a written policy on that subject had ever existed, and if not, why not.[5]

6. Inquiring About Discrepancies Between Practices and Policies

Inquiries about practices and policies may reveal that an organization's practices do not match its policies. For instance, you may discover that while a governmental agency's policy provides for a formal hearing for every permit application for discharges of waste into streams, the agency's actual practice does not always include hearings. However, before arguing that a conflict supports a helpful argument, inquire into any reasons or justifications for the conflict. Doing so can help you determine whether

---

5. If a deponent testifies that no written or unwritten policy has ever existed, you might follow up by asking the deponent if such a policy was ever considered and, if so, the reasons why the policy was never adopted.

your adversary is likely to be able to successfully undermine your argument.

7. Inquiring About Discrepancies Between Practices & Policies and What Happened in Your Client's Case

When you discover that there are discrepancies between a practice or policy and what happened in your client's case, you also typically want to inquire into all the potential justifications or reasons for the discrepancies. Once again, you'll want to consider whether the justifications undermine arguments you plan to make.

CHAPTER 20

DEPOSING EXPERTS

To acknowledge the obvious, experts are ubiquitous in civil litigation. Evidence rules have generally widened the scope of acceptable expert testimony, experts have developed increasingly narrow specialties and lawyers have become more creative in using experts to transmit opinions to judges and jurors.[1] Under the Federal Rules of Civil procedure, parties have a right to depose experts who are likely to testify at trial.[2] Therefore, deposing experts is usually a crucial pretrial activity.[3] The bulk of this Chapter describes deposition questioning strategies for deposing adverse experts, i.e,. experts retained by an adverse party. These questioning strategies apply no matter what a particular adverse expert's field of expertise.

1. For a discussion of the qualifications required of expert witnesses, see ROBERT S. HUNTER, FEDERAL TRIAL HANDBOOK—CIVIL § 48:6 (4th ed. 2010).

2. Only under exceptional circumstances can you depose a retained adverse expert who is not going to testify at trial. See Wright, Miller, & Marcus, Federal Practice and Procedure: Civil 2d § 2032.

3. If you are the deposing party, FRCP 26(b)(4)(C) normally requires you to pay reasonable compensation either to the expert or to the adverse party who retained the expert.

The Chapter concludes with a brief discussion of considerations that arise when you depose a percipient expert, e.g., an emergency room physician who treated a plaintiff but has not been retained as an expert witness.

1. Mandatory Disclosures

Parties who anticipate offering expert testimony at trial must make disclosures concerning that testimony.[4] That is, pursuant to FRCP 26(a)(2)(B) a party must voluntarily provide a report to adverse parties which discloses the following with respect to each expert the party may call as a witness at trial:[5]

* an expert's opinions;

* the bases and reasons for those opinions;

* information considered by the expert in arriving at the opinions;

* any exhibits that will be used at trial to summarize or support the opinions;

* the expert's qualifications and publications authored within the previous ten years;

* the amount of the expert's compensation; and

* a list of other cases in which the expert has testified (either in a deposition or at trial) during the preceding four years.[6]

4.　FRCP 26; most states have similar disclosure rules.

5.　Typically, parties must make the disclosures required by FRCP 26 at least 90 days before a case's trial date. For experts hired solely to contradict an adversary's expert, you must make such disclosures within 30 days "after disclosure" by an adverse party. See FRCP 26(a)(2)(C).

6.　FRCP 26(a)(2)(B).

Thus, at the time you're preparing to depose experts, you'll likely be able to anticipate much of their testimony.[7]

2. Beginning Adverse Expert Depositions

A. *Give Admonitions*

Even if an expert has participated in more depositions than you, it makes sense to begin the expert's deposition with the same admonitions you would give to any other witness. Admonitions tend to discourage adverse witnesses, whether or not they are experts, from changing their testimony later in a case. The reason is that admonitions allow you to undermine explanations that witnesses commonly give to justify changed testimony.

You may want to supplement the admonitions you give to a lay witness with a few questions that may prevent an expert from giving opinions at trial that were not given in the deposition. You might, for example, ask questions such as the following:

Q: Are you willing and able to state all the opinions at this deposition that you believe you will express at trial?

7. Your preparation is also likely to be aided by your own experts, whose specialized knowledge you will often rely on to undermine the opinions of adverse experts. If you are unfortunate enough not to have your own expert, you will greatly benefit from thoroughly researching the area of expertise of the adverse expert prior to the deposition. The more you know about the adverse expert's area of expertise, the better you will be able to identify areas of inquiry that might help to undermine the adverse expert's opinions.

A: Yes.

Q: Do you realize that you may be prevented from giving an opinion at trial if you do not disclose it at this deposition?

A: Yes.

Such testimony may help you to convince a judge to prohibit an expert from giving an opinion at trial that is not provided to you at the deposition.[8]

B. *Confirm That You Have All Relevant Documents*

Reports that you receive pursuant to FRCP 26 (a)(2) usually include or at least refer to the principal documents that adverse experts relied on in forming their opinions. However, at deposition you want to confirm that you have been provided with copies of all documents an expert reviewed, considered or prepared.[9] For example, indicate to an expert the documents you have been provided with and then ask questions such as:

8. See, e.g., Jones v. Moore, 80 Cal.App.4th 557, 95 Cal. Rptr.2d 216 (2000); Amtower v. Photon Dynamics, Inc., 158 Cal.App.4th 1582, 71 Cal.Rptr.3d 361 (2008).

9. Of course, you would like to obtain all relevant documents prior to a deposition. You might obtain such documents either through a Request for Production under FRCP 34, a Subpoena Duces Tecum Re Deposition under FRCP 45, or by an agreement with opposing counsel. See Wright, Miller, & Marcus, Federal Practice and Procedure: Civil 2d §§ 2202 and 2456. Documents provided to an expert by opposing counsel are generally not protected by the work product or attorney client privileges. See Wright, Miller, & Marcus, Federal Practice and Procedure: Civil 2d § 2031.1 n.10.

Q: Have you considered any documents in connection with this case other than the ones I just
mentioned?

Q: Did you generate any documents in connection with this case other than the ones I just
mentioned?

Q: Did you generate any interim or draft reports
in this case?

Q: Did you look at any documents in connection
with this case other than the ones I just mentioned?

Having all the documents an adverse expert reviewed, considered or prepared helps to inform your
questioning through out the deposition. For example, such questions might unearth an interim opinion that contradicts the expert's opinion at the
deposition.

C. *Obtain Background Information*

Since a specialized background is what enables
experts to offer opinions, background questioning of
experts may be extensive. For example, you are
likely to probe an expert's background thoroughly
when you anticipate asking a judge to exclude an
opinion as unreliable.[10] Moreover, careful parsing of

10. Arguments that expert opinions are unreliable may be
based on a witness' personal lack of qualifications, or the unrelia-
bility of an expert's methodology. In some states, you might also
challenge an opinion because the underlying methodology has
not been generally accepted by a relevant field of experts. For a
discussion of what factors a judge should consider when assess-
ing the reliability issue, see FRE 702; Daubert v. Merrell Dow
Pharm., Inc., 509 U.S. 579 (1993); Kumho Tire Co. v. Carmicha-

an expert's background may promote credibility arguments based on your expert's having more impressive qualifications and experience than your adversary's.

Topics that are often useful to pursue during background questioning include:

* An expert's education and professional training, including both academia (undergraduate, graduate and post-graduate education) and professional or on-the-job training.

* An expert's work experience, including when relevant such matters as work in private industry, government-sponsored research, teaching (whether in academia or elsewhere), and reasons for changing jobs.

* Awards or honors received and publications authored.

* Organizational affiliations, such as service on the boards of professional organizations or pri-

el, 526 U.S. 137 (1999) (holding that the reliability requirement in Daubert applies to all expert testimony); see also, Johnson v. Manitowoc Boom Trucks, Inc., 484 F.3d 426 (6th Cir. 2007) (explaining how the factors test should be applied); Daubert v. Merrell Dow Pharm. Inc, 43 F.3d 1311, 1317 (9th Cir. 1995) (considering whether expert prepared the opinion for litigation, or based the opinion on previous work unrelated to the litigation); General Elec. Co. v. Joiner, 522 U.S. 136, 146 (1997) (judge should consider whether the expert's conclusion is supported by the data); Claar v. Burlington Northern R. Co., 29 F.3d 499 (1994) (failure to rule out alternative explanations can be reason to exclude expert testimony); but *cf.* Ambrosini v. Labarraque, 101 F.3d 129 (DC Cir. 1996) (failure to rule out alternative explanation should go to the weight of expert testimony, not to its admissibility).

vate companies, editorial services for peer-reviewed publications.

* Previous experience as an expert witness, including number and types of cases, interests an expert has represented, and the number of times an expert has qualified as such in court.

Credibility arguments that you might make as a result of such questioning include:

* An adverse expert is a generalist (e.g., a real estate appraiser) testifying to subject matter in a field in which some experts are specialists (e.g., an appraiser of industrial real estate).

* An adverse expert has academic qualifications, but lacks practical experience. For example, in a legal malpractice case a legal academic may qualify to deliver an opinion about whether a situation amounted to a conflict of interest such that an attorney should have advised a client to seek alternate legal counsel. However, the fact that the academic has never practiced law may cause a factfinder to question the academic's credibility.

* An adverse expert's training and practical experience is not a precise "fit" with the facts of a given case. For example, an adverse expert appraiser's experience is in commercial real estate in County A, whereas the property involved in your lawsuit is industrial real estate in County B.

3. Obtain a Chronology of Case Related Activities

Generally, the meat of expert depositions consists of eliciting and challenging opinions. Before doing so, however, you should generally first elicit a detailed chronology of an expert's case-related activities. An expert's chronology consists of the significant case-related activities from the date of **first contact** by opposing counsel to the **date of deposition.**[11] Obtaining such a chronology promotes thoroughness and helps you understand and later probe the bases of an expert's opinions. For example, by eliciting a chronology, you generally:

* Learn when the expert agreed to serve and what the expert was aware of at that time. If an expert agreed to serve before reviewing pertinent information, you may argue that the expert's evaluation and opinion is less than objective.

* Learn what information opposing counsel provided to the expert, and when it was provided. If your adversary has given an expert incomplete information, or if the information was delayed, you may argue that the expert's conclusions are based on a distorted picture of the evidence. Uncovering the substance of opposing counsel's discussions with an expert, particularly during deposition preparation sessions, may reveal information about counsel's view of the strengths and weaknesses of a case.[12]

11. Chapter 3 describes useful questioning strategies for obtaining a chronology.

12. For cases indicating that communications between counsel and a testifying expert are discoverable, see In re Pioneer Hi–Bred Intern., Inc., 238 F.3d 1370, 1375 (Fed. Cir. 2001) ("[T]he Federal Rules of Civil Procedure make clear that documents and information disclosed to a testifying expert in connection with his testimony are discoverable by the opposing party, whether or

* Develop a picture early on of what an expert
did to arrive at her opinions. For example, what
methodology did an expert use? What tests did
the expert conduct or fail to conduct? What re-

not the expert relies on the documents and information in
preparing his report."); see also TV–3, Inc. v. Royal Ins. Co. of
Am., 194 F.R.D. 585 (S.D. Miss. 2000) (explaining that correspondence between counsel and expert witnesses is discoverable
under Rule 26 and its Advisory Committee Note); B.C.F. Oil Ref.
v. Consolidated Edison Co., 171 F.R.D. 57 (S.D.N.Y. 1997) (stating that conversations between attorneys and experts are discoverable); Cornell Research Foundation, Inc. v. Hewlett Packard
Co., 223 F.R.D. 55, 78–79 (NDNY 2003) (entire document given
to expert is discoverable, even though his opinion will only be on
some of the subject areas in the document; document can't be
redacted to just include portions he will testify on, everything the
expert was given is discoverable); South Yuba River Citizens
League v. National Marine Fisheries Service, 257 F.R.D. 607 (ED
Cal 2009). (work product exception does not apply to materials
the expert considered as a legal consultant because he was also
testifying); Herman v. Marine Midland Bank, 207 F.R.D. 26, 29
(DCNY 2002) (defendant must be given an unredacted report
shown to plaintiff's expert witness in preparation for testifying
because the expert disclosure requirement "trumps" work product protections); Elm Grove Coal Co. v. Director, Office of
Workers' Compensation Programs, 480 F.3d 278, 302 (4th Cir.
2007) (attorney-expert communications are not entitled to protection); Regional Airport Auth. of Louisville v. LFG, LLC, 460
F.3d 697, 715–717 (6th Cir. 2006) (mandating disclosure of all
documents, including attorney opinion work product, given to
testifying experts). Fidelity Nat'l Title Ins. Co of NY v. Intercounty Nat'l Title Ins., 412 F.3d 745, 751 (7th Cir. 2005) (a
testifying expert must disclose communications even if in the end
he does not rely on them in formulating his expert opinion). Not
all courts have required disclosure of such communications. See
Nexxus Prod. Co. v. CVS New York, Inc., 188 F.R.D. 7 (D. Mass.
1999); Karn v. Ingersoll–Rand Co., 168 F.R.D. 633 (N.D. Ind.
1996); In re Teleglobe Communications Corp., 392 B.R. 561
(Bkrtcy.D.Del. 2008); Krisa v. Equitable Life Assur. Soc., 196
F.R.D. 254, 255 (M.D.PA 2000).

search did the expert conduct or fail to conduct? What interim reports or documents did the expert create or receive, and what witnesses did the expert speak with and when?

* Identify assistants or independent third parties and their contributions to an expert's investigation. This information helps you decide if you need additional depositions.

* Identify exhibits the expert has prepared for use at trial, and find out when the exhibits were prepared and what information the expert had at the time they were prepared.

* Learn what the expert did to prepare for the deposition. Whom did he talk to? Did he talk to opposing counsel? What was said? What documents did he review? Why did he review those documents but not other documents?

When you conclude a chronology, you might also ask whether an expert anticipates extending an investigation beyond the date of deposition. If so, you might follow up by asking what the expert intends to do and why the expert needs to do it. You can then attack credibility if the expert neglects to follow through. Alternatively, if the expert does intend to conduct further investigation, you may want to postpone the conclusion of the deposition until after the investigation is complete.[13]

13. To do so, do not adjourn the deposition when you have finished questioning. Instead, try to have opposing counsel agree to continue the deposition at a date when the expert will have completed her work. This saves you the trouble of trying to

One approach to eliciting a chronology is to elicit details as the chronology emerges. For instance, if the first event in a chronology is a "January 26 phone call," you might find out as much as you can about the call before finding out what happened next.

Alternatively, and especially when a chronology is likely to be lengthy, you may want to obtain a brief overview of activities before exploring any of them in depth. An overview often helps you make judgments about which events are most important, thus promoting efficiency. The following example suggests how you might elicit a chronological overview. Assume that you are deposing Lex Purt, an engineer retained by the defendant in a product liability case involving the alleged substandard design of a bicycle helmet. Overview questioning might go as follows:

Q: What's the first time that you heard about this case?

A: It was on January 10, when I got a phone call from Jean, the defense attorney. Jean gave me some basic information and asked if I'd be willing to evaluate the case. I agreed to do so, and she said that she'd send me a copy of the file.

Q: Then what happened?

A: I called Jean a couple of days later. I'd read the file, and I told her I'd be willing to look into what happened and give her an opinion, and that

notice a second deposition, for which you usually need court permission under FRCP 30(a)(2)(A)(ii).

I'd be available to testify if it came to that. We made some fee arrangements.

Q: What's the next thing you can recall happening in connection with this case?

A: I'd asked Jean to send over transcripts of depositions that had previously been taken, and I read through those. Around the same time I looked through a treatise, "Bicycle Helmet Design in a Nutshell" and talked with Jack Aranda, who I believe at the time was the President of the National Association of Bicycle Helmet Manufacturers.

Q: What time period are we talking about when you're reviewing transcripts and the treatise and talking to Mr. Aranda?

A: Probably late January. Jean had told me that the case was on a fast track and that I needed to gather information quickly.

Q: Okay, what happened next that is in any way related to this case?

A: I toured the defendant's factory. I talked to various employees, particularly in the quality control department, and got copies of design specifications and other records.

Q: Between the time you reviewed the transcripts and before you toured the factory, did anything else happen related to this case?

A: Well, I talked to Jean to set up the tour of the factory.

Q: Now, after touring the factory, what happened next?

A: . . . .

4. Obtain **All** Expert Opinions

The voluntary disclosures required by FRCP 26 (a)(2)(B) should state all the opinions to which an expert will testify at trial. A chronology of an expert's activities typically surfaces the opinions that an expert will give at trial. Nevertheless, before beginning to probe each opinion, it makes sense to ask experts whether they have any opinions that they have not yet mentioned.[14] For example:

1. Q: Ms. Jetson, showing you what has been marked as Exhibit 23, this is the report you prepared in this case, correct?

2. A. Yes.

3. Q: In Exhibit 23, you state that it is your opinion that my client's car was traveling at a speed of 65 m.p.h. when it struck the bridge abutment, correct?

4. A: Yes.

5. Q: Do you have any opinions in any way related to this case in addition to the opinion that my client's car was traveling at a speed of 65 m.p.h. when it struck the bridge abutment?

14. If you obtain a complete list of all of an expert's opinions at deposition, you may then be able to prevent the expert from testifying to additional opinions at trial. See, e.g., Jones v. Moore, 80 Cal.App.4th 557, 95 Cal.Rptr.2d 216 (2000); Amtower v. Photon Dynamics, Inc., 158 Cal.App.4th 1582, 71 Cal.Rptr.3d 361 (2008).

6. A: No.

7. Q: So you do not have any opinion about whether or not my client lost control of the car before striking the abutment, do you?

8. A: No, I was not asked to give an opinion on that.

9. Q: And you do not have any opinion about whether or not my client was driving negligently on the day of the accident, correct?

10. A: That is correct.

11. Q: And you do not have any opinion about what caused my client's car to strike the abutment, correct?

12. That's right. My only opinion relates to the speed of the car at impact.

In this example, Nos. 1–6 establish that the expert has only one opinion in the case. You could have concluded your question with question No 6. However, questions such as in Nos. 7–12 provide added assurance that an expert will not provide additional opinions at trial. If the expert did try to provide additional opinions at trial, Nos. 7–12 help you to convince a judge to exclude them.

5. Obtain the Basis for Each Opinion

When an expert provides an opinion, the expert typically reaches that opinion by evaluating case-specific evidence or factual information[15] in light of

15. An expert opinion need not be rooted in the facts of a specific case when an expert delivers what is often called an "advisory" opinion. For example, an expert in cognitive psycholo-

one or more premises drawn form an expert's specialized knowledge. For example, a medical expert's **opinion** that injuries to a child were intentionally inflicted may be based, in part, on case specific **evidence** of x-rays showing that the child's leg had a spiral fracture, and the expert's specialized knowledge that validates the **premise** that such a spiral fracture generally results from an intentional twisting of the leg.

For each opinion, you typically want to obtain **both** the evidentiary basis and the relevant specialized knowledge relied on by the expert.

A. *Obtain the* Evidentiary *Basis for Each Opinion*

To obtain the evidentiary basis for an opinion, you can simply ask the expert for **all** the evidence supporting an opinion. Experts can rely on many different types of information as the evidentiary basis for an opinion. For example, the evidentiary or factual basis for an expert's opinion may include:

*Tangible evidence, e.g., a blood sample, a fingerprint or a hair sample.

*Information obtained by the expert from reviewing written discovery, witness statements, deposition transcripts, and other documents.

gy might testify to factors that in general affect the reliability of eyewitness identifications, but express no opinion about the accuracy of eyewitness testimony in a specific case. In such a situation, your challenge would relate to the expert's specialized knowledge.

*Information generated directly by the expert, e.g., test results or the results of interviews or other activities conducted directly by the expert.

*Factual assumptions made by the expert at the direction of the retaining party, e.g., an expert calculating damages in a wrongful termination case may have been told to assume that the plaintiff would have worked at the company until the age of 60 if she had not been discharged.

In some cases, the evidentiary basis for an opinion may consist only of one or two items of evidence. For example, assume that an expert testifies the drug your client manufactured had an inadequate warning label because it failed to warn users not to consume alcohol when taking the drug. The evidentiary basis for the opinion may be simply what the warning label says and does not say. On the other hand, the evidentiary basis for an opinion may be extensive. For example, an arson expert who testifies that a fire was intentionally set may rely on information in several witness statements, fire department reports, blueprints of the burned building and evidence obtained from the expert's own observations of the scene.

When an evidentiary basis is extensive, you may need to ask a series of questions to uncover all the information an expert relies on.[16] For example, you may begin with a general question like "What are the facts in this case that you believe support that

---

16. The T–Funnel questioning pattern discussed in Chapter 2 will help you to exhaust the expert's evidentiary basis for an opinion.

opinion?" To be sure you have obtained a complete evidentiary basis, you can follow up with more narrowly focused questions, such as:

"What information did you obtain from any of the witnesses in this case that supports that opinion?"

"What information did you obtain from any of the discovery documents provided to you in this case that supports that opinion?"

"What information did you obtain as a result of your own investigation into what happened in this case that supports that opinion?"

"What assumptions, if any, did you make in order to reach that opinion?"

B. *Obtain the* Specialized Knowledge *Underlying Each Opinion*

The statutory background factors which qualify experts to render opinions include "knowledge, skill, experience, training or education."[17] This specialized knowledge usually falls into one or all of the following categories:

***Experience**

***Training and education**

***Authorities (e.g. treatises, research studies, industry standards, etc.)**

For each opinion render by an expert you will typically want to obtain the specialized knowledge that the expert relies upon to reach that opinion.

17. See FRE 702.

For example, return to the case of the medical expert who opined that injuries to a child were intentionally inflicted based on x-rays showing that the child's leg had a spiral fracture. To obtain the expert's specialized knowledge support this opinion you might ask questions such as the following:

- Tell me all the reasons you believe a spiral fracture indicates that the fracture was the result of an intentional injury.

- What training do you have that supports your opinion that a spiral fracture indicates an intentional injury?

- Is there anything in your educational background that you rely on to support your opinion that a spiral fracture indicates an intentional injury?

- What medical authorities support your opinion that a spiral fracture indicates an intentional injury?

6. Undermining an Expert Opinion

You can typically undermine an adverse expert's opinion by challenging one or both of the following:

(1) The accuracy or sufficiency of the evidentiary basis for the opinion.

(2) The adequacy of the specialized knowledge of the expert.

The remainder of the Chapter examines a variety of questioning strategies for challenging adverse experts' opinions on one or both of these grounds.

Typically, the strategies you pursue in any individual case depend on factual disputes in the case and the areas of disagreement between an adverse expert's opinions and the conflicting opinions of your own expert. Your own expert will often be able to suggest which of the strategies discussed below are most likely to be effective, and may even be able to suggest specific lines of inquiry. You may use one or more of these strategies with respect to each opinion of an adverse expert.

7. Challenge #1—An Expert's Specialized Knowledge Is Inadequate

Recall that the statutory background factors which qualify experts to render opinions include "knowledge, skill, experience, training or education."[18] Thus, you may undermine an opinion by probing the adequacy of an expert's specialized knowledge.[19] Here, your questions are likely to concentrate on the three topics that typically serve as the sources of specialized knowledge: experience, training and education, and authorities.

For an illustration of how you might probe an expert's specialized knowledge, assume that you represent the defendant manufacturer of an automobile tire that ruptured and caused a serious accident. You are deposing the plaintiff's expert, who has opined in a report provided to you that a manufacturing defect caused the tire to fail, and

18. See FRE 702.

19. As you probe specialized knowledge, you may discover that an expert may have an insufficient background to qualify as an expert under FRE 702.

there was no miss use of the tire by the plaintiff. You contend that the rupture was caused by misuse of the tire. To attempt to undermine the adequacy of the expert's specialized knowledge, you might proceed as follows:

Q: What is your opinion as to why the tire failed?

A: A manufacturing defect caused the tire to rupture.

Q: What is there about the tire that leads you to conclude that there was a manufacturing defect?

A: My inspection of the tire indicated that the tread had separated from the tire's inner steel belt. When that happens, if the separation isn't the result of misuse, such as under-inflating the tire, then the separation must be due to a defect in the way the tire was made or designed. In my opinion, this separation was not the result of misuse.

Q: Let's first address your opinion that the separation was not caused by misuse. What evidence supports your opinion that the tire was not misused?

A: When a tire is misused, I'd expect to find physical symptoms consistent with misuse. These symptoms are greater tread wear on the shoulder than on the center of the tire, bead grooves on the inside of a tire's rim, deteriorated side walls, and marks on a tire's rim flange. Unless I find at least two of these symptoms, I conclude that there was no misuse. I didn't find two of those symptoms in this case.

Q: Is there any other evidence that supports your opinion that the tire was not misused?

A: No. Not in this case.

Q: What **experience** do you have that allows you to say that there is no misuse unless at least two of these symptoms are present?

A: I have an engineering degree and I worked for Goodstone tire company for 15 years, specializing in tire failure analysis.

Q: What other **experience** do you have that allows you to say that there is no misuse unless at least two of these symptoms are present?

A: I don't have any other such experience.

Q: We'll talk about your work at Goodstone a little later. Right now I'd like to know how many ruptured tires have you examined to try to determine whether at least two of these symptoms are necessary to conclude that the tire was misused?

A: I've only done that three times, when I have been asked to testify as an expert in litigation.

Q: How many of these cases involved the same make of tire as the one involved in this case?

A: None.

(Additional questions about these three cases are omitted).

Q: Now, have you received any **training** where you were told that there is no misuse unless at least two of these symptoms are present on a tire?

A: No. Not specifically. But my approach is based on my experience and my education and training as an engineer.

Q: Are you aware of any research reports, articles, opinions by other experts or any other **authorities** that support your opinion that there is no misuse unless at least two of these symptoms are present?

A: No. I developed this methodology on my own. . . .

Arguments that you might be able to make after probing these three specialized knowledge factors include:

* An opinion is entitled to little weight because an expert's education and training took place many years ago.

* An opinion is entitled to little weight because an expert's experience relates to situations different from those involved in your case.

* An opinion is entitled to little weight because an expert's methodology is not generally accepted in the scientific community.

* An opinion is entitled to little weight (or is inadmissible) because an expert's knowledge is based on unreliable methodology.

8. Challenge #2—"Exceptions" Detract From an Opinion's Accuracy

As noted above, expert opinions rest on one or more premises. And such premises are often true less than 100% of the time. For example, based on the premise that spiral fractures in young children are <u>generally</u> the result of an intentional injury, a medical expert might testify to an opinion that a child with a spiral fracture was a child abuse victim. Similarly, based on a premise that speakers <u>usually</u> make unique speech sounds, a linguistics expert might testify that a comparison of two voices indicates that both are the voice of the same person. Because the premises relied on by experts are typically not true 100% of the time, almost all expert opinions are subject to "exceptions." Depositions give you an opportunity to probe for such "exceptions." Consider the following example.

Assume that you represent an oil company that owns an oil tanker that ran aground and caused property damage and a variety of environmental harms. Your adversary claims that the tanker ran aground because the captain was drunk and therefore unable to recognize that the tanker was off course. The deponent is Dr. Peter Laddy, a voice identification expert. Based on his analysis of the captain's voice recorded by the ship's audio tapes before and after the ship ran aground, Dr. Laddy arrived at the opinion that the captain was under the influence of alcohol at the time that the ship ran aground. Dr. Laddy's factual support for this conclusion is that the captain's voice was deeper and huskier, and the captain spoke more slowly, around the time of the grounding than before and after the grounding. Your search for exceptions might proceed as follows:

1. Q: Dr. Laddy, is it fair to say that your opinion is that as a general rule, evidence that a speaker's voice was deeper and huskier than normal indicates that the speaker was under the influence of alcohol?

2. A: Yes.

3. Q: Are there factors other than the consumption of alcohol that might cause a person's voice to become deeper and huskier than usual?

4. A: Yes. Many drugs that would have that effect.

5. Q: Are there factors other than drugs that might make a person's speech deeper and huskier than normal?

6. A: Yes. There have been some research findings that the speech sounds of people who talk under conditions of stress are deeper and huskier than normal. A study by Dr. Allenson is perhaps the best known research in this area. However, this has never been a consistent finding—all the studies indicate that the speech patterns of some subjects are unaffected by stress.

7. Q: Nevertheless, some research indicates that speech patterns may sometimes be affected by stress?

8. A: Yes.

9. Q: And that effect is to make a person's voice huskier and deeper than normal?

10. A: Yes.

11. Q: Are there any factors, other than drugs and stress, that might make a person's speech deeper and huskier than normal?

12. A: Well, someone can consciously make their voice deeper and huskier.

13. Q: Are there any factors, other than drugs, stress and a conscious attempt to alter one's voice that that might make a person's speech deeper and huskier than normal?

14. A: I don't think so, no.

15. Q: Well, when a person speaks within a minute after being awakened, might that have a tendency to make the person's voice deeper and huskier than normal?

16. A: That would be a possibility, yes.

17. Q: Tape C was recorded minutes before the ship ran aground, correct?

18. A: That's correct.

19. Q: I want you to assume that at the time Tape C was recorded, the captain was under stress and had just been awakened a couple

of minutes before Tape C was recorded. Would those assumptions make you less confident in your opinion that the captain was under the influence of alcohol at the time that Tape C was recorded?

20. A: Not really.

21. Q: Why not?

22. A: Because my opinion is also based on the fact that the captain's voice was slower than normal, that is, that his voice was slower on Tape C than it was on Tape A or B.

23. Q: Let's talk about that. Dr. Laddy, is it fair to say that it is your opinion that as a general rule, someone's talking more slowly than normal is evidence that the speaker is under the influence of alcohol?

24. A: Yes.

25. Q: Are there things, other than the consumption of alcohol, that might make a person's speech slower than normal?

26. A: Yes...

Here, the expert's opinion rests on the premise that deeper, huskier and unusually slow speech tends to prove that a speaker has consumed alcohol. (Nos. 1–2; 23–24). Instead of trying to directly challenge the validity of this premise, you have identified exceptions to the premise that when a speaker's voice is deeper and huskier it tends to show that a speaker has consumed alcohol. (Nos. 3–16). And you have begun to search for exceptions for the premise involving unusually slow speech. (Nos. 25–26). If you can show that the facts supporting an exception are likely to be present, you can undermine the expert's opinion.

9. Challenge #3—Conflicting Authorities Undermine an Opinion

Probes for exceptions generally assume the validity of a premise underlying an expert's opinion. Another type of challenge is to attack directly the validity of underlying premises. Typically, this type of challenge involves searching for or confronting an expert with authorities (e.g. treatises, research studies, industry standards etc.) that conflict with the premises on which the expert relies.

For example, assume that a medical expert has testified to an opinion that a fracture of a three-year-old child's arm was intentionally inflicted. The expert's opinion relies heavily on x-rays showing that the child had a spiral fracture. Questioning about contrary authorities might proceed as follows:

Q: Dr. Weil, you testified that the fact that the child had a spiral fracture of the humerus bone supports your opinion that the fracture was the result of an intentional injury, correct?

A: That's correct.

Q: Are you aware of any authorities that conclude that spiral fractures to the humerus bones of young children generally do not indicate intentional injury, but rather are consistent with accidental injury.

A: Yes. There have been 2 studies recently reported in medical journals saying that.

Q: Other than these two studies, are you aware of any other authorities that conclude that spiral fractures to the humerus bones of young children generally do not indicate intentional injury, but rather are consistent with accidental injury?

A: No.

Q: Given these two recent studies that you mentioned, why do you say that the spiral fracture tends to support your opinion that the injury in this case was intentional?

A: I think both of those studies were seriously flawed.

Q: Please tell me all the ways in which you think these studies were flawed.

A: Well. . . .

Note that after uncovering a conflicting authority, you ask the expert why he nevertheless maintains his opinion. If the expert has a reasonable explanation, better that you learn it now than later in the case.

10. Challenge #4—An Opinion Is Based on Inaccurate Information From Third Parties

As discussed above, the evidentiary basis for an expert's opinion may be information gleaned from such third party sources as discovery responses, witness statements, deposition transcripts or other documents. At deposition, one way to challenge an opinion is to establish that an expert has assumed the accuracy of such information. You may be able to challenge the opinion by later showing that the information is not accurate.

Example

You represent Pat, one of a group of police officers who has been sued by an arrestee, Mr. Kang, for allegedly using "excessive" force during Kang's arrest. You are deposing Kang's expert, who earlier testified to an opinion that the force was excessive, in part because Pat should not have kicked Kang in the head after Kang was lying on the ground. Pat denies kicking Kang in the head and contends that Kang's head was injured when Kang fell and hit it on a curb. Your questioning proceeds as follows:

1. Q: Your opinion is that Officer Pat used excessive force, in part because he kicked Mr. Kang in the head?

2. A: That's right.

3. Q: Would you tell me all the information you are aware of that indicates that Officer Pat kicked Mr. Kang in the head?

4. A: Mr. Kang testified in his deposition that he was kicked in the head by Pat. And the medical records indicate that Kang had a severe contusion on the right side of his head where he said he was kicked.

5. Q: Is there any other information that you are aware of that indicates that Officer Pat kicked Mr. Kang in the head?

6.   A: No, not that I know of.

7.   Q: You were <u>not</u> asked to undertake an investigation or an analysis of the facts of this case to determine whether Mr. Kang was telling the truth when he said he was he was kicked in the head, correct?

8.   A: That's true.

9.   Q: You are assuming that Mr. Kang is telling the truth about being kicked in the head, correct?

10.   A: I suppose that's true, but it seems to me that Mr. Kang's testimony is consistent with the medical records.

11.   Q: You have no medical training, correct?

12.   A: That's correct.

13.   Q: So you don't know whether the medical records are consistent with Mr. Kang having hit his head on a street curb when he fell to the ground as the officers were attempting to arrest him, correct?

14.   A: That's true.

15.   Q: And you never personally talked to Mr. Kang about what happened on the night of his arrest, correct?

16.   A: That's true.

17.   Q: Now, if you found out that Officer Pat did not kick Mr. Kang in the head, would that change your opinion about whether the

officers used excessive force on the night in question?[20]

18. A: No, because there are other reasons that the force used by the officers was excessive.

19. Q: If you found out that Officer Pat did not kick Mr. Kang in the head, would you be less confident in your opinion about whether the officers used excessive force on the night in question?

20. A: No, I would not.

21. Q: Why not?

22. A: Because even if Pat did not kick Kang in the head, the officers hit him in the legs with their batons after he was lying on the ground and offering no resistance, and that constitutes excessive force.

23. Q: Would you tell me all the information you are aware of that indicates that when the officers hit Kang in the legs with their batons he was not offering resistance?

24. A: Well. . . .

20. Evidence rules generally allow you to pose hypothetical questions to experts. See FRE 703. A good use of hypothetical questions at expert depositions is to demonstrate that additional information, if accurate, might affect an expert's opinion. Of course, hypothetical questions are effective only if you prove that the facts assumed in your hypothetical are true. Thus, if at trial you could show that the officers did not kick Kang in the head, you would be able to use the deposition questions to undermine the expert's opinion.

In this example, you first elicit all the information the expert is aware of that indicates that Pat kicked Kang in the head. (Nos. 3–6). Next, you establish that the expert has no first-hand knowledge of that information's accuracy. (Nos. 7–16).

Note that after establishing the expert's lack of firsthand knowledge, you try to establish that the expert's opinion, or his confidence level in that opinion, would change if the information from the third party proved false. (Nos. 17–22). Such concessions are important if you can produce evidence undermining the accuracy of the information on which an opinion rests. In addition, you might argue that an expert's insistence that an opinion would be unaffected by a drop in evidentiary support is implausible.

11. Challenge #5—Undermine the Results of Scientific Tests or Technical Procedures

Evidence supporting an expert's opinion may consist of the results of scientific tests or procedures. For example, an expert testifying that your client was under the influence of alcohol at the time of an auto accident may rely on the results of a breathalyzer test. And an expert's opinion that property is contaminated with toxic waste may be based on the results of a soils test.[21]

The topics you inquire into to undermine the results of a test or procedure obviously vary dra-

---

21. In each instance, experts may have personally conducted the tests on which they rely, or they may rely on tests conducted by a third party.

matically from case to case. And your own expert's input will be particularly helpful when developing lines of inquiry for this challenge. There are, however, several areas you should at least consider probing to try to undercut the accuracy of test results and procedures:

* **Procedural Irregularities**—Generally, the accuracy of test results hinges on proper procedures. Thus, you can inquire into topics such as whether an expert knows what procedures were followed when a test was given, and if so the propriety of those procedures. For example, before using a breathalyzer to test for the percentage of alcohol in blood, a technician should first conduct an "open room test." This test determines whether chemicals that might interfere with the accuracy of a test are present in the room where a test is given.[22] Results may therefore be inaccurate if an open room test is not performed.

* **Inherent Uncertainties**—Test results can be inaccurate even if proper procedures are followed. Thus, you can inquire into a test's accuracy. For example, has accuracy been investigated, and if so has an error rate been established? For example, some instruments measure the amount of alcohol in a person's blood by passing infrared light through a breath sample and measuring the amount of infrared light absorbed by the alcohol

22. R. Erwin, <u>Defense of Drunk Driving Cases</u> § 22.04[2] (3rd ed. 2001).

molecules in the sample.[23] Even when all proper procedures are followed, however, molecules other than alcohol that absorb infrared light may be present in a person's breath. The presence of such molecules in a breath sample therefore tends to produce inaccurate test results.

* **Sample Errors**—Test results are inaccurate when the wrong sample is used or when a sample becomes contaminated before testing by age or by improper storage or handling. In addition, a sample may become contaminated or degraded as a result of prior tests or procedures.

* **Failure to Conduct Additional Tests**— Opinions that rely on test results may be undercut with evidence of an expert's failure to conduct additional, reasonable investigation. For instance, if a medical expert bases an opinion that brain damage is permanent on the results of lab tests and x-rays, you might ask whether other tests, such as a "CAT" scan, were performed. If not, elicit an expert's reasons for not doing so.[24]

* **Reliability of Methodology**—Under the Federal Rules of Evidence as currently interpreted by the U.S. Supreme Court, an expert opinion may be inadmissible at trial if based on evidence resulting from unreliable methodologies or proce-

23.   Id. at § 22.06[4][c].

24.   If an expert admits that further testing could reasonably have been done, you may probe the likelihood that additional information might have altered an opinion or an expert's degree of confidence in an opinion.

dures.[25] No single standard of reliability exists. Factors that judges may consider include whether experts' methods have been generally accepted in the community of experts with relevant expertise; whether methods have been published in peer-reviewed journals; and whether methods have been scientifically tested and error rates established. You may want to inquire into such topics at deposition, particularly if an adverse expert's opinions are based on novel or untested methods. The information you develop may lead to arguments concerning both the weight and the admissibility of opinions.

12. Challenge #6—An Investigation Is Incomplete or Untimely

You may be able to show that an expert's investigation was insufficient or incomplete. For example, if an arson expert relies exclusively on burn pattern evidence when concluding that a fire was intentionally set, you might probe to determine whether the expert could have talked to the warehouse manager and the night watchman working on the night of the fire to obtain further relevant information. Or if an engineer testifies that a tire ruptured due to a manufacturing defect, you might probe to determine why the expert only looked at pictures of the ruptured tire rather than examining the tire itself.

You may also be able to undermine an expert opinion by showing that the expert's investigation was untimely. For example, assume that an expert

25. See footnote 10, supra.

opines as to the cause of a mudslide that damaged a residence. You may be able to show that the expert first visited the site several weeks after the slide first occurred. If so, you can then probe to determine whether the expert knows if the conditions that she observed were the same as the conditions immediately after the slide. If the conditions may have changed, you have undermined the expert's opinion.

13. Challenge #7—An Expert Is Biased

In theory, experts are neutrals with no stake in lawsuits' outcomes. In practice, of course, this is seldom true. And depositions provide an opportunity to explore topics that might yield grist for an argument that an adverse expert is biased and therefore not credible. Common topics relevant to bias include:

* An expert's relationships with opposing counsel and parties. For example, has opposing counsel previously employed an expert? If so, how often and in what cases? Does an expert have a personal relationship with opposing counsel or the opposing party?

* The percentage of an expert's time and income devoted to testifying as an expert. Jurors may distrust "professional witnesses" whose main occupation consists of hiring themselves out as experts.

* If not included in a required disclosure report, the number and types of cases in which an expert has previously been retained, and by which party (plaintiff or defendant) an expert was retained. Repeatedly taking the same position (e.g., that doctors were not negligent) suggests that an expert's opinion reflects a pre-existing bias rather than an independent analysis of the evidence in a particular case.

* <u>An expert's compensation.</u> To the extent that complete information is not set forth in a disclosure report, you can ask how much an expert has been paid to date, and how much additional compensation an expert expects to receive for post-deposition work, including testifying at trial. Although compensation of experts is routine, overly generous compensation arrangements may suggest that an expert is biased.

* <u>Prior inconsistent statements.</u> Ideally, prior to deposition you will be familiar with relevant statements an expert has made in books, articles, prior cases, etc. At deposition, you might confront the expert with conflicts between prior and current statements to determine if the expert has a reasonable explanations for the conflicts.

14. Garner Support for Your Expert's Opinion

In addition to trying to undermine an adverse expert's opinion, you may also question the expert with an eye toward garnering evidence supporting your own expert's opinion(s). You cannot, of course, expect the adverse expert to abandon an opinion in favor of one championed by your expert. But you can often get an adverse expert to acknowledge one or more of the following:

* Evidence relied upon by your expert is accurate (or at least that the adverse expert has no reason to believe it is not accurate);

* Evidence relied upon by your expert is consistent with or supports your expert's opinion.

* Authorities relied upon by your expert are reliable, are generally relied on by others in the field, and have been relied on by the adverse expert in the past.

* The tests conducted by your expert are likely to produce results that are relevant to your expert's opinion, and the methods used to conduct the tests are proper.

* Your expert's experience and training are generally likely to provide someone with the specialized knowledge that is relevant to your expert's opinion.

* Your expert has a good reputation in her field of expertise.

In each of the areas, if an adverse expert will not make the acknowledgement you seek, you might follow up by asking for the basis for any refusal. For example, if an adverse expert will not acknowledge that evidence relied upon by your expert is consistent with or supports your expert's opinion, you might ask for an explanation of why the evidence is not consistent with your expert's opinion. This information helps your expert prepare for deposition or trial.

15. Opposing Party's Duty to Supplement Expert's Deposition Testimony

Opposing parties have an obligation to supplement the answers in their expert witness deposition testimony with information learned after the expert has been deposed.[26] The FRCP imposes no such explicit obligation to supplement deposition testimony of a <u>lay witness</u> with information learned after the deposition is complete.[27]

26. FRCP 26(e).

27. See Advisory Committee Notes for 1993 Amendments to Federal Rules of Civil Procedure, Fed. R. Civ. P. 26 ("The revision also clarifies that the obligation to supplement responses to formal discovery requests applies to interrogatories, requests for production, and requests for admissions, but not ordinarily to deposition testimony."); 6–26 Moore's Federal Practice § 26.131 (Mathew Bender 3d. ed. 2010) ("The duty to supplement and correct generally does not extend to disclosures made as part of deposition testimony. However, with respect to experts for whom a disclosure report is required, the duty extends both to information contained in the report and to information provided through the expert's deposition.")10 John Kimpflen et. al., Fed. Proc., L. Ed. § 26:65 (2010). ("While the Advisory Committee Notes state that the obligation to supplement responses to formal discovery requests applies to interrogatories, requests for production, and requests for admissions, but not ordinarily to deposition testimony, it has been held that the duty to supplement expert testimony extends to any changes or additions to the information provided in a deposition.") 8A Charles Allen Wright et. al., Fed. Prac. & Proc. Civ. § 2049.1 (3d ed. 2010). ("Ordinarily, the duty to supplement discovery responses applies only to interrogatory answers and document production, but Rule 26(e)(2) goes further with regard to an expert... directing as follows: [T]he party's duty to supplement extends... to information given during the expert's deposition.")

16. Preparing Your Own Expert for Deposition

When preparing your expert to testify at deposition, your conversations are typically **not** protected by the attorney-client privilege, and may be inquired into by opposing counsel at deposition. As a result, you may need to make strategic decisions about how much to prepare your expert and think carefully about what you say in the preparation session. These issues are discussed in Chapter 23.

17. Deposing Percipient Experts

This Chapter has focused on strategies and techniques for deposing adverse experts, i.e. experts retained by an adversary for the purpose of giving testimony. Some experts, however, are not retained; they are percipient witnesses. Examples:

* An emergency room physician who treated a plaintiff immediately after an auto accident and will testify to the nature and extent of the injuries.

* A county health inspector who inspected an apartment house and will testify to the extent to which the building complied with building codes.

Unlike retained experts, percipient experts generally are not required to provide voluntary disclosures. Nevertheless, from documents you've subpoenaed or from talking with them directly, you'll often be able to anticipate much of what percipient experts are likely to say at deposition. If so, the following considerations arise when you decide whether to depose percipient experts:

* If a percipient expert's testimony is likely to be damaging, you might elicit the expert's version of significant events, attempt to undermine harmful evidence, and search for helpful testimony. To the extent that a percipient expert provides damaging opinions, you may attempt to challenge them using the strategies described earlier in the Chapter. However, you generally should not search for harmful evidence. Such a search often makes sense when you depose adverse witnesses because opposing counsel usually has the opportunity to develop additional harmful evidence after a deposition concludes. By contrast, opposing counsel is less likely to have access to a percipient expert outside the confines of a deposition. Thus, if you don't bring out harmful evidence at deposition, opposing counsel may never learn of it.

* If a percipient expert's testimony is likely to be helpful, consider whether it makes sense to depose the expert. Typical downsides of taking a deposition in these circumstances are the expense of a deposition, and providing your adversary with a venue for undermining the helpful testimony. Moreover, a deposition may be unnecessary because percipient experts typically leave paper trails of their observations, and much of that trail is likely to be admissible in evidence (say, as a business record) even if the expert is unavailable to testify at trial. Especially since

these records may be sufficient to support your position at settlement negotiations, you may decide to forgo taking a deposition. On the other hand, if a case justifies the expense, or if an expert's records are of poor quality or are unlikely to be admissible in evidence, you may want to take a deposition to preserve the helpful testimony.

* If you do decide to depose a percipient expert whose testimony is likely to be helpful, elicit the helpful testimony and foundational testimony establishing that the testimony is accurate. To the extent that an expert can testify to helpful opinions based on specialized knowledge, elicit foundational evidence establishing the expert's qualifications to testify as an expert.

CHAPTER 21

DEPOSING YOUR OWN WITNESS OR A NEUTRAL WITNESS

Ordinarily, you do not depose your own witnesses. However, deposing you own witnesses to preserve their helpful testimony makes sense in at least the following two situations:

* You think that your client or a witness associated with your client will be unavailable to testify at trial or to provide an affidavit to support a pretrial motion. For example, a friendly witness may be gravely ill. In this situation, a deposition to preserve testimony often serves as a substitute for live testimony at trial.[1]

* You fear that one of your witnesses may become hostile. For example, if your witness is an employee who your client intends to fire, you may think that the employee's pre-firing version of events will be more helpful to your client than the post-firing version.[2] If a deponent becomes a

1. You are authorized to read in admissible portions of the deposition testimony in these circumstances by FRCP 32(a)(4) and FRE 804.

2. Indeed you will often ask corporate defendants to notify you before taking adverse personnel actions against important witnesses.

turncoat witness at trial, the deposition transcript will be available to impeach changed testimony.[3] In addition, a deposition to preserve testimony may serve as a substitute for live testimony if the deponent becomes unavailable.

You can also take a deposition to preserve the helpful testimony of a "neutral," third party witness who you believe will provide evidence helpful to your case. For example, in an assault case a bystander who observed the altercation may tell you or your investigator that your client did not strike the first blow and acted only in self defense. This witness may be unavailable or hard to subpoena later in the case. You may decide to preserve the bystander's favorable testimony via deposition.[4]

This Chapter examines strategies and techniques for taking depositions of your witness or a neutral witness to preserve their helpful testimony.

1. Pre–Deposition Preparation

Since depositions to preserve testimony often serve as substitutes for live testimony at trial, you typically prepare a friendly witness for a deposition the same as you would for a direct examination at trial. Typical trial preparation techniques include conducting a mock direct examination and provid-

3. Under FRE 801 a prior inconsistent statement in a deposition is admissible for its truth.

4. Because a deposition to preserve testimony often substitutes for a direct examination at trial, you may want to add impact to the testimony by visually recording the deposition. See Chapter 22.

ing feedback on a witness' answers.[5] You may use documents to refresh the witness' recollection, though you may have to show those documents to your adversary.[6] Since your adversary can question a deponent after your deposition questioning concludes, you may also want to help the witness prepare to respond to opposing counsel's deposition questioning.[7]

2. Questioning Strategies and Techniques

The subsections below suggest questioning strategies and techniques for conducting depositions to preserve testimony. These strategies and techniques mirror those that you typically use when conducting direct examinations at trial. At deposition, you have to be even more careful than at trial to conform your questions and a deponent's answers to evidence rules. Usually, an adversary's failure to object to an improper question or answer at trial acts as a waiver, making the evidence admissible. By contrast, at deposition a variety of objections are "auto-

5. If you are preparing a non-client witness for deposition, what you say to the witness during preparation may not be covered by the attorney client or work product privileges. Consequently, opposing counsel may inquire at deposition or at trial regarding your conversations with the witness. As a result, you may decide not to prepare such a witness for deposition. If you do decide to prepare a non-client witness for deposition you will need to exercise care to prevent your preparation of the witness from exposing the witness to charges of bias. See Chapter 23, Section 4.

6. See FRE 612. See Chapter 13 for a discussion on when you may have to produce documents used to refresh a witness' or a deponent's recollection.

7. See Chapter 23.

matically preserved," meaning that an adversary can sit silent at deposition and then raise evidentiary objections when you seek to use deposition testimony at trial.[8]

A. *Elicit Background Evidence*

As a general rule, after completing the admonition[9], begin depositions to preserve testimony by eliciting background evidence of the type you would elicit at trial. For example, you might ask about a deponent's occupation and job duties. Background inquiries are helpful both because they tend to relax deponents, and because the inquiries help to personalize a deponent if you offer a deposition into evidence at trial. Aspects of a deponent's background may also strengthen the credibility of a deponent's testimony. For example, if a lawsuit involves complex financial transactions, evidence of a deponent's training and experience with accounting principles may add luster to the deponent's

8. For a discussion of objections that are automatically preserved, see Chapter 15.

9. See Chapter 13 for an example of a typical admonition. Your admonition in a deposition to preserve testimony may not be exactly the same as your admonition when you depose an adverse witness. But you will want to indicate for the record that the deponent knows he is testifying under oath, knows he is not to guess, should wait for you to finish your question before answering, etc. In addition, if a neutral witness is nervous at the beginning of a deposition, some portions of the admonition may help the witness relax. For example, you might explain that the witness should feel free to ask to look at documents to refresh recollection during the deposition. You will probably have explained these procedures during preparation, but a reminder at the beginning of a deposition may help ease an apprehensive witness into the substantive testimony.

description of events. In such cases, background questioning can be extensive.

B. Elicit a Selective Chronology

Once you have decided on the information you intend to elicit, you generally want to organize that information in chronological order. A chronology tends to foster a factfinder's understanding of testimony and bolster a deponent's credibility. Moreover, chronologies respond to the way that judges and jurors usually approach decision-making, which is to develop stories about what they believe really happened.[10] Finally, chronologies tend to stimulate recall of past events, and therefore may help deponents testify completely and accurately.

Reaping the benefits of chronologies does not require you to slavishly determine the earliest event to which a deponent will testify, and proceed sequentially from there. You may choose other starting places, reflecting your judgment about what portions of a story are most important or what a factfinder will be most anxious to hear. But wherever you break into the story, the events should typically unfold chronologically.

By the same token, an effective direct examination, whether live or read from a deposition transcript, is not simply a chronological run-through of everything a deponent knows about a case. Such testimony would be tedious, and irrelevant details would undoubtedly eclipse the helpful evidence sup-

10. See W. Bennett & M. Feldman, Reconstructing Reality In the Courtroom (1981).

porting your claims. Thus, the stories you elicit must be selectively told. Emphasize important, helpful information and touch lightly on or even ignore other portions.

When stories consist of several strands of events, trying to elicit a single chronology may impede both a deponent's recall and a factfinder's understanding. Consider instead separate chronologies, one for each strand of a total story. For instance, assume that you represent an employer who is defending a claim for illegally firing an employee on the basis of age. A supervisor will testify on the employer's behalf that the firing resulted from several work-related deficiencies, including improper work attire, acts of insubordination and drinking on the job. Here, instead of trying to cram all the deficiencies into a single chronology, you might break the story into three sub-chronologies: one devoted to improper work attire, another to insubordination and the last describing the instances of drinking. This ordering emphasizes each deficiency yet retains the benefits of chronology.[11]

11. You need be less concerned with a chronological organization of testimony at the friendly witness' deposition than during a live direct. When you read the deposition in at trial, you need not read it in the order in which it appears in the transcript. With a judge's permission, during your case in chief you may read in only the portions that you want the jury to hear. Consequently, you may be able to read the testimony in chronological order at trial through selective editing of the transcript. Nevertheless, eliciting the deposition testimony in chronological order will help the deponent to testify accurately and completely and make it much easier for you to later read in a chronological direct from the transcript at trial.

C. Elicit Important Testimony Through Open Questions

Open questions call for a narrative response, rather than a "yes" or "no" answer. As at direct examination at trial, open questions are a staple during depositions to preserve testimony. Examples of open questions include:

1. "What happened after the meeting?"

2. "What was said during the conversation?"

3. "Why was this location chosen?"

Eliciting important information with open questions has several advantages:

> Just as is true at trial, leading questions are generally objectionable at deposition when you are examining your own witness or a neutral witness on an important matter.

> Open questions tend to enhance credibility because they afford deponents substantial latitude to select responses' content and wording.[12]

> Open questions tend to be efficient. With a single response, deponents can often cover territory much more quickly than with a series of responses to narrower questions.

12. See W. O'Barr, Linguistic Evidence: Language, Power, and Strategy in the Courtroom 76–83 (1982) (Studies on styles of courtroom speech indicate that narrative testimony, as opposed to fragmented testimony, enhances witness credibility because it makes a more favorable impression on the jury. Narrative testimony was considered to be long and full responses, whereas fragmented testimony was brief, incisive, non-elaborative responses).

Jurors tend to pay more attention to the fuller responses that open questions tend to produce as compared to brief responses to narrow questions.[13]

D. *Emphasis Techniques*

In addition to eliciting selective chronologies, you can emphasize important testimony through a number of other techniques.

1. *Incorporate Important Evidence into Subsequent Questions*

A common emphasis technique involves incorporating evidence from a previous answer into a successive question. For example, assume that you are deposing Larry Wendt, a witness in an auto accident case. You want to prove that the defendant, Mr. Dennis, was under the influence of alcohol at the time of the accident. After the accident, Wendt walked over to the defendant's car and noticed a bottle of whiskey on the front seat. To emphasize Wendt's testimony about the whiskey, your questioning may proceed as follows:

1. Q: Tell us what you did after you saw the accident.

2. A: I walked over to the scene to see if I could help.

13. S. Hamlin, <u>What Makes Juries Listen</u> 212–13 (1985) (explains that using open-ended questions to stimulate direct and full witness responses helps the jury stay interested and follow the examination); see also J. Tanford, <u>The Trial Process: Law, Tactics and Ethics</u> 268–269 (2d ed. 1993).

3.   Q: Did you look inside the red car at that time?

4.   A: Yes, I did.

5.   Q: Tell us what happened when you looked inside the red car?

6.   A: I saw a bottle of whiskey on the front seat.

7.   Q: What led you to believe that the object you saw on the front seat of the car was a bottle of whiskey?

8.   A: It was a clear bottle, the liquid inside was the color of whiskey, and the car smelled of whiskey.

9.   Q: When you first saw the whiskey bottle in the red car, where were you standing?

10.   A: I was right next to the window on the passenger's side of the car.

11.   Q: Was this whiskey bottle on the driver's side or the passenger's side of the front seat of the red car?

12.   A: The driver's side.

13.   Q: How big was the bottle of whiskey you saw in the red car?

14.   A: It looked like a quart-size bottle.

15.   Q: After you saw the whiskey bottle in the red car, what did you do?

16.   A. I went....

Once Wendt testifies to seeing the whiskey, you emphasize that evidence by incorporating it into subsequent questions. The technique allows the factfinder to hear about the whiskey bottle evidence several times, and reduces the possibility that a momentarily inattentive factfinder will "miss" this important evidence.

2. *Front Load Important Testimony*

A factfinder's attention is typically at its height when you begin a witness' examination. This is especially likely to be true when you read testimony from a deposition transcript or even if you show a deposition on videotape. Therefore, you may want to begin friendly witness depositions by quickly highlighting the most significant testimony. For example, assume that you represent a tenant seeking to establish that an apartment was uninhabitable. One of your witnesses is a building inspector who inspected the apartment on three separate occasions and found housing code violations each time. After eliciting evidence of the witness' occupation, experience, and job duties, you may continue as follows:

1. Q: Now, did you inspect Apartment 3 at 11359 Bolas Street during the months of February and March of this year?

2. A: I did, three different times.

3. Q: And did you find violations of the building code during those inspections?

4. A: Yes, I did.

5. Q: Please briefly summarize the violations you found.

6. A: All right. They consisted of an unvented heater, a cockroach infestation and no hot water.

7. Q: Did you notify the owner, Leona Trump, of these violations?

8. A: Yes, I did.

9. Q: OK. Now, I'd like to take you back to the first time you visited the apartment. When was that?

10. A: It was on. . . .

Here, you emphasize key evidence at the deposition's outset, providing a perspective for the details that are to follow. Limiting the initial recitation to a brief summary enables you to cover the same territory later in the deposition without giving a factfinder the impression that "I've heard all this already."

3. Elicit a String of Denials

One way to emphasize what <u>did</u> happen is with a series of questions showing what did <u>not</u> happen. For example, assume that you represent Hurt, who is suing Dempsey for injuries suffered in a barroom brawl. Hurt claims that he did nothing to provoke Dempsey's attack. To emphasize Hurt's version of events, you might ask the following series of questions:

Q: And then what happened?

A: Dempsey just walked over and started shoving me.

Q: Before the defendant started shoving you, did you touch him?

A: No.

Q: Did you touch him at all?

A: No.

Q: Before he started shoving you, did you say anything to him?

A: No.

Q: Were you even looking in the defendant's direction before he started shoving you?

A: No.

Q: All right, after he started shoving you, then what happened?

E. *Help Forgetful Deponents*

No matter how well you've prepared them, the pressure of testifying under oath at deposition may result in deponents' forgetting or neglecting to mention important evidence. There are several techniques for dealing with this problem.

1. Follow a Closed/Open Questioning Sequence

While open questions do have several advantages, a potential disadvantage is that they do little to cue deponents to the evidence you want to elicit. Consequently, when responding to open questions, deponents may neglect to mention helpful evidence you want in the record. Thus, if you've been proceeding primarily with open questions, switching to a "closed/open" questioning sequence can stimulate a deponent's recall. Consider the following example:

1. Q: What happened after your car came to a stop?

2. A: The plaintiff, Mr. Sander, got out of his car and came over to talk to me.

3. Q: What did Mr. Sander say at that time?

4. A: He said that I shouldn't have tried to make a left turn until all the traffic had cleared. Then he said that he wanted the name and telephone number of my insurance agent.

Assume that in response to No. 3, you expected the deponent to testify that Sander also said that he didn't think that he had been hurt in the accident. A closed/open sequence may surface the omitted evidence:

5. Q: When he came over to talk to you, did Mr. Sander say anything about how he was feeling?

6. A: Yes.

7. Q: What did he say?

8. A: He said that he felt fine, and he didn't think he had been hurt.

Here, the closed question (No. 5) gently reminds the deponent of the omitted subject matter, which you then elicit through an open question (No. 7). Note that the closed question should not include the substance of the desired testimony. That is, you do not ask in No. 5, "When he came over to talk to you, did Mr. Sander say he didn't think he had been hurt?" That question is arguably leading and therefore improper. Even were a judge to permit it, the important testimony would come from your mouth rather than the deponent's and thus might lack credibility.

It may take more than one simple closed/open combination to elicit omitted testimony. For example, assume that based on pretrial interviews, you have learned that a defendant made representations concerning three topics during a meeting in early January. The representations involved installation dates for a new computer system, the system's price, and software programs that would be included with the computers. Assume further that with respect to installation dates the defendant made three representations at this meeting: (a) the electrical wiring for the computers would be installed by February 15th; (b) three of the computers would be installed and ready to use by March 1st; and (c) all ten of the computers would ready to use by March 15th. At deposition, you want the deponent to testify to the above information. The testimony about this meeting proceeds as follows:

1.   Q: At the meeting in early January, what did you and the defendant Ms. French discuss?

2.   A: We talked about what we'd be getting and how much each of the computers would cost. And Ms. French told me that if we made a down payment of $5,000 right then we could get everything for a total price of $42,000. I thought that was a fair deal so I agreed and wrote her out a check at the meeting.

3. Q: During this January meeting, did Ms. French say anything about software programs?

4. A: Yes, she did.

5. Q: What did she say about software programs?

6. A: She said that the computers would have an Easy Rite software program loaded into the hard drive of each computer when they arrived.

7. Q: Was anything mentioned at this meeting about when the computers would be ready for you to use?

8. A: Yes, we discussed that.

9. Q: What did Ms. French say about when the computers would be ready?

10. A: She promised me that they'd have three of the computers installed and ready to go by March 1st and the rest of them would be ready by March 15th.

11. Q: At the January meeting was there any discussion about work that Ms. French's company would be doing before the computers arrived?

12. A: Yes. She said that they would have to put in some additional electrical wiring for the computers. She told me they would put the wiring in on a weekend, so they wouldn't disrupt our business.

13. Q: Did she tell you when the electrical wiring would be installed?

14. A: Yes, she gave me a specific date. She told me the wiring would be finished by February 15th.

Here, you employ a series of closed/open questions to elicit testimony that the deponent fails to provide in response to the initial open question. Each closed question calls the deponent's attention to the omitted subject matter, but does not include the desired evidence. This closed/open technique is particularly attractive because it often allows you to elicit the "forgotten" testimony without calling the jury's attention to the initial failure of recollection.

2. *Use Documents to Refresh Recollection*

Documents are a second method of eliciting testimony from forgetful witnesses. You may use any document to refresh recollection, regardless of whether a deponent prepared it or has ever seen it. Consider the following example:

1. Q: What happened after your car came to a stop?

2. A: The plaintiff, Mr. Sander, got out of his car and came over to talk to me.

3. Q: What did Mr. Sander say at that time?

4. A: He said I shouldn't have tried to make a left turn until all the traffic had cleared. Then he said that he wanted the name and telephone number of my insurance agent.

5. Q: When he came over to talk to you, did he say anything about how he was feeling?

6. A: I don't remember.

7. Q: I am showing you what the reporter has marked as Exhibit A. Would you read it silently to yourself.[14]

(The deponent reads the document and returns it to you.)[15]

8. Q: Is your memory now refreshed as to what else, if anything, Mr. Sander said to you?

9. A: Yes. Sander also said that he felt fine and he didn't think he had been hurt.

Once a deponent has testified to an absence of recollection (No. 6.) you can use a document, or anything else,[16] to attempt to refresh recollection.

Recognize that this technique has limitations. You may not want to make a document available to your adversary by using it to refresh recollection. And, especially when used extensively, this technique can call into question your deponent's credibility.

14. Remember, your adversary typically has the right to examine what you show to the witness to refresh recollection.

15. Technically, you should remove the document from the witness before you elicit the desired information. This is required, as the assumption (undoubtedly sometimes fictional) is that the witness is testifying from present recollection refreshed, not to whatever the document happens to say. Your opponent may object on lack of foundation or hearsay grounds if the deponent is merely reading from the document.

16. For example, you could play a song to help refresh a witness' recollection. This is seldom done, but it illustrates the point that anything may be used to refresh a witness' recollection. For a humorous account of the possibilities, see Baker v. State of Maryland, 35 Md.App. 593, 371 A.2d 699 (1977).

F. Consider Steering Around Unfavorable Testimony

Because information may be unfavorable or of marginal relevance, you may want friendly deponents to omit mention of it. You can use a closed/open questioning sequence to navigate around information you want to omit. For example, assume that your client (Ms. Jones) is a plaintiff in a wrongful termination matter. Ms. Jones had a meeting with her supervisor a week before she was discharged. At this meeting, they discussed the strengths and weaknesses of Jones' work performances and her goals for improvement during the next review period. At the deposition of an employee representative who attended the meeting, you want to omit any mention of the discussion of goals for improvement. If you ask an open question, (such as, "What was discussed at this meeting?"), the answer may include the information you want to avoid. Examine how the closed/open sequence can steer the deponent around the unwanted information:

1. Q: Did you attend a meeting between Ms. Jones and her supervisor shortly before her discharge?

2. A: Yes.

3. Q: And at that meeting, did the supervisor talk about the strengths and weaknesses of Ms. Jones' work performance?

4. A: Yes.

5. Q: Let's take the strengths first. Tell us what was said during this meeting about Ms. Jones' strengths as an employee.

6. A: Well, the supervisor said that. . . .

7. Q: And now tell us what the supervisor said about her weaknesses.

8. A: The supervisor said. . . .

In this sequence, the second closed question (No. 3) defines the topics you want the deponent to describe. The question is permissible since it is not leading, i.e. it does not refer to the substance of what was said, but refers only to whether a discussion of a particular topic took place. The open questions (Nos. 5 and 7) then ask the deponent to talk only about the defined topics. Testimony about other unwanted topics is thus excluded from the deposition.

You can also use the closed/open sequence to steer around specific time periods that you want a deponent to ignore. For example, examine the following portion of a deposition of a witness to an assault:

1. Q: After the two men arrived, what happened?

2. A: There was a fight.

3. Q: Could you tell us what happened during the fight?

4. A: [Deponent narrates].

5. Q: Now, after the fight was over did you call anyone on the telephone?

6. A: Yes. I called the police.

7. Q: Please tell us what happened after you called the police.

8. A: Well ...

Here you use the closed/open sequence (Nos. 5 and 7) to steer the deponent around what happened between the end of the fight and the time the deponent called the police.

3. Redirect Examination

After your examination concludes, your adversary has an opportunity to question the deponent. Following an adversary's examination, you may want to conduct redirect examination. As at trial, redirect at deposition allows you to respond to issues raised during your adversary's examination of the witness. For example, if opposing counsel obfuscates the order of events, on redirect you may review the proper chronology. Or if opposing counsel develops an apparent implausibility during her questioning, during redirect you might ask a deponent for an explanation.

An adversary's examination of the deponent may be less damaging than you anticipated. For instance, you may be aware of inconsistent statements which an adversary neglected to put on the record. In such cases, you may want to forego redirect and conclude a deposition as quickly as possible. If you instead conduct a redirect examination, you give your opponent another opportunity to question the deponent and bring out damaging testimony.

4. Responding to Objections

When opposing counsel objects to questions, you are usually entitled to answers notwithstanding the objections.[17] But if an objection is valid—that is, if it might be sustained by a judge when you want to use the testimony—you generally need to cure the objection with a proper question.[18]

If in your opinion an objection is clearly without merit, you may ignore it and proceed with your examination.

Opposing counsel may object to a deponent's answer as well as to your question. Most commonly, opposing counsel objects to answers on the ground that they are non-responsive. To cure this objection, simply ask questions that render the answers responsive. For example:

1.   Q: When Mr. Smith came to your office on the 4th, what, if anything, did he say anything about renegotiating the loan?

2.   A: When Mr. Smith came in on the 4th, he was already in default.

17.   See Chapter 15 and FRCP 30(c)(2) which provides that when an objection is made at deposition "the examination shall proceed, with the testimony being taken subject to the objections." And opposing counsel can obviously not instruct your witness not to answer a question.

18.   See Chapter 15.

3. [Opposing lawyer] Objection. Move to strike. The answer is non-responsive.

4. Q: When Mr. Smith came into your office on the 4th, what was the status of his loan?

5. A: His loan was in default.

6. Q: And when Mr. Smith came to your office on the 4th, what if anything did he say anything about renegotiating the loan?

7. A: Well he asked.....

No. 4 is a question that renders the answer in No. 2 responsive. No. 6 allows the witness to provide a responsive answer to your initial question.

An objection to an answer may be a delayed objection to your question. As such, an objection to an answer can raise any of the objections that might have been timely raised to a question. You typically cure such a valid, but belated, objection as you would a timely one. Consider the following example:

1. Q: What physical defects, if any, did Mr. Bird have at that time?

2. A: He was hard of hearing.

3. [Opposing lawyer] Objection. Move to strike. There is no showing that the deponent has personal knowledge that Mr. Bird was hard of hearing. There was no foundation for that question.

4. Q: At that time, did you think that Mr. Bird was hard of hearing?

5. A: Yes, I did.

6. Q: What made you think that at that time Mr. Bird was hard of hearing?

7. A: He was wearing a hearing aid in his left ear. Also prior to that day, he was always telling me to speak louder because he had trouble hearing.

8. Q: Is there any other reason you felt at that time that Mr. Bird was hard of hearing?

9. A: Only that when his wife asked him a question, he didn't answer her.

Reminder: An adversary's failure to object at deposition may be a tactical ploy. If an objection is one that is automatically preserved,[19] an adversary may intentionally forgo making the objection in an effort to prevent you from recognizing and overcoming evidentiary shortcomings in questions and answers. Thus, no matter what an adversary does, you must monitor the evidentiary propriety of your questions and answers.

19. For a discussion of which objections are automatically preserved even if not made at the deposition, see Chapter 24.

CHAPTER 22

VISUALLY RECORDED DEPOSITIONS

As technology becomes more accessible and judicial acceptance of it increases, lawyers increasingly elect to visually record depositions.[1] This Chapter explores the major procedural and strategic considerations surrounding visually recorded depositions.

1. Ground Rules for Visually Recorded Depositions Under the FRCP

The FRCP set forth simple procedures for visually recording depositions. For example, FRCP 30(b)(2) provides that a deposing party may unilaterally arrange visual recording by indicating in the notice of deposition that it will be visually recorded.[2] And FRCP 30(b)(2) provides that a visually recorded deposition need not be recorded stenographically.[3]

1. A visual recording will obviously also include an audio recording of the deponent's testimony. For ease of reference through out this Chapter we will refer to the combined audio/visual recording as a "visually recorded" deposition.

2. Many states have similar rules permitting a party to notice visually recorded depositions. See, e.g., Cal. Civ. Proc. Code § 2025.330(c) (2004).

3. The language of FRCP 30(b)(3)(A) and 30(b)(3)(B) is ambiguous on the question of whether the noticing party may designate two or more methods for recording the deposition.

Under FRCP 30(b)(3), any party, not just the party taking a deposition, can arrange for visual recording. The party requesting visual recording bears its expense. Consequently, if your opponent notices a "regular" deposition, i.e., one to be steno-graphically recorded by a court reporter, you may serve a notice that the deposition will also be visual-ly recorded at your expense.[4]

FRCP 30(b)(4) provides that unless all parties stipulate otherwise, a visually recorded deposition must be conducted before an "officer," i.e., a court reporter or some other disinterested person author-ized to administer oaths under FRCP 28.[5] The officer must be present even if the visually recorded deposition is <u>not</u> being stenographically recorded.

Section (b)(3)(A) is written in the alternative, arguably limiting the noticing party to a single method of recording the deposition. And Section (b)(3)(B) indicates that other parties can designate additional methods of recording the deposition in addition to "the" method specified by the person taking the deposition. The language of both these provisions suggests that the person taking the deposition may not be authorized to visually record the deposition and simultaneously record it stenographically and/or on audio tape. But the statute clearly contemplates more than one method of recording a deposition, and there would seem to be no obvious reason to prohibit the noticing party for stating that two methods would be used to record the deposition. <u>See also</u> Wright, Miller & Marcus, Federal Practice and Procedure: Civil 2d. § 2115.

4. Similarly, under FRCP 30(b)(5), if your opponent notices a deposition which will be visually recorded, but not stenographi-cally recorded, you may serve a notice that the deposition will be also be stenographically recorded at your expense.

5. The officer may not be a relative or employee of counsel, or anyone with a financial interest in the case. See FRCP 28(c).

The Federal Rules provide little guidance for recording methods. FRCP 30(b)(4) simply provides that the appearance or demeanor of a deponent or counsel shall not be distorted through camera or sound recording techniques. Local court rules in your jurisdiction may have additional provisions governing visually recording methods.

At the beginning of the first visually recorded session, the presiding officer must administer the oath and state for the record: (a) the officer's name and business address; (b) the date, time and place of the deposition; and (c) the name of the deponent. The officer also identifies all persons present at a deposition. If a deposition requires more than one recording unit, e.g. more than one DVD or visually record, the officer must repeat items (a)–(c) at the beginning of each new recording unit.

At the end of a deposition, the officer must state on the record that the deposition is complete and indicate the terms of any stipulations of counsel regarding the custody of the recording units and any exhibits, or any other stipulations of counsel.

After a deposition is concluded, the officer must provide deposing counsel with a copy of the recording unit(s), which deposing counsel must maintain under "conditions that will protect it against loss, destruction, tampering, or deterioration."[6] The officer must also keep a copy of the recording unit(s) and, upon payment of reasonable costs for copying,

6. See FRCP 30(f).

make copies available to the deponent or to any party.[7]

2. Advantages of Visually Recording Depositions

A visual recording has several potential advantages compared to a written transcript.

A. Adds Impact to Impeachment at Trial

Deposition testimony can be admissible at trial to impeach a non-party deponent's inconsistent trial testimony.[8] A visual recording tends to heighten the impact of impeachment because the judge or jury sees and hears a witness' contradictory deposition testimony.[9] So much the better for you if the visual recording also depicts the deponent's unfavorable body language, intonation, pauses between question and answer, conferences with counsel before answering, and other cues that indicate hesitation, uncertainty, evasiveness or sarcasm. Such visual and auditory indicia of poor credibility are lost when impeaching testimony is read from a transcript.

While visually recorded impeachment can be dramatic and effective, implementation can be difficult and expensive. Prior to trial, you may not know whether conflicts will arise between an adverse witness' trial and deposition testimony. When a

7. See FRCP 30(f).

8. See FRCP 32(a)(2).

9. You will typically have to provide the court with a transcript of the portions of the visually recorded depositions which you use at trial. See FRCP 32(c).

conflict does arise and you want to impeach, a visual recording can be unwieldy. You'd need to quickly locate the impeaching portion of the deposition, before a judge's patience wears out and jurors forget the inconsistent testimony.

Technologies for overcoming the limitations of visually recorded depositions evolve constantly. At the moment, one useful preparation practice is to generate a bar code for each line of deposition testimony. You then have a bar code for each question you ask the witness on cross. If the witness testifies inconsistently with the deposition, you sweep an electronic wand across the appropriate bar code, and the appropriate portion of the deposition immediately shows on a screen for the jury to see.[10]

B.   *Adds Impact to an Adverse Party's Helpful Deposition Testimony*

Use of an adverse witness' deposition is not limited to impeachment. Under FRCP 32(a)(2), you can offer an adverse **party's** deposition testimony into evidence at trial for any purpose.[11] If you do choose

10.   For a discussion of the use of bar coding, see Jill M. Brannelly & John J. O'Connor, Massachusetts Discovery Practice § 12.2.3 (2009).

David M. Malone et al, Effective Deposition: Techniques and Strategies That Work 274 (3rd ed. 2007).

11.   Of course, the deposition testimony is only admissible to the extent that it would be admissible if the deponent were testifying live at trial. See FRCP 32(a)(1). Thus, for example, you can not introduce inadmissible hearsay simply because it comes from a deposition. You may, however, be able to admit otherwise inadmissible evidence, if it was not objected to at the deposition. See Chapters 13 and 24.

to offer any part of an adverse party's deposition testimony into evidence (typically because you consider it helpful), the testimony is likely to have greater impact if you show it on television rather than have it read. Again, the impact will be even greater if the adverse party appears evasive or hostile.

C. Adds Impact to Preserved Testimony of a Friendly, Unavailable Witness

When a friendly witness is likely to be unavailable to testify in person at trial, you can "preserve" testimony by deposing the witness and then offering the deposition testimony at trial in lieu of live testimony.[12] Again, a visually recorded deposition is likely to add impact to the deposition testimony. If all you have is a written deposition transcript, the questions and answers have to be read orally to a jury or by the judge. Even if in a jury trial you enlist the aid of another person who reads the answers while you read the questions, oral dialog is unlikely to have the impact of a visual recording of the actual witness' testimony. In an age dominated by visual media such as televisions and computers, jurors are used to seeing rather than hearing about events and may even expect you to offer evidence visually.

D. Adds Impact to Demonstrations or Re-Enactments

You may properly ask deponents not merely to describe events verbally, but also to demonstrate

12. See FRCP 32(a)(3) and Chapter 21.

what happened physically.[13] If so, capturing the demonstration on a visual recording can make it easier for the trier of fact to understand the deponent's testimony.

For example, assume that in a product liability case you ask the adverse party to demonstrate how he was using your client's equipment at the time an injury occurred. Your purpose is to show that the product was not being used for its intended purpose. While you might elicit and then introduce into evidence at trial the party's verbal description of what happened, a visual demonstration may be much more effective.

E.   Creates Illustrative Exhibits for Trial or Settlement

You can excerpt portions of visually recorded depositions to add impact to opening statement or closing arguments.[14] For example, you might assemble a montage of inconsistent statements by your adversary's main witness which were admitted into evidence to show to the jury during closing argument. The recording may well carry greater impact than verbal references to the witness' inconsistent testimony.

13. See Emerson Electric Co. v. Superior Court, 16 Cal.4th 1101, 68 Cal.Rptr.2d 883, 946 P.2d 841 (1997) (deponent may be required to perform demonstration or reenactment); see also Howard v. Michalek, 249 F.R.D. 288 (N.D.Ill. 2008) (police station employee is not ordered to re-enact her actions in the video surveillance room at time of prisoner suicide, but court does discuss situations where re-enactment order would normally be granted).

14. You will need to get the court's prior approval to do so.

Settlement discussions offer other opportunities for using portions of visually recorded depositions. In a personal injury case, for example, you might combine a visual recording of a day in the life of your seriously injured client with the most damaging visually recorded portions of the defendant's deposition testimony to show to an arbitrator, settlement conference judge, or insurance adjuster.

F.   Discourages Inappropriate Behavior by Opposing Counsel

Even if opposing counsel's picture is not visually recorded, their voice will be recoded. Consequently, a visual recording is generally much more effective than a written transcript for providing evidence of improper behavior such as objections made for the purpose of coaching a deponent, pre-answer consultations between opposing counsel and a deponent, and the like.[15] Consequently, a visual recording tends to discourage such behavior. If opposing counsel nevertheless behaves improperly, you have a visual record to show to a judicial officer to justify a request for a protective order and sanctions or the recovery of attorneys' fees.

G.   Reduces Deposition Costs

While visually recording is not necessarily a cost-saving device, you can realize cost savings if you frequently visually record depositions. You can invest in your own equipment and if necessary hire

15. You may want to put both opposing counsel and the deponent in the picture. However, no rule requires that opposing counsel be in the picture.

an experienced videographer to set it up.[16] Thereafter, for each deposition you need only a camera operator and a notary public authorized to administer oaths; the same person can serve in both capacities.[17] If you visually record in lieu of a stenographic transcript, you also save the expense of a court reporter. Under these conditions, the costs of a visually recorded deposition may be lower than for a stenographically-recorded one.

H. *Improves Feedback From Mock Jury Trials*

Visually recorded deposition testimony is useful for presenting cases to mock juries. "Jurors" can then provide realistic feedback on witness credibility. Such feedback can help you decide what, if any, deposition portions to show at trial. Moreover, the feedback may help you prepare your own witnesses for trial. Finally, feedback as to the outcome of a case and the significance of particular items of evidence may be more reliable when mock jurors have seen and heard the actual witnesses who will testify at trial.

I. *Improves Your Witness' Trial Testimony*

Typically, you visually record a friendly witness' deposition because you think the witness will not be available to testify at trial. If it turns out that your witness is available to testify, you may want to use

16. The National Court Reporter's Association provides guidelines for visually recorded depositions and a "Legal Video Specialist" certification.

17. You may not, however, use your employee or anyone else interested in the case as a deposition officer. See FRCP 28(a) and 30(b)(5).

the visually recorded deposition to improve the witness' trial testimony. Together, you and a witness can watch a visually recorded deposition and discuss how to eliminate flaws in testimonial style which might unfairly diminish credibility.[18]

3. Disadvantages of Visually Recording Depositions

Visual recording, like every other strategy, has potential disadvantages.

A. *The Visual Recording of Your Witness Will Be Available for Your Adversary's Use at Trial*

When you visually record your own witness's deposition, an adversary's examination will also be visually recorded. Your opponent will be able to use the visually recording, as discussed above, to enhance his impeachment during cross of your witness.

In addition, your adversary can show helpful portions of the deposition of your witness during his case in chief.[19] This can be particularly damaging if

18. Of course, if your communications during preparation of a witness to testify at trial are not protected by the attorney client privilege, you may not want to review a visually recorded deposition with the deponent. Such a preparation session would provide opposing counsel with an opportunity to question the deponent about what occurred in the preparation session. See Chapter 24. Even if a client's deposition testimony were not visually recorded, you could visually record a practice direct and cross exam in the privacy of your office and use that recording to improve your client's trial testimony.

19. See FRCP 32(a)(3) providing that the deposition of an adverse witness may generally be used at any time and for any purpose at trial.

your witness appears evasive or less than credible on the visual recording.

In short, when you visually record your own witness' deposition, your adversary will be able to show the most damaging aspects of your witness' testimony, rather than having to read that damaging testimony in from a transcript.

In light of the above, you are most likely to visually record the deposition of your own witness when all three of the following are true:

*Your witness is likely to be unavailable at trial.

*Your witness' testimony is extremely important to your case. As a result, you would be likely to benefit by having the testimony presented visually rather than read in through a transcript.

*Your witness appears credible, i.e. your witness is likely to make a favorable impression on a factfinder and not likely to be hurt badly on cross examination at trial. As a result, your adversary is not likely to benefit from being able to use the visually recorded deposition at trial.

B. The Visually Recording of an Adverse Witness May Be Available for Your Adversary's Use at Trial

When you visually record an adverse witness, your adversary will be able to play helpful portions of the deposition if the witness is unavailable at trial.[20] The visual recording may provide more compelling evidence than reading in a transcript.

20. See FRCP 32(a)(4).

C. Technological Risks

A possible corollary of Murphy's Law is that when you rely on electronic technology, the technology will fail at the absolutely worst moment. Therefore, unless you are confident with your own technological skills or have expert assistance, consider the possibility of a mechanical breakdown as a risk of visual recording. Common risks include equipment breaking down, an operator's failure to hit the "record" button, and defective recoding units. Such problems can result in the loss of testimony, which can potentially prevent the use of the visually recorded deposition or require you to get court approval to take a second deposition.[21] Similarly, if for any reason the quality of a visually recorded deposition is poor, you may be prohibited from using it at trial.[22] Consequently, make sure you run a "test" before the beginning of a deposition to be sure that picture and sound quality are acceptable. And, especially when you are recording at an unfamiliar location or with an operator you have never worked with before, you may want to indicate in your deposition notice that you will also record the deposition with a court reporter as a backup.

D. Increased Expense

While visually recording depositions can be more economical than recording them stenographically,

21. See FRCP 30(a)(2)(A)(ii).

22. See Tsesmelys v. Dublin Truck Leasing Corp., 78 F.R.D. 181 (1976) indicating a recording may be excluded from evidence if the prejudicial effect of the poor quality of the recording outweighs its probative value.

this is not always true. To obtain a high quality visual record, you may have to hire a videographer to attend the deposition and supervise the recording of the testimony. If you are recording outside of your usual office location, the videographer should accompany you, set up the equipment, and supervise the recording. In either case, videographer fees can dramatically increase the cost of the deposition.

Another common expense associated with visually recording arises when you want to use all or a portion of a visually recorded deposition either as part of a pre-trial motion or at trial. In either event, you must provide opposing counsel and the court with a written transcript of any portions of a visually recorded deposition you rely on.[23] Thus, you'll have to pay for a written transcript of any portion of a deposition that you plan to use.

E. *Inconvenient to Review*

When you prepare for additional depositions or for trial, written deposition transcripts are easy to review. You can quickly move around in a transcript, with or without the help of an index prepared by yourself or a paralegal. Review of visually recorded depositions requires a machine, and moving backwards and forwards to different parts of testimony can be cumbersome. You can, of course, have your staff prepare a transcript from the visual record, but that may involve considerable additional expense.

23.   See FRCP 26(a)(3)(A)(ii) and 32(c). The statute does not require that the transcript be made by a court reporter.

4. Strategies for Preparing Friendly Deponents

When you visually record a friendly witness' deposition, the usual reason is that the witness may not be available for trial. If so, the deposition is in essence the witness' direct examination at trial and you should prepare accordingly. Here are a few suggestions.[24]

A. *Visually Record a Practice Session*

If possible, conduct and visually record a practice deposition, consisting of the questions you intend to ask and that you think your adversary is likely to ask. Watch the recording with the witness and try to correct any visual or oral flaws that might damage credibility. People who are unused to appearing in front of a camera may display distracting mannerisms, such as touching their faces with their hands, looking around rather than directly into the camera and swiveling back and forth in the chair. Watching a recording of a practice session is the best way for witnesses to see for themselves how such unconscious habits can detract from credibility. Although you may not be able to eliminate the habits of a lifetime in one or two practice sessions, you may be able to improve a witness' performance.

You may not want to visually record a mock deposition with a witness unless your conversations and the recording are protected by the attorney-client privilege. If your conversations are not privi-

---

24. For a discussion of how to organize a direct examination of your own witness, see Chapter 21.

leged, the practice session may be inquired about by your opponent at the deposition and be used to support an argument that the witness is biased.

B. Show a "Good" Performance

A picture may be worth a thousand helpful suggestions. Before or after visually recording a practice deposition, consider showing a prospective deponent a positive example of another deponent's effective deposition testimony. Such a concrete positive example may help your witness more than anything you say. If you visually record friendly witnesses frequently, you may even invest in a "standard" example that you show to all deponents.

C. Discuss What to Wear

A witness' manner of dress is obviously more important in a visually recorded than in a transcribed deposition. Generally, it makes sense to give the same clothing advice for a visually recorded deposition as for trial. However, television adds an additional wrinkle, and a professional videographer may advise you about what sort of clothing tends to create a favorable impression.

5. Strategies for Taking Visually Recorded Depositions Effectively

A. Complying With FRCP 30(b)(4)

No matter the size of your deposition budget, you must comply with the mandate of FRCP 30(b)(4) that the appearance or demeanor of the deponent or counsel may not be distorted through camera or sound recording techniques. (Again, local rules in your jurisdiction may have additional requirements.)

To insure that a recording complies with this rule and is of good enough quality for use in court, perform a dry run and check on the following before a deposition begins:

* Check the Sound. Determine where microphones need to be placed to permit you, the witness and opposing counsel to be heard clearly when speaking in a normal voice. A mixer (a device which controls the volume of each microphone for each speaker) allows you to easily adjust volume for all participants. To the extent possible, arrange microphones so as to avoid picking up background noise from inside or outside the deposition room.

* Check the Lighting. Proper lighting is essential for fairly capturing a deponent's appearance and demeanor. In some locations, you may need to arrange for special lighting to produce a recording of satisfactory quality.

* Check the Temperature. If you are deposing a friendly witness and especially if you are using special lighting, try to ensure a normal temperature inside the deposition room. A room that is too warm may cause a deponent to perspire and otherwise appear uncomfortable.

* Check the Camera Set Up. A deponent should be able to look directly into the camera when answering questions. Yet most deponents have a natural tendency to look at the questioner. There-

fore, set up the camera so that a deponent can easily look both at you and the camera. The camera should provide a straight-on head and shoulders shot of a deponent.

* Check That You Can See the Picture. Place the monitor so that you can see it from where you are asking questions. That way you can detect any changes in recording quality. Such an alignment is especially important if you want to use any of the "big budget" techniques described below.

If you have a larger deposition budget and want to make a professional quality visual record that rivals what jurors are likely to see on television, you may well need to hire a videographer. Here are some of the issues you might want to review with a videographer:

* Use of Multiple Cameras: Multiple cameras allow you to use a variety of shots from different camera angles. The variety makes a recording look more professional and may stimulate a jury's interest.

* Zoom In and Out: Zooming is another way to give a professional appearance to a visually recorded deposition. For example, you can ask the camera operator to zoom in for close ups of documents or exhibits or of you or opposing counsel. If you are deposing an adverse witness, you might want to zoom in when the deponent is being evasive or hostile. If you are deposing a friendly witness, you might want to zoom in when the deponent is providing crucial testimony.

  * <u>Vary Who is on Camera</u>: A camera may remain focused on a deponent at all times; or may alternate between a deponent, counsel, and exhibits. Multiple cameras also allow for a "split screen," say with you and a deponent in the picture at the same time.

  * <u>Communicating With the Camera Operator</u>: If you do use any of these special techniques, you have to work out with the camera operator in advance a system for advising the operator of the type of image you want.

  "Big budget" procedures such as these may impel opposing counsel to object that the taping procedures violate Rule 30(b)(4) because they "distort" the deponent or counsel. Of course, you should fairly respond to valid concerns, and if you can reach agreement put the agreement on the record at the start of a deposition. If you cannot agree, you will have to conduct a deposition subject to opposing counsel's objections.[25] Of course, you may be prohibited from using a visually recorded deposition if a court later rules that your procedures did distort the deponent or counsel. If this is a concern, you may want to have a court reporter transcribe a deposition as a back up.

B. *Bring an Assistant to the Deposition*

  Especially when you depose a friendly witness, consider bringing a paralegal or other assistant to a deposition. While you concentrate on your questions and the deponent's answers, your assistant can concentrate on such concerns as whether the depo-

  25. See FRCP 30(c)(2).

nent is looking directly at the camera, whether the witness looks fatigued or uncomfortable, and the like.

C. *Monitoring Your Own Conduct*

In any deposition, you should maintain a professional and courteous manner toward all witnesses and opposing counsel during the deposition.[26] This is especially important when your voice or image will be on display for a judge or jury. To state the obvious, at a visually recorded deposition you should conduct yourself as you would before a judge and jury.

6. Strategies for Defending Visually Recorded Depositions

By and large, you defend a visually recorded deposition as you would one that is stenographically recorded. The subsections below address particular concerns that arise when you defend visually recorded depositions.

A. *Visually Record a Practice Session*

If possible, conduct and visually record a practice deposition, consisting of the questions you think your adversary is likely to ask. Your adversary may show the deposition of your witness during settlement negotiations or at trial. As a result, you should prepare the witness for the deposition as you would prepare a witness to testify at trial.

Watch the recording of the practice session with the witness and try to correct any visual or oral

26. See Chapter 14.

flaws that might damage credibility. Under the pressure of examination by opposing counsel, even sophisticated and experienced people who are used to speaking to groups may appear evasive or non-responsive, or display distracting mannerisms, such as touching their faces with their hands, looking around rather than directly into the camera and swiveling back and forth in the chair. Watching a recording of a practice session is the best way for witnesses to see for themselves how their demeanor can detract from credibility. Although you may not be able to eliminate the habits of a lifetime in one or two practice sessions, you may be able to improve a witness' performance.

Again, you may not want to visually record a mock deposition with a witness unless your conversations and the recording are protected by the attorney-client privilege. Absent the privilege, the practice session may be inquired about by your opponent at the deposition and be used to support an argument that the witness is biased.

B. Ensuring Fair Visually Recordings

Before a deposition begins, ask deposing counsel to conduct a short off the record "dry run" so that you can see and hear a deponent[27] Also, ask for a "time and date generator" to appear on the record-

27. If the deposition is at an unfamiliar or unusual location, you may want to visit it prior to the day of the deposition. If you have any concerns about the suitability of the site for a visually recorded deposition, you can raise them with opposing counsel prior to the day of the deposition.

ing. The time record enables you to recognize when the portions of a recording are missing.

If you have any concerns about lighting, sound, camera angles, zoom shots, use of multiple cameras or any other taping procedures, try to work them out with opposing counsel before a deposition begins. If you can not reach a satisfactory arrangement on these issues, state your objections on the record at the start of the deposition. You can then raise these objections later if your adversary tries to use the visual record in connection with a motion or at trial. If you do not put these objections on the record at the start of the deposition, or as soon thereafter as you become aware of any objectionable procedures, you probably have waived your right to object.[28]

If your concerns about the way your witness' is being depicted on the recording are serious enough, you might want to consider terminating the deposition and moving for a protective order. Remember, however, that FRCP 30(b)(4) simply provides that the appearance or demeanor of the deponent or counsel shall not be distorted through camera or sound recording techniques. If your witness' appearance is not distorted, obtaining a protective order is problematic.

Once a deposition begins, you need to object on the record to any conduct during the deposition that might adversely affect your client's appearance on the recording. Examples:

28.   See FRCP 32(d)(3)(B).

* The camera operator may zoom in for an extreme close up whenever a deponent hesitates before answering an important question;

* If opposing counsel moves away from the camera and (as is usually the case) the deponent looks at counsel and not at the camera when answering questions, the deponent may come across as evasive. You may respond by objecting that by moving away from the camera, opposing counsel is distorting the deponent's appearance.

C. Avoid Conferences While on the Record

While on the record, you should not confer with a deponent unless it is for the purpose of deciding whether to assert a privilege.[29] Avoiding improper

29.   See In re Stratosphere Corp. Sec. Litig., 182 F.R.D. 614, 621 (D. Nev. 1998) ("When there is a question pending neither the deponent nor his or her counsel may initiate the interruption of the proceeding to confer about the question, the answer, or about any document that is being examined, except to assert a claim of privilege (conform to a court order or seek a protective order)."); In re Amezaga, 195 B.R. 221, 228 (Bankr. D.P.R. 1996) ("Counsel for the deponent has a very limited role during the taking of a deposition and conversing with the witness is limited to discussions about whether the objection of privilege should be asserted."); Armstrong v. Hussmann Corp., 163 F.R.D. 299 (E.D. Mo. 1995); Hall v. Clifton Precision, 150 F.R.D. 525, 527 (E.D. Pa. 1993) ("[C]ourts have held that private conferences between deponents and their attorneys during the taking of a deposition are improper unless the conferences are for the purpose of determining whether a privilege should be asserted."); Tuerkes–Beckers, Inc. v. New Castle Assocs., 158 F.R.D. 573, 575 (D. Del. 1993) ("Counsel for a witness may not consult with that witness about the subject matter of his or her testimony while that witness is under examination by an opposing party.") Plaisted v. Geisinger Medical Center, 210 F.R.D. 527 (M.D.Pa. 2002); United States v. Philip Morris Inc., 212 F.R.D. 418, 420 (D.D.C. 2002)

conferences is particularly important in a visually recorded deposition. Your behavior might seem suggestive if that portion of the recording is shown to a jury. Moreover, a deponent may whisper something embarrassing or damaging in a conference that would not be heard by a court reporter at a stenographically recorded deposition (and therefore would not become part of the record), but will be picked up by the microphone and become part of the record. In short, if you need to confer with your witness, be sure you are off the record and the recording device is turned off.

D. Make Objections as You Would Before a Jury

Generally speaking, you should raise objections at a visually recorded deposition as you would in the absence of the camera.[30] At a visually recorded deposition, however, you need to be especially careful not to coach, or appear to coach, the witness while making objections.

(communications between attorney and client during the actual deposition are not appropriate, even if deposition lasts several consecutive days); Calzaturficio SCARPA Spa v. Fabiano Shoe Co. Inc., 201 F.R.D. 33, 39 (D. Mass. 2001). For further discussion of when you may confer with your witness at deposition see Wachen, David S. "Can We Talk? Nationwide Survey Reveals Wide Range of Practices Governing Communication with Witnesses while Defending Their Deposition" www.abanet.org/litigation/committees/pretrial/articles.html. For a discussion of whether communications with a deponent during a deposition or during recesses are protected by the work product or attorney client privilege, see Chapter 25.

30. For a discussion of the proper form of objections, see Chapter 25.

E.   Take Adequate Breaks

Adequate "rest stops" help deponents to look fresh on camera. Therefore, you may want to take more frequent breaks in a visually recorded than in a stenographically transcribed deposition.

F.   Prohibit Improper Use of the Recording

If you are concerned that opposing counsel or an opposing party may distribute the recording to the press or public in an effort to embarrass or otherwise damage a deponent or your case, you should either enter into a stipulation with opposing counsel or obtain a protective order prohibiting such use.

PART FOUR

DEFENDING DEPOSITIONS

Part Four (Chapters 23 and 24) explores strategies and techniques for preparing both clients and non-clients for a deposition and for defending depositions taken by an adverse party.

CHAPTER 23

PREPARING DEPONENTS

Pre-deposition meetings with deponents can ease their anxiety and help them respond effectively at deposition. In addition, such meetings may alert you to the need to gather more information and/or documents before a deposition begins. This Chapter focuses on strategies for preparing clients,[1] and concludes with a section devoted to preparation of non-clients.

1. Your Pre–Meeting Preparation

The subsections below examine steps that you may take prior to pre-deposition preparation meetings with clients.

A. *Review the Validity of Document Requests*

The Notice of Deposition or Subpoena Duces Tecum that requires your client's attendance may request the production of documents.[2] If so, decide

1. In instances where the person being prepared is an employee of a private or public entity that has retained you, the discussion assumes that the employee qualifies as a client for the purpose of asserting the attorney-client privilege. For a discussion of when the law treats an entity's employees or agents as clients even though they have not individually retained an entity's lawyer, see Wright, Miller, & Marcus, Federal Practice and Procedure: Civil 3d § 2017.

2. See FRCP 45(a)(1)(C).

whether you intend to object to any portion of the request. You need to file any objections pursuant to FRCP 34 or FRCP 26(b).[3]

B. Review Pertinent Documents

Prior to meeting with clients, gather and review the documents you will produce in response to deposing counsel's request at the deposition as well as any other documents that may be pertinent to a client's testimony. For example, you might want to examine all case-related documents that bear a client's name, documents that may refresh a client's memory, and documents about which a client is likely to be questioned.

C. Prepare a Case Chronology

If you have not already done so, prepare a case chronology reflecting each party's versions of the significant events in a case.[4] Reviewing relevant portions of a chronology with a client can refresh the client's recollection and help the client testify accurately.[5]

D. Help Identify FRCP 30(b)(6) Deponents

If opposing counsel notices a FRCP 30(b)(6) deposition,[6] you should make a reasonable effort to help

3. With respect to objections to notices to produce, see FRCP 34(b)(2). With respect to objections to documents sought by subpoena duces tecum, see FRCP 45(c)(2)(B) or FRCP 26(b)(3).

4. For advice on preparing case chronologies, see Chapter 16.

5. If you show the client the chronology and it is used to refresh the client's recollection, you may have to provide it to your adversary. See infra note 9. You can, of course, go over the information in the chronology without showing the document to a client and avoid any risk of having to produce it.

6. For a discussion of 30(b)(6) depositions, see Chapter 18.

your client (i.e., a corporation, partnership or government entity) identify and produce the person(s) most knowledgeable with respect to the subjects listed in the notice. If a client does not currently have a person who is knowledgeable about subjects listed in the notice, inform the client that it has an obligation to take reasonable steps to educate a representative to testify on any such subject.[7]

E.   Arrange to Meet the Client

When it comes to scheduling a client's preparation meeting, your primary considerations include how many meetings may be needed and how far in advance of deposition to meet.

You may need more than one meeting to prepare a client, especially when:

* A case is complex;

* A deposition is likely to be lengthy;

* A client is unsophisticated and nervous;

* Events likely to be asked about are no longer fresh in a client's mind.[8]

On the other hand, a single meeting may be adequate if a deposition is likely to be short and a client's testimony is straightforward.

7. See Wright, Miller, & Marcus, Federal Practice and Procedure: Civil 3d § 2103. For further discussion of FRCP 30(b)(6) depositions, see Chapter 18.

8. Of course, you must also take into account a client's willingness to spend time and pay fees for the preparation.

Whether or not you hold a single meeting or multiple ones, hold meetings far enough in advance of deposition to allow clients to gather additional information or documents should such actions be necessary.

2. Tell Clients What Documents to Review

Any case-related document that a client reads in preparation for deposition may have to be turned over to an adversary—even if the document would otherwise be privileged.[9] Therefore, tell clients what

9. The basic rule for requiring disclosure of a document that a deponent has used to refresh recollection in preparation for a deposition is found in FRE 612. In essence, this rule provides that if a witness uses a writing to refresh memory for the purpose of testifying, an adverse party is entitled to have the writing produced at the hearing if a court in its discretion determines it is necessary in the interests of justice. While FRE 612 pertains to testimony at trial, case law makes clear that the rule also applies to testimony at deposition. See, e.g., Sporck v. Peil, 759 F.2d 312, 317 (3rd Cir. 1985); Magee v. Paul Revere Life Ins. Co., 172 F.R.D. 627 (E.D.N.Y. 1997); Stone Container Corp. v. Arkwright Mutual Ins.Co., No.93 C 6626, 1995 WL 88902 (N.D. Ill. Feb 28, 1995); Auto Owners Ins. Co. v. Total-tape, Inc., 135 F.R.D. 199, 202 (M.D. Fla. 1990); Parry v. Highlight Industries, 125 F.R.D. 449, 452 (W.D. Mich.1989); James Julian, Inc. v. Raytheon Co., 93 F.R.D. 138, 144 (D.C. Del. 1982); Heron Interact, Inc. v. Guidelines, Inc., 244 F.R.D. 75, 77 (D. Mass. 2007); Coryn Group II, LLC v. O.C. Seacrets, Inc., 265 F.R.D. 235, 240 (D. Md. 2010); Frazier v. Ford Motor Co., 2008 WL 4809130 (W.D. Ark. 2008); Medtronic Xomed, Inc. v. Gyrus ENT LLC, 2006 WL 786425 (M.D. Fla. 2006).The extent to which courts have found that the interest of justice requires that privileged documents used to refresh the deponent's recollection prior to the deposition be turned over to an adversary varies greatly. For examples of cases requiring disclosure of privileged documents, see S & A Painting Co., Inc. v. O.W.B. Corp., 103 F.R.D. 407, 409 (D.C. Pa. 1984); James Julian, Inc., 93 F.R.D. at

documents they should and should not review when preparing to meet with you.[10]

Clients may also have to disclose the identities of anyone they talk to when preparing for deposition, as well as the content of any such conversations. Consequently, advise clients to whom they may speak concerning case-related subjects.

Advice you may give a client with respect to these matters may go as follows:

Jenni, between today and the time we meet next Thursday, it will be useful for you to review your correspondence file with Trans Co. relating to

145–46; Prucha v. M & N Modern Hydraulic Press Co., 76 F.R.D. 207, 209–10 (D.C. Wisc. 1977); Thomas v. Euro RSCG Life, 264 F.R.D. 120, 122 (S.D. N.Y. 2010); Coryn Group II, LLC v. O.C. Seacrets, Inc., 265 F.R.D. 235, 240 (D. Md. 2010); Heron Interact, Inc. v. Guidelines, Inc., 244 F.R.D. 75 (D. Mass. 2007); United States ex rel. Bagley v. TRW, Inc., 212 F.R.D. 554 (C.D. Cal. 2003); Sperling v. City of Kennesaw Dept., 202 F.R.D. 325 (N.D. Ga. 2001). For cases holding that privileged documents need not be disclosed even though a deponent used them to refresh memory, see Sporck, 759 F.2d at 317; Bogosian v. Gulf Oil Corp., 738 F.2d 587 (3rd Cir. 1984); Derderian v. Polaroid Corp., 121 F.R.D. 13 (D. Mass. 1988); Al–Rowaishan Establishment Universal Trading & Agencies, Ltd. v. Beatrice Foods Co., 92 F.R.D. 779, 780 (D.C.N.Y. 1982); In re Teleglobe Communications Corp., 392 B.R. 561, 587 (D. Del. 2008); Scanlon v. Bricklayers and Allied Craftworkers, Local No. 3, 242 F.R.D. 238, 247 (W.D. N.Y. 2007); In re Managed Care Litigation, 415 F.Supp.2d 1378 (S.D. Fla. 2006); U.S. E.E.O.C. v. Continental Airlines, Inc., 395 F.Supp.2d 738, 744–45 (N.D. Ill. 2005); Suss v. MSX Intern. Engineering Services, Inc., 212 F.R.D. 159, 163 (S.D. N.Y. 2002).

10. In addition to wanting to protect privileged documents, you might also want to protect documents that an adversary has not previously sought through a request for production of documents.

this project. Be sure to review carefully the transcripts I sent you of the depositions of George Murray and Nancy Iorillo. However, I don't want you to look over the memo you sent me in February of last year. If you look that over, we may have to turn that memo over to Billings' lawyer and I prefer not to do that. Also, please don't talk to anyone about the case and your deposition between now and the time we meet unless you clear it with me first.

3. Conducting Preparation Meetings

The subsections below describe matters you are likely to address when you meet to prepare clients for deposition.

A. *Explain What a Meeting Entails*

Simple, brief explanations of what you plan to do during a preparation meeting can help ease the anxiety of a client who is unfamiliar with the deposition process. An explanation may go as follows:

Bob, as you know, next week the lawyer for Billings is going to take your deposition and will ask you about what happened when the deal with Billings went sour. What I'm going to do today is go over with you once again what happened. We filed this suit three years ago and reviewing what occurred will give both of us an opportunity to refresh our memories about exactly what took place. After we've done that, I'll explain what usually takes place during depositions and then give you a chance to practice answering questions of the type that Billings' lawyer is likely to ask you. Any questions before we get going?

Offering clients an opportunity to ask questions can surface concerns you would not have anticipated. Alleviating clients' concerns early on helps clients pay attention to your inquiries rather than dwell on private misgivings.

B. *Review a Client's Version of Events*

Typically, a preparation meeting's main event consists of reviewing, updating and probing a client's version of events. Much time probably will have passed since you and a client discussed a case in detail. Thus, absent refreshment, a client's memory may be stale or incomplete.[11] Moreover, in the interim, both you and a client are likely to have gained additional information. Some of this additional information may raise questions that you did not anticipate when you and a client last discussed a case in depth, and may even appear to create gaps and/or inconsistencies in a client's account. Therefore, conducting a thorough review of a client's version of events can provide several benefits. For example:

* You may realize that you need to gather more information and/or documents before a deposition begins.

* Refreshing both your and a client's memory helps a practice question-answer session proceed without repeated interruptions to clarify facts.

11. Recall that if you show documents to a client to refresh recollection, you may have to provide the document to your adversary. See supra note–9.

* At the deposition, you may recognize that a client's testimony is erroneous, and as a result you may give the client a chance to clarify and correct the erroneous testimony during the deposition.[12]

* You may recognize that a client has failed to disclose helpful information that you want to put in the deposition record.

Depending on such factors as the complexity of a case, the extent of a client's involvement in significant events and a client's litigation budget, reviewing a client's version of events may take less than an hour or more than a day.

C. Briefly Explain What Will Occur During the Deposition

Unless a client has previous deposition experience, you can also help to ease a client's anxiety by briefly explaining what will likely happen at the deposition. Your explanation may cover such matters as:

* Who will be present.

* That the client will be placed under oath, just as in court.

* That the deposing lawyer will probably begin by explaining the deposition procedures and asking questions about any medications or drugs the client may be taking.

12. For a discussion of how and when to correct inaccurate testimony, see Chapter 24.

* That after the deposing lawyer asks questions, you will then have a chance to ask questions to clarify any evidence that may have come out muddled and to bring out helpful information that the deposing lawyer neglected to ask about.

When potentially sensitive or embarrassing subjects are relevant to a case, and therefore are likely to be inquired into by deposing counsel, you might also advise a client to expect such inquiries. For example, in a sexual harassment case in which your client contends that she was touched inappropriately at work, you might advise the client to expect detailed questioning about such matters as exactly where she was touched and how she reacted to being touched.

D. Conduct a Practice Session[13]

Practice sessions are an essential aspect of preparing clients for depositions. During practice sessions, you ask clients to respond to questions that you believe deposing counsel is likely to ask. Thus, practice sessions give clients a realistic and concrete preview of what will happen at deposition. At the same time, such sessions give you a chance to educate clients about how to translate their knowl-

13. This Chapter's organization makes it appear that "reviewing a client's version of events" occurs separately from and prior to a practice session. In reality, the demarcation may not be so distinct. For example, while conducting a practice session you may become aware of an important topic that you have not yet reviewed with a client. If so, you may choose to temporarily halt the practice session and review the client's version of events with respect to that topic. You may then return to the practice questioning.

edge of a case into effective answers. The subsections below explore strategies for conducting useful practice sessions.

1. *Devote Practice Questioning to Selected Topics*

Time considerations are likely to necessitate limiting practice questioning to selected topics. The topics should be those that you believe deposing counsel is almost certain to cover as well as those that you consider significant. When possible, include in a practice session both topics that are likely to produce testimony harmful to your case as well as topics that are likely to produce helpful testimony.

2. *Explain the "Golden Rules" for Answering Questions*

Clients often are unsure of how they are supposed to answer questions at deposition. To help clients understand the basic lay of the deposition land and perhaps correct any misperceptions they may have, explain the following "golden rules" before beginning to ask practice questions.

* <u>"Answer Honestly"</u>

Atticus, I know you'd do this anyway, but the first thing I tell all my clients is to answer all questions at the deposition honestly.

This rule may seem self-evident and thus unnecessary to articulate. However, the advice can usefully remind clients that they should not try to outsmart the adversary's lawyer by either withholding or inventing information.

* "If You Don't Know or Don't Remember, Say So"

At some point, Sylvia, you'll probably be asked a question where you feel like you should know the answer, but you either don't know the answer or, even if you knew the answer at one time, you just can't remember the answer at the deposition. If you honestly can't remember or don't know the answer to a question, just say so. That's no problem. But if you don't know or can't remember and you take a guess at what the answer is, that's when we might have problems.

This bit of advice is consistent with the earlier reminder to "answer honestly." Here, you remind clients that answers such as "I don't know" and "I don't remember" may be truthful. Such advice may be particularly valuable when questions ask for information that clients don't know but think they "ought" to know. For example, a client who actively participated in a meeting may think that she ought to be able to remember what was discussed. Rather than look foolish by truthfully confessing to a lack of memory, the client may guess at what probably happened.

* "If You Don't Understand The Question, Say So"

Their lawyer, Ms. Hsu, may ask you some questions that you don't understand. If she does, don't answer the question. Just tell her that you don't understand her question and wait for her to ask a question you do understand. It's her job to ask clear questions and you shouldn't guess at what she's trying to get at. Make her do her job.

Daily life socializes us to guess at the meaning of ambiguous questions. As a result, clients may guess at the meaning of deposition questions rather than tell deposing counsel that they don't understand the question. For example, a client who isn't sure may guess that a question pertains to a "June 8 meeting." If the client's guess is incorrect, the client may give erroneous testimony.

* "Answer Questions Completely"

When you do understand a question, answer that question as completely as you can. Don't try to give just a partial answer, give the best answer that you can. For example, if the lawyer asks you what problems you had with the condensers, don't just mention one problem and stop; tell her all the problems with the condensers that you can recall.

Despite your admonition to answer questions honestly, some clients may be tempted to withhold information by providing only partial, and misleading, answers. Consider the following example:

Deposing Lawyer: Let's turn to the meeting that occurred on May 4th. Tell me what Mr. Jones said at that meeting about delivery dates.

Client: He said that the computers would be delivered by September 17th.

Assume that the client remembers that what Jones said at the May 4th meeting was, "We'll have the computers delivered by September 17th if we can get the hard drives from the supplier in Korea by the first of September. But if we can't, we may not be able to make delivery until the beginning of November." The client may privately congratulate himself on hiding information while giving a technically accurate answer.[14] However, partial, misleading answers such as these may damage a client's credibility with a judge or jury. For example, the client may be impeached with the deposition testimony at trial if he includes Jones' entire statement in his trial testimony. Similarly, other witnesses or documents may contradict the client's deposition testimony. Finally, deposing counsel may conclude that "cute" answers such as the one above are likely to make the client a poor trial witness and in any settlement negotiations discount much of what the client says. Consequently, this golden rule encourages clients to provide complete answers to deposition questions.[15]

14. Case law on perjury apparently accepts this distinction. The general rule is that an incomplete answer, even if intentionally misleading, does not provide a basis for a perjury prosecution if the answer is technically true. See Bronston v. United States, 409 U.S. 352, 360 (1973).

15. The potential disadvantage to this golden rule is that it may encourage clients to volunteer information beyond that called for by the question. You may be able to at least partially offset this disadvantage by advising clients not to volunteer information and to answer only the questions that deposing counsel asks. See infra Subsection 4. In any event, all but the

3. Ask Questions as Deposing Counsel

A practice session largely consists of your asking questions that you anticipate opposing counsel will ask at deposition and having clients answer as they would at deposition.[16] For example, you may use leading questions and press for details that opposing counsel is likely to pursue.[17]

Before embarking on practice questioning, advise clients that you will temporarily be assuming the role of deposing counsel when asking practice questions. For example, you may say something along these lines:

> Edith, now that you have some idea of what will take place in the deposition and how to respond to Ms. Silver's questions, I want to give to ask you. We'll assume for the moment that I'm Ms. Silver. I'll ask you questions in the way she is likely to question you, and please answer as though this were the actual deposition. As you

most hardened deposition veterans inevitably volunteer information at deposition no matter what advice you give.

16. You may want to visually record this practice session and show it to your client. When it comes to providing feedback on a client's performance, a visual recording may be worth a thousand words.

17. You might even adopt an aggressive or even hostile tone during practice questioning. Doing so has risks and benefits. A client may benefit from such realistic practice. On the other hand, some clients may become terrified of the upcoming deposition or get the sense that you no longer have faith in their case. If you do want a client to experience a hostile questioning manner and if resources permit, consider preserving rapport by having a colleague who does not know the client play the role of deposing counsel.

respond, I may make a few suggestions. We won't have time to cover everything that Ms. Silver is likely to ask about, but this practice session will give you a pretty good sense of what to expect.

4. Improve Answers With Feedback and Advice

As a practice session unfolds, you can drop out of the role of deposing counsel to provide feedback and advice that may improve clients' deposition performance. The subsections below describe advice and feedback that you may want to give. Realize, however, that under the pressure of testifying at deposition, some clients are likely to have difficulty remembering and trying to apply your advice. If you overload clients with too many suggestions about how to answer questions, clients may focus too much on trying to remember your advice and too little on questions and their answers.[18]

* Reinforce Golden Rules

Often, you can improve upon a client's answer simply by reinforcing a golden rule. Illustrating a golden rule in a concrete context tends to help clients understand how to apply the rule.

Example ("Answer Completely")

You: Let's turn to the meeting that occurred on May 4th. Tell me what Mr. Jones said at that meeting about delivery dates.

---

18. In general, the risk of overload is less with sophisticated clients who have previous deposition experience.

Client: He said that the computers would be delivered by September 17th.

You: Now, that answer is technically accurate, but as I understand what you've told me all along it may not be complete. My understanding is that at the May 4th meeting, Jones said something like the computers would be delivered by September 17th if they could get the hard drives from the supplier in Korea by the first of September. And Jones said that if they couldn't get the hard drives, delivery might not be made until the beginning of November. Is my understanding correct?

Client: Yes, but I wasn't sure that I was supposed to say all that.

You: That's okay, that's why we're doing this practice session. If you have more information that responds to a question, go ahead and mention it. Try to give a complete answer to each question. So let's try that question again . . .

* Advise Clients Not to Volunteer

In general, you do not want clients volunteering information beyond that called for by a question. The volunteered information may be harmful to your case. However, even if the information is helpful, it may be information that you would prefer that a client not disclose in the absence of a question that requires its disclosure. The dialogue below demonstrates how you might provide advice when a client volunteers information during a practice session.

You (Q): They told you that the hard drives might not be delivered by the 17th of September, didn't they?

Client: They did say that, but since at that time we had plenty of inventory on hand, we weren't that focused on the precise delivery date.

You (Comment): Mario, your answer goes beyond what you were asked. A "yes" answer would have been a complete answer to the question. You didn't need to volunteer the other information about the inventory and the precise delivery dates. When you are at the deposition, listen to questions and give complete answers but don't volunteer by going beyond what you're asked. You don't have to worry about getting out all the important information when their lawyer is questioning you. Remember, if we need to bring out any additional information, I'll have an opportunity to ask questions after their counsel is finished.

While such advice may make it less likely that a client will volunteer information at deposition, giving the advice has potential drawbacks. Clients may be confused by what may be an elusive line dividing **advice to give "complete answers" from advice not to volunteer information**. Moreover, some clients may wrongly interpret your advice not to volunteer as a tacit signal that they should intentionally withhold damaging information even if it is called for by a question.[19] Finally, a frequent

19. Particularly likely to be troublesome are suggestions that clients not volunteer information with respect to particular top-

bottom-line reality is that such instructions are often unavailing. Verbose clients are likely to follow their natural tendencies acquired over a lifetime regardless of your request not to volunteer. Consequently, if you continually press a natural rambler not to volunteer, you may end up either alienating the client or making the client excessively anxious.

* Suggest Appropriate Responses

You can sometimes improve upon clients' answers by advising them of what information to include in their answers. Assuming that your advice is based on information that a client has previously disclosed, this strategy is legally proper.

Example

You (Q): How did the lack of heat in the apartment affect your children?

A: They were really suffering during most of March.

You (Comment): John, if you're asked about how the lack of heat affected the kids, you really want to talk about the problems that you told me about

ics. For example, assume that you say something like: "Don't volunteer any information about the meeting in February unless you are specifically asked." A client may interpret this suggestion as an instruction to intentionally withhold information even when called for by a question. If a client makes an intentional withholds information about a material matter (i.e., commits perjury), you are obligated to take corrective action. See A.B.A. Comm'n on Ethics and Professional Responsibility, Formal Op. 93–376 (1993); Steven H. Goldberg, *Heaven Help the Lawyer for a Civil Liar*, 2 Geo. J. Legal Ethics 885 (1989); Charles W. Wolfram, *Client Perjury*, 50 S. Cal. L. Rev. 809 (1977).

earlier. In whatever words you want to use, you should talk about the kids missing school due to colds and infections, and the effect of the dampness on Marcia's asthma.

As in this example, when suggesting appropriate responses you might also mention that clients needn't parrot your exact words. Otherwise, you may overburden clients and inhibit them from testifying naturally and effectively.[20]

* Advise Clients Not to Hold Back

Before beginning to practice with respect to a particular topic, you might want to remind a client that the topic is important to a favorable outcome and therefore merits a full and detailed answer. For example, you might say something along these lines:

Rachel, now we're going to turn to the problems you had with the condensers. This is an important area for our case, and to help us in settlement talks we really want to get our side out at the deposition. So when I ask you these next questions that deal with the problems you had with the condensers, please try to give a much detail as you can.

As you are no doubt aware, a comment such as this is merely a variant on the golden rule to

---

20. In rare instances, you may need to tell clients precisely what words to use when answering a question. For instance, assume that a client with limited English language ability refers to mortgage payments as rent. You might want to instruct the client to refer to the payments as mortgage payments and not as rent.

"answer completely." You might use this variation when you want the details relating to helpful information to come out in response to deposing counsel's questions. The information may have more credibility if it comes out during deposing counsel's questioning than if it comes out during your follow-up questioning.

Comments such as these have at least one potential disadvantage. An instruction to "not hold back" may be difficult for many clients to reconcile with an instruction not to volunteer. Consequently, you might want to give such advice only to articulate and confident clients who have previous deposition experience, and then only on a very small number of topics.

E. Concluding Preparation Sessions

1. Explain Objections and Instructions Not to Answer

Before concluding a preparation session, explain that you may object to questions, and that if you do so a client should nonetheless answer them.[21] Based on examples of trials in popular culture, deponents who lack deposition experience tend to expect that objected-to questions need not be answered. Thus, your explanation is likely to avoid client confusion at deposition.

You might also explain that on some occasions it might be necessary for you to instruct a client not

21. "An objection ... must be noted on the record, but the examination still proceeds; the testimony is taken subject to any objection." See FRCP 30(c)(2).

to answer a question. Simply indicate that if you do so, the client should refuse to answer the question based on your advice.

2. Final Instructions

Before closing a preparation session, take a few moments to provide a few common sense final instructions. Typical concluding advice includes:

* Clients should not bring any documents to the deposition other than those you have indicated.

* If necessary, talk to clients about what to wear so that they will make a positive impression and feel appropriately dressed.

* Remind clients of exactly where and when a deposition will take place.

* Advise clients not to converse beyond normal social niceties "off the record" with opposing parties, deposing counsel, or anyone but you.

* Remind clients not to talk with friends or colleagues about: (1) the upcoming deposition, (2) the facts of the case, or (3) what took place during the preparation session. Discussions with friends and colleagues are usually not privileged and may be inquired into during the deposition.

4. Preparation Meetings With Non–Clients

This section examines strategies for preparing non-clients who are supportive of your client's position and are willing to meet with you. Such a non-client may be, for example, a lower echelon employ-

ee of a corporate client, or a bystander who observed an auto accident.

At the outset, realize that non-clients may be
uncertain as to the legitimacy of meeting with you
prior to deposition. They may also be uncertain
about what to say if deposing counsel asks about
what took place during the meeting. To reassure
non-clients, you may begin a meeting by saying
something along these lines:

> Mr. Williams, I appreciate your willingness to
> meet with me today. As you know, I'm the attor-
> ney for Susan French. First off, you should know
> that there's absolutely nothing wrong with us
> meeting in advance of your deposition. It's com-
> mon and I simply want to answer any questions
> you may have about what will happen, and go
> over what happened so that you can give accurate
> testimony. There's nothing confidential about
> anything that I or you say, and if Ms. Asimow,
> the attorney who will be asking you questions,
> asks about whether we met and what was said
> between us, you can tell her exactly what we
> talked about. Do you have any questions about
> this?[22]

Risks attend holding preparation meetings with
non-clients. Since the meeting is not protected by
the attorney-client privilege, anything that happens
may be inquired into by the deposing attorney.
Moreover, a deposing attorney may try to exploit

22. Even experienced witnesses may need to be reminded of
this absence of confidentiality.

the fact that you met to try to suggest that the non-client is biased.

Nonetheless, pre-deposition preparation meetings are often of benefit. Just as with clients, you may:

* Briefly explain what will take place at deposition, including that the fact that objected-to questions are normally to be answered. Such information is likely to ease the anxieties of non-clients who lack deposition experience.

* Review a non-client's version of events. So doing may refresh a non-client's recollection of helpful information. You may choose to elicit the information should deposing counsel's questions fail to do so.

* Explain the golden rules for answering questions. The information tends to help non-clients testify efficiently and accurately.

How much more you do at a preparation session is a matter of personal judgment. For example, do you want to conduct a practice session? Doing so may enable a non-client to testify more fully and accurately. On the other hand, practice sessions with non-clients are fraught with risk. Among the risks are the following:

* A non-client asked about what took place during a practice session may misinterpret your feedback and respond to deposition questions in a way that suggests that you tried to influence the non-client's deposition testimony during the practice session.

* You may inadvertently disclose strategies which a non-client later reveals to deposing counsel. For example, if deposing counsel asks a non-client to disclose the topics you reviewed during a practice session, the non-client's answers may reveal your litigation strategies.

* A non-client may interpret what you say in a practice session as an effort to influence their testimony, perhaps leading a non-client to back-pedal on favorable testimony.

For all these reasons, your may not want to conduct practice sessions with non-clients. And should you choose to conduct a practice session, you may decide not to offer suggestions as to how a non-client should answer questions.

CHAPTER 24

DEFENDING DEPOSITIONS

To defend a deposition is to attend a deposition that your adversary notices and takes. Typical defending strategies include: making objections; instructing client deponents not to answer; consulting with deponents during deposition breaks; and questioning deponents after the adversary's questioning concludes. This Chapter explores these defending strategies in three common deposition situations in which you might find yourself:[1]

* The deponent is "your witness"—that is, your client, a person associated with your client, or your expert.

* The deponent is a "neutral" witness—a witness who is not associated with a party.

* The deponent is friendly to your adversary—either the adverse party or a person associated with the adverse party. An adversary who takes such a deposition probably seeks to preserve the deponent's testimony for eventual use in a motion or at trial because the deponent is likely to become unavailable. Hence, this type of deposition

1. For a discussion of special concerns when defending visually recording depositions, see Chapter 22.

is often called a "trial deposition" or a "deposition to preserve testimony."[2]

The Chapter concludes with a discussion of when you might terminate a deposition because it has exceeded the FRCP's one day/seven hour presumptive time limit.[3]

1. Defending Depositions of Your Witnesses

A. *Objections*

The sections below explain rules and strategies relating to deposition objections, perhaps the most frequently misunderstood aspects of defending depositions.

1. *Purpose of Objections*

FRCP 30(c) provides that when an objection is made at deposition, "the examination shall proceed, with the testimony being taken subject to the objections."[4] Consequently, deposition objections do not

---

2. For a discussion of how to take a deposition to preserve the testimony of your own witness, see Chapter 21.

3. FRCP 30(d)(1).

4. The courts have interpreted FRCP 30(c)(2) to mean what it says: questions must be answered notwithstanding an objection. See Redwood v. Dobson, 476 F.3d 462, 467–68 (7th Cir. 2007) (even though deposing attorney was asking inappropriate and not relevant questions instruction not to answer inappropriate where there was no claim of privilege); Pilates, Inc. v. Georgetown Bodyworks Deep Muscle Massage Ctrs., Inc., 201 F.R.D. 261 (D.D.C. 2000) (objections by counsel were not based on privilege, so witness was ordered re-deposed and directed to answer questions where privilege was not asserted); Amari Co. v. Burgess, 2009 WL 1269704 (N.D. Ill. 2009): Eggleston v. Chicago Journeymen Plumbers' Local No. 130, 657 F.2d 890 (7th Cir.

prevent deponents from having to answer questions.[5]

Rather, the purpose of deposition objections is to "preserve" objections to a later time when your adversary may want to use a deposition transcript at trial or in support of a motion. In other words, if you raise a valid objection at deposition which your adversary does not "cure," a judge should later rule that the objected-to testimony is inadmissible. On the other hand, if you neglect to object at deposition, and the objection was one which is waived if not made, the objectionable testimony will be admissible.

Example 1—A Valid Objection

1.   Q: Can you tell me when your meeting with my client took place and when the Vice President, Ms. Lester, told you she had decided to fire my client?

2.   You: Objection. Compound.

3.   A: It was some time before his last performance report.

1981); Ralston Purina Co. v. McFarland, 550 F.2d 967 (4th Cir. 1977); United States v. International Bus. Machines, Corp., 66 F.R.D. 180, 186 (S.D.N.Y. 1974) (relevance objections should be noted and the question answered). However, if deposing counsel harasses the deponent by repeatedly insisting on answers to highly argumentative questions, repetitive questions, or questions clearly beyond the scope of discovery, especially when they seek personal information, you may terminate the deposition and move for a protective order and sanctions against deposing counsel. See FRCP 30(d)(3).

5. For a discussion of when you can instruct a deponent not to answer, see Section B below.

Your deposition objection is timely and proper. Therefore, your adversary should not be able to read in this portion of the transcript at trial or use the transcript in connection with a pre-trial motion to establish that the decision to discharge the plaintiff occurred before the last performance report. However, assume that the deposition had gone as follows:

Example 2—An Objection is Waived

1.   Q: Can you tell me when your meeting with my client took place and when the Vice President, Ms. Lester, told you she had decided to fire my client?

2.   A: It was some time before his last performance report.

Your adversary again seeks to read in this portion of the transcript at trial or in connection with a motion to establish that the decision to discharge the plaintiff occurred before the last performance report. At that point, you object that the answer is inadmissible because it came in response to a compound question. Your belated objection would probably be to no avail, and your adversary could use the deposition testimony.

By putting the onus on you to raise certain objections at deposition, the law prevents you from "sandbagging" deposing counsel. As a result, in many situations you may not sit silently as objectionable questions go by, and then spring an objection at trial or in connection with a motion, when an adversary may no longer have an opportunity to correct a deficiency.[6] Instead, you must often give an adversary a chance to "fix" an evidentiary failing by objecting at deposition. Return to the same deposition:

Example 3—An Objection is Cured

1. Q: Can you tell me when your meeting with my client took place and when the Vice President, Ms. Lester, told you she had decided to fire my client?

2. You: Objection. Compound.

3. A: It was some time before his last performance report.

4. Q: Did Ms. Lester tell you anything about when had she decided to fire my client?

5. A: Yes.

6. What did Ms. Lester say about when she had decided to fire my client?

---

6. See Cabello v. Fernandez–Larios, 402 F.3d 1148, 1160 (11th Cir. 2005) Objection based on failure to have an official administer an oath at the deposition in Chile. The deponents offered to get a Chilean official, who was authorized to administer the oath under Chilean law, but the defendant's counsel declined the offer. The court said the deposition testimony was correctly admitted at trial because defendant's counsel waived objection. Id.; See also Kansas Wastewater, Inc. v. Alliant Techsystems, Inc., 217 F.R.D. 525 (D. Kan. 2003) (no objection at deposition that question was asked and answered, so objection was waived); Roy v. Austin Co., 194 F.3d 840, 844 (7th Cir. 1999) (objection to leading questions waived if not made at the deposition); State Farm Mut. Auto. Ins. Co. v. Dowdy ex rel. Dowdy, 445 F. Supp. 2d 1289, 1293 (N.D. Okla. 2006); Bahamas Agric. Indus. Ltd. v. Riley Stoker Corp., 526 F.2d 1174, 1180 (6th Cir. 1975).

7.   She told me she had decided to fire him some time before his last performance report.

Here, in response to your objection, your adversary corrected a problem involving the form of a question (No. 4).

2.   "Curable" and "Non–Curable" Objections

As mentioned above, you waive an objection by failing to make it at deposition **only if the objection is "curable."**[7] As a general rule, judges consider an objection to be "curable" if through further questions deposing counsel could have obviated the evidentiary problem raised by an objection. On the other hand, objections which <u>cannot</u> be obviated even if raised at deposition are preserved, and can be raised for the first time after the deposition.[8]

Whether an objection is curable is an issue that can't be fully addressed in the abstract. The reason is that curability depends not only on the ground for objection, but also on the unique legal and factual issues of individual cases. However, for your general guidance, Section "a" below identifies common "use them or lose them" objections to questions that you'll probably waive if you don't make at deposition. As you'll see, most "curable" objections involve the form of questions rather than their content. Section "b" identifies a second set of

7. Most of your objections will be directed to deposing counsel's questions. If you have objections to the behavior of the court reporter or anyone else present at the deposition, you also waive those potentially curable objections if you do not raise them at the deposition. See FRCP 32(d)(3)(B).

8. FRCP 32(d)(3)(B).

common objections to questions that typically cannot be cured and so are likely to be preserved even though you don't make them at deposition.

a.   Objections That Commonly Are Curable

The following objections are ones which you typically must make at deposition or waive the ability to assert later. The "possible cures" which the examples include demonstrate that your objection does afford an adversary a realistic opportunity to fix the evidentiary failings.[9]

—Compound

A question is compound because it is essentially two questions phrased as one.

* Example: "Who was at the party and which of them had you met previously?"

* Possible Cure: Divide the question into two or more smaller questions, e.g. "Who was at the party?" and "Which of them had you met previously?"

—Vague

A question is vague when it does not make clear what information is being sought.

---

9.   This section does not discuss objections based on privilege. If you contend that a question seeks information that is privileged, you should both raise the privilege objection and also instruct the deponent not to answer the question.

* Example: "Before that meeting, what was going on between you and Mr. Pell?" The question is unfocused and uncertain as to time.

* Possible Cure: "During the month before that meeting, did you and Mr. Pell have any arguments at work?."

—Assumes Facts Not in Evidence

A question assumes facts not in evidence when it incorporates information to which a deponent has not testified.

* Example: A deponent who has not testified to talking to a Mr. Pell prior to a meeting is asked: "When you and Mr. Pell met before the termination meeting, what did you talk about?"

* Possible Cure: Ask a question which establishes the assumed fact: "Did you and Mr. Pell meet before the termination meeting?"

—Leading

A leading question is one which either by its wording or through the questioner's tone of voice suggests the answer the deponent should give. If deposing counsel is deposing your client, a witness "identified with your client" or a "hostile witness," you should not object on this ground since leading questions are permitted with such witnesses.[10] If the deponent is a neutral witness, leading questions are usually improper.

* Example: "Isn't it true that you met with Mr. Pell before the meeting?"

* Possible Cure: "Had you met Mr. Pell before you went to the meeting?"

—Misquotes or Mischaracterizes Testimony

A question that misstates what a deponent said earlier in the deposition falls into this category.

* Example: Your adversary asks a deponent who had testified that your client, Ms. Anderson, "shouted" dur-

---

10. FRE 611(c). For a discussion of the meaning of "identified with your client," see Wright & Gold, Federal Practice and Procedure: Evidence § 6168; see also Haney v. Mizell Memorial Hosp., 744 F.2d 1467 (11th Cir. 1984); Ellis v. City of Chicago, 667 F.2d 606 (7th Cir. 1981); Stahl v. Sun Microsystems, Inc., 775 F.Supp. 1397 (D. Colo. 1991). For a discussion of the meaning of "hostile" witness, see Wright & Gold, Federal Practice and Procedure: Evidence § 6168; United States v. Cisneros–Gutierrez, 517 F.3d 751, 762 (5th Cir. 2008); United States v. Mora–Higuera, 269 F.3d 905 (8th Cir. 2001); Gell v. Aulander, 252 F.R.D. 297 (E.D.N.C. 2008); SEC v. World Info. Tech., Inc., 250 F.R.D. 149 (S.D.N.Y. 2008); National R.R. Passenger Corp. v. Certain Temp. Easements Above R.R. Right of Way, 357 F.3d 36 (1st Cir. 2004); Thomas v. Cardwell, 626 F.2d 1375 (9th Cir. 1980); United States v. Brown, 603 F.2d 1022 (1st Cir. 1979). When you are unsure if the deponent is "identified with your client" or "hostile" toward deposing counsel or his client, you may decide to make leading objections to avoid a waiver.

ing a performance review: "When Ms. Anderson raised her voice during the performance review, do you think anyone outside your office could have heard what Ms. Anderson said to you at that time?"

* Possible Cure 1: Restate the question and correct the mischaracterization: "When Ms. Anderson allegedly shouted during the performance review...."

* Possible Cure 2: Delete the reference to the prior testimony: "During the performance review, do you think anyone outside your office could have heard what Ms. Anderson said to you at that time?"

—Calls for a Narrative

A question "calls for a narrative" when it is overly broad in scope and so may permit a deponent to testify to inadmissible evidence before you can object to it.

* Example: "Please tell me everything that led up to the decision to purchase the new computer system."

* Possible Cure: Narrower, more focused questions, such as, "Did you attend any meetings in which the purchase of the new computer system was discussed?" If the answer is yes, then the questioner might continue by saying, "Please tell me what happened at the first meeting in which purchasing a new computer system was discussed."

—Argumentative

An argumentative question asserts a questioner's argument or comment on testimony in the form of a question.

* Examples: "Doesn't the fact that you can't remember who was present show that you never were at that meeting?" "Since Mrs. Green's report was written right after the meeting, why shouldn't we believe Mrs. Green's report rather than your testimony?"

* Possible Cure: Delete the comment or argument and ask only for information that might support the argument. "Do you believe Mrs. Green's report is inaccurate?" "Why do you think it is inaccurate?"

—Lack of Personal Knowledge (Lack of Foundation)

These objections are appropriate when the record does not indicate that a deponent had first hand knowledge.

* Example: The adversary asks, "What did Ms. Julian do after she left

the meeting?" However, the record doesn't indicate that the deponent was in a position to know what Ms. Julian did after she left the meeting.

* Possible Cure: Establish the deponent's personal knowledge: "Did you see Ms. Julian after she left the meeting?"

—Calls for Speculation

This objection is similar to the objection for lack of personal knowledge. The objection is appropriate when the question asks a deponent to testify about a matter which the deponent would appear to have no basis for knowing.

* Example: Your adversary asks, "Why was Ms. Julian worried about the decision to purchase computers?" The question calls for speculation because a deponent cannot perceive another's thoughts.

* Possible Cure: Establish the deponent's personal knowledge: "Did Ms. Julian tell you what she thought about the decision to purchase computers?"

—Inadmissible Opinion

This objection usually asserts that an opinion is (a) not rationally based on the deponent's perceptions or (b) not helpful to a clear understanding of the deponent's testimony.[11]

* Example: A deponent who testified that "I caught a quick glimpse of the driver" is asked, "Did the driver appear to be driving carefully?" (In this example, a "quick glimpse" suggests that the opinion may not be rationally based on the deponent's perceptions.)

* Possible Cure: Establish that the deponent has an adequate basis for the opinion: "How long did you watch the driver?" "Over what distance?"

This objection can also raise the issue of whether a question calls for an expert opinion from a witness who has not been qualified as an expert. Your adversary can cure this problem by qualifying the deponent as an expert.

—Hearsay

Whether a hearsay objection is curable typically depends on whether your adversary can elicit foundational evidence satisfying a hearsay exception or exemption.[12]

* Example: Your adversary asks a deponent who saw an automobile accident, "What did the passenger in the

11. See FRE 701.
12. See FRE 801, 803, 804.

defendant's car say when you first went over to the car?"

* Possible Cure: Elicit foundational evidence establishing that the passenger's statement falls within the "excited utterance" exception to the hearsay rule: "How long after the collision did you speak to the passenger?" "What was the passenger's demeanor at the time you spoke to the passenger?"

—Lack of Foundation For, or Failure to Authenticate, a Document

Deposing Counsel can often cure "lack of foundation" or "failure to authenticate" objections to documents by laying the proper foundation for the document.[13]

—Violates the Best Evidence Rule

The "best evidence rule" provides that, subject to exceptions, (1) the original of a document must be used to prove its contents; and (2) the contents of a document can not be established through oral testimony.[14] Thus, this objection may assert that your adversary has used a copy instead of the original of a document, or has attempt-

13. For a discussion of the proper foundation for documents, see Chapter 10.

14. See FRE 1002–1007.

ed to prove the contents of a document through oral testimony.[15]

* Example: "What did the report say about the reason for the decline in sales?"

* Possible Cure: Authenticate the report, ask the deponent to read from it and ask the court reporter to attach a copy to the deposition transcript.

b. Common "Incurable" Objections That You Can Raise Later Even if You Don't Make Them at Deposition

The following objections generally cannot be cured by deposing counsel at deposition. Consequently, you can raise them later even if you don't make them at deposition.

—Asked and Answered

This objection asserts that your adversary has asked the same question previously in the deposition, and that the deponent has answered it. This objection is typically inappropriate at deposition.[16] However, since making an ob-

15. See FRE 1002–1007.

16. See, e.g., Plaisted v. Geisinger Med. Ctr., 210 F.R.D. 527, 534 (M.D. Pa. 2002); Caplan v. Fellheimer, Eichen, Braverman, & Kaskey, 161 F.R.D. 29, 32 (E.D. Pa. 1995) ("During the course of a routine deposition, a lawyer is free to revisit areas already examined, so long as that does not become oppressive or harassing."). See also Applied Telematics, Inc. v. Sprint Corp., No. 94–CV–4603, 1995 WL 79237, at *2 (E.D. Pa. Feb. 22, 1995); First Tennessee Bank v. Fed. Deposit Ins. Corp., 108 F.R.D. 640, 641

jection would not allow your adversary
to cure the problem by "unasking" the
earlier question, the objection is incurable and you should be able to make it
later even if you don't make it at deposition.

—Inadmissible Legal Conclusion

If a question asks for an improper legal conclusion, your adversary can't
cure the problem through further
questioning. Hence, the objection is
preserved even if you don't make it.

—Irrelevant

Typically, your adversary can do nothing to cure this objection; evidence is
either relevant or it is not, depending
on the contentions at the time your
adversary seeks to use the evidence.
Hence, you usually need not make relevance objections at deposition.[17]

(D.C. Tenn. 1985); but cf. Kansas Wastewater, Inc. v. Alliant
Techsystems, Inc., 217 F.R.D. 525 (D. Kan. 2003) (No objection
at deposition that question was asked and answered, so it was
waived.); State Farm Mut. Auto. Ins. Co. v. Dowdy ex rel. Dowdy,
445 F. Supp. 2d 1289, 1293 (N.D. Okla. 2006). You are not, of
course, entitled to ask the same question an unlimited number of
times. At some point, repeating the exact same question and
insisting on an answer may constitute harassment and justify
deposing counsel's termination of the deposition to seek a protective order.

17. See FRCP 30, advisory committee's notes, reprinted in
146 F.R.D. 664–65 (1993), stating that objections that do not
relate to the form of the question or the responsiveness of the

—Not Reasonably Calculated to Lead to Admissible Evidence

This objection asserts that evidence is irrelevant even by broad discovery standards. If your adversary later seeks to use evidence which is irrelevant by discovery standards, you would simply object that the evidence is irrelevant regardless of whether you objected at deposition.[18]

3. *Objections to Deponent's Improper Answers*

A deponent's answer to a proper question may either refer to inadmissible evidence or be non-

answer are generally preserved for trial and therefore "should be kept to a minimum during a deposition." But see Kirschner v. Broadhead, 671 F.2d 1034, 1038 (7th Cir. 1982) (indicating that any objection that might be cured, including a relevance objection, must be raised at the deposition or it is waived); Bahamas Agric. Indus. Ltd. v. Riley Stoker Corp., 526 F.2d.1174, 1180 (6th Cir. 1975) (indicating that any objection that might be cured must be raised at the deposition or it is waived).

18. As amended in December 2000, FRCP 26(b)(1) provides that relevant information is discoverable if it is reasonably calculated to lead to the discovery of admissible evidence. However, this same provision limits discovery, absent a court order, to information that is relevant to the claim or defense of any party; while information that is only relevant to the subject matter of the action is discoverable only if a court so orders. It is not clear how these recent amendments will effect the scope of permissible questioning at deposition. It would appear, however, that at a minimum, information that is reasonably calculated to lead to the discovery of admissible evidence with respect to a claim or defense of a party should be discoverable at deposition. For a further discussion of the effect of the 2000 amendment to FRCP 26(b)(1), see Wright, Miller & Marcus: Federal Practice and Procedure: Civil 2d. § 2008.

responsive. Yet, no different from improper questions, the problem in the answer may be curable. If so, in order to preserve your right to later object to use of the answer, you should move to strike the answer and identify the ground of your motion.[19]

Example 1

1. Deposing Counsel: After Mr. Bradley came out of the meeting what happened next?

2. A: Mr. Bradley went into Ms. Gardener's office and told her what happened at the meeting.

3: You: I move to strike the answer on the grounds that the witness lacks personal knowledge.

The deponent's answer indicates that what Bradley said to Gardener took place in Gardener's office. Therefore, the deponent may not have personal knowledge of what Bradley said to Gardener. This defect might be cured, perhaps by further questioning showing that the deponent was in Gardener's office and heard the conversation. As the defect may be curable, failure to move to strike may result in a waiver of your right to object later.

Example 2

1. Deposing Counsel: At the time you first talked with Ms. Stoffer about a loan, did she tell you how much the monthly payments would be?

2. A: I was so concerned about refinancing my house I'm not sure I paid close attention to what the monthly payments were.

19. See FRCP 32(d)(3)(B).

3. You: Move to strike the answer as non-responsive.

Here, as deposing counsel may be able to cure the problem by eliciting the non-responsive testimony ("concern for refinancing my house") in response to another question, failure to move to strike at deposition would probably result in a waiver of the right to do so later in the case.

4. Objecting to Improve a Deponent's Answers

A second reason to object at deposition is to improve a deponent's answers. When you prepare a client or other friendly witness for deposition, you are likely to emphasize that the deponent should listen closely to questions and make sure they know what they are being asked before answering.[20] Yet, as depositions tend to be stressful and mentally tiring, inexperienced deponents in particular tend to lose focus and guess at questions' meanings. If you detect this happening, you may use <u>legitimate and properly phrased</u> objections to remind deponents to make sure they understand the questions.

<u>Example 1</u>

Deposing Counsel: At that time, were you solely responsible for the development of the new product line?

You: Objection. The question is vague.

A: Do you mean was that my only responsibility or are you asking if I was the only one responsible?

---

20. For a discussion of preparing clients for deposition, see Chapter 23.

Example 2

Deposing Counsel: In light of your concerns about the financing, why did Johnson decide to move forward with the purchase?

You: Objection. Lack of foundation, lack of personal knowledge, calls for speculation.

A: I don't know why Johnson decided to move forward. You'd have to ask him.

In each of these examples, your objections may remind deponents to listen closely to and ask for clarification of the questions. In this way, objections such as these tend to promote the accuracy of testimony.

5. *Forgoing Objections*

You needn't object at every valid opportunity. For example, it makes sense to forgo objecting when an answer is obviously helpful to you, or if a topic is trivial. More subtly, you may forgo a legitimate objection to prevent deposing counsel from inquiring into an area that hurts your case. Consider the following example.

Example **(Forgoing Objection):**

Deposing Counsel: Did your supervisor agree with your decision to remove my client from the University's account?

A: Yes, he did.

Deposing Counsel: After my client was removed from the University's account, who was assigned to that account?

A: Well.....

Example (Making Objection)

Deposing Counsel: Did your supervisor agree with your decision to remove my client from the University's account?

You: Objection. Lack of foundation, calls for speculation.

Deposing Counsel: Well, let me lay a foundation. Did you have a conversation with your supervisor about whether or not my client should be removed from the University's account?

A: Yes.

Deposing Counsel: And would you tell me everything that your supervisor said in that conversation?

A: He said that he was glad we had an excuse to remove your client from the account because he wanted to put a younger person in charge. He said he thought a younger person would be able to relate better to the new administrator at the University. He also said that ...

Although the lack of foundation objection in the second example is certainly valid, raising it led to deposing counsel's inquiring about damaging testimony that may not have come out had you not objected.

Obviously, prior to the deposition you need to determine what your deponent's testimony will probably be so you can intelligently exercise your judgment about whether raising an objection will encourage deposing counsel to uncover information that damages your case. When you do not know what a deponent's testimony will likely be, predicting whether an objection will backfire is particularly difficult.

6.　*Phrasing Objections Properly*

If objections are to give fair notice to deposing counsel as to curable evidentiary problems, it follows that to object properly you should identify your ground or grounds for objection. FRCP 30(d)(1) also requires that objections at deposition be stated "concisely and in a non-argumentative and non-suggestive manner." Thus, your objections need and should refer only to their legal basis or bases. For example:

* "Objection. Hearsay."

* "Objection. Lack of foundation, lack of personal knowledge, inadmissible opinion and calls for speculation."[21]

* "Objection. The question is compound."

* "Objection. The question assumes facts not in evidence."

Avoid "speaking" objections, i.e., objections that include both a legal ground for objection and argument. Such speaking objections violate FRCP 30(d)(1) because they disrupt a deposition and/or "coach" a deponent by suggesting how the deponent should respond to a question. The following examples illustrate improper speaking objections.

---

21. When you in good faith believe that you have multiple grounds for objecting to a question, state each such ground.

Example 1

A: Bob said that he thought the sample was inadequate and that we should insist on a larger one. Mr. Fazio disagreed.

Deposing Counsel: After Mr. Fazio voiced his approval of the sample, what is the next thing that occurred with respect to the sample?

You: Objection. Misstates the testimony. The witness didn't say anything about Fazio having approved of the sample. Maybe all Mr. Fazio said was that he didn't think the sample was adequate. Maybe Mr. Fazio was commenting on the issue of insisting on a larger sample. If you want to know what happened, ask a question but don't put words in the witness' mouth.

Example 2

1. Deposing Counsel: Did anyone else at the meeting have an opinion about Karen's performance?

2. A: Yes, Monty did.

3. Deposing Counsel: What were Monty's thoughts?

4. You: Objection. Speculation. Also, lack of personal knowledge. How can this witness possibly know what were the thoughts of someone else? If you want to ask her what she thought, you can certainly do that. But don't ask her a question that calls on her to speculate about someone else's state of mind.

These "speaking" objections violate FRCP 30(d)(1) because they go beyond providing notice of the grounds of your objection and interrupt the flow of deposing counsel's examination or suggest how the deponent should respond to the question. If you repeatedly make such improper "speaking" objections, deposing counsel would have the right to terminate a deposition and seek a protective order and sanctions against you.[22]

B. *Instructions Not to Answer*

You can properly instruct a deponent not to answer a question only when one or more of the following is true:[23]

* Deposing counsel's question calls for information protected by a recognized privilege,[24]

22. Speaking objections have consistently been interpreted as violating the FRCP and justifying the issuance of a protective order and sanctions pursuant to FRCP 26(c) and 30(d)(2) and (3) See also Morales v. Zondo, Inc., 204 F.R.D. 50, 54 (S.D.N.Y. 2001); Craig v. St. Anthony's Med. Ctr., 2009 WL 690210 (E.D. Mo. 2009); Amari Co. v. Burgess, 2009 WL 1269704 (N.D. Ill. 2009); Armstrong v. Hussmann Corp., 163 F.R.D. 299, 303 (E.D. Mo. 1995); Hall v. Clifton Precision, 150 F.R.D. 525, 530 (E.D. Pa. 1993); Van Pilsum v. Iowa State Univ. of Sci. & Tech., 152 F.R.D. 179 (S.D. Iowa 1993) (The Van Pilsum court also granted a protective order to prevent similar behavior at future depositions, appointed a master to preside over future depositions, and imposed part of the cost of the master on the attorney who engaged in the disruptive behavior necessitating the master's appointment.); American Directory Serv. Agency, Inc. v. Beam, 131 F.R.D. 15, 18 (D.D.C. 1990).

23. See FRCP 30(c)(2) and 30(d)(3).

24. FRCP 30(d) uses only the term privilege, but courts agree that work product falls within the definition of privilege as used

* Deposing counsel's question violates a prior court ordered limitation on discovery, or

* You are suspending the deposition to seek a protective order because deposing counsel is conducting the deposition in bad faith or in such manner as unreasonably to annoy, embarrass, or oppress the deponent or a party.[25]

1. Instructions Not to Answer to Preserve a Privilege

When you instruct a deponent not to answer based on a claim of privilege,[26] you must articulate

in 30(d). See Banks v. Senate Sergeant-at-Arms, 241 F.R.D. 376 (D.D.C. 2007); SEC v. Nacchio, 614 F. Supp. 2d 1164, 1176–77 (D. Colo. 2009); SEC v. Buntrock, 217 F.R.D. 441, 444–45 (N.D. Ill. 2003) (questions seeking how a party intends to marshal facts and evidence, and inferences need not be answered); Tuerkes–Beckers, Inc. v. New Castle Assocs., 158 F.R.D. 573, 575 (D. Del. 1993) ("Counsel may not instruct a witness not to answer a question, unless (1) answering the question would require the disclosure of information that is protected from disclosure as privileged or work product. . . ."); see also Roper v. Exxon Corp., No. CIV. A. 97–1971, 1998 WL 341838, *2 (E.D. La. June 25, 1998) ("If at any time during the examination of the witnesses it appears that a question calls for the disclosure of privileged communications or attorney work product, defendant is free to employ the procedure authorized by Fed. R. Civ. P. 30(d)(1) and (3) to protect such privileged information."). For a general discussion of what privileges are recognized by Federal courts, see Wright & Graham, Federal Practice and Procedure: Evidence § 5423. You may be able to assert a work product privilege when the deponent is asked to marshal all the facts, including the facts uncovered by counsel while investigating the case, that support one of your client's legal or factual contentions. See Equal Opportunity Comm'n v. American Intl. Group, No. 93 Civ. 6390 (PKL) (RLE), 1994 WL 376052 (S.D.N.Y. July 18, 1994); S.E.C. v. Morelli, 143 F.R.D. 42, 47 (S.D.N.Y. 1992).

25. For a discussion of the making of such motions, see Wright, Miller, & Marcus, Federal Practice and Procedure: Civil 2d § 2116.

the facts on which the privilege claim is based with sufficient detail to "enable other parties to assess the applicability of the privilege."[27] For instance, if you base an instruction not to answer on the attorney-client privilege, you must not only state the grounds for the instruction but also the basis for it.

For example, assume that you represent a corporate plaintiff seeking to enforce a three-year non-competition clause in an employment contract signed by the defendant, Gary Blasi. The CEO of the corporation is being deposed by Blasi's lawyer and the questioning proceeds as follows:

1.　Deposing Counsel: After the company terminated Mr. Blasi, did you direct the company to change the term in the non-competition clause of its standard employment contract from three years to two years?

2.　A: Yes.

3.　Deposing Counsel: Did an attorney for the company suggest that this change be made?

If you want to instruct the CEO not to answer this question on the ground of attorney-client privilege, you must do more than merely state, "I in-

26.　Of course, you are not required to instruct a deponent not to answer a question that calls for privileged information. The client is typically the holder of the privilege and as such may decide to waive it. But you will want to discuss the pros and cons of waiving the privilege with your client before allowing him to disclose privileged information.

27.　See FRCP 26(b)(5).

struct you not to answer on the ground of attorney-client privilege.'' You must also indicate why the privilege applies. Hence, you might say something like the following:

4: You: I instruct you not to answer that question on the ground of attorney-client privilege. The question is improper because it seeks to elicit information about what counsel for the company may have told this deponent about the non-competition clause.

2. *Instructions Not to Answer Based on a Prior Court Order*

You may properly instruct a deponent not to answer when the question violates a prior court order limiting the scope of discovery. For example, if a court has ordered that certain business practices should not be inquired into in order to preserve trade secrets, you may simply instruct your client not to answer any questions relating to those practices on the ground that the inquiry is forbidden by court order.

3. *Instructions Not to Answer to Suspend a Deposition to Seek a Protective Order*

When deposing counsel conducts the deposition in bad faith or in such a manner as to unreasonably annoy, embarrass, or oppress the deponent or a party, you may instruct a deponent not to answer.[28] When you instruct the deponent not to answer on this ground, you are required to also suspend the deposition and move the court for a protective or-

28. FRCP 30(c)(2) and 30(d)(3).

der.[29] Your motion for a protective order may seek
sanctions from your adversary and request the
court to terminate the deposition or "limit the
scope and manner of the taking of the deposition."[30]

4. *Risks of Improper Instructions Not to An-swer*

If you've taken at least a few depositions, you are
probably well aware that defending attorneys are
prone to instruct deponents not to answer even
when proper grounds for such an instruction are
non-existent. For example, instructions not to answer such as the following are common but improper:

* "Objection. The question calls for hearsay and I
  instruct the witness not to answer."

29. FRCP 30(d)(3). See also Biovail Labs., Inc. v. Anchen
Pharms., Inc., 233 F.R.D. 648 (C.D. Cal. 2006); Redwood v.
Dobson, 476 F.3d 462, 470 (7th Cir. 2007) (Court finds that even
though the deposing attorney was asking inappropriate and not
relevant questions, the witness's counsel should have ended the
deposition and asked for a protective order. For failing to seek
protective order, counsel was censured.) Hearst/ABC–Viacom
Entm't Servs. v. Goodway Mktg., Inc., 145 F.R.D. 59 (E.D. Pa.
1992); Smith v. Logansport Cmty. Sch. Corp., 139 F.R.D. 637
(N.D. Ind. 1991); Hanlin v. Mitchelson, 623 F.Supp. 452
(S.D.N.Y. 1985); Stewart v. Colonial W. Agency, Inc., 87 Cal.
App.4th 1006, 105 Cal.Rptr.2d 115 (2001). The burden is on the
terminating party to establish that the deposition was conducted
in bad faith or in an oppressive manner. See Caplan v. Fellheimer, Eichen, Braverman, & Kaskey, 161 F.R.D. 29 (E.D. Pa. 1995);
Smith, 139 F.R.D. at 640. For a discussion of the process for
obtaining a protective order, see Wright, Miller, & Marcus,
Federal Practice and Procedure: Civil 2d § 2035.

30. See FRCP 30 and FRCP 26(c).

* "Objection. The question calls for information not calculated to lead to the discovery of admissible evidence and I instruct the witness not to answer."

* "Objection. This line of questions is oppressive and constitutes bad faith. I instruct the witness not to answer."

The first two instructions are improper because the questions neither ask for privileged information nor violate a court order. The third is improper because the objector did not follow the instruction by terminating the deposition to move for a protective order.

What risks do you run by improperly instructing deponents not to answer? Is a judge likely to sanction you or your client? A realistic answer depends on numerous factors, including customs in your local practice area. No matter where you practice, however, the risk of sanctions probably depends in part on the nature of the impropriety.

The risk of sanctions should be lower if you instruct a deponent not to answer burdensome and oppressive questions without terminating a deposition.[31] First, deposing counsel would be unlikely to seek a court order that such questions be answered. Second, a judge may decide not to sanction you for

31. See, e.g., Landers v. Kevin Gros Offshore, L.L.C., 2009 WL 2046587 (E.D. La. 2009); Eckert v. Hurley Chicago Co., 638 F.Supp. 699 (N.D. Ill. 1986); Lapenna v. Upjohn Co., 110 F.R.D. 15 (E.D. Pa. 1986); but cf. Stewart, 87 Cal.App.4th at 1013, 105 Cal.Rptr.2d at 119; Redwood v. Dobson, 476 F.3d 462 (7th Cir. 2007).

ordering your client not to answer burdensome or oppressive questions.

On the other hand, the risk of sanctions goes up if you instruct deponents not to answer questions on the ground that they call for hearsay, are compound, lack foundation, seek irrelevant information or on similar evidentiary grounds. The rule that deposing attorneys are entitled to answers to questions that might be improper at trial is well established, and deposing counsel is likely to seek and obtain an order that the questions be answered and that you be sanctioned for improperly instructing deponents not to answer such questions.

Sanctions are not the only penalty you and your client may incur if your adversary obtains an order for questions to be answered. The delay occasioned by going to court gives the deposing attorney an additional chance to prepare questions, in essence getting two bites at a deposition rather than one. As a result, the deposing attorney may elicit damaging testimony that might have been overlooked had the deposition been completed in a single session.

5. An "Early Warning System" Alternative Strategy

Instructions not to answer are a common source of friction between attorneys. Though the grounds for such instructions are actually quite limited, defending attorneys commonly issue them anyway out of what they perceive of as a right or even a duty to protect clients against improper questions. Moreover, the rules create burdensome choices for both counsel. Deposing attorneys have to go to court to overcome improper instructions not to answer, and defending attorneys have to go to court to seek a protective order against bad faith or oppressive questioning.

As a defending attorney, therefore, consider using an "early warning strategy" as an alternative to an instruction not to answer. This middle ground strategy might prevent a deponent from having to answer improper questions yet relieve you from the risks of an improper instruction not to answer. Consider these examples of an early warning strategy:

Example 1

Deposing Counsel: And at this meeting, what did you tell my client about the reasons for his discharge?

You: Objection. Asked and answered. Counsel I will permit my client to answer this question. But I want to note for the record that you've asked this same question about four times now and I've let it go. Repeating the same question over and over is oppressive. If you continue to do that, I will have no choice but to instruct my client not to answer and seek a protective order and sanctions.

Example 2

Deposing Counsel: Mr. Foster who owns stock in the Wiltern Corporation?

A: I do and my brother does. He owns 75% and I own 25%. It's been that way ever since we set up the company ten years ago.

Deposing Counsel: When you set up the company, why did you get 25% of the stock and your brother 75%?

You: Objection. That's irrelevant and not reasonably calculated to lead to the discovery of admissible evidence. Counsel, this case isn't about the shareholders, it's about whether the Wiltern Corporation is liable for what you allege was a defective product. You are just asking this question to prolong the deposition and embarrass my client by going into personal matters that are not related to this litigation. I will permit him to answer this question, but I will instruct him not to answer if you continue along this line.

Perhaps such warnings will be sufficient to move deposing counsel away from the improper areas without your having to issue an instruction not to answer. Admittedly, when you issue such a warning on the record, deposing counsel may be reluctant to "lose face" by backing down, especially if deposing counsel's client is present. Consequently, if your personal relationship with deposing counsel permits, consider giving the early warning privately. For example, request a break and make a statement similar to the one above but in a private, non-confrontational and off the record conversation. Of course, if your on the record or your private conversation is unsuccessful, you may have to instruct a deponent not to answer and terminate a deposition to seek a protective order against bad faith and oppressive questioning.

A risk of the early warning strategy is that deposing counsel and a judge might interpret a warning as an improper "speaking objection." Thus, if you routinely issue such warnings, it may be your adversary who terminates and obtains sanctions against you. However, if you issue such a warning sparingly and only when warranted, a judge is likely to consider the warning an admirable attempt to resolve a dispute without having to stop a deposition and run to court.

C. Consulting With Deponents

1. Conferences During Deposing Counsel's Examination

Unless you are conferring with your client for the purpose of deciding whether to assert a privilege, you should not confer with a deponent during deposing counsel's examination.[32] For example, you

32. See Plaisted v. Geisinger Medical Center, 210 F.R.D. 527 (M.D.Pa. 2002); United States v. Philip Morris Inc., 212 F.R.D. 418, 420 (D.D.C. 2002) (communications between attorney and client during the actual deposition are not appropriate, even if deposition lasts several consecutive days); Calzaturficio SCARPA Spa v. Fabiano Shoe Co. Inc., 201 F.R.D. 33, 39 (D. Mass. 2001); In re Stratosphere Corp. Sec. Litig., 182 F.R.D. 614, 621 (D. Nev. 1998) ("When there is a question pending neither the deponent nor his or her counsel may initiate the interruption of the proceeding to confer about the question, the answer, or about any document that is being examined, except to assert a claim of privilege (conform to a court order or seek a protective order)."); In re Amezaga, 195 B.R. 221, 228 (Bankr. D.P.R. 1996) ("Counsel for the deponent has a very limited role during the taking of a

should not suggest responses to pending questions. Nor should deponents confer with you if they are unclear about the meaning of a question. Instead, they should indicate their uncertainty to examining counsel.[33]

Of course, some conferences between you and your client, although a technical violation of the Federal Rules, are unlikely to concern your adversary. Consider the following examples:

Example 1

1. Deposing Counsel: What, if anything, did Sara say in response?

2. A: She said that she didn't give a damn about the stupid policy.

deposition and conversing with the witness is limited to discussions about whether the objection of privilege should be asserted."); Armstrong v. Hussmann Corp., 163 F.R.D. 299 (E.D. Mo. 1995); Hall v. Clifton Precision, 150 F.R.D. 525, 527 (E.D. Pa. 1993) ("[C]ourts have held that private conferences between deponents and their attorneys during the taking of a deposition are improper unless the conferences are for the purpose of determining whether a privilege should be asserted."); Tuerkes–Beckers, Inc. v. New Castle Assocs., 158 F.R.D. 573, 575 (D. Del. 1993) ("Counsel for a witness may not consult with that witness about the subject matter of his or her testimony while that witness is under examination by an opposing party.") For further discussion of when you may confer with your witness at deposition see Wachen, David S. "Can We Talk? Nationwide Survey Reveals Wide Range of Practices Governing Communication with Witnesses while Defending Their Deposition" www.abanet.org/litigation/committees/pretrial/articles.html.

33. Id. See also Birdine v. Coatesville, 225 F.R.D. 157, 159 (E.D. Pa. 2004): ("defense counsel should have allowed the witness to answer the question or to ask for clarification for himself if he did not understand the question.")

[Deponent whispers to you in a voice that the reporter cannot hear.]

You: My client has just advised me that he has an appointment at 5 P.M. and he'd like to know if the deposition will be concluded in time for him to make that appointment. If not, he'd like to take a break soon so he can call and cancel.

Example 2

1.   Deposing Counsel: Why do you think Phillips agreed with Johnson's decision to terminate the contract for failure to perform after finding out about the problems in February with the disks delivered in early January?

[Deponent looks totally confused and briefly whispers to you.]

You: My client's having difficulty understanding your question. Perhaps you could rephrase it.

In neither of these examples do the conferences constitute attempts at coaching or otherwise influencing the deponent's testimony. Consequently, deposing counsel may well ignore these conferences or politely ask your client to speak to her rather than you when questions are confusing.

Despite the FRCP's prohibition on conferences during questioning, the traditional practice for many lawyers has been to whisper advice in a client's ear when a question is pending or assert that they have the right to confer with their client "at any time." A growing number of cases make clear, however, that these practices are prohibited by the Rules and expose defending attorneys to a risk of sanctions.[34] How great the risks are depends on the local customs in your jurisdiction.

2. Conferences During a Recess or Break

Deposition recesses give you an opportunity to provide moral support to a deponent and review matters that you touched on during pre-deposition preparation. For example, you might reassure a deponent that she is doing a fine job and remind her not to answer a question if she is uncertain of its meaning. When you confer with a client during a break in the deposition, your conversations are generally protected by the attorney-client privilege.[35] If the deponent is not your client, however, such conversations may be inquired into when the deposition resumes.[36]

34. You may be sanctioned pursuant to FRCP 26(c) and 30(d)(2) and (3). See also Morales v. Zondo, Inc., 204 F.R.D. 50, 52–54 (S.D.N.Y. 2001); (counsel sanctioned for private conferences with client out of hearing of deposing counsel, telling client how to answer questions, and telling client not to answer questions.) State Farm Mut. Auto. Ins. Co. v. Dowdy ex rel. Dowdy, 445 F. Supp. 2d 1289, 1293 (N.D. Okla. 2006). Armstrong, 163 F.R.D. at 303; Hall, 150 F.R.D. at 530; American Directory Serv. Agency v. Beam, 131 F.R.D. 15 (D.D.C. 1990).

35. See Henry v. Champlain Enters., Inc., 212 F.R.D. 73, 92 (N.D.N.Y. 2003) (court refuses to allow deposing counsel to ask what was said to deponent by counsel during break); In re Stratosphere, 182 F.R.D. 614, 619–21 (D.Nev. 1998). But see Hall, supra, 150 F.R.D. at 528.

36. If the deponent is an agent or employee of a corporate client, you will need to determine whether your communications during recesses are protected by the attorney-client privilege.

D.   Resolving Disputes Via Telephone

If you are unable to resolve disputes with deposing counsel, pursuant to a local rule the judge (or magistrate) in charge of your case may be willing to resolve the dispute over the telephone during a deposition recess. When available, this procedure typically saves considerable time, money and inconvenience for all concerned. You should, of course, resort to a telephone call only after you have made a good faith effort to resolve a problem with deposing counsel.

E.   Should You Ask Questions?

When an adversary has completed questioning, you too have the right to ask questions. If a deposition has gone better than you expected, with deposing counsel failing to inquire into areas that would have badly damaged your case, you may well decide not to exercise this right. Not only might damaging information come out in response to your questions, but also deposing counsel will have a second chance to ask questions when you are finished. However, in at least the three following situations you may want to consider questioning your own witness:

* The deponent may be unavailable at trial;

* The deponent has apparently made mistakes during the deposition; or

* The questioning has failed to bring out helpful evidence that you intend to stress during settlement negotiations or at trial.

The following sections explore each of these situations.

1.   The Deponent May Be Unavailable at Trial

If a deponent is likely to be unavailable to testify at trial, you may want to question the deponent yourself.[37] Even if all or almost all the helpful information the deponent can provide has emerged in response to deposing counsel's questions, the information is unlikely to have come out in a way that will be persuasive if the deposition transcript is eventually read into the record at trial. By examining a deponent as you would on direct examination,[38] you may elicit a comprehensible and credible story that is both admissible and persuasive when read from a deposition transcript or shown on visual recording at trial.[39]

2.   The Deponent's Answers Have Been Inaccurate

If your client makes a misstatement while testifying, you may recognize the error immediately and decide to talk to the client during a break and suggest that when the deposition resumes, the

37.   Although FRCP 30(c) states that examination at deposition may proceed as at trial, when you question your client at deposition, your examination is not limited to the subjects covered by deposing counsel in the initial examination. See FCC v. Mizuho Medy Co., 257 F.R.D. 679, 682 (S.D. Cal. 2009) (Topics at cross-examination are not limited to those mentioned in the notice of deposition.); Smith v. Logansport Comty. Sch. Corp., 139 F.R.D. 637 (N.D. Ind. 1991).

38.   For a discussion of how to conduct such an examination during deposition, see Chapter 21.

39.   Presenting deposition testimony at trial via a visual recording rather than through a reading of the transcript is often

client volunteer a correction.[40] Immediate correction may reduce the impact of impeachment if your adversary uses the incorrect deposition testimony to impeach the deponent's trial testimony.[41]

If your client does not volunteer a correction during deposing counsel's examination, you may question your client to elicit a correction. One strategy for correcting inaccurate testimony is to explicitly confront a client with the prior testimony and ask whether it is correct. A second strategy is to ignore the erroneous testimony and simply inquire into the same subject matter, assuming that the client will give the correct response the second time around. Under either strategy, after a deponent has testified correctly, ask the deponent to explain why the earlier testimony was inaccurate. Hopefully, the correction in combination with the explanation will vitiate any subsequent attempt at impeachment of the deponent by your adversary.

The following examples illustrate each of these approaches for making corrections.

preferable. For a discussion of videotaping depositions, see chapter 22.

40. The discussion in the text assumes that your client has made an innocent misstatement. If your client has made an intentional misstatement about a material matter (i.e., committed perjury) you are obligated to take corrective action. See A.B.A. Comm'n. on Ethics and Professional Responsibility, Formal Op. 93–376 (1993); Steven H. Goldberg, Heaven Help the Lawyer for a Civil Liar, 2 Geo. J. Legal Ethics 885 (1989); Charles W. Wolfram, Client Perjury, 50 S. Cal. L. Rev. 809 (1977).

41. The possibility of successful impeachment at trial if a correction is not made during the deposition will be especially strong should the deponent subsequently sign the deposition without making a correction.

a. Explicit Reference to Incorrect Testimony

1. You: Ms. Stussman, earlier you testified that the first time you found a sample of contaminated water in the stream was on the tenth of August. Think carefully, had you ever noticed contaminated water in that stream prior to that date?

2. A: Well, now that you mention it, I believe we did find contamination in the water before that date.

3. You: When did you first find contamination?

4. A: I believe it was in mid-May when I went to the site with Ms. Carlson.

5. You: If the first time you found contaminated water in the stream was in mid-May, why did you state earlier that you first noticed contaminated water in the stream in August.

6. A: I really don't know. I guess I made a mistake.

7. You: Can you explain why you made a mistake?

8. A: I really can't say; I guess I wasn't thinking carefully.

9. You: Was it in mid-May that you first noticed the contamination in the stream?

10. A: Yes it was.

11. You: Why can you now remember that it was in mid-May when you first noticed the contamination?

12. A: Because I recall it was before I went to Colorado and I went there in June.

b. Cover Same Subject Matter

1. You: Ms. Stussman, earlier you testified about visiting the stream, during the prior year did you ever visit the stream with Ms. Carlson?

2. A: Yes.

3. You: Why did you go to the site with Ms. Carlson?

4. A: Mr. Terry had told Ms. Carlson that he thought the river was contaminated around that site, and we went to see if perhaps Mr. Terry was correct.

5. You: Was anyone else present on that occasion when you went with Ms. Carlson to determine if Mr. Terry was correct?

6. A: No. We were the only people there.

7. You: On that occasion, did you test the water for the presence of contamination?

8. A: Yes I did.

9. You: And did that test verify what Mr. Terry had said?

10. A: Yes. A sample disclosed that pollution was present.

11. You: Now did you go with Ms. Carlson before or after August first?

12. A: Oh, we went in the spring sometime, probably around mid-May.

13. You: And at that time you and Ms. Carlson found a sample of contaminated water?

14. A: Yes.

15. You: So the first time you found a sample of contaminated water in the stream was in mid-May?

16. A: Yes.

17. You: If the first time you found a sample of contaminated water in the stream was in mid-May, why did you testify earlier in response to Mr. Stark's questions that the first time you found a sample of contaminated water in the stream was on August first?

18. A: All I can say is that I made a mistake.

19. You: Can you explain why you made a mistake?

20. A: I really can't say; I guess I wasn't thinking carefully.

21. You: Was it in mid-May that you first noticed the contamination in the stream?

22. A: Yes it was.

23. You: Why do you now remember that it was in mid-May when you first noticed the contamination?

24. A: Because I recall it was before I went to Colorado and I went there in June.

25. Q: Is it correct then that the first time you found a sample of contaminated water in the stream was in mid-May?

26. A: Yes it is.

As the second approach appears to be less suggestive, it may make a deponent's change of testimony more credible to your adversary and eventually to a judge or jury. Moreover, the second approach is more likely to result in corrected testimony, as you ask a deponent to recall details in the context in which they occurred. Increasing the probability of such recall is particularly likely to be important in those instances where you have not had an opportunity to speak with a deponent in detail before a deposition. On the other hand, the first approach has the advantage of "cutting to the chase" quickly and therefore may be a more efficient choice, especially when a pre-deposition interview convinces you that the deponent will readily correct the error. Ultimately you must rely on your judgment in determining which approach to adopt.

3. *Bringing Out Helpful Evidence*

Your adversary's questioning may fail to uncover evidence helpful to your client. Your combative instinct may be to let such evidence sleep until you can spring it on your adversary at trial. However, if you think it likely that a case will settle before trial, eliciting the favorable evidence yourself can improve your settlement position.[42] Typically, settle-

42. Note that the idea is not to bring out the entirety of a deponent's probable testimony at trial. Rather, the notion is a

ment negotiations based on what you can prove at trial are more persuasive if you can support your positions with actual deposition testimony rather than your naked assertion of what a witness will testify to once trial begins.[43] An adversary who has seen "the whites of a deponent's eyes" is more likely to be persuaded than an adversary who has heard only what appears to be your "negotiation puffery."

When eliciting favorable evidence, conduct the questioning as you would a direct examination at trial. For example, elicit testimony through open rather than leading questions.[44] Taking this approach should enhance the likelihood that an adversary will see a deponent's responses as credible.

2. Defending Non–Party Clients

You may appear at a deposition as counsel for your client even when your client is not a party to the lawsuit in which the deposition is taken. For example, your client may have witnessed an assault that resulted in a lawsuit. Of course, when people have no potential legal exposure, they don't normally incur the expense of legal representation at deposition. If you do represent a disinterested non-party

much more limited one. Bring out only those particular matters you would like to emphasize during settlement negotiations.

43. Deciding to bring out favorable evidence is not an all or nothing proposition. You can always decide to elicit some favorable evidence while reserving other such evidence for trial.

44. For a further discussion of how to question a deponent as though the deponent were a witness on direct examination, see Chapter 21.

client, your main objectives at the deposition will probably be limited to:

    * Consulting with your client before disclosing privileged information;

    * Preventing deposing counsel from harassing your client with abusive questioning;[45] and

    * Providing moral support.[46]

Since you and your client are by definition indifferent to the outcome of the underlying case, you need not make objections to prevent examining counsel from using your client's deposition testimony later in the case.

If a non-party client is willing to pay you to be present at a deposition, the likely reason is that the client may at some time after the deposition become a party either to the same or a related lawsuit. If so, you would defend the deposition as if your client were already a party. For example, assume that a city has sued a contractor for submitting fraudulent invoices for work allegedly never performed. Your client was a foreman for the contractor and, while not a named party in the city's suit, is scheduled to be deposed. Here, your client may realistically fear

45. You may only instruct your client not to answer questions, however, to preserve a privilege, to enforce a court order limitation on discovery, or if you are terminating the deposition to move for a protective order to prevent abusive behavior. See FRCP 30(c)(2). If you instruct your client not to answer for any other reason, you may be sanctioned by the court.

46. Prior to the deposition, you will typically have a preparation session with your client. For a discussion of what you might do at this preparation session, see Chapter 23.

being added as a defendant in the civil case or being charged in a criminal complaint. Therefore, you would defend as though your client were already a party, including making objections.

3. Defending Depositions When You Do Not Represent the Deponent

You will routinely attend depositions of a "neutral witness," i.e., someone with whom you do not have an attorney client relationship. For example, as attorney for a party to an auto accident, you might attend the deposition of a bystander/ neutral witness who observed the auto accident and knows neither of the parties in the case. This section discusses how to defend such neutral witness depositions.

A. *Making Objections*

Objections at neutral witness depositions have the same purpose as in any other depositions: you want to prevent your adversary from using deposition testimony against you later in the case. Thus, you must raise curable objections at the deposition or waive them. "Leading" is the one objection you may make at a neutral witness' deposition that you need not make when deposing counsel deposes your witness. Leading questions are ordinarily objectionable when asked of a neutral witness.[47] If you do not raise this objection at deposition, you waive it.

Your general policy should be to make all legitimate curable objections during neutral witness depositions. A neutral witness is more likely than a

47. See FRE 611(c).

party or a person affiliated with a party to be unavailable to testify in person at trial. If so, your adversary may seek to read portions of the unavailable witness' deposition into evidence at trial. If you objected at deposition and the deposing attorney did not or could not cure the objections, your adversary may be unable to use portions of the deposition testimony. Of course, just as when you defend a client's deposition, you may choose not to make an objection for fear of making damaging testimony even more damaging.[48]

B. Instructions Not to Answer

If deposing counsel conducts a neutral witness deposition in bad faith or in such a manner as unreasonably to annoy, embarrass, or oppress the deponent or your client, you may instruct the deponent not to answer the pending question if you also suspend the deposition to seek a protective order in court.[49] Your motion for a protective order may request the court to terminate the deposition or "limit the scope and manner of the taking of the deposition."[50] You should, of course, generally try to work out the problem with deposing counsel before suspending the deposition to move for a protective order.

You may also instruct the deponent not to answer if examining counsel's questions violate a court ordered limitation on the scope of discovery.[51]

48. See discussion supra § 1, 5.

49. FRCP 30(c)(2) and 30 (d)(3). For a discussion of the process for obtaining a protective order, see Wright, Miller, & Marcus, Federal Practice and Procedure: Civil 2d § 2035.

50. FRCP 30(d)(3).

51. FRCP 30(c)(2).

When a question calls for information protected by a privilege held exclusively by the neutral witness deponent, you do not have the authority to instruct the deponent not to answer, since the deponent could decide to waive or fail to assert the privilege.[52]

C. Consulting With a Neutral Witness During the Deposition

You are generally prohibited from consulting with neutral witnesses with respect to how to respond to pending questions. If you nevertheless do consult with a neutral witness when a question is pending, or if you do so during a break in the deposition, your conversation is not privileged and the deposing attorney may ask the deponent to testify about the conversation.

D. Should You Question a Neutral Witness?

As with any other deposition, when defending a neutral witness deposition you may question the deponent after your adversary's questioning is complete. Your primary options are these:

* **Ask No Questions.** If the deponent's testimony is favorable to your case, you may decide not to ask questions. If you have not talked to the neutral

---

52. On the question of whether you can advise the deponent that a question calls for privileged information and that the deponent may therefore decide to refuse to answer, see <u>Morris Stulsaft Foundation v. Superior Court of San Francisco</u>, 245 Cal.App.2d 409, 54 Cal.Rptr. 12 (1966).

witness prior to the deposition, you will not know whether your questioning might inadvertently elicit damaging evidence. And the neutral witness may well be unavailable at trial. If so, any damaging testimony that the witness might give will never be heard by a settlement judge or the factfinder if you pursue this option.

* Improve Helpful Testimony. A second option is to question the deponent in an effort to clarify or strengthen helpful answers the deponent has already given. This option also tends to reduce the risk that your questioning inadvertently elicits damaging testimony. You do, however, give deposing counsel a second bite at the apple. During your questioning, deposing counsel may think of additional questions to ask that will make the overall record less helpful to your case.

* Question Extensively. Your third option is to question the neutral witness with many of the same goals you would have if you were deposing an adverse witness. Thus, you might obtain the deponent's version of significant events,[53] try to undermine harmful evidence, exploit inconsistencies, search for and strengthen helpful evidence, etc. You are most likely to pursue this alternative when the witness' testimony has, on balance, hurt your case. When pursuing this option, however, you may well

53. You will obviously already have some information relating to the deponent's version of events as a result of deposing counsel's examination. But you may want to check for gaps in areas already covered and go well beyond the events covered by your adversary.

decide <u>not</u> to search for harmful evidence as you would with an adverse witness. The risk of being surprised by harmful evidence that you do not uncover at deposition may be outweighed by the risk that you will educate deposing counsel.

If the neutral witness is unavailable for trial, you will have to read in the deposition transcript (or show the visual recording of the deposition) at trial. When you think the witness is likely to be unavailable at trial, you should try to organize your questions so that the testimony will be comprehensible and persuasive when read or shown to a factfinder.

4. Defending an Adversary's Deposition to Preserve Testimony

Attorneys do not normally depose their own clients or witnesses. When they do so, the reason is usually that an attorney wants to preserve the testimony of a deponent who is likely to be unavailable to testify in person at trial. (Attorneys commonly refer to such a deposition as a "deposition to preserve testimony" or a "trial deposition".)[54] However, an attorney may also want to lock up a friendly witness' testimony before the witness becomes much less friendly. For example, in a wrongful termination suit, the defendant employer is likely to count heavily on evidence from the plaintiff's former supervisor. If the employer intends to sack the former supervisor, the employer's attorney may want to take the supervisor's trial deposition before the sacking takes place.

---

54. Chapter 22 discusses how you might take such a deposition.

As when you defend neutral witness depositions, it generally behooves you to make all appropriate curable objections (including "leading") when your adversary takes a trial deposition. Your adversary will probably not take a trial deposition unless the resulting testimony is going to be favorable, so you want to preserve all legitimate objections until later in the case. Again, just as when you are defending your client's deposition, you may sometimes choose not to make an objection for fear of making damaging testimony even more damaging.[55]

Since the deponent is adverse, you normally also want to thoroughly question after your adversary's questioning is complete. As with any adverse witness, you'll normally want to elicit the deponent's version of significant events,[56] try to undermine harmful evidence, exploit inconsistencies, and search for helpful evidence.

5. Terminating a Deposition That Exceeds the "One Day of Seven Hours" Time Limit

FRCP 30(d)(2) provides that a deposition is limited to "one day of seven hours," absent a stipulation by all parties[57] or a court order to the contrary.

55. See discussion supra § 1,5.

56. You will have some information relating to the deponent's version of events as a result of deposing counsel's examination, but you may want to check for gaps in areas already covered and go well beyond the events covered by your adversary.

57. If the deponent is not a party, the deponent's consent is not required to extend the length of a deposition. See FRCP 30(d)(1).

Therefore, absent such an agreement by the parties or a court order:

   * You, or any other party, may terminate a deposition when it exceeds seven hours. When calculating the seven hours, you must exclude time for lunch breaks and other breaks in the testimony.[58]

   * Even if a deposition does not exceed seven hours, you, or any other party, may terminate a deposition at the end of the first day of testimony.[59]

58. The FRCP advisory committee's notes (2000) indicate that the "only time to be counted is the time occupied by the actual deposition." See Also Condit v. Dunne, 225 F.R.D. 100, 112 (S.D. N.Y. 2004) ("[T]he 2000 Advisory Committee notes to Rule 30(d) clearly state that only the time taken for the actual deposition, not breaks, counts toward the 7 hours...") Dow Chemical Co. v. Reinhard, 2008 WL 1735295 (E.D.Mich. 2008); Wilson v. Kautex, A Textron Co., 2008 WL 189568 (N.D.Ind. 2008). Tmie taken by objections by opposing counsel do count, unless the objections are in bad faith. FRCP 30(d)(1) states that "the court must allow additional time consistent with Rule 26(b)(2) if needed for a fair examination of the deponent or if the deponent or another person, or other circumstance, impedes or delays the examination." See Also Plaisted v. Geisinger Medical Center, 210 F.R.D. 527, 533 (M.D. Pa. 2002) (holding that the administrators' counsel could re-depose witnesses because the medical center's counsel did not state objections concisely in a non-argumentative and non-suggestive manner and the objections went on for pages); Miller v. Waseca Medical Center, 205 F.R.D. 537, 538 (D. Minn. 2002) (allowing additional time for the completion of depositions that were impeded by objections inconsistent with Rule 30(d); Armstrong v. Hussmann Corp., 163 F.R.D. 299, 303 (E.D. Mo. 1995) (granting the defendant's motion to re-depose witnesses because the plaintiff's attorneys violated Rule 30(d)(1) when they made constant interruptions and objections in bad faith during the depositions).

59. The FRCP advisory committee's notes (2000) provide:

FRCP 30(d)(2) applies to all depositions. Thus, you have the statutory right to terminate a deposition which exceeds the time limits of FRCP 30(d)(2) if the deponent is your client or a witness associated with your client, a neutral third party witness, or an adverse party or someone associated with an adverse party (i.e. when you are defending a deposition where deposing counsel is deposing her own witness).

If you choose to terminate a deposition because it exceeds the limits provided in FRCP 30(d)(2), an adverse party can, of course, seek a court order to extend the deposition.[60]

If you believe that you might want to exercise your right to terminate a deposition under FRCP 30(d)(2), you may want to so state on the record at the beginning of the deposition. By putting deposing counsel on notice that you may decide to enforce these time limits, you may encourage deposing

"The limitation is phrased in terms of a single day on the assumption that ordinarily a single day would be preferable [to more than one day]; if alternative arrangements would better suit the parties, they <u>may</u> agree to them" (emphasis added). The FRCP advisory committee's notes (2000) also indicate that "[t]he court may also <u>order</u> that a deposition be taken for limited periods on several days" (emphasis added). This language would seem to indicate that absent an agreement by the parties or a court order, a deposition would be limited to one calendar day.

60. The court must generally grant additional time if it is needed for a fair examination of the deponent or if the deponent or any other person has impeded the examination of the deponent. See FRCP 26(b)(2) and 30(d)(1). According to the FRCP advisory committee's notes (2000), the party seeking the court order to extend the time is "expected to show good cause to justify such an order."

counsel to structure questioning so as to conclude the deposition within the time limits. And if you do ultimately decide to terminate the deposition because it exceeds these limits, your advance notice to deposing counsel may discourage a court from granting an order extending the length of the deposition.

You obviously have to decide on a case by case basis whether to exercise your right to terminate under FRCP 30(d)(2) or to agree to extend the time limits. Factors you may want to take into consideration include:

* <u>Whether you wish to examine the deponent after your adversary has completed questioning.</u> If you terminate the deposition after seven hours of testimony by your adversary, you will not be able to examine the deponent. Similarly, if all parties do not agree to extend the time limits of FRCP 30(d)(2), any party may terminate the deposition, even if you have not yet had an opportunity to examine the deponent. Thus, for example, in the absence of an agreement extending the time limit in FRCP 30(d)(2), deposing counsel may question your client for seven hours and then terminate the deposition before you have a chance to ask questions. You would then have to get a court order in order to resume the deposition.[61]

61. Such a result seems to have been contemplated by the drafters of the 2000 amendments to the FRCP. The FRCP advisory committee's notes (2000) indicate that should the law-

* Whether the deposition can reasonably be completed within the time limits of FRCP 30(d)(2). A reasonable examination of the deponent often requires more than one day of seven hours. For example, if the case is complicated, the deponent requires an interpreter, the deponent must review and be questioned about many documents, several parties wish to examine the deponent after one counsel has completed questioning, or the deponent is an expert witness, you may want to agree to extend the time for the deposition.[62]

* Whether you anticipate needing additional time to complete your depositions. If you will be taking depositions that require more than one day of seven hours, you may want to agree that other parties may also exceed the limit.

6. Requesting That the Deponent Have a Right to Review the Transcript

A deponent has a right to review and make changes to the deposition transcript, only if the deponent or a party requests the right to do so.[63]

yer for the deponent wish to ask questions, "that may require additional time" (emphasis added).

62. The FRCP advisory committee's notes (2000) contemplate that counsel will often agree to extend the time limits in such cases. ("[I]t is expected that in most instances the parties and the witness will make reasonable accommodations to avoid the need for resort to the court.")

63. See FRCP 30(e). Generally speaking, a deponent may make any change the deponent desires, but some courts have imposed limits on the types of changes allowed. For a discussion of what types of changes are permitted, see Wright, Miller & Marcus, Federal Practice & Procedure: Civil 2d. § 2118; Glen-

When defending a deposition of your witness, you typically want to request on the record that your witness have such a right. After the deposition, you may decide that such a review is not necessary. Nonetheless, at the deposition you want to preserve your witness' right to review.

7. Supplementing Deposition Testimony After the Deposition Is Signed

After parties have completed an initial response to answers to interrogatories, requests for production of documents, requests for admission and voluntary disclosures under FRCP 26(a), they are required to supplement their initial responses to these types of discovery information learned after the initial response. They must supplement their initial responses whenever it is necessary to prevent their initial responses from being materially incomplete

wood Farms, Inc. v. Ivey, 229 F.R.D. 34, 35 (D.C. Me. 2005) (Even substantive changes to deposition testimony are permissible as long as reasons are provided and the original testimony remains on the transcript.); Hambleton Bros. Lumber v. Balkin Enters., 397 F.3d 1217, 1225 (9th Cir. 2005) (Explanations for corrections in the transcript are required to determine whether or not changes "have a legitimate purpose." Changes without explanations deemed inadmissible.): Reilly v. TXU Corp., 230 F.R.D. 486 (N.D. Tex. 2005)–(Changes are permissible so long as there is an explanation provided.). Of course, both the original testimony and any changes may be admissible at trial. See Wanke v. Lynn's Transportation Co., 836 F.Supp. 587 (N.D. Ind. 1993). And at trial a deponent may be questioned about changes made in the deponent's deposition testimony. A failure to provide a reason for a change may invalidate it. See Bongiovanni v. N.V. Stoomvaart–Matts "Oostzee," 458 F.Supp. 602, 605 n.4 (D.C.N.Y. 1978).

or incorrect.[64] The FRCP imposes no such explicit obligation to supplement deposition testimony of a lay witness with information learned after the deposition is complete. Consequently, once a deposition has been read and signed by a deponent, a party is generally not required to supplement the deposition testimony with information learned after the deposition has been signed.[65]

64. FRCP 26(e).

65. See Advisory Committee Notes for 1993 Amendments to Federal Rules of Civil Procedure, Fed. R. Civ. P. 26 ("The revision also clarifies that the obligation to supplement responses to formal discovery requests applies to interrogatories, requests for production, and requests for admissions, but not ordinarily to deposition testimony."); 6–26 Moore's Federal Practice § 26.131 (Mathew Bender 3d. ed. 2010) ("The duty to supplement and correct generally does not extend to disclosures made as part of deposition testimony. However, with respect to experts for whom a disclosure report is required, the duty extends both to information contained in the report and to information provided through the expert's deposition.")10 John Kimpflen et. al., Fed. Proc., L. Ed. § 26:65 (2010). ("While the Advisory Committee Notes state that the obligation to supplement responses to formal discovery requests applies to interrogatories, requests for production, and requests for admissions, but not ordinarily to deposition testimony, it has been held that the duty to supplement expert testimony extends to any changes or additions to the information provided in a deposition.") 8A Charles Allen Wright et. al., Fed. Prac. & Proc. Civ. § 2049.1 (3d ed. 2010). ("Ordinarily, the duty to supplement discovery responses applies only to interrogatory answers and document production, but Rule 26(e)(2) goes further with regard to an expert … directing as follows: [T]he party's duty to supplement extends … to information given during the expert's deposition."); Encore Entertainment, LLC v. KIDdesigns, Inc., 2005 WL 2249897, at * 9 (M.D. Tenn. Sept. 4, 2005) (noting that "the supplementing duties of Rule 26(e) do not extend to deposition testimony, other than that of expert witnesses"); Intermedics, Inc. v. Cardiac Pacemakers, Inc., 1998 WL

35253493, at *2 (D. Minn. April 10, 1998) (stating that "the remarks of the Advisory Committee merely confirm the common sense proposition that, having once been deposed, a witness is under no duty to continuously review his testimony in order to revise his answers as a result of subsequently occurring events";. Ransdell v. Russ Berrie and Company, Chicago, Inc., 1996 WL 242961, at *5 (N.D. Ill. May 8, 1996) (holding that the plaintiff was not required to supplement deposition answers because "the duty to supplement does not apply ordinarily to deposition testimony"); Coleman v. Keebler Co., 997 F.Supp. 1102, 1107 (N.D. Ind. 1998) (citing to Moore's Federal Practice for the notion that "The duty to supplement and correct generally does not extend to disclosures made as part of deposition testimony"); Eli Lilly and Co. v. Actavis Elizabeth LLC, 2010 WL 1849913. At *3 (D. N.J. May, 7 2010) (citing to Moore's Federal Practice for the notion that "The duty to supplement and correct generally does not extend to disclosures made as part of deposition testimony").

INDEX

References are to Pages

ADMISSIONS
Strategies & Techniques to obtain, See Chapter 4
Using documents to obtain, 213

ADMONITIONS
Example of, 248
Expert depositions, in, 412–414
Purposes of, 247

AGGRANDIZE THE LIE, 145

ANSWERS, TYPES OF, See also OBJECTIONS TO ANSWERS
Evasive, See Evasive Answers, Hints, 176
Hyper-technical, 180
"I don't know," 196
"I don't remember," 186
Non-responsive, 175
"What do you mean by" 178

ARGUMENTS
Communicating to opposing counsel at deposition, See Chapter 12

AUTHENTICATING DOCUMENTS, 202

BACKGROUND QUESTIONING
Expert depositions, 414–416
Generally, 265
Masking during, 98

BEGINNING DEPOSITIONS, See Chapter 13
Admonitions, See ADMONITIONS
Background questioning, 265
    See also MASKING

BEGINNING DEPOSITIONS—Cont'd
Deponent's preparation, questions regarding, 260
Stipulations, 244
Time limits, 244

CEMENTING, See Chapter 5
Asked & answered objections, responding to, 128
Benefits of, 113
Defined, 112
Impeachment, techniques for facilitating, 114
Risks of, 115
Techniques for, 115

CHRONOLOGY
Asking a deponent for,
   See Timelines Chapter 3
Benefits of, 49
Creating in preparation, 340
Deponent can't remember, 66
Depositions to preserve testimony, use in, 456
Documents, using to obtain, 206
Expert deposition, use in, 416–422
Obtaining details when chronology not available, 66

COMMUNICATING ARGUMENTS, See Chapter 12
Selecting arguments, 238
Techniques for, 234
Timing of, 243

CONCLUDING DEPOSITIONS, 267
Stipulations, 267
Transcript review, 267

CONCLUSIONS
Ask for basis of, 225
Undermining, 143, 148

COURT REPORTER
Qualifications of, 376
Treatment of, 232

CREDIBILITY
Challenging
   See HARMFUL EVIDENCE
   See IMPLAUSIBILITIES
   See INCONSISTENT STATEMENTS

CROSS EXAMINATION, 233–234

DEFENDING DEPOSITIONS, See Chapter 24
Conferring with clients, 556
Depositions to preserve testimony, 524, 573
Duty to supplement deposition testimony, 579
Instructions not to answer, 547
    Grounds for, 547–551
    Neutral witness, 570
    Risks of improper instructions, 551
Neutral witness deponent, 524, 569–573
Non-party clients, 567
Objections to answers, 540
Objections to questions, 525
    Curable, 528, 529–538
        Argumentative, 534
        Assumes facts not in evidence, 531
        Best Evidence Rule, 537
        Compound, 530
        Hearsay, 536
        Inadmissible Opinion, 535
        Lack of Foundation, 534, 537
        Lack of Personal Knowledge, 534
        Leading, 531
        Mischaracterizes testimony, 532
        Narrative, 533
        Speculation, 535
        Vague, 530
    Forgoing, 543
    Non-curable,
        Asked and Answered, 538
        Inadmissible Legal Conclusion, 539
        Irrelevant, 539
        Not reasonably calculated to lead to admissible evidence, 540
    Phrasing, 545
    Purpose of, 525
    Waiver of 527
Preparing the witness, See PREPARING WITNESSES FOR DEPOSITION
Questioning a client or friendly deponent, 560
Resolving disputes by telephone, 560

DEFENDING DEPOSITIONS—Cont'd
Review of transcript, requesting, 578
Terminating a deposition,
    Time limits exceeded, 574
    To seek protective order, 550
Visually recorded depositions, See VISUALLY RECORDED
    DEPOSITIONS

DEMEANOR
Advantages of professional demeanor, 271
Building rapport, 273
Of deponents, See EVASIVE ANSWERS
Of deposing counsel, See Chapter 14
Visually recorded depositions, in, 493

DEPONENT'S VERSION OF EVENTS
Examples of, 2
Experts, 416–422
Obtaining, illustration of, 47
Risks of obtaining, 5
Why obtain, 4

DEPOSING EXPERTS, See Chapter 20
Admonitions, 412–414
Background, 414–416
Bias, establishing, 445
Challenging expert opinions, 427–446
Chronology of activity, 416–422
Opinions
    Obtain all, 422
    Obtain evidentiary basis for each, 424
    Obtain specialized knowledge re opinions, 426
    Undermining, multiple strategies for, 427–446
Percipient experts, 449
Pre-deposition disclosures, 411
Report of, 411
Supplementing deposition testimony, 446
Use in preparing your expert, 449
Your expert
    Garnering support for, 446
    Preparing for deposition, 270

DEPOSITIONS TO PRESERVE TESTIMONY, See Chapter 21
Direct examination, akin to, 454
Harmful testimony, avoiding, 469
Preparing deponent for, 453

DEPOSITIONS TO PRESERVE TESTIMONY—Cont'd
Questioning strategies and techniques, 454–471
Redirect examination, 471
Responding to objections, 472
Why take, 452

DIAGRAMS, 214

DOCUMENTS, See Chapter 10
Authentication, 202
Chronologies, use in obtaining, 206
Exhibits
    Copies for opposing counsel, 201
    Marking, 198
    Numbers for, 198
    Referring to, 198
Foundation for use at trial, 202
History of, 211
Memory refreshment, use in, 205
Production of
    At deposition, 373
    From non-party, 375
    Necessity for subpoena duces tecum, 375
    Prior to deposition, 374
Reviewed by deponent to prepare, 338
Using to obtain chronology, 206
Using to obtain helpful answers, 213
Using to stimulate memory, 205
Words & phrases in, learning meaning of, 210

"ESPECIALLY WHEN" TECHNIQUE
Magnifying implausibilities, 170
Use in preparation, 346

EVASIVE ANSWERS, 175
Hyper-technical deponents, responding to, 180
Types of, & responses to, See Chapter 9

"EXCEPT WHEN" TECHNIQUE
Undermining expert opinion, 432
Undermining harmful testimony, 144
Use in preparation, 348

EXHIBITS, See DOCUMENTS

EXPERTS, See DEPOSING EXPERTS

588

INDEX

References are to Pages

EXPLOITING BIAS
Defined, 89
Illustrations of, 93
Preparing to use, 358
Risks of 94
Techniques for, 89

FORGETFUL DEPONENTS, See also MEMORY
Illustrations of, 186
Techniques for probing, 188–194

GENERALIZATIONS
See ESPECIALLY WHEN AND EXCEPT WHEN

GESTURES, CLARIFYING, 231

GOALS AT DEPOSITION
Deponent's version of events, obtaining, 2
    Benefits of, 4
    Risks of obtaining, 5
Harmful Evidence, uncovering & undermining, 7
Helpful evidence,
    Confirming accuracy of, 6
    Searching for, 6
Neutral witnesses, 10
Order of pursuing, 10

GOLDEN RULES, 509

GUESSING
Admonition regarding, 250

HARMFUL EVIDENCE
Aggrandize the lie, 145
Attacking the inference, 143
Challenging accuracy of, 130
Checklist for undermining, 153
Conclusions, undermining, 143, 148
Opinions, undermining, 148
Undermining, See Chapter 6
    Delaying, 152
Why search for, 7

HEARSAY
Asking for, 219, 183–186
Objecting to, 536
Responding to, 305

HELPFUL ANSWERS
Cementing, See CEMENTING
Documents to obtain, 213
Leading questions to obtain, 73
Preparing to obtain, 110,
Searching for, goal of, 6
Techniques for obtaining, See Chapter 4
    Exploiting bias, 89
    Masking, 94, 98
    Plausibility chains, 74
    See also PLAUSIBILITY CHAINS

HISTORICAL RECONSTRUCTION, 344

HYPER–TECHNICAL DEPONENTS
Responding to, 180

"I DON'T KNOW" ANSWERS, See EVASIVE ANSWERS

"I DON'T REMEMBER" ANSWERS, See EVASIVE ANSWERS

IMPEACHMENT AT TRIAL
Cementing to improve, 114
Inconsistent statements, use of, See Chapter 7
Visually recording to improve, 478

IMPLAUSIBILITY
Deferring inquiry into, 171
Defined, 169
Magnifying, techniques for, 170
    "Especially when," 170
Seeking explanations for, 172

IMPROPER BEHAVIOR BY OPPOSING COUNSEL
Coaching the witness, 321
Conferences with a deponent, 324, 328
Disruptive objections & statements, 312
    Protective order to prevent, See PROTECTIVE ORDER
    Responding to, 311
Speaking objections, 322

INCONSISTENT STATEMENTS, See Chapter 7
Deponent's prior inconsistent statement, 155
Options for dealing with, 155–164
Third person's conflicting statement, 164

INSTRUCTIONS NOT TO ANSWER
Early warning system, 553
Obtain an Order to Compel an Answer, 287

INSTRUCTIONS NOT TO ANSWER—Cont'd
Responding to invalid instructions, 278
Risks of, 551
Valid Grounds for, 277

LEADING QUESTIONS, 73
Using to communicate arguments, 234

LENGTH OF DEPOSITIONS
Preparation, consider during, 364
Time limits on, 244–247, 367

MASKING
Background questioning to mask, 98
Defined, 94
Illustrations of, 95
Impeachment and, 107
Preparing to use, 358

MEMORY
Refreshing, techniques for, 20–21, 205

METHOD OF RECORDING TESTIMONY AT DEPOSITION, 369

NEUTRAL WITNESS
Deposing, See Chapter 21
Goals when deposing, 10
Preparing for deposition, 520

NON–RESPONSIVE ANSWERS, See ANSWERS

NOTE TAKING, 19

NOTICING DEPOSITIONS, See Chapter 17
Arranging for court reporter, 376
Contents of, 369
Location of depositions, 371
Number of depositions 367
Method of recording testimony, 369
Priority of depositions, 367
Production of documents at deposition, See DOCUMENTS
Subject matter depositions, 382
Subpoenas, necessity for, 373
When depositions can be taken, 370
Who can be deposed, 366
Written notice required, 367

NUMBER OF DEPOSITIONS, 367

OBJECTIONS TO ANSWERS, 308

OBJECTIONS TO QUESTIONS, MAKING, See DEFENDING DEPOSITIONS

OBJECTIONS TO QUESTIONS, RESPONDING TO, See Chapter 15
Common Objections, 298
    Curable objections, 294, 299
        Argumentative, 301
        Assumes facts not in evidence, 299
        Best Evidence Rule, 306
        Compound, 299
        Hearsay, 305
        Inadmissible Opinion, 304
        Lack of Foundation, 303, 306
        Lack of Personal Knowledge, 303
        Leading, 301
        Mischaracterizes testimony, 302
        Narrative, 300
        Speculation, 303
        Vague, 300
    Non-curable objections, 306
        Asked and Answered, 307
        Inadmissible Legal Conclusion, 307
        Irrelevant, 308
        Not reasonably calculated to lead to admissible evidence, 308
Disruptive objections, 312
During depositions to preserve testimony, 472
Obtaining answers to objectionable questions, 290
Objections used to coach deponent, 321
Protective orders, seeking, 331
Responding to curable objections, 316
Speaking objections, 322
Stipulations for preserving objections, 318

OPINIONS, See CONCLUSIONS

OPPOSING COUNSEL, See IMPROPER BEHAVIOR OF OPPOSING COUNSEL

PARKING, 25, 58

PERJURY, 562 footnote 40

PERSON MOST KNOWLEDGEABLE, See SUBJECT MATTER
DEPOSITIONS

PLAUSIBILITY CHAINS
Accepting imperfect answers, 79
Based on prior statements, 80
Common features of, 77
Illustrative examples, 74–89
Preparing to use, 358
Risks of, 94

PRACTICE & POLICY DEPOSITIONS, See Chapter 19
Purposes of, 394
Questioning strategies during, 395, 399–409
Who to depose, 397

PREPARING TO TAKE A DEPOSITION, See Chapter 16
Chronology, 340
Document review, 338
Outline, creating, 357
    Strategic decisions in finalizing, 357–365
Steps in Preparation, 334
    Step 1, Identify Crucial Factual Contentions, 335
    Step 2, Identifying Topics, Events and Documents to Explore
        at Deposition, 338–357

PREPARING WITNESSES FOR DEPOSITION, See Chapter 23
Conduct a practice session, 508
    Explain "Golden Rules," 509
    Explaining objections, 519
    No discussion of with others, 520
    Review client's version, 506
    Suggesting appropriate responses, 517
    Volunteering information, instructions regarding, 515
Deposition to preserve testimony, 453
Non-clients, 520
Pre-meeting preparation, 500
    Prepare case chronology, 501
    Review document requests, 500
    Tell client what documents to review, 503
Visually recorded depositions, 488–489

PRIOR STATEMENTS
Inconsistent Statements, 155
Plausibility chains based on, 80
Third person's conflicting statement, 164

PROTECTIVE ORDERS, 331, 550

QUESTIONING OWN CLIENT AT DEPOSITION, 560

QUESTIONING TIPS, See Chapter 11

RAPPORT, See DEMEANOR

REFRESHING RECOLLECTION, See MEMORY

SANCTIONS, 331–332, 551

SETTLEMENT
Communicating arguments to enhance, See Chapter 12
Consider during preparation, 363
Enhancing through professional demeanor, 276

SEVEN HOUR RULE, 244–247
See also TERMINATING DEPOSITIONS

STIPULATIONS, 244, 267

SUBJECT MATTER DEPOSITIONS, See Chapter 18
Defined, 380
Limit on number, 382, 390
Limitations on questions at, 389
Notice for, 382
Obtaining adverse party's contentions, limits on, 391
Questioning the deponent, 383–390
Scope of, 389
Why take, 381

SUBPOENA RE DEPOSITION, 373

SUPPLEMENTING DEPOSITION TESTIMONY, 579

TERMINATING DEPOSITIONS
Time limits exceeded, 574
To seek protective order, 550

T–FUNNELS, See Chapter 2
Benefits of, 20
Combining with Timelines, 61
Common T–Funnels, 32
Getting details of events, 228
Illustration of, 12, 14
Inverted, 30
Note taking, 19
Omitting closed questions, 27

T–FUNNELS—Cont'd
Parking, 25
Problems to avoid, 22
Secondary, 15, 18
Series of, 15

TIME LIMITS, 244–247
See also TERMINATING DEPOSITIONS

TIMELINES, See Chapter 3
Abandoning, 66
Basic Timeline pattern, 45
Benefits of, 49
Chronology, obtaining, 45
Combining with T–Funnels, 61
    Illustrations of, 62–66
Defined, 44
Gaps in 47, 57
Illustration of, 47
Obtaining details when chronology not available, 66
Parking, 58
Problems to avoid, 51–61
What are Timelines, 44

TRANSCRIPTS
Right to review, 578
Supplementing, 579

TRIAL DEPOSITIONS, See DEPOSITIONS TO PRESERVE TESTIMONY

UNDERMINING HARMFUL ANSWERS, See HARMFUL EVIDENCE

VISUALLY RECORDED DEPOSITIONS, See Chapter 22
Advantages of, 478–484
Disadvantages of, 484–487
FRCP relating to, 475
Preparing friendly deponent for, 488–489
Settlement, use in, 481
Strategies for defending, 493–498
Strategies for taking, 489–493
Technical considerations, 489–492

WAIVER OF FRCP REQUIREMENTS FOR DEPOSITIONS, 377

WHO CAN BE DEPOSED, See NOTICING DEPOSITIONS

WHY QUESTIONS
Why ask why, 220, 222

†